THINKING STRAIGHT

PRENTICE-HALL ENGLISH COMPOSITION AND
INTRODUCTION TO LITERATURE SERIES

Maynard Mack, Editor

THINKING STRAIGHT

Principles of Reasoning for Readers and Writers

BY

MONROE C. BEARDSLEY

Swarthmore College

SECOND EDITION

Englewood Cliffs, N. J.

PRENTICE-HALL, INC.

First printing........January, 1956
Second printing......January, 1957
Third printing.......January, 1958
Fourth printing.........July, 1958
Fifth printing.......February, 1959
Sixth printing.........May, 1960
Seventh printing........April, 1961
Eighth printing....September, 1961
Ninth printing........August, 1962
Tenth printing.........June, 1963
Eleventh printing......May, 1964
Twelfth printing.....January, 1965

PRINTED IN THE UNITED STATES OF AMERICA

91814-C

Acknowledgments

Those who are acquainted with the earlier edition of *Thinking Straight* will observe that for the present edition it has been thoroughly revised and its contents rearranged. I am much indebted to many teachers and students whose criticisms and suggestions have helped me enormously in the task of making this addition more interesting, clear, and useful.

But I should also like again to express my gratefulness to those whose aid was acknowledged in the first edition, for the basic principles, method, and point of view have been preserved. They are: Mr. William A. Pullin; Professor Maynard Mack, Department of English Literature, Yale University; Professor Thomas C. Pollock, Dean of Washington Square College, New York University; Professor Ernest Nagel, Department of Philosophy, Columbia University; Professor Henry W. Sams, Chairman of the College English Staff, the University of Chicago; Professor Glenn Leggett, Department of English Literature, the University of Washington; Professor John Gerber, Department of English Literature, the Iowa State University; Professor Bruce Dearing, Department of English Literature, Swarthmore College; Professor Alburey Castell, Department of Philosophy, University of Oregon; Professor Richard B. Brandt, Department of Philosophy, Swarthmore College; Professor Roderick Firth, Department of Philosophy, Harvard University; Professor Sidney Morgenbesser, Department of Philosophy, Columbia University; and, most especially, Professor William K. Wimsatt, Jr., Department of English Literature, Yale University, and Professor Elizabeth Lane Beardsley, Department of Philosophy, Lincoln University.

M.C.B.

Contents

Preview

Suppose you lived in one of those cities that have suffered in recent years from regular attacks of smog. (If you don't live in such a city, you soon may, for many more cities are working up to it.) You wake up to a clear, sunny morning. About 9:00 a.m. a murky haze begins to form, getting thicker and thicker until it blots out the sun. In the early afternoon a breeze may blow all, or most, of it off to the mountains—or it may stay on day after day. You go about your business coughing and dabbing at your smarting and bloodshot eyes. The vegetables in your garden, your flowers and grass, become discolored and show signs of burning and necrosis. People with lung ailments die unexpectedly.

No doubt all these conditions will produce a good deal of consternation. On street corners, in bars, over store counters and dinner tables, people complain about the smog and say that Something Should Be Done About It. There are letters to the editor, and sharp words over the radio. All sorts of suggestions are offered, with plenty of feeling. Somebody should be fired. Somebody should be thrown in jail. Prayers should be offered. The National Guard should be called out. Oil refineries should be fined. All industrial plants should be closed down for a week. The Mayor should consult an astrologer or Swami So-and-so.

What we want to know is how to stop the smog. But before we can answer this question, we first have to ask another: what is the *cause* of it? Smoke from the incinerators in every back yard? The exhaust from thousands of cars in the streets? Sulphur dioxide gas from oil refineries? Or something else? If you lose your temper, it will be easy to find a scapegoat. It's that private utility plant you have always objected to. Or the factories in that detestable city a few miles away. Or maybe spacemen in those flying saucers you've heard about. Thoughts like these afford emotional satisfaction, and we are likely to cling to them with some affection. But if someone keeps cool long enough to get help from the Air Pollution Control Association, and experts go to work on the problem, we will find that their way of operating is in marked contrast to that of the hysterical accusers.

First, they will make sure that they know what the problem *is* before they rush around trying to solve it. A chemist will take a bag full of the stuff, and analyze it. And it will probably turn out that strictly speaking it isn't smog at all. The word "smog" was coined (by a Dr. Des Voeux) in 1905, and meant what it seems to mean: a combination of smoke and fog. But when a new kind of murk descended upon cities like Los Angeles, and people labeled it "smog," they were jumping to conclusions. For that murk was neither smoke nor fog but something much more mysterious. And the misleading label set prevention campaigns off on the wrong track for years.

Once the investigators have a fairly clear idea of what it is they are trying to cope with, they will no doubt bring to bear upon the problem whatever relevant knowledge they can lay their hands on. And with the help of this knowledge, they will think of various possible explanations. Perhaps the irritant particles in the air are formed by chemical reactions in the upper atmosphere from substances that are contained in certain kinds of smoke and gas but are not at all harmful before the reaction takes place.

Finally, they will test their explanations, as carefully and as fully as they can. They will have to forget what newspapers and aldermen are saying, and refuse to be hurried by political pressures. They will have to withhold their conclusion until they are sure the evidence is adequate. And when their report appears, it will have several notable features. It will be as clear and exact as possible. It will set forth the facts that are taken to support the conclusion, so they can be inspected by any competent reader. It will list some of the alternative explanations, with the facts that seem to make them unacceptable. The investigators will say how confident they are of the conclusion they have reached; whether they think it is almost certain or only tentative. They will mention other questions that haven't yet been answered, and they may suggest how the answers to some of these would strengthen their conclusion or weaken it.

Of course, all this sounds a good deal smoother and easier than it really is. There are many ways in which the investigation might be temporarily blocked, or shunted aside, before it gets to the end. And it may end in defeat: that is, the investigators may discover that not enough is known about the behavior of certain chemicals, or about certain meteorological conditions, to solve their problem, so that the solution must wait until other investigations have been carried out. But if *anything* is to be found out, whether positive or negative—if any progress is to be made toward dealing with the unpleasant and dangerous situation that started the whole thing off—it is evidently going to take a good deal of *thinking*.

On Answering Questions

In a broad sense, you can call anything that passes through your mind "thinking." But this is not the sense in which we use the word when we say to someone who makes a quick and careless reply to a question, "You're not thinking." In this remark we assume a distinction that is, in fact, important. All sorts of feelings, recollections, images, and symbols may run after one another in your mind. You may regret something, or mechanically repeat that nine times nine is eighty-one, or vividly and breathtakingly picture to yourself someone you once knew long ago; or one image may call up another by a process of free association. But you aren't *thinking* unless you have a problem.

When a series of ideas is set off by a question that it aims to answer, it is more than just a series of ideas. It doesn't wander all over the lot, as the whim takes it; it has direction, for it is aimed toward providing an answer to the question, and it is controlled by the implicit conditions of the question. When you daydream, you aren't thinking. But when you ask, for example, whether the permanent membership of the United Nations Security Council should be changed, then you have something to think *about*. That is, you have something to think *from* (a situation in which someone is puzzled or baffled or in doubt what to believe), and you have something to think *toward* (a way out).

Of course, the problem doesn't have to be a practical one, like the problem of revising the U. N. charter. A while back, an advertisement in a Sunday book review started out with this question, in black letters: "HAS THE INVASION OF EARTH BY BEINGS FROM ANOTHER WORLD ALREADY BEGUN?" If that didn't make you sit up and take notice, there was a list of other questions to worry, or at least bewilder, you: "Has the earth been under observation by extra-terrestrial visitants for more than 1200 years? ... How many of the mysterious disappearances of men and women in 1948-55 were abductions aboard flying saucers? ..." Meaty questions, indeed—and the advertisement promised that the book would answer them all.

Now, you might call this a practical problem, except that the advertisement clearly suggested that the situation was out of control, with disguised visitors from Outer Space already infiltrating our cities. If it's too late to do anything, the question is academic. Still, it's a challenging question, and something you can think about. You can ask yourself what sort of information would help to decide whether those people who mysteriously disappeared did so from earthly causes (amnesia, kidnaping, or getting fed up with it all) or from heavenly ones (being whisked off in a space ship). This isn't going to be a simple problem, since you can't ask them what happened to them. But there may be clues that will point toward the invasion theory, or against it. In any case, there is presumably some truth to be gotten at—either there is an invasion, or there is not—and to think, in the strictest sense, is always to aim at discovering, and establishing, a truth.

Truth is what thinking is after. Even if you are thinking of the best way of deceiving someone, you want the truth about how the deception is best accomplished. Otherwise, you only deceive yourself.

Thinking is good thinking when it eventuates in knowledge, whether the problem that started it was practical or theoretical. This distinction between theory and practice is often misleadingly made. There is a difference, of course, between putting out a house that is on fire and studying the techniques of fire fighting in a training school for air raid wardens. And one can be interested in merely learning those techniques, just as one can be interested in studying astronomy or genetics without the slightest interest in shifting planets about or breeding Supermen. To know is not necessarily to do; but there is no problem about doing unless there is a need of knowledge. It is this need that thinking aims to fill.

Creative and Critical Thinking

Looking back over the problem with which we started—the elimination of municipal murk—we see that the thinking going on there

PREVIEW

has two different aspects. They are not completely independent, and in a difficult investigation we may shift back and forth from one aspect to another, but when we are considering how to improve our thinking, we have to deal with them separately. Thinking has a *creative* aspect; it also has a *critical* aspect.

Creative thinking is what it takes to get new ideas—to conceive of *possible* answers to a question, so that we have something to try out. Whoever first thought up the theory that the murk may be due to chemical reactions in the upper atmosphere was thinking creatively. Maybe this theory isn't true. We may have to scrap a dozen theories before we get the right one, but the wrong ones may lead us to the right ones, and we can't scrap them until we have them. Whoever first suggested that the murk might be due to spacemen was thinking creatively, too—only not so well. His theory was bold (and there is always the possibility that the startling theory is the right one), but it was not adequately connected with available information about the laws of nature.

In the broad sense, of course, there is creative thinking involved in writing a story, constructing a melody, or designing a picture—whereever, in fact, there is at work what we call "imagination": the capacity to see possibilities that have not yet turned up in our actual experience. To create a work of art is not in itself to solve a problem, but the process of creation is one in which problems are continuously encountered and solved, and each opens up hitherto unrealized possibilities for the artist's imagination. And this is not so very different from what goes on in the mind of one who sees a way out of an impasse at an international conference, or devises a new method of manufacturing cortisone, or produces an explanation of the fact that the moon appears larger near the horizon, or suggests a solution of the four-color map problem.

We recognize creative thinking in phrases such as these: "If announcements won't get a quorum out to the annual membership meeting, *why don't we try* a square dance?" "Boxers have been among the best-tempered and friendliest dogs I have known; this may be a coincidence, but I *wonder if* perhaps all boxers are good-tempered." "There appear to be ghosts on the television screen; *it may be* that the aerial has been turned around by the wind."

Now, of course, just getting a new idea is not enough to make it true—the idea has to be checked, sometimes over and over again.

This is the *critical* aspect of thinking: trying out a suggestion, testing a theory against relevant experience. It is critical thinking that considers the ways and means of having a square dance, and projects the probable consequences to see whether it will or will not achieve its purpose. It is critical thinking that estimates the likelihood that there are bad-tempered boxers, or that the television aerial has been turned around; and, in the last analysis, it is critical thinking that leads you out to look for bad-tempered boxers or makes you climb up on the roof.

These two aspects of thinking don't exist apart, of course. Some people are better at one than at the other—better at thinking of ideas than at checking them, or better at checking other people's ideas than at thinking of new ones themselves. But an individual or a group can't deal adequately with its problems, and get hold of the knowledge it needs, unless it can do both to some extent. And it is convenient to distinguish them. In the problem of the municipal murk, it is one thing to think of a possible explanation—it is another thing to line up the chemical and meteorological facts that would decide whether the explanation is correct, and to test the explanation by means of them.

Now, when we ask how we can *improve* our thinking, this question turns out to have two parts, too. How can we make our thinking more creative? How can we make our thinking more critical?

It is safe to say that we do not know very much about answering the first question. We know a little of the psychology of creative thinking. There is evidence that people can develop their imaginations to some degree, and widen the range of the original ideas they can invent. This is one of the reasons for studying imaginative literature. But we must still be rather tentative on some of these points. It is evident that if you work in a job where you are continually faced with problems of a certain kind, such as dissatisfied workmen or record players that need fixing, you get better and better at thinking of ways to handle the problems. But that doesn't mean you get better at thinking creatively about problems in general.

Some interesting work is being done on this question, and we shall know more before long. But perhaps creative thinking will never be reduced to rules. Rules for creative thinking seem as odd, in a way, as a mechanical music composer or a formula for beautiful paintings. There is a good deal more to be said about the second aspect of thinking. Critical thinking does have some mechanical elements. They can be reduced to rules; and the work of logicians and other philosophers since ancient Greek times has placed us in a position where we can say, in many cases quite exactly, whether a particular fact refutes or strengthens a particular theory.

Logic and Language

Good critical thinking is what we colloquially call "straight thinking." Its task is to subject ideas to critical scrutiny, to determine whether they are true or false, and it is straight thinking when it goes about this task in an efficient and effective way.

This is what we shall be concerned with in this book. It will probably not make you more fertile in devising ingenious solutions to puzzles, or in inventing fruitful and original answers to the questions that come up to trouble you. But it should help you to decide whether or not to accept the answers you *can* think up, or can borrow from someone else. In short, it will deal with the techniques of critical thinking. And it will deal with the *applications* of these techniques, rather than the theory behind them.

The central principles of straight thinking are principles of logic. They are the principles that determine whether or not our thinking is correct. If our ideas were always perfectly clear, and if we could carry on our thinking in a pure and wordless way, we would need no other principles. But for the most part we do our thinking in a *medium*. For a physical scientist this medium may consist of mathematical symbols, but for most of us, in our daily life, it consists of words. We think in a language.

Maybe there is such a thing as nonlinguistic thinking—there may be hunches and sudden insights that come to us first as a vague idea that has to be put into words, and we may have to grope a little for the words we want. But an idea does not grow into a fullfledged thought, a theory or a proposal or a plan, until it is formulated in words. We cannot be sure it is clear, for it is not ready to be critically examined, until we verbalize it in some way. You can play chess without a chessboard or pieces—just in your mind—but you can't play it without *names* of pieces and *rules* to define their capacities for movement.

The words of a natural, spoken language such as English, are, as we all know, powerful and dangerous tools that can be used in all sorts of ways. Their behavior is much more complicated, and more difficult to understand and master, than that of artificial symbols as in projective geometry or the calculus. If you're better at writing letters than differentiating equations, it's because you have had a lot more practice with English; a mathematician might be able to manipulate non-Euclidian geometry with the greatest of ease but yet be incapable of reading a daily newspaper intelligently.

⌐ It is in ordinary English that we have to do most of our thinking about the things that matter most to us as human beings and as citizens of a democracy. In the first place, most of the *data* with which we have to do our thinking come to us in words—from newspapers, books, magazines, radio and television programs. And what an enormous flood of words is poured out upon us every day! We are constantly called upon to make up our minds about vital problems—whether to vote for So-and-so or write a Senator about such-and-such a bill, to invest in this stock or support that municipal school bond issue. And the information we need to cope with these problems becomes more and more difficult to get—partly because it becomes more and more complicated, but partly because the facts we need are obscured by *misinformation,* wittingly or unwittingly thrown at us.⌐

In the second place, the theories we invent to explain the things that baffle us, and the projects we construct to escape our difficulties, have to be put into words, as clearly as possible, before we can see what they involve, how they are to be worked out, and whether they will serve. And in the third place, we can do little to help our most important and pressing troubles, whether disease, poverty, or war, unless we can act in groups, cooperatively—and this requires communication, the sharing of information, and agreement upon theories and projects.

Critical thinking involves the critical use of language, critical reading (or listening), and effective writing (or speaking). We need techniques for getting at the meaning of what we read, discriminating what is significant, tracing the path of the reasoning so that we can scrutinize its twists and turns. Only in that way can we hope to make a fair success at separating what is true in it from what is false.

Not that we are always reading (or writing) for the sake of knowledge. We watch or act a play, we read or tell a story, for other reasons, just as good—perhaps because we want, or want others to have, a peculiarly valuable experience, whether it gives new information or not. A religious ceremony or a football rally doesn't reveal, or convey, hitherto unknown facts; it is a witness to and a celebration of something the group finds memorable. But some of the important reading (and listening) we do aims to supply us with true beliefs about matters of fact in the natural or social world around us. And some of the important writing (and speaking) we do—in reports or committee meetings, for example—aims to share with others the true beliefs that we already have. It is this sort of language that we shall be especially interested in—though the principles of logic *can* be applied to any discourse, if you care to apply them.

How to Use This Book

This book, then, is an introduction to applied logic, with special emphasis upon the principles for handling ordinary English. It is designed to be useful to anyone who wishes to be as rational as he can in solving his share of the problems of man—personal, domestic, political, and international.

There are several points about the book that might well be kept in mind from the start.

First, it is planned for orderly study as well as for flexibility. There is an opening chapter introducing a half-dozen basic terms that are used throughout the book. It is probably best to read this chapter first.

Chapters 2 and 3 present some widely applicable principles of logic. These are (to use a phrase of I. A. Richards) the "logical machinery" of the book, and it has been kept quite simple and plain, though it includes a few indispensable distinctions usually left out of elementary treatments. It is a good idea to think of these principles as "logical machinery," for they are brought in to do a certain job, and they are to be judged according to their success, whether or not they occasionally creak or look awkward. The problem in these two chapters is: how do we know when a train of thought, leading from one idea to another, is *correct*? There is more than one way of setting up the rules of correctness; and our rules could be more sharply defined, or extended further. Moreover, in this space we cannot lay down all the rules. We shall examine a few of the most general and useful ones, and try to become clear about what correctness is—which may help us to recognize it even without the aid of rules.

The last four chapters distinguish various features of language and meaning that a critical reader must be aware of, and present techniques for dealing with certain kinds of verbal behavior that are likely to give trouble to readers and writers—for example, ambiguity, emotive language, and metaphor.

In some ways it is easier to understand the problems of language after you have a general idea of what thinking looks like when it is clear and correct; that is why the two chapters on logic are placed after Chapter 1. But some teachers may prefer to take up the principles of language first, and this is perfectly feasible, for the last four chapters do not presuppose Chapters 2 and 3, and the few terms that are introduced in Chapters 2 and 3 and used later can be looked up in the index and their definitions easily found. The sections in each chapter build upon one another to some extent, but each completes a topic, so that a teacher who is pressed for time can leave out sections without leaving gaps in the exposition.

Part of what this book aims to supply is a vocabulary for talking about logical and linguistic matters. We shall make a number of distinctions that are a powerful aid to straight thinking, though some of them are blurred by common speech. Where everyday language fails us, we have to introduce technical words to mark our distinctions; these unfamiliar words are not numerous, and they are carefully defined and illustrated. Many of the other important words in this book are common enough, but they are often used loosely and carelessly: for example, "assumption," "prove," "valid," "theorem," "evidence," "derive," "logical," "deduce," "induce," and "implies." When you know how to use these words, you have some very handy tools. You know what to look for in what you read, what sort of thinking it involves, and what sorts of crooked thinking it is apt to fall into. And you can explain clearly and convincingly to others why you think that a plan is good or bad, why you think that an opinion is right or wrong.

This helps you achieve a degree of calm in reading about highly emotional or sensational issues. Before you can think straight about such matters, you have to be somewhat detached and objective. Of course this is something that logic by itself can't give you. Still, if you try applying the principles to cases where it is not hard to be fairly detached, you can develop a tendency to look at what you read and hear this way, when you want to. And this in turn helps make it easier to keep your eye on the words themselves, rather than succumb to them. It is something like the way a surgeon goes to his task, or an arachnologist might overcome a distaste for spiders. The surgeon can control his natural feelings about blood because he's got something to do, and he knows how to do it—and the critical thinker is in a similar position with respect to a piece of violent propaganda or a particularly malicious bit of character assassination.

That is why this book, which is above all designed to be practical, contains a large number of things to do. First, after each section in a chapter, there is a Check-up Quiz, a relatively quick and simple exercise to help you make sure you understand the main points of that section. There are thirty of these. Second, at the end of each chapter there are several longer exercises, considerably varied, and generally harder and more searching. Some of them contain more items than you may be able to do in a single assignment; you might do half of them when you first read the chapter, and the other half when you are studying for a test. There are forty of these exercises, of which the last three are set apart at the end of the book. These three consist of longer passages that illustrate mistakes of all sorts, and each can be used as a general review of the whole book or of any part of it. To help you with these, there is, finally, a list of nineteen fallacies discussed in the book, with brief definitions and examples.

You will learn a good deal if you also collect your own examples of confused and crooked thinking—and of especially good thinking—while you are studying this book. If you keep a lookout while you are reading the newspaper or your favorite magazines, you will probably find examples of most of the mistakes we shall be discussing.

Nobody can start from scratch in studying a book like this; if you didn't have some grasp of the differences between good thinking and poor thinking, you wouldn't be able to study logic in the first place. What you are after is (first) to clarify and sharpen your understanding of what is going on in the cases you can already recognize to be crooked, so that (second) you can deal more safely and efficiently with the harder cases. You will get most out of this book if you know what you are looking for in it. A good way to begin, then, is to try the following PRELIMINARY QUIZ. See what you can do with these twenty-five examples before you study the book, and then, after you have finished it, see how well you think you did earlier. (At the end of each paragraph there is a reference to the section that takes up the principles that apply to it particularly.)

A PRELIMINARY QUIZ.   How good is the thinking in the passages below? Read each passage carefully. If you find that the thinking is confused or crooked, try to explain briefly in your own words exactly what is wrong.

A. SHOULD THE CONSTITUTION BE AMENDED TO PERMIT 18-YEAR-OLDS TO VOTE?

In the second session of the 83d Congress, the Administration, as it had promised earlier, submitted to Congress a bill proposing a 23d amendment to the Constitution, which, when ratified by three-fourths of the states, would lower the legal voting age to 18. This bill was debated at length in the Senate on May 21, 1954; it was discussed in magazine articles, editorials, letters to editors, and radio forums. Here are some of the comments that were made:

1. Anyone who is considered old enough to go into the army and fight for his country must be a mature person, and anyone old enough to vote must be a mature person, too. Hence, anyone old enough to fight is old enough to vote. (See §12)

2. It is all very well to say that 18-year-olds are qualified to vote. But let me remind you that Russia, and the satellite countries behind the Iron Curtain, have lowered the voting age to 18. And let me remind you that in all the history of the world there has been no such terror and slavery as in those hapless lands. (See §30)

3. Tradition has drawn a clear line between youth and maturity, fixing it at the 21st birthday. If we abandon this demarcation, where can we logically stop? If 18, why not 17½? If 17½, why not 17? And so on. Shall we then wind up by carrying infants to the polls, placing ballots in their little hands, and letting them vote by putting the ballot into either a pink or blue ballot box, whichever strikes their fancy? (See §19)

4. There is one state in the Union that already allows 18-year-olds to vote, and that is Georgia. What we learn from observing the politics of that state, its recent preferences for Governor, and other things,

makes it clear that to allow 18-year-olds to vote is a very great mistake. (See §7)

5. It has been argued that boys who are old enough to fight are old enough to vote. This is argued by those who say that 18-year-olds are old enough to vote. But does it follow that 18-year-old girls are also old enough to fight, and to be logical would we not have to draft them into the Army? (See §12)

6. Those who are in favor of this amendment are in effect going to the people of the great state of Texas and saying to them: "Do you believe that Washington bureaucrats should tell Texans what age they should fix for voting?" I challenge anyone to do that. (See §29)

7. I don't believe in depriving citizens of their chance to vote, and certainly not those draftees who stand ready to give their lives for our liberty. But I do say that only people who have the opportunity to keep in close touch with what is going on in politics should vote, and soldiers in training don't have this opportunity. (See §13)

8. The American people, acting through their elected representatives, have declared that citizens shall not be denied the right to vote by reason of color (the 15th amendment) or sex (the 19th amendment). In exactly the same way, we are now proposing that they shall not be denied this right by reason of being only 18 years old; the three are exactly the same in principle. (See §9)

9. What is the proposal before the Senate? The proposal is merely to have the Senate pass the resolution so that it can be sent on to the states for their consideration. What are those who are opposing the resolution afraid of? What is their hidden aim? Why do they want to prevent the states from expressing themselves? (See §30)

10. If we follow to its logical conclusion the argument of those who say anyone old enough to fight is old enough to vote, we shall have to say that men over the draft age should not be allowed to vote, because they are not of fighting age. (See §12)

11. I am sure that 18-year-olds today have more maturity of judgment than 18-year-olds did one or two generations ago. I have a daughter who is now 20, and I feel that at 18 she was at least as well equipped to decide who she wanted to have for president as I was at 21. (See §7)

12. I am in favor of 18-year-olds voting, but I am not in favor of forcing states to set their voting age at 18 if they don't want to. Obviously

if it were a matter of life and death, an amendment to the Constitution would be in order. But obviously it is not a matter of life and death. Therefore, a constitutional amendment is not in order. (See §15)

13. But let us set aside the dry legalistic aspects of this issue, and get to the simple heart of the matter, which can be put in a nutshell. Picture, if you will, the young lad sent off to service abroad, by the vote of his Senator or Congressman. He has nothing to say about it; he is pushed around by his so-called "representatives," but he cannot vote; he can only silently grieve . . . (See §30)

B. Should "comic" books be censored?

A special Senate subcommittee that was investigating juvenile delinquency in the spring of 1954 heard testimony from various people on so-called "comic" books and their effect upon children. More than a billion of these are sold every year in the United States, most of them at 10 cents each. Partly as a result of the subcommittee's discoveries, various proposals have been made to censor or regulate the sale of comic books more drastically, and to prohibit the sale of objectionable ones. These proposals have been opposed as violating freedom of the press, and there has been much public discussion. Here are some comments:

14. In one comic book which I found my children had bought, there was a story about an orphan boy who is cared for very solicitously by foster parents because, as he discovers, they are vampires who suck his blood when he goes to sleep. Justice triumphs in the end, however, because this boy turns into a werewolf and eats his foster parents. Now this is rather gruesome, to be sure, but it didn't seem to give bad dreams to my children, and I'm sure therefore that it won't have bad effects on other healthy children. (See §7)

15. It is absurd to think that mere stories and pictures can have any noticeable effect upon the way healthy, normal children behave. Of course comic books don't do them any harm. Children just read them —they don't go out and cut people in pieces or push them off cliffs just because the people in the comic books do. But this is only the negative side of the case—on the positive side, it can be said that comic books can inspire a moral point of view, patriotism, Americanism, admiration of strength and courage, and so on, so that many healthy children who read them probably are in fact led to act better than they did before. (See §14)

16. The whole question comes down to this: has any of our red-blooded American children ever been ruined merely by a comic book? The suggestion is laughable. There's your answer to the question about their harmfulness. (See §30)

17. Comic books are sometimes condemned because they are read by so many adults, and they are sarcastically called "escape literature" because they take people's minds off their problems and keep them from solving their problems (so it is said). Now let's dispose of this term once and for all. A problem is a situation that perplexes or worries someone so that there is a need to change it. Now, if a book takes a person's mind off a situation, there is no perplexity or worry, and there is therefore no problem. But if there is no problem, there is nothing to escape from, and no "escape"; in fact the comic book does away with the problem. (See §20)

18. Books that are really comic ought to be permitted to be sold without restriction, but some comic books are not really comic; it follows that they ought not to be permitted to be sold without restriction. (See §12)

19. It is not enough to say that every parent should decide what his own child should read, any more than we can leave it up to each parent to decide what medicine his child should take. That's like saying we can leave it up to a parent to decide whether he will risk polio infection or quarantine his children for measles. You can't fight a disease in your own home if it's all around you. And the poisonous virus spread about by comic books is the same. As Dr. Frederic Wertham, the psychiatrist, says in his book *Seduction of the Innocent*, they should be controlled by civil authorities, and the worst ones destroyed before they do irreparable harm. (See §9)

20. As with most issues, this one can easily be settled by a few clear definitions. Definitions, of course, are arbitrary, and I choose to define "juvenile delinquency" in my own way. I say a child is delinquent if he is involved—in word, thought, or deed—with antisocial behavior. When he reads stories of crime, he naturally *thinks* of crime, and therefore in my sense crime comics make children delinquent. (See §24)

21. The test is obvious when we reason correctly. If comic books are bad, we would expect them to have a disturbing effect upon a child who reads them over a period of time. My younger child, who has read them for some time, shows signs of being disturbed. It logically follows that comic books are bad. (See §15)

22. Comic books may be divided into several kinds: funny ones (like "Donald Duck"), classics (like "Treasure Island"), and horror-mystery-crime (like "Eerie Comics"). The great majority of them seem to belong in the first group, but the popularity of the third kind among children is on the increase. (See §8)

23. Those who object to regulating the sale of horrible and obscene comics generally defend their view on the ground of aesthetic freedom, thus assuming that there is no fundamental difference between comic books and genuine literature. But surely this assumption is false, for it fails to give an account of the distinctive qualities of true literature that are missing from comic books. (See §16)

24. All I can say is, those who tackle the problem of juvenile delinquency by burning books are throwing paper pellets to scare away a tiger, and they will fall flat on their faces. (See §26)

25. There are two things we can do: we can try, by various kinds of pressure, to improve the level of comic books, or we can try, so to speak, to inoculate our children against them. It seems clear to me that we *should* try to work on the children, by education in taste and by helping their mental health, and it follows necessarily, then, that we should *not* do anything about the comic books themselves. (See §15)

THINKING STRAIGHT

Sizing up an Argument

Suppose you open a book, unfold a newspaper, turn the page of a magazine, listen to a news broadcast, or see someone rise at a meeting to make a proposal. Or suppose you become aware that your acquaintance at lunch is neglecting his coffee in order to tell you his convictions about politics, race, modern art, food, sex, or himself. What you are reading or hearing consists of a series of words in a particular language, more or less connected according to the general rules that make up the grammar of that language. For the sake of brevity, we shall call any such series of words (whether spoken or written) a **discourse**. A discourse may be long or short, in prose or verse, serious or trivial, valuable or worthless. A newspaper editorial is a discourse, and so are James Joyce's *Ulysses*, a shampoo commercial, "The Shooting of Dan McGrew," a shaggy dog story, *Macbeth*, *Mein Kampf*, and the Emancipation Proclamation.

A discourse may be accompanied by pictures, graphs, charts, or music, which may have important connections with the words, but the words themselves are the discourse.

There are a great many ways of looking at a discourse, and there may be a number of things in a single discourse in which you can be interested. You can be interested in its grammatical peculiarities, its sound, its wit, its beauty; in what it shows about social conditions; in how well it takes your mind off an unpleasant task or puts you to sleep. You can be interested in it as a clue to mental disorder, as a source of income, as an aid to selling plywood or mouth wash, or as a means of getting votes. These features of a discourse are the concern of all sorts of specialists: the linguist, the song-writer, the gagster, the literary critic, the historian, the sociologist, the person who is bored, the insomniac, the psychiatrist, the journalist, the adman, the politician.

But you can also be interested in whether or not you ought to believe it, and to act upon that belief.

When you pay attention to a discourse and notice your own mental processes as they are affected by it, you find many things going on in your mind. You may be moved, irritated, bored, cheered, soothed, or disgusted. But in order to think clearly about it, you must concentrate, not on your own feelings, but on the discourse itself. Before you can decide whether there is something in it that ought to be believed, you must recognize the *kind* of discourse it is; you must see what, if anything, it has to *say*.

A discourse is a *whole*. The sentences and words that make it up are not quite like blocks or bricks that just lie quietly side by side, or one on top of the other. The words, somewhat like a colony of living things, throw out all sorts of links to one another, and the sentences, though somewhat more detachable than the words, develop their own interrelations, throwing light or confusion, giving life or deadening, building up or cancelling one another. But to get a firm grip on a discourse, so that we can be sure to know how much of it we can believe, and how confidently we can believe it, we have to analyze it. The special vocabulary and principles of logic are devices for prying a discourse apart to examine the way it works. This does not mean that we cannot put it back together again, or that we must miss the wood for the trees, for we need not lose sight of our aim, which is to understand and pass judgment upon the discourse as a whole. But we must begin by getting a clear idea of the working parts. And the first parts to notice particularly are the individual sentences.

§1. STATEMENTS

When someone sneezes, you may be able to tell that he has hay fever. If you feel sorry for him, you may say, "Too bad!" But you don't say, "That's true." His sneeze *shows* that he has hay fever, but doesn't *say* it. It would be different if he had said, "I have hay fever"—then you could agree with him. But you can't agree with a sneeze: a sneeze is neither true nor false.

It is the same with laughing, crying, groaning, or measles spots:

they may be symptoms of someone's feelings or state of health, but they are not words. If someone groans when there's nothing wrong with him, and makes you think he is in pain when he isn't, you can say he has deceived you, but he hasn't exactly lied.

Sneezes and groans are not discourse, for a discourse is a string of words. But some discourse is like them in one very important respect. There are two very different kinds of sentences: (1) those that are (like sneezes) neither true nor false, and (2) those that are either true or false.

The first kind includes sentences of three familiar grammatical types. (1) Most *interrogative* sentences are neither true nor false: "What is my line?" "How can world trade be increased?" "What causes cancer?" (2) Most *imperative* sentences are neither true nor false: "Close cover before striking matches." "Let's get out of here!" "Thou shalt not kill!" (3) Most exclamations are neither true nor false: "Ouch!" "Oh, dear!" "Hooray!" (Some grammarians would call "Ouch!" a "nonsentence," but that doesn't affect the point here.)

The second kind includes most *declarative* sentences (whether in the indicative or subjunctive mood): "Some species of centipede have one hundred and seventy-three pairs of legs." "She was a phantom of delight." "If Lee had won the battle of Gettysburg, the South would have won the War Between the States."

The sentences we have put in our first group are questions, commands, or ejaculations. Although there are important differences among them, they all have something in common: they cannot make *assertions*. If someone asks, "What time is it?" it makes no sense to reply, "I agree" or "I disagree." If someone says, "Please open the window," it makes no sense to reply, "I believe it" or "I don't believe it."

But most declarative sentences are quite different. They can be true or false. If someone says, "It's three o'clock," or "The window is shut," it does make sense to agree or disagree; something is said that can be believed or disbelieved. Sentences that are either true or false we shall call **statements.** Any group of words that can be asserted is a statement: reports, opinions, affirmations, denials, comments, remarks, judgments, propositions. To make a report or to express an opinion is to utter a declarative sentence, or a number of declarative sentences, and that is to make a statement.

There are some cases where you may feel that the distinction between statements and other sentences is not very sharp: "No smoking!" certainly is *not* a statement, but "It is against the rules to smoke here" certainly *is*. Still, for some practical purposes these are not very different, and in between them we can find borderline sentences like "You ought not to smoke here." It would take us into some fairly difficult philosophical questions to decide definitely about this last example, and we will have to be content for the time being with a rule-of-thumb distinction. Our principle will be this: Any sentence that can be understood in a way that makes it susceptible of being affirmed or denied is a statement. Sentences built around the word "ought" are readily affirmed or denied in ordinary speech, and therefore, by our principle, they will be counted as statements.

Most declarative sentences, then, are statements, and most other sentences are not. But this is not much help unless we are clear what the exceptions are. You can't come to grips with a discourse unless you know when it is saying something and when it is not: the better you understand this distinction, the more quickly you can get at what is significant in what you read or hear.

There is one sort of declarative sentence that we shall count as an exception to the general rule that declarative sentences are state-ments. It is a rather odd sort, and fortunately doesn't turn up very often, but it is worth noting. Suppose a friend of yours in a foreign country, who gets his American news in a roundabout way, tells you that he believes the Sultan of Wisconsin has a beard, "Is that not so?" You might be puzzled about the best way to set him straight. Since (at last report) there is no Sultan of Wisconsin, you don't want to say that it's *false* that the Sultan of Wisconsin has a beard, and of course you don't want to say it's *true* either. There is nobody for it to be true or false *about*. So sentences like "The Sultan of Wisconsin has a beard," or "The Shangri-La Board of Education is conservative," can be said to be neither true nor false, and hence, by our definition, not genuine statements. There is an interesting way of interpreting such sentences so that they *are* true or false (by this interpretation they become, in fact, false), but we shall not concern ourselves with that possibility here, for in ordinary conversations, it seems evident, we would say they cannot be simply accepted or rejected as they stand. Their peculiarity is that they contain a refer-ence to something that does not exist, and thereby rest upon a false assumption about the world; if you have no sister, the question, "Is your sister a blonde?" cannot be answered either "Yes" or "No."

Except for these false-assumption sentences, then, we can say that all declarative sentences are statements. But in some cases we have too little information about the circumstances in which a sentence is written or uttered to *know* whether it is a statement or not. If you don't happen to know whether or not there *is* an Akond of Swat, then you don't know whether there are statements to answer the famous questions in Edward Lear's poem:

> Do his people like him extremely well?
> Or do they, whenever they can, rebel,   or PLOT,
>   At the Akond of Swat?
>
> If he catches them then, either old or young,
> Does he have them chopped in pieces or hung,   or SHOT,
>   The Akond of Swat?

More important are sentences like "I'm hungry" and "It's cold today," which are incomplete in certain ways—they don't have a definite meaning for us until we know *who* is speaking, or *when* he is speaking. Since they contain the words "I" and "today," which refer to the speaker and to the circumstances under which he is speaking, a vital ingredient is missing from them when they are extracted from those circumstances and considered by themselves. They are not detachable. Before we can find out whether they are true or false, we have to know what the circumstances are.

This is rather like trying to make sense of a scrap of a letter found on the sidewalk, or a fragment of a telephone conversation. "He told me you said not to tell her about it" is impenetrable to an outsider. But even in this case, though we don't know *what* is supposed to be kept from *whom*, and on *whose* authority—that is, we don't know the antecedents or referents of the key pronouns—we do have evidence that the pronouns are being used to refer to *somebody*, and if we knew the circumstances, we could fill out the missing places in the sentence and reconstruct the whole message. Therefore, we shall call these sentences "statements" because, taken in their circumstances, they can be agreed to or disagreed with by someone who understands them. They are incomplete as they stand, but they *can* be completed by those who use them, and when completed they would be full-fledged statements.

Generally speaking, then, declarative sentences are statements, whether *affirmative* ("Buttons are useful") or *negative* ("Coffee is not fattening"). Moreover, some *parts* of declarative sentences are also statements: for example, nonrestrictive clauses that are introduced by relative pronouns. For such clauses may be agreed with, or objected to, on their own account. And with a little ingenuity they can be transformed into independent sentences.

Take the following sentence: "The workers refused to join the union, which was controlled by the company." This sentence has two clauses, and can be broken down into two simple sentences: "The workers refused to join the union. The union was controlled by the company." It is not recommended that you translate complex sentences, wherever possible, into simple ones, of course, though sometimes this is an excellent way of making complicated meanings clear. But to read a complex sentence intelligently you must know whether it contains more than one statement, and the test is whether the parts of it can be made into independent sentences without distorting the meaning.

In the example just given, the translation brings out the importance of the comma. For if there were no comma after the word "union," the sentence would not have been equal to two statements, since the clause would have been restrictive. The sentence, "He talked to the committeemen, who were at home," says two things: that he talked to the committeemen *and* that they were at home. But in the sentence, "He talked to the committeemen who were at home," the subordinate clause merely tells *which* of the committeemen he talked to. Similarly, the sentence, "Only a poet like E. E. Cummings would think of 'swaggering cookies of indignant light,'" says that any poet who would think of that phrase would have to be like Cummings. But the sentence, "Only a poet, like E. E. Cummings, would think of that phrase," says that anyone who would think of that phrase is a poet, *and* that Cummings is a poet, too.

Just as there are parts of statements that are statements, so there are parts of other sentences that are statements, even if the sentences as a whole are not declarative sentences. There are certain kinds of questions, commands, and exclamations that contain true or false ingredients, and these questions, commands, and exclamations must, for our purposes, be treated as statements.

First, consider *questions*. Direct questions, like "Did it rain yesterday?" merely ask for information; they do not give it. But questions that have a negative form like "*Didn't* it rain yesterday?" are more complicated. "Didn't it rain yesterday?" is like saying, "It did rain yesterday, didn't it?" and such a question, though it is perhaps a rather tentative sort of statement, is a statement nevertheless. Negative questions, then, can be partly translated into statements to make the implicit assertion explicit. The question, "If you prick us, do we not bleed?" includes the statement, "If you prick us, we do bleed."

Next, consider *commands*. Simple and direct commands, like "Vote!" or "Watch out" or 'Drop dead!" get their results just by indicating the action to be performed. But some commands go beyond this. "Remember that you have a duty to vote!" includes the statement, "You have a duty to vote." And "Don't tangle with Murgatroyd, who has it in for you" includes the statement, "Murgatroyd has it in for you."

Finally, consider *exclamations*. Some exclamations, like "Ugh!" or "Ah!" are no more than expletives, that is, involuntary responses to an affecting situation. But other exclamations contain clauses. "How ugly that painting is!" includes the statement, "That painting is ugly." And "Oh, how the mighty have fallen!" includes the statement, "The mighty have fallen."

Now, of course, there will be borderline cases, where even after careful examination you can't be sure whether something is being stated or not. It is important not to miss statements that are made in a discourse, but it is just as important not to read into a discourse something that isn't there. Both kinds of mistakes can get you into trouble, whether you are reading a love letter or an insurance policy or instructions for assembling a kitchen cabinet. One precaution against this trouble is to be clear about what is, and what is not, a statement.

A CHECK-UP QUIZ. Which of these sentences either are or include statements? If only part of a sentence is a statement, write out that part.

1. "For this reason, all of us who believe in the aims of this program should join together to elect Republican Senators and Congressmen, who will work effectively with leaders of the Executive Branch toward the fulfillment of that program." (A Presidential message in August, 1954.)

2. What shall we do now?

3. All generalizations are untrue, including this one.

4. Report at 7:00 A.M. to begin your job, which has already been explained.

5. Long live the king!

6. Wouldn't it be better to reconsider the provisions of the treaty in the light of these developments?

7. How difficult it is to get a clear picture of the situation!

8. Many are called, but few are chosen.

9. All aboard!

10. I gave her one, they gave him two,
    You gave us three or more;
    They all returned from him to you
    Though they were mine before.

FURTHER READING: Morris Cohen and Ernest Nagel, *An Introduction to Logic and Scientific Method*. New York: Harcourt, Brace and Co., 1934, ch. 2, sec. 1.   P. F. Strawson, *Introduction to Logical Theory*. New York: John Wiley and Sons, 1952, ch. 6, sec. 3. L. M. Myers, *American English*. New York: Prentice-Hall, Inc., 1952, Part III.

§2. ASSERTION

Truth and falsity are the central notions that we use in approaching discourse from a logical point of view. There are many things about a statement that one can be concerned about, but in this book we only want to know how to tell, as well as we can, whether it is true or false.

Now there are some statements that you might hesitate to call true or false because it seems unlikely that you can ever decide conclusively (or at least that people will ever all agree) that they are true or false. A statement like "American policy toward China during World War II was responsible for its going Communist" is such a crude description of such a very complicated matter, that most of us wouldn't want to discuss its truth or falsity as it stands, without making a number of distinctions. At least we know that yes-or-no debates over such questions are generally pretty futile because the truth, if it can be obtained, is a mixture of a number of truths. Moreover, statements like "The veto power should be taken away from members of the Security Council of the United Nations" and "Alaska and Hawaii should be admitted to the Union as states," are the subject of widespread and sometimes bitter disagreement, with something to be said on both sides. Of course, that doesn't mean that no *more* can be said on one side than on the other, but they are open questions; their truth or falsity is still in the balance.

Sometimes such statements as these are said to be *neither* true nor false because they are "mere opinions" or because their truth is "relative" to some point of view. In this way of speaking, "opinions" are contrasted with "facts." Thus the statement, "The Washington Monument is 555 ft., 5⅛ inches high," is said to be a "fact," whereas the statement, "Washington was wrong in warning us against foreign entanglements" is said to be an "opinion," or, sometimes, a "proposition," the difference being that the former is not "debatable," whereas the latter is.

This is a very confusing way of describing the difference, however. Facts, it is true, are not debatable, but that is only because facts are statements whose truth is thought of as securely established. You call the statement about the Washington Monument a "fact" because you assume that the measurements have been carried out carefully, and checked, and rechecked; if the statement about foreign entanglements were as conclusively shown to be true (and a growing number of people think the evidence is fairly conclusive), it, too, would be called a "fact." An opinion is a statement that is believed, or ought to be believed, tentatively and without too much confidence—say, that rockets will take us to the moon in thirty years, or that the Dodgers will win the next World Series—but an opinion is not an opinion unless it is an opinion *about* something. We may not *know* whether it is true—as we do not know whether there are four hundred and sixty-two mountains on the other side of the moon, or whether Xerxes often had nightmares—but we know that it must be either true or false.

In this book, we shall treat sentences about what is right and wrong, good and bad, as statements. There are, it is true, many puzzling features of value-judgments, and it must be admitted that present-day philosophers are far from complete agreement about them. But these difficult questions we have to set aside. As they appear in ordinary speech, statements about right and wrong are commonly used like other statements; they are affirmed and denied, attacked and defended, and they are understood to commit those who utter them to definite courses of action. In short, they are regarded as statements.

Whether or not a sentence can be used to make an assertion is a good test of whether it is a statement or not. But this is no help unless we are clear about what it is to make an assertion. Ordinarily, when you utter a statement, or write it down for someone else to read (or for yourself to read later), you believe that what you write down is true, and you expect your hearer or reader to believe it too. Of course, you can lie, but to lie with any hope of success you have to let on that you believe what you are saying, and so you are soliciting the belief of your audience. When someone, then, utters or writes a statement in such a way (that is, with such a tone of voice, or in such circumstances) that he appears to believe what he is saying, and appears to invite others to believe it as well, we shall say that he is **asserting** the statement, or making an assertion.

There are several ways of uttering or writing statements *without* asserting them. You may put them into indirect discourse: when you say, "Medieval people thought the earth is flat," you are not yourself asserting that the earth is flat. You may put them inside quotation marks: the Bible contains the statement, "There is no God," but it is not asserted, for it is preceded by the words, "The fool hath said in his heart." The statements that are printed in small type in this book are not asserted *by the author*, but presented as examples of someone else's assertions, except where otherwise noted. In speaking, you may utter a statement in a tone of skepticism or mockery that shows you are only echoing another person's incredible stupidities: "Oh, you know Max. No *sacrifiss* is too great for *A-a-art!*"

Perhaps the most noteworthy examples of statements that are written without being asserted are those that occur in literary works. Here we touch upon a very interesting and difficult philosophical problem, to which more than one answer has been given. Of course, we can't deal with it adequately here, but it needs a little discussion, at least to make more clear the kind of discourse that we are concerned about in this book.

When you tell someone a joke or a tale, you show him that it is only a joke, that you don't believe it really happened or expect him to believe it; you may even tell him you made it all up. A writer of fiction does something like this when he labels his work a "novel" or a "mystery story," and also by much subtler means. Of course, some of the sentences in his novel may be not quite statements at all, like the one about the Sultan of Wisconsin; the Wizard of Oz and the Forsaken Merman are also nonexistent people. But other sentences in the novel may be true or false: "At 4:30 P.M. on November 26, 1939, a young man wearing a gabardine topcoat was waiting for a Washington train in Pennsylvania Station, ..." We don't *care* whether the statement is true or false, and would not take the trouble to find out because we don't have to know in order to enjoy the story; but presumably it *could* be true or false, nevertheless.

Though our discussion of this problem about the difference between literature and other types of discourse, or between fiction and nonfiction, is very sketchy, it may be enough to show some of the reasons why we generally do not treat the sentences in novels or poems as materials for logical analysis. In many of the greatest literary works, of course, there are implicit theses or doctrines about politics, society, life, or God. In so far as *Paradise Lost* or *An Essay on Man* lays claim to our assent, it is assertive. And if we want to we can examine its assertions like any others to find out whether we should believe them. But where nothing is asserted, where no information is proffered or requested, the question of truth or falsity simply doesn't arise.

The distinction we have been making, between, let us say, assertive and nonassertive discourse, is quite often mixed up with a very different distinction with which it is connected. Writers on logic and language usually distinguish between various "uses" or "functions" of language: the "informative" (to convey truth), the "expressive" (to vent feelings or excite them), and the "incitive" (to get people to do things). Usually literary works turn up, in this classification, as examples of the "expressive" use of language, and this is thought to take care of them. It would carry us too far from our chief business here to consider the difficulties in this view of literature; the main point to keep in mind is that this classification is neither a very clear nor a very helpful one. No doubt language can be used in thousands of different ways, that is, as a means of realizing an unlimited variety of purposes, and no doubt this variety can be collected under three, or six, or some other number of headings. But the important question about any discourse that confronts us is not "What is its function?" but "What is it?" If it is, or contains, an assertion, or purports to be true, then it invites belief, and it is up to us to decide whether to accept that invitation. We must keep our mind on this problem, no matter if at the same time the discourse is expressive, evocative, or incitive.

A statement, then, is, by definition, something that *can* be asserted, though it may *not* be asserted on a particular occasion. And the statements that we shall, for the most part, be concerned with are statements that *are* asserted, and not only that, but often believed both by those who assert them and by those who read or hear them. These are the ones it is important to think straight about.

A CHECK-UP QUIZ. Which of the following statements *in italics* are probably asserted by the speaker, and which are not?

1. Some people believe that *euthanasia is wrong.*
2. I believe that *euthanasia is not wrong.*
3. *Weather tonight: cloudy and continued warm.*
4. All right, I'll tell you a story. *Once upon a time there was an enormously fat king who had three daughters . . .*
5. If economic conditions continue as foreseen, *we shall balance the budget.*
6. *There was a young belle of old Natchez,*
   Whose garments were always in patchez . . .
7. *In 1275 Marco Polo reached the court of Kublai Khan after a journey of three and a half years.*
8. Aristotle said, "*Man is a rational animal.*"
9. As Aristotle said, *man is a rational animal.*
10. Friends, *Shakespeare cigarettes are cooler, milder, tastier, less irritating and more free from harmful ingredients.*

FURTHER READING: Irving M. Copi, *Introduction to Logic.* New York: Macmillan Co., 1953, ch. 2, secs. 1–3.

§3. EXPOSITION AND ARGUMENT

Now let us consider those discourses that contain asserted statements. Here is a passage that might appear in a history book:

. . . The Smoot-Hawley Tariff Act, passed in June, 1930, raised import duties on many goods considerably above the already high levels. But the Democratic Administration which took over in 1933 began, in 1935, to sponsor the Hull system of bilateral trade agreements. Many of the unfortunate effects of the high-tariff laws were then alleviated. World trade was somewhat expanding in 1939, when the Second World War....

Notice that this passage consists of a series of assertions, and nothing more. The following passage on the same subject might appear in an economics book:

> ... In the short run, a high tariff on high-quality shoes seems to benefit shoemakers in America by keeping British shoes out of effective competition. But in the long run, the tariff works to every-one's disadvantage. For it keeps the price of shoes high, and therefore absorbs money which consumers could be spending on other things —money which would increase production of other goods and lower *their* price. Moreover, it keeps the shoemakers employed in work that is economically unsound, when they could be making other things that the United States can produce more efficiently than other countries. . . .

Here the statements are placed in a certain relation to each other by the words "for" and "therefore": some of the statements are offered as *reasons* for other statements. When a discourse not only makes assertions, but also asserts that some of the assertions are reasons for other ones, we shall call it an **argument**. Discourse that does not give reasons we shall call **exposition**.

In common speech, as when someone says, "Let's not get into an argument," the word "argument" often means a dispute, or a some-what acrimonious disagreement between two people. In the language of logic it is used in a more inclusive sense, as when we speak of some-one "arguing for" something. An argument in this sense is a discourse that contains at least two asserted statements and the claim that one statement ought to be believed because another is true.

To believe a statement because you think it follows from another statement is to make an *inference*. And making inferences is *reason-ing*, that is, seeing reasons and seeing what they are reasons for. The relation between reasoning and argument is this: Reasoning is the mental process, and the argument is its verbal record.

The word "exposition" also has a broad sense here. Books on rhetoric often classify discourses in another way, as "exposition," "argument," "description," and "narration." Some description and narration, as in poems or stories, may not in fact be assertive at all, but, if we are speaking about assertive discourse. it seems more logical, and more useful, to let the word "exposition" cover all discourse that asserts but does not argue. Then *description* will be a special kind of exposition: it is exposition that deals, in the main, with fairly concrete matters. We describe a house, a bonfire, a girl, or a baseball game. *Narration* will be a special kind of description: it is a description of a happening, or a series of happenings. A narrative is about a baseball game, a revolution, a courtship, or a human life.

There are arguments of all imaginable degrees of complexity, but what holds them together is always the same: the idea of some statements being reasons for others. Probably the clearest and most direct word for this idea is the word *"therefore."* With this word, we can, so to speak, construct the simplest possible model of an argument and stop to study it closely before going on to more complex arguments, somewhat the way an aeronautics engineer constructs a small-scale working model of a new jet plane in order to see how it will behave in a wind tunnel. Consider this one:

> The sunset was very red tonight. *Therefore,* it will be a fine day tomorrow.

This is a stripped-down model. It's not quite the natural way of putting the argument in ordinary speech; we would be more likely to say something like, "I'll bet it will be a fine day tomorrow because the sunset was very red tonight." But the logical connection is the same.

Any argument, or piece of an argument, consisting of two statements can be written in the "therefore" form. The statement that goes in front of the "therefore" we shall call simply the *reason,* and the statement that goes after the "therefore" we shall call the *conclusion.* The conclusion is the statement we are being invited to believe; the reason is the statement that is supposed to support it. Thus a two-statement argument can be set up in this way:

Reason

therefore:

Conclusion

How, then, are we to decide when a discourse is an argument and when it is not? In many cases this is quite easy, providing we know which words in our language show that a certain statement is a conclusion from another statement. It is a significant fact about ordinary language that it gives us a remarkable number of ways of saying this. These words and phrases we shall call *logical indicators*; they show that inference is going on, and they point out the *direction* in which the inference is going.

To the critical reader, these logical indicators are important signals; he looks for them the way a sailor looks for buoys or a runner on second looks to the third-base coach. Each of the following words or phrases usually shows that the statement following it is a conclusion:

> therefore ...
> which shows that ...
> proves that ...
> hence ...
> thus ...
> so ...
> indicates that ...
> consequently ...
> you see that ...
> implies that ...
> entails ...
> allows us to infer that ...
> I conclude that ...
> we may deduce that ...
> points to the conclusion that ...
> suggests very strongly that ...
> leads me to believe that ...
> bears out my point that ...
> from which it follows that ...

And each of the following words or phrases usually shows that the statement following it is a reason:

> since ...
> for ...
> because ...
> for the reason that ...
> in view of the fact that ...
> on the correct supposition that ...
> assuming, as we may, that ...
> may be inferred from the fact that ...
> may be deduced from ...
> as shown by ...

> as indicated by . . .
> as is substantiated by . . .

This does not pretend to be a complete list of logical indicators; it contains most of the words and phrases whose main job is marking an argument, but there are many others that do this job on a part-time basis. If there seem to be rather too many, that need not discourage us. They all have their distinct uses to the writer, in particular contexts, and a sensitive reader must understand the differences between them. But at the moment we are not concerned about their differences: what they have in common is the idea that one statement logically depends upon another. And whenever any of them appears in an argument, it will always be possible to substitute the word "therefore" and arrange the statements in such a way that the reason comes first and the conclusion second.

Take for example the sentence:

> The proposal to construct Panther Mountain Dam is a betrayal of the people, since it would destroy beautiful scenery, a bird sanctuary, valuable hunting preserves, and one of the finest golf links in the state.

The word "since" tells us that what follows it is the reason, and what precedes it the conclusion. We can thus restate the argument in this way:

> It [constructing Panther Mountain Dam] would destroy beautiful scenery, a bird sanctuary, valuable hunting preserves, and one of the finest golf links in the state.

> *Therefore*:

> > The proposal to construct Panther Mountain Dam is a betrayal of the people.

The main source of difficulty in deciding whether or not a given discourse is an argument is that in some arguments there is no logical indicator at all. A discourse of this sort, though it does not explicitly assert that one statement is a reason for another, may still be an argument if it clearly and definitely *suggests* that this is so. Suppose someone remarks, "The sky is full of dark clouds. It's going to rain." You would probably agree that this is an argument, in which the first statement is taken to be a reason for the second. There is an implicit "therefore" between them.

Arguments minus their logical indicators usually occur in informal conversation. The surrounding circumstances or tone of voice take the place of the indicator, and if there is any doubt, you can ask the speaker about it. If a writer doesn't take the trouble to let you know when he is making inferences, and expecting you to make them, the chances are his work is not worth bothering very much about. But *you* can make sure, when you construct your own argument, that it *is* an argument, and can be recognized as one.

In this book we shall be especially (though not exclusively) concerned with arguments. This covers more ground than you might think. Perhaps the word "argument" calls to mind debates, editorials, and Supreme Court decisions. But as a matter of fact, a great deal of the discourse you run across in the ordinary affairs of life, apart from songs, stories, and plays, is argument. It is very hard to write *pure* exposition, as you will discover if you try it. Even historical narratives, if they are interesting, and official reports, if they are significant, contain some reasoning, and require the reader to do some reasoning, too. You are reasoning when you interpret a poem, decide whether to buy a house, defend a political proposal, explain how to run a mink farm, or criticize a movie. Outside of literature and entertainment, most writing contains argument.

In this book we are interested in whether or not an argument is a sound one—that is, in whether or not a statement is a *good* reason for another, or, to put it more carefully, *how* good a reason it is (as compared with other reasons). When a reason is very good, we can say that the argument is a *proof*. And a critical reader is one who makes an effort, when he is reading an argument that matters, to find out whether or not the argument comes close to being a proof. That is the main theme of this book.

A CHECK-UP QUIZ. Each of the following items is an argument. What is the conclusion, and which are the logical indicators of each?

1. "Any man's death diminishes me, because I am involved in mankind" (John Donne).

2. Since no senator is willing to be counted against the bill in an election year, it will inevitably be passed.

3. There's no use in her trying to be an actress. You can't make a silk purse out of a sow's ear.

4. It is clear that his testimony is not very reliable because psychologists have shown that people who are excited are not good observers.

5. Roberts is the best pitcher in both leagues. He is the only 6-year 20-game winner.

6. It is important for every citizen to feel responsible for his country; consequently, everyone should pay at least some income tax.

7. Criminal trials should not be conducted in front of television cameras, for that only puts a premium on sensationalism and emotionalism.

8. Henry has been spending a lot of time playing golf. He has not been attending to his job.

9. That car you bought was no bargain. The motor needs a complete overhauling.

10. There is no limit to the power of Congress to investigate. Any fact could be relevant to some possible legislation.

FURTHER READING: Alburey Castell, *A College Logic*. New York: The Macmillan Co., 1935, topic 1.

§4. GETTING THE POINT

Once you know that you are confronted by an argument, you next want to know what it is aiming at. An argument is a discourse that is going somewhere, and before you can hope to say whether or not it is a good argument, you have to get the *point*.

In any argument, no matter how small or large, we find (a) some statements that are given as reasons for other statements, and (b) some statements that are given as conclusions, that is, supported by reasons. There may be some statements that are *both* reasons and conclusions at the same time. Some of the reasons, in other words, will in turn be supported by other reasons; but when you trace them back, you ultimately find certain statements that are not supported by any other statements *in that argument*. These we call the *basic reasons* of the argument. They are the rock-bottom statements on which the whole argument rests (though, of course, they might be conclusions in another argument at another time and place).

Moreover, you find that there is at least one statement (perhaps more than one) that is a conclusion, but not a reason, in that argument. This we call the *final conclusion* of the argument. The final conclusions are the statements that the argument aims to make convincing; they are the **point of the argument.**

The little two-statement arguments that we have used as examples contain only one basic reason. They are somewhat condensed, to be sure; in most of them, you can see that the basic reason wouldn't be a very *good* reason for the conclusion unless some important assumptions were made. And these other assumptions are, in a way, part of the argument, too. In his famous speech on the French Revolution, Edmund Burke said:

> The constituent parts of a state are obliged to hold their public faith with each other, and with all those who derive any serious interest under their engagements, as much as the whole state is bound to keep its faith with separate communities. Otherwise competence and power will soon be confounded, and no law be left but the will of a prevailing force.

When we turn this argument around so that it goes in the direction of the inference, and rephrase the reason, and put in an arrow to stand for "therefore," it looks like this:

> [If the constituent parts of a state did not keep faith with each other,] competence and power would soon be confounded, and no law left but the will of a prevailing force.
>
> The constituent parts of a state are obliged to hold their public faith with each other.

The statements have been abbreviated, but the gist of the argument is clear. Evidently some important assumptions have been left out of the argument; it is incomplete. Later, we will take up the problem of finding out and supplying what is left out of arguments like this. But before we come to that, we always have to be clear about the logical relationships between the statements we *do* have, and the most important part of this is to see which statements are the final conclusions.

The chief difficulty in finding the point of an argument is illustrated by the following passage:

Joyce Kilmer's "Trees" is a popular poem, and one that is often reprinted. Let us look at it closely. It compares the tree to a human being who presses her mouth against the ground while she lifts her arms in the air to pray. This utterly mixed metaphor puts the tree into an impossible posture. The tree is like a nursing infant, a chaste young maiden, and an overdressed woman who goes around wearing birds in her hair. All these figures are connected in the most superficial way, with a banal remark to sum them up. The rhythm is monotonous and trivial.

It is clear that this writer takes a dim view of "Trees," but if we search for a single sentence that contains the conclusion, we cannot find it. However, the statements it does contain all tend in the same direction, so that we can hardly help supplying an implicit conclusion, even if we are not sure exactly how it should go: let's say, " 'Trees' is not a good poem."

When a discourse is apparently an argument, in that some fairly definite conclusion could easily and reasonably be drawn from it, we can regard the conclusion as suggested, though not stated. (This distinction will be clarified in a later chapter.) Before we criticize the discourse, we have to make explicit the conclusion at which we think it aims, and treat this as the point of the argument. Some discourses, it is true, are so wandering that it is hard to know whether to treat them as confused exposition or as aimless argument. They seem pointless. In such a case, where the circumstances do not make it clear, you could still say whether it *would* be a good argument *if* it had such-and-such a conclusion. But this is a waste of time unless you judge that someone else might *think* it proves something.

A further comparison of argument with exposition may be helpful here. An exposition, by definition, does not have a point, but it may have, and be held together by, a *theme*. An exposition, like an argument, has a *subject*, which is what it is mostly about: the United Nations, yaks, radar, science fiction, the rules of parliamentary procedure. An exposition, like an argument, also *asserts* something about the subject, and the general tenor of its assertions can be summarized by such phrases as these: the importance of strengthening the United Nations, the health-giving properties of yaks' milk, the difficulty of repairing radar, the literary values of science fiction, the faults of some rules of parliamentary procedure. These are *themes*. In an exposition, the statements may be organized in any one of several ways: for example, according to a chronology of events (as in a history of the United Nations) or according to the subdivisions of the subject (the anatomical parts of the yak, or the chemical constituents of its milk). But they do not have the ". . . therefore . . ." pattern.

When you have singled out the final conclusions of an argument, you next need to trace out the main lines of thought. The logical *structure* of the argument is a sort of skeletal pattern in which reasons and conclusions are fitted together. To know whether the reasons are good ones, or the conclusions justified, you may have to take the argument apart and examine it piece by piece. But you will get its pieces mixed up or mislaid unless you first understand the general hang of it. This is easy when the argument is presented in a plain and tidy shape, with the statements set out in an orderly row, and all the inferences clearly marked by logical indicators. The arguments we are most likely to encounter in the ordinary course of events, however, have their skeletons hidden, and sometimes carefully disguised, so that a certain amount of dissection is needed to discover what is going on.

When the structure of an argument is really troublesome to grasp, it will be helpful to work it out with a *diagram*. By numbering the separate statements, and by using the arrow introduced above as an abbreviation for "therefore," you can show very simply the supports on which the conclusion is supposed to rest. If the argument is not too elaborate, you can put in every element; if it is long, you would do better to begin by summarizing it, and diagramming the main lines of force, leaving the less important statements for later consideration. It may seem a little artificial at first to reduce an argument to a diagram, but practice in this will help you in two ways: it is a good method for getting the drift of any argument, no matter how complicated it may be, and it will get you used to looking for, and sizing up quickly, the structure of an argument.

Before diagramming any argument, read it all the way through carefully:

> A common international language, like Esperanto or Interlingua, would be of tremendous benefit to the world. For the failure in understanding between peoples of different nations is responsible for much of their mutual mistrust. Moreover, the lack of an easy

medium of communication among business men and among scientists causes a great waste of time, money and effort. We must teach mankind an international language as soon as possible (to supplement, not to replace, existing tongues), especially since such a vast educational project would itself be a practicable field for desperately needed cooperation between nations. Let us not forget the tower of Babel!

Now you can break it down into its separate statements. This may take three steps. (1) Separate the statements by brackets, and number the usable ones. Some of the sentences or clauses may not be directly relevant to the argument and, though they are not to be forgotten, they can be temporarily set aside when you are only concerned with the logical structure of the argument. If we leave out the last sentence and the phrase in parentheses, we have five distinct statements in the present argument. (2) Underline the logical indicators, and supply any others that are required to make explicit the implicit connections. For instance, the word "for" shows that the second and third statements are reasons for the first, and the word "since" shows that the fifth statement is a reason for the fourth; it also appears, on further inspection, that the fourth statement is a conclusion from the first statement, so we can insert a "therefore" in front of the fourth statement. (3) In order to get the individual statements completely independent of one another, you may have to fill in parts of sentences that have been skipped, and supply the antecedents of pronouns. The phrase "such a vast educational project" refers back to "teach(ing) mankind an international language"; if the latter phrase is inserted in the fifth statement, it can stand by itself in a diagram.

The argument for an international language then looks like this:

① [A common international language, like Esperanto or Interlingua, would be of tremendous benefit to the world.] *For* ② [The failure in understanding between people of different nations is responsible for much of their mutual mistrust] and ③ [The lack of an easy medium of communication among businessmen and among scientists causes a great waste of time, money, and effort.] (*Therefore*) ④ [we must teach mankind an international language as soon as possible,] *since* ⑤ [such a vast international project (as teaching mankind an international language) would itself be a practicable field for desperately needed cooperation between nations.]

Now it is easy to transfer the statements to a diagram. When they are short, or easily abbreviated, you can put them directly into the diagram; otherwise, just use the numbers:

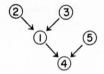

This shows that 1 and 5 are both reasons for 4, and that 1 is in turn supported by 2 and 3.

In some ways this argument is a fairly easy one to diagram, though it illustrates most of the usual problems. If we were diagramming the argument about "Trees," we would have to write in the conclusion in our own words, in parentheses, and then divide up the reasons given. If we cut out a certain amount of apparent repetition, and abbreviate here and there for convenience, the argument can be diagrammed this way:

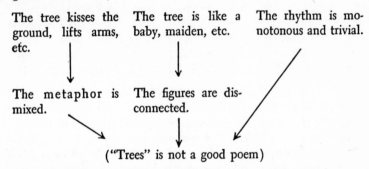

This diagram brings out the structure clearly. Three reasons are given for asserting that "Trees" is poor (if the first two reasons are really different), and the first two of these reasons are themselves backed up by more basic reasons.

Now, when you have a tool like the diagram method for analyzing other people's arguments, you get only half the good of it if you don't apply it to your own. When you construct an argument, your problem is to let your reader know, with the least trouble, which of your reasons belong with which conclusions. When you have a number of statements to make, you can't set them down all at once:

you have to put them in a sequence. And if you want to make your point, and show how everything else relates to that point, your task is to choose the sequence that will bring this out as clearly as possible. There are two general rules to keep in mind.

First, there is the *Rule of Grouping*. Suppose you have a number of reasons for the same conclusion. You will only dissipate their force if you scatter them about with other, irrelevant conclusions in between. It may not matter whether the reasons come before or after the conclusions, but they should be kept as close together as possible. It is confusing to write: "The College Toasty is losing money, so it needs a new manager, and besides it is inefficient," where the first and third statements are both reasons for the second.

Second, there is the *Rule of Direction*. Suppose you have a series of statements, the first being a reason for the second and the second for a third. You will only send your reader off on a wild-goose chase if your inference goes one way and then backtracks. It may not matter in which direction the argument goes, but it should be kept moving as much as possible in the *same* direction. It is confusing to write: "The Council is hopelessly divided, and therefore should be dissolved, because it hasn't reached a decision in weeks," where the third statement is a reason for the first, and the first for the second.

Suppose you were handed the following argument and assigned the task of rewriting it to make its logical structure more clear:

> It is all too apparent that television has never grown up: the programs hit a consistently low level of taste, humor, and value, and the sales-promotion is relentless and vulgar (which shows that television badly needs a new code for commercials). The fact that television presents too many old movies and feeble comedians bears out the point made above, and consequently commercial television should be supplemented by state-supported noncommercial stations.

When we diagram this argument, we find that it violates both the Rule of Grouping and the Rule of Direction. Moreover, it contains two final conclusions, one of which seems the main one, and the other of which (stated in parentheses) might better be saved for another day. But even if it must be put in here, the course of the argument can still be made a good deal smoother. After studying our diagram to get clear about the logical connections among the statements, we might try rewriting the paragraph this way:

Commercial television should be supplemented by state-supported noncommercial stations, for television as it is now has never grown up. This is evident from the fact that the programs hit a consistently low level of taste, humor, and value; from the fact that television presents too many old movies and feeble comedians; from the fact that its sales-promotion is relentless and vulgar (which also shows that it badly needs a new code for commercials).

This is by no means a perfect paragraph, but it can't be improved very much without expanding the base and scope of the argument itself. In any case, it eliminates some of the circumlocutions, and puts the statements in an order that calls attention to, instead of distracting attention from, the inferences that are made from one to another. Of course there is more to a good argument than that—but if you *have* a good argument to offer, you give it its best chance of working when you make its structure plain.

A CHECK-UP QUIZ. Here are some three-statement arguments. Which of the three different types of structure diagrammed below does each one have?

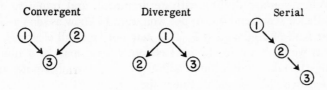

Convergent   Divergent   Serial

1. Since he is industrious, and has had a great deal of experience, he's a good man for the job.
2. He's lazy and he's shiftless. He's not the man for this job.
3. This "inside story" of the Roosevelt Administration was written by a man who was fired by the President, which means that it gives a one-sided picture, so it will be welcomed by ardent anti-New Dealers.
4. Mars is probably uninhabited, for it must be very cold, and its atmosphere is thin.
5. Everything possible must be done to cut down the evils of traffic accidents, so we must have compulsory liability insurance, and we must have compulsory car inspection.

6. Congress should pass the Housing Bill, and it should clamp down on the housing lobby. Remember, its duty is to "promote the *general* welfare."

7. His advice should be taken. He's well-informed about plastics. He has been in the business for many years.

8. The safe was opened very neatly, so it's probably a professional job. This is also suggested by the fact that the jewels have been disposed of through a "fence."

9. The new tax bill will stimulate investment, for it increases exemptions for income derived from stock dividends, and consequently it will promote the prosperity of all.

10. This must be a wildcat strike, since the Union leaders say they oppose it, which means that they will probably take steps to end it soon.

See also Exercises 1, 2, and 3, pages 32-37.

FURTHER READING: Irving M. Copi, *Introduction to Logic.* New York: The Macmillan Co., 1953, ch. 1.

§5. THE TWO TYPES OF ARGUMENT

When you are dealing with an argument, and trying to discover whether it is a sound one or not, you want to know as soon as you can what *kind* of argument it is. This may not be at all clear right away, for as we shall see in the next chapters there may be a number of things to take into account before you can even be quite sure you *understand* the argument. But while you are making out the details of its meaning, you will best be guided by a general conception of what kind of argument it could turn out to be.

According to an old tradition, there are many types of argument: the argument from definition, the argument from similitude, the argument from circumstance, the argument from consequences, the argument from contraries, and others. Most of these distinctions are worth noting, and we shall have something to say about them later; but there is a more fundamental distinction that underlies them all: the distinction between *deductive* and *inductive* arguments. The traditional types of argument are subdivisions of these two basic types.

To be clear about the distinction between deductive and inductive arguments, we must first pay attention to a very important feature that some arguments have and others lack. Consider the following simple inference:

Sally is Susan's cousin.
Therefore: Susan is Sally's cousin.

We can all agree that *if* the first statement is true, the second statement is *necessarily* true; it simply *can't* be false. And it is easy to think of any number of arguments of which we can say the same thing. *If* the dollar is in your wallet, and the wallet is in your pocket, then the dollar is necessarily in your pocket. *If* Sally reads faster than Susan, and Susan reads faster than Bobby, then Sally *must* read faster than Bobby. In each case, the conclusion follows with certainty from the reason. Of course, this doesn't guarantee that the conclusion is certainly *true*; that depends on whether the *reason* is certainly true. But it is certain that *if* the reason is true, then the conclusion is true.

Now consider the following inference:

Sally is Billy's sister.
Therefore: Billy is Sally's brother.

Let's suppose that the name "Billy" may be (as it sometimes in fact is) either a boy's nickname (for "William") or a girl's nickname (for "Wilhelmina"). In that case, the conclusion does *not* follow necessarily from the reason, for Billy may be either Sally's brother or her sister. And again it is easy to think of any number of arguments in which the conclusion *may* be true if the reason is true, or may not be true. *If* you put the nickel in your pocket ten minutes ago, and haven't taken it out, it is probably still there—though it *may* have fallen through a hole. *If* the Weather Bureau says it will rain tomorrow, it probably will rain—though the Bureau could be wrong. In these two arguments, the reason creates a certain *likelihood*, or probability, that the conclusion is true, but it does not *necessarily* make it true. The reason could be true and the conclusion could conceivably be false.

Now, if an argument clearly moves from reason to conclusion with logical necessity, it is a deductive argument. But even if it doesn't actually achieve this degree of conclusiveness, it may implicitly claim, or be set forth as claiming, that the conclusion follows necessarily. Someone may say:

I have a dollar bill, three halves, one quarter, a dime, two nickels, and a penny. Therefore I must have exactly $2.86.

Since he claims that the figure he names is the sum of the bills and coins he has listed, and since adding up numbers is an attempt to get a necessary conclusion (two plus two is *necessarily* four), we can say that his argument is a deductive argument, even though, this time, he happens to have made a mistake in his addition. In the same way, if someone argues that:

> All communists are atheists, and all materialists are atheists, from which it follows that all materialists are communists,

we can call his argument a deductive argument, even though it is not a good one. A **deductive** argument, then, is an argument that either *is* one, or *claims* to be one, in which the conclusion follows necessarily from the reason.

If an argument is not deductive, then it is **inductive**: that is, it claims only that the reason contributes to the probability that the conclusion is true. The probability may be very great, as when the evidence is piled up against someone who is accused of a crime:

> X bought the weapon three weeks before the murder; he was overheard telling someone that he hated Y; he wrote in his diary several times that he intended to kill Y when he got the chance; he bought a plane ticket a week ahead so he could get out of town on the night of Dec. 3; *therefore*: the crime was premeditated in the legal sense.

(But even here, of course, the conclusion does not *necessarily* follow because, for one thing, all those actions *might* have been part of an elaborate joke.) Or the probability may be very small, as when people jump to conclusions:

> It is well known that X and Y had a violent argument six months ago; *therefore*: X is guilty of Y's murder.

As soon as we begin comparing sound arguments (whether deductive or inductive) with unsound ones, of course we raise a great many interesting questions about them—questions that we shall take up in the next two chapters. Here it will be convenient to make a few observations, and introduce some terms that will be useful throughout all the other chapters of this book.

In a deductive argument, the statements that make up the reason are called **premises**, and the conclusion is said to be "deduced," whether correctly or incorrectly, from the premises. In an inductive argument, the statements that make up the reason are called the **evidence**, and the conclusion is said to be "induced from," or "supported by" the evidence.

Thus there are two basically different kinds of reasoning that we do. In one kind, we try to dig out of a premise, or set of premises, what seems to be necessarily implied by them. In the other kind, we try to discover what is probably true in the light of whatever evidence we have on hand. There are many other words for different kinds of reasoning, for example: guessing, suspecting, calculating, predicting; but these can all be understood in terms of deduction and induction. To guess is to make an induction from practically no evidence, to suspect is to make an induction from slight or inadequate evidence; to calculate is to carry out a deduction in symbols of some sort; to predict is to deduce something about the future from a general statement that has already been induced.

The difference between success and failure in reasoning is not decided by whether or not you feel satisfied with the results. The reasoning is *reasonable* if, and only if, there is a logical connection between the conclusion and the reason that makes the truth of one depend either completely or partly upon the truth of the other. It is the business of the logician to study such connections and to reduce them, as far as possible, to *rules*. When we have such rules, we can say that an argument is good if it obeys them, and not good if it doesn't, and we can find out whether an argument is good or bad (or how good it is) by applying the relevant rules. Such rules we shall call **rules of inference**. They are like traffic regulations that control the flow of reasoning. If an argument can justify itself by a rule of inference, it is sound; if it seems to appeal to some rule of inference but actually violates that rule, then it is said to commit a **fallacy**.

A fallacious argument conforms to the rules up to a point, and so at first glance it may seem to be all right. But if you are clear in your own mind as to what the rule is, and what it permits, and if you have practiced analyzing fallacious arguments of a similar sort, you can keep from being fooled by it. For then you can *expose* it, that is, make it *look* as fallacious as it really is. This book will explain and illustrate various rules of inference, in terms of which we can give an account of what sound thinking is. At the same time, you will become familiar with common ways in which those rules are violated, and thus learn to recognize unsound thinking when you run across it.

But there is an important difference between deductive and inductive arguments that we shall have to keep in mind. When the conclusion of a deductive argument actually does follow necessarily from
the premises (so that if the premises are true the conclusion *must* be
true), the argument is said to be **valid**. Validity is something the
argument either has or doesn't have—there's no third possibility. And
logicians have found ways of setting up the rules of inference for
deductive arguments so rigorously and completely that, if we wish,
we can decide exactly and conclusively whether a deductive argument
is valid or invalid—once we understand the argument. If some of the
deductive arguments we find in ordinary speech make it hard for us
to be perfectly sure whether they are valid or invalid, this is not
because of any lack of precision in the rules of inference, but because
of a lingering doubt about just what the argument *is*. That is why we
shall spend so much of our time in this book on the problem of
getting the *meaning* of a discourse, and understanding what sort of
argument, if any, it contains, *before* applying the rules of inference.

The situation is very different for induction. Here you do not, so to
speak, win or lose in some decisive way; you only make more or less
reliable inductions. The rules of inductive inference are not complete
guarantees of success or failure, they are more like *policies* to be
followed—policies that have been well studied and found helpful in
getting at inductive truths in the long run.

Sometimes it is illuminating to think of reasoning as a serious
game in which each inference is like a move. The *deductive* rules of
inference are like those rules that tell how to decide when the game is
over and won: the winner is the player with the most tricks after all
the cards have been played; or the winner is the player who gets all his
counters to the goal first. The *inductive* rules are like the advice we
get from professional players telling us not how to play, but how to
play *well:* don't lead from a king high; or, keep all your counters
moving, without letting any get too far behind.

Before you can criticize an argument, you have to know whether
it is deductive or inductive. Of course, the more experience you have
with the rules of inference for each type, the more easily you can
recognize the inference being made in a particular case. But it is a
good idea at this point to be fairly clear about the differences between
the two types. Unfortunately, there are in English no perfectly dependable signals to show whether an argument is deductive or induc-

tive. If the argument clearly exhibits the sort of necessity we discussed above, it is deductive. If it lacks this necessity, but its logical indicators or its circumstances show that it *claims* necessity, then it is deductive. If it contains words like "probably," "apparently," or "likely" that show it is being offered as a sensible inference from the evidence presented, it is inductive.

Beyond these general considerations, there are others taken from the nature of the statements themselves. If the argument moves from a large group to a smaller group ("All human beings have an appendix; therefore, Americans have an appendix") or from a group to an individual ("All Americans have an appendix; therefore, Billy has an appendix") it is probably a deductive argument. If it goes from a smaller group to a larger one ("Billy, Susan, and Sally go to school; therefore, most children in this village go to school"), it is probably an inductive argument. If the reasons build up a strong case for a conclusion, but it is clear that this is not the *only* conclusion that could be drawn from them, the argument is probably an inductive argument. We shall consider all these patterns of argument later.

A CHECK-UP QUIZ. Is each of the following arguments *deductive* or *inductive*?

1. Susie's mother is the cousin of Sally's mother; therefore, Susie and Sally are second cousins.

2. Every time I have eaten artichokes, I have had something wrong; therefore, I am allergic to them.

3. Killybegs is south of Portnoo, which is south of Inishfree; therefore, Killybegs is south of Inishfree.

4. Today is Tuesday; therefore, tomorrow is Wednesday.

5. The handwriting on this check is like yours; therefore, you wrote it.

6. This discourse is an argument; therefore, it has a conclusion.

7. Bradley was in Memphis at noon yesterday; therefore, he was not in New York at noon yesterday.

8. Bradley was in Memphis at noon yesterday; therefore, he was not in New York at 2:30 yesterday.

9. There are five aces in the deck; therefore, somebody is cheating.

10. General Motors is a company; therefore, the president of General Motors is the president of a company.

See also Exercise 4, page 37.

FURTHER READING: A. A. Bennett and C. A. Baylis, *Formal Logic*. New York: Prentice-Hall, Inc., 1939, ch. 1, secs. 1.1 to 1.6. Morris Cohen and Ernest Nagel, *Introduction to Logic and Scientific Method*. New York: Harcourt, Brace and Co., 1939, ch. 1.

Outline-Summary of Chapter 1

Sentences are divided into (A) those that are either true or false (*statements*) and (B) those that are neither true nor false (chiefly questions, commands, and exclamations). A statement is asserted if it is uttered in such a way as to show that the speaker (or writer) believes it and wants others to believe it.

Discourses are divided into (A) those that contain assertions and (B) those that do not contain assertions. Discourses that contain assertions are either (1) arguments or (2) expositions. Arguments are either (a) deductive or (b) inductive.

An argument consists of at least two asserted statements plus the claim that if one or more of these statements are true, then others are either necessarily true (deductive arguments) or probably true (inductive arguments). An argument (for example, "The light is on; *therefore*, Henry is at home") contains:

1. One or more conclusions ("Henry is at home");
2. One or more reasons ("The light is on") for each conclusion; and
3. One or more logical indicators (*"therefore"*) that show which conclusions are inferred from which reasons.

In a sound argument, the conclusion is drawn in accordance with a logical rule of inference, which (A), in a deductive argument, prescribes the conclusion that follows necessarily from the premises, or (B), in an inductive argument, describes what conclusions are made more or less likely to be true by the evidence. If an argument appears to conform to a rule of inference but actually violates it, the argument commits a fallacy.

Exercise 1

Read the following paragraphs carefully, and decide whether each one is exposition or argument. If it is an argument, write out the conclusion, or, if the conclusion is only implicit, supply it in your own words.

1. In accordance with the President's directive of November 2, the Committee proceeded to the scene of the disaster; it interviewed all those in any way connected with the disaster; it examined all official documents bearing on the matter at hand; it deliberated for three weeks before presenting the Report which follows.

2. Eighteen-year-olds are considered old enough to marry, manage their households, and bring up children. They drive cars, run businesses, and take part in politics. They are called upon to fight for their country, and even give their lives for it. Despite all this, there are, strangely enough, people who question whether eighteen-year-olds should be allowed to vote in all states as they do in Georgia. They "doubt whether eighteen-year-olds are wise and mature and responsible enough" to have a voice in deciding who shall represent them in Washington. They talk about zoot suits, bobby sox, and juvenile delinquency as though these outweighed all the positive evidence of the capabilities of American youth.

3. You can have all the productive capacity in the world; but it doesn't seem to help business if business doesn't have buyers. The best business stimulant at a time like this is customers walking in the front door with money in their pants. . . .

The function of democratic capitalism is not just making things; the system works only as it gets the things it makes into the lives of people who can use them. So my own belief is that in the present situation the emphasis should be on encouraging consumption. (Adlai Stevenson, at Charlotte, N.C., April 2, 1954)

4. The steps by which, after the fall of Alba, Rome, now mistress of a territory comparatively considerable, and, we may venture to say, the leading power in the Latin confederacy, extended still further her direct and indirect dominion, can no longer be traced. There were numerous feuds with the Etruscans and the Veientes, chiefly respecting the possession of Fidenae; but it does not appear that the Romans were successful in acquiring permanent mastery over that Etruscan outpost, which was situated on the Latin bank of the river not much more than five miles from Rome, or in expelling the Veientes from that formidable basis of offensive operations. On the other hand, they maintained undisputed possession of the Janiculum and of both banks of the mouth of the Tiber. . . . (Mommsen, *History of Rome*)

5. The only freedom which deserves the name, is that of pursuing our own good in our own way, so long as we do not attempt to deprive others of theirs, or impede their efforts to obtain it. Each is the proper guardian of his own health, whether bodily, or mental and spiritual. Mankind are greater gainers by suffering each other to live as seems good to themselves, than by compelling each to live as seems good to the rest. (John Stuart Mill)

Exercise 2

Show the structure of each of the following arguments by a diagram.

1. On the obvious principles that the more experienced members of Congress will probably have a better grasp of legislative processes, and that they are less likely to be swayed by lobbying pressure groups, it will be seen that the Senators who have had the longest term of service should have positions of greatest authority and trust. This is the justification of the rule that Committee chairmanships in the Senate should be assigned on the basis of seniority.

2. The only rewards and punishments are those, however feeble and fallible, that are awarded to man by man himself. There is no Hell, because guilt and good conscience are but psychological states (only the most naive still think of hell as a real place and genuine threat), and there is no Heaven either.

3. Advertising, one of man's most ingenious inventions, keeps the consumer dissatisfied with what he possesses and thus stimulates him to desire, and purchase, new products as they become available. Moreover (as the Advertising Federation has pointed out), it preserves a steady demand for old products, because it keeps the prestige of well-known brand names always in the public mind. Advertising certainly plays an important role in our constantly expanding economy.

4. Anyone who thinks about the matter can see that to deny jobs to qualified people merely because of race, religion, or national origin is unjust, and that it is uneconomical, since it deprives society of the fruits of their labor, makes them a burden on the rest, and withholds from them opportunities that are left open to others.

5. The great masses' receptive ability is only very limited, their understanding is small, but their forgetfulness is great. As a consequence of these facts, all effective propaganda has to limit itself only to a very few points and to use them like slogans until even the very last man is able to imagine what is intended by such a word. (Adolf Hitler, *Mein Kampf*)

6. When the divorce rate goes up every year, and the crime waves come faster and faster, isn't it evident that Americans are suffering from a fundamental lack of discipline? This, in turn, is a proof that a severe moral crisis imperils our age. "Where there is no faith, the people perish." You can see this lack of discipline everywhere: in progressive educators who say that children are being taught to read too early; in churchmen who object to the discipline of military training; in adolescents who avoid regular church attendance. And there is no more conclusive evidence of the moral crisis—which has reached proportions suggesting the collapse

of the Roman civilization—than the cynical selfishness of the laboring class, as evidenced by their desire to get more wages for less work. "In the sweat of thy brow shalt thou eat thy bread." (From a sermon)

7. It may seem strange to some man, that has not well weighed these things, that Nature should thus dissociate, and render man apt to invade, and destroy one another: and he may therefore, not trusting to this Inference, made from the Passions, desire perhaps to have the same confirmed by Experience. Let him therefore consider with himselfe, when taking a journey, he armes himselfe, and seeks to go well accompanied; when going to sleep, he locks his dores; when even in his house he locks his chests; and this when he knows there bee Lawes, and publike Officers, armed, to revenge all injuries shall bee done him; what opinion he has of his fellow subjects, when he rides armed; of his fellow Citizens, when he locks his dores; and of his children, and servants, when he locks his chests. Does he not there as much accuse mankind by his actions, as I do by my words? (Thomas Hobbes, *Leviathan*)

8. Equal justice to the South, it is said, requires us to consent to the extending of slavery to new countries [the Kansas-Nebraska Territory]. That is to say, inasmuch as you do not object to my taking my hog to Nebraska, therefore I must not object to you taking your slave. Now, I admit this is perfectly logical, if there is no difference between hogs and Negroes. But while you thus require me to deny the humanity of the Negro, I wish to ask whether you of the South yourselves, have ever been willing to do as much? . . . The great majority, South as well as North, have human sympathies, of which they can no more divest themselves than they can of their sensibility to physical pain. These sympathies in the bosoms of the Southern people, manifest in many ways their sense of the wrong of slavery, and their consciousness that, after all, there is humanity in the Negro. If they deny this, let me address them a few plain questions. In 1820, you joined the North, almost unanimously, in declaring the African slave trade piracy, and in annexing to it the punishment of death. Why did you do this? If you did not feel that it was wrong, why did you join in providing that men should be hung for it? The practice was no more than bringing wild Negroes from Africa, to sell to such as would buy them. But you never thought of hanging men for catching and selling wild horses, wild buffaloes, or wild bears. (Lincoln, speech at Peoria, Illinois, October 16, 1854)

Exercise 3

In each of the following arguments, the logical connection of the statements is somewhat obscured by the order in which they are given. Rewrite

each argument to make it as brief and orderly as you can. It may be helpful to diagram the arguments before rewriting them.

1. There are many points about the United Nations that we should
think carefully about before hastily withdrawing from it because we disagree with some decision it makes. It has accomplished a great deal in
helping unfortunate peoples fight poverty and disease, so it has in this
way contributed to peace, also because it has reduced want and provided
a forum for the airing of grievances that might otherwise smoulder into
flame. Thus it has increased the nations' understanding of one another,
and encouraged discussion and negotiation, and helped to keep peace.
Moreover, to abandon it to Russia now would give her a tremendous
propaganda point, and so, besides the fact (as suggested above) that it
deserves our support, it would be expedient to stay in it, which is what
I think we should do.

2. We should stop giving Post Office mural-painting jobs and other
Federal funds and encouragement to modernist abstract painters, unless
they promise to paint no more such pictures. In the first place, abstract
paintings are influenced by foreign and leftist schools of art. Yes, abstract
art is un-American. For, because abstract painters chop up the human
figure by putting an arm down here, a leg up there, an eye or half an eye
over somewhere else, the pictures mock the dignity and divine likeness of
man. And also when they do paint a recognizable human being, it is
usually distorted and out of shape. Not only that, but only a small clique
of self-styled connoisseurs and aesthetes can appreciate the "beauty" of
these daubs, and therefore the paintings are inherently undemocratic.

3. Mr. Johnson's letter casting aspersions on the Citizens' Committee,
which you published recently, is beneath contempt. He does not care for
our report, in which we urged that the Mayor stop whitewashing the
Welfare Department, and, instead, concentrate on a thorough overhauling of its personnel. I wish to refute Mr. Johnson, who doesn't know what
he is talking about.

The Mayor's own figures show that the Welfare Department is spending $40 a week for every person it takes care of. Maybe these people are
deserving—I know some deserving people myself—but this is a wasteful
and inefficient business, obviously. The cost is too high, especially because
there is indication of not only this wastefulness but deliberate fraud. You
can see this in the unwillingness of the Department to allow the Committee to examine its records or talk with people on relief, and also there
is the fact that the Department is using all sorts of outmoded methods of
keeping records, thus taking time, energy, and money, which the city
could save. After all, time is money, too—as Benjamin Franklin said.

Moreover, while we are on the subject of dishonesty, and so on, we might mention that 30 per cent of the people on relief are in Ward 3, which is the chief support of the Mayor's party. (A letter to a newspaper)

Exercise 4

Say whether each of the following arguments is deductive or inductive, and give your reasons for saying so.

1. The homicide rates for Michigan, Maine, Minnesota, North Dakota, Rhode Island, and Wisconsin, which have all abolished capital punishment, are lower than the average for the rest of the nation. This shows that capital punishment does not deter murderers.

2. It has often been noted that the number of violent crimes in New York often rises sharply after a highly publicized execution: partly, perhaps, because the newspaper accounts arouse sympathy for the doomed convict, and this stirs up deep resentments against the social order and the law. Apparently capital punishment actually stimulates crime.

3. As the Declaration of Independence states, human beings have an *inalienable* right to life—that is, a right that no man, not even the judge or the executioner, can take away. It follows that capital punishment is a violation of individual rights.

4. Wherever there is a chance that a mistake can be made, justice requires that every precaution must be taken to avoid mistakes that in the nature of the case can never be corrected. We know that innocent people have been convicted of murder, and even put to death for it, through prejudice or carelessness, and they cannot be brought back to life, even if, as sometimes happens, someone later confesses to the crime. It is certain, then, that capital punishment has caused injustice that life imprisonment would not have caused.

5. Juries are much less willing to convict a murderer when they know that the penalty is death. Thus capital punishment tends to undermine the law by protecting the guilty.

2

The Weight of the Evidence

In recent years a number of problems have plagued American city administrators and worried thoughtful citizens: for example, traffic congestion, noise, smoke, street litter, slums. But the worst problem, to many people, has been (and still is) the increasing crime among adolescents and children—the problem of juvenile delinquency. Communities have been shocked by gang warfare, petty thievery, armed robbery, and even killing—sometimes apparently for sheer sadistic enjoyment.

Here is a problem with so many elements and so many ramifications that its solution may require the combined resources of parents, welfare workers, psychiatrists, economists, teachers, and municipal court judges. It has occasionally been possible to get such experts together to make plans. Of course, when public opinion is aroused, nearly everyone will have his own solution, whether or not he knows anything of family relations, psychiatry, economics, education, or law. And usually his solution will be simple. Cut progressive education out of the schools—back to "the three R's," perhaps with more emphasis on Religion, as a fourth "R." Double the police force. Stop coddling delinquents in juvenile courts. No more self-demand schedules for babies: more rules, discipline, and spankings. A teen-age curfew at 11:00 P.M. Fire all working mothers so they will have to stay home with their children. Make Bingo illegal. Burn the comic books.

Now, all these suggestions take for granted that there is some *connection* between the state of affairs we want to eliminate and the action proposed. Burning comic books won't help unless in some way the reading of comic books is one of the factors involved in *producing* juvenile delinquency. Do we have any solid reason for believing that babies fed on self-demand schedules are more likely than other babies to rob gas stations when they grow up? And making mothers stay home with their children may do more harm than good unless we know how to take care in some other way of whatever economic needs and psychological frustrations caused them to go to work in the first place. Unless you know the *causes* of crime, you cannot know the *effects* of the proposed cures. You might as well distribute lollypops, put on rain dances, or paint the city hall blue.

If someone appoints a qualified committee to study the problem, there is some hope of a rational solution. Before they start suggesting remedies, they will first examine the nature and scope of the disease. How much has the crime rate risen? Which age groups are chiefly involved? From what family, economic, national, or regional backgrounds do they come? Instead of jumping to the first conclusion that occurs to them (or falling back on one of their favorite villains, like progressive education, Marxism, Wall Street, radioactivity, or immigrants), they will consider several possible causes, and several possible cures.

And when they present their report, it will reflect these features of the inquiry. The facts that serve as the basis of the report will be clearly and fully presented. The assumptions that are made, as working principles, will be explicitly stated and defended. The theories that are rejected will have cited along with them the facts that make them rejectable. And the theories that are accepted will be stated as clearly as possible, along with the facts that make them acceptable. Such a report will be, in short, an *inductive argument*, and a good one.

There has been attributed to a certain corporation counsel a remarkable comment upon the much discussed idea of "guilt by association": "If I frequent Ebbets Field," he said, "it's a fair assumption that I am a Dodger fan." As *The New Yorker* pointed out, "It may be a good guess, but it is a foul assumption." Now, if this counselor is neutral about the Dodgers (and who is?), he won't mind being publicly accused of being a Dodger fan. But suppose it were illegal, or scandalous, or likely to cost him his job if word got around

—then we ought to have some better evidence before we go about accusing him. As *The New Yorker* added:

> It is conceivable that the man is nothing more sinister than a sports reporter who has been associated briefly with the Dodgers in order to observe their queer ways. Or maybe he is a seller of pop, homing with the day's receipts. . . . He may even be a Dodger hater who went to the game in the hope of seeing the team fall flat on its face.

When people reason like the counselor, they seem to have no notion of how to distinguish between good evidence and bad. Or perhaps they are less interested in cutting down juvenile delinquency than in insulting their neighbors. It is said that a few years ago an American diplomatic representative abroad was recalled because in his reports of the nation in which he was stationed "he painted the situation as black as it was." Let us hope this is an exaggeration. Still, people can be so bent on fooling other people that they don't care how much they have to fool themselves in order to do it.

If we want the truth about anything, however, there is only one way to get it, and that is to get good evidence for our conclusions. Induction is a matter of weighing evidence. "Weighing" is misleading if it makes you think that there might be an exact scale on which weighing can be done. It is more like *hefting* the evidence, as you might heft two stones to judge that one is *about* twice as heavy as the other. There is no exact science of hefting, but there are good hefters and poor ones. And it is something we are doing much of the time—most successfully, in the long run, when we are most deliberate about it; that is, when we know clearly what we are doing. There are no strict rules for inductive reasoning, but there are some general principles that are useful and widely applicable. Some of these we shall consider in the present chapter.

§6. THE PROCESS OF INDUCTION

The foundation on which an inductive argument is built is a set of statements that are taken to be *facts*. These facts are the evidence you are given to work with in that argument. They may be called the *data* for the induction.

The data of one inductive argument may have been the conclusions of earlier arguments. The facts an engineer has on hand for determining the feasibility of a bridge or tunnel at a certain place are, for him, basic, but he may have got them from others who had to infer them as conclusions from other facts. Thus one argument builds upon another. But in any particular argument we can, and indeed must, distinguish clearly the evidence *sup*posed from the conclusion *pro*posed.

Induction, then, is a constructive activity like that of a chassis assembly plant; it receives parts that have already been shaped or partly put together, and it sends out something more developed and organized. The work involves some interesting problems, and we shall come to them shortly. But first we shall consider in a general way two questions about induction: What is the source and nature of the ultimate raw materials? And what sort of products does induction aim to supply?

In the last analysis, the data of induction come from experience. But each of us distinguishes, within his own experience, what he himself perceives from what others tell him they perceive. What you know directly through your senses—the color of a flower, the shape of a dog biscuit, the smell of hay—you know by *direct observation*. What you haven't observed, but are told about by others—the color of the Taj Mahal, the path of an electron in a magnetic field, the political maneuvers of Abraham Lincoln—is *testimonial* evidence.

There are two kinds of observation. In one kind there is some manipulation of the environment—sterilizing the test tube, exposing the cow to atomic radiation, running the rat through the maze—and this is controlled observation, or *experiment*. In the other, there is simply looking, or listening, or sniffing, or tasting, or feeling, with no attempt to set up special conditions. But the line isn't sharp because even to taste something you have to put it in your mouth, and that is rearranging the world a little, though it is a far cry from the elaborate arrangements a chemist or nuclear physicist makes before he is ready to observe the results.

Testimonial evidence is *expert* testimony when the informant is (a) truthful, (b) especially well qualified to observe what he claims to have observed, and (c) capable of reporting his observations accurately. In general, we regard our own firsthand observation as better evidence than the testimony of others who are no more expert in the matter than we are. This is sensible. But we also often regard the testimony of experts as better than even our own firsthand observation. And this is sensible, too, for the real expert is a *trained* observer. That means he notices things we don't. It also means he can keep clearly distinct, whether in his own observations or the testimony of others, what is actually *observed* and what is really *inferred*.

Suppose somebody tells you that he, with his own eyes, saw A picking B's pocket. That's his testimony. If you care anything about A's reputation, you don't leave it at that. You ask the witness to describe, as carefully as he can, exactly what he *saw*. Perhaps it turns out, after some questioning, that he saw A take his hand out of his coat pocket, insert it into B's coat pocket when B wasn't looking, and put his hand back in his own pocket. That A was stealing is not something observed; it is something inferred: it is not an *observation*, but a *conclusion*. The argument is:

> A removed his hand from his coat pocket, placed it in B's coat pocket when B wasn't looking, and replaced it in his own pocket.
>
> *Therefore*:
>
> A was picking B's pocket.

A might have been putting something *into* B's pocket—perhaps some money he felt he owed B for tickets to a fight, though B did not want to accept it. This is just as good a conclusion from what is actually observed.

Now, of course, this more charitable conclusion could be wrecked by further evidence. If A's hand appeared empty when it went into B's pocket and appeared to contain a wallet when it came out, that would be different. But the point here is that a good observer knows what he *has* actually observed and what he has *not* observed, but merely inferred.

The problem of expert testimony is part of the general problem of *authority*. We have to depend upon other people for most of the information on which we base our own conclusions about what is going on in the world, and our decisions about what to do. This information does not come to us as pure report of sense experience; it has already passed through other minds, and is selected, sifted, rearranged, and mingled with conclusions, guesses, and surmises. Consequently, we are often faced with the problem of evaluating the sources of our information, or, in other words, deciding how much confidence to place in them. When someone tells us that certain air force appropriations will be sufficient for a secure national defense, or that if we eat wheat germ and blackstrap molasses we will be a great deal healthier, or that the happiness and welfare of American Indians requires that their tribal organizations be broken up as quickly as possible, we want to know how much of an *authority* he is on the subject he is talking about.

It is easy to define an authority, but it may be very hard to tell when you've got one. He is a person (a) who is in a position to have obtained the facts he claims to have, (b) who is qualified, by his intelligence and training, to draw sound inductive inferences from those facts, and (c) who is free from prejudices and emotional attachments that would prevent him from drawing the most reasonable inferences or from communicating them clearly and truthfully to others. In some fields the authorities are widely recognized, and there are various ways of finding out who they are. For example, we will certainly put more trust in an article in the *Journal of the American Medical Association*, reporting a new discovery in dietetics, than in a popularized report for *Newsweek*, but we will put more trust in the latter than in a statement by a food company that its product will increase our energy and eliminate tooth decay. In other fields there is much less agreement. For example, when apparent, or self-styled, authorities seem to disagree about the correct method of teaching children how to read, which authority shall we accept? But even here, though we cannot be dogmatic, we can distinguish the better from the worse. Presumably, a man who reads a few articles in education journals and writes a lively best-selling book is less of an authority than the people who wrote the articles, and even among the latter, if we care to look into it, we shall find that some of them base their conclusions on more experience, and more careful observation, over a longer time, on a greater number and variety of pupils, and show that they have weighed both sides of the issue more thoroughly and judiciously, than others.

Some people have a lot of curiosity about isolated facts—who invented the bobby pin, what post office issued the first adhesive stamps, what is the National League record for strikeouts in double-headers played on Sunday afternoon, and so forth. For these people, facts are something to collect, like china dogs, first-day covers, and baseballs hit into the stands at major league games. They are data, if you like; that is, they are given, but they don't become evidence until they are used to establish a conclusion, until they are evidence *for* something. As thinkers, rather than as collectors, our question is always, what can we *do* with the facts; how can we make them yield new knowledge of something that we want to know about?

There are certain characteristics that are found in all inductive arguments, but these are best understood by first making a distinction between the two kinds of inductive argument and seeing the differences. All the conclusions that can be drawn inductively fall into two groups: there are *generalizations*, and there are *hypotheses*. And though both are supported by evidence, the way they are supported is somewhat different.

The kind of inductive argument that results in a generalization has a comparatively simple structure. Suppose we get interested in a certain class of things: rats, mathematicians, television programs, cigarettes. And we want to know something special about them: Are all rats color-blind? Are all mathematicians good at music? Do violent television programs increase juvenile delinquency? Does smoking cigarettes cause lung cancer? Some generalizations are answers to questions like these. If some of these questions obviously have "no" for an answer, we can ask better questions: What *proportion* of mathematicians are good at music (most? all? 79.2 per cent?)? *To what extent* is children's behavior affected by what they see on television? Does smoking cigarettes *tend* to increase the likelihood that one will die of lung cancer? Many generalizations are answers to questions like these.

How do we go about answering such questions? We can't examine all rats; some are dead, some yet unborn. We can't (and we don't need to) test all mathematicians for their musical ability, study every child who watches television, obtain the medical history of all cigarette smokers, past, present, and future. We get information about *some* of the members of the class, and on the strength of this information we make a tentative statement about what is true of all, or most, or many members of the class: "All ripe pineapples are sweet," or "73.66 per cent of farmers are in favor of crop control." Then we are *generalizing*.

If we should set out our reasoning in its simplest form, it would shape up like this:

> Rat #1 is color-blind;
> Rat #2 is color-blind;
> Rat #3 is color-blind; . . .
>
> *Therefore:*
>
> All rats are color-blind.

Or consider this one:

> On the basis of a twenty-month study of data on 187,766 men between the ages of 50 and 70 years, Dr. E. Cuyler Hammond of the American Cancer Society concluded that cigarette smokers between these two ages have a 52 per cent higher death rate from all causes than other men in the same age group, and men who smoke more than twenty cigarettes a day have a 75 per cent higher death rate.

Of course, this is only part of the actual story, but it will serve as an example.

At first glance the second example may look quite different from the first. That is because the data here are telescoped, or summarized. But logically speaking, the two examples are the same. In both cases, there is a generalization about a certain percentage of the members of a given class: rats, cigarette smokers. And the *evidence* for the generalization consists of statements about some of the members of the class: the rats tested, the smokers studied. Argument goes from *some* to *more* than that some. The conclusion is more general than the evidence; that is what is meant by calling it a **generalization**.

The individual objects or people that have been observed, and on which the generalization rests, are said to be *instances* of the generalization. Every muddy little boy is an instance of the generalization "All little boys get muddy" (it is also an instance of "13.5 per cent of little boys get muddy," and "All muddy human beings are little boys"). The argument for a generalization is not a deductive argument; no matter how many instances we have, so long as they are fewer than the class covered by the whole generalization, the conclusion does not follow *necessarily*. Yet every instance we collect is *some* reason (however small) for believing the generalization it is used to support. Thus when we generalize we are reasoning by a very important principle that might be stated this way:

> *Every instance of a generalization is positive evidence that the generalization is true.*

The kind of inductive argument that results in a hypothesis is somewhat more complicated. In this kind of argument we are interested in something about a particular individual person or thing or event or state-of-affairs. Was Mr. Blank guilty of espionage? What disease did Mozart die of? Has the earth been visited by flying saucers from outer space? Hypotheses are answers to questions like these.

How do we go about answering such questions? They can't be answered by direct observation. Mr. Blank was found taking home a briefcase full of secret documents; but that isn't *seeing* him spying. He says he was catching up on his office work in the evening, and that he was sorry if he was careless. Even if Mozart's doctor knew all that our present-day doctors know, he still wouldn't *see* the disease kill Mozart; he would have to infer it from the symptoms and laboratory tests. People *do* "see" flying saucers, or rather they have certain experiences that they judge to be experiences of seeing flying saucers (not merely of imagining them), but they are making *inferences* when they think the shapes or lights they see are ships whirling in from distant worlds. Yet all these hypotheses are *based* on observation; the secret documents in the briefcase are certainly evidence, and they can be seen and touched; Mozart's thinness and swollen legs could be seen; and if we should conclude that there are flying saucers, this conclusion would have to be backed up by the observations of trained observers.

An argument for a hypothesis, when explicitly set forth, will look like this:

> The house across the street has shown no signs of life in some days;
> Some rolled-up, rain-soaked newspapers lie on the front steps;
> The grass needs cutting badly;
> Salesmen who ring the doorbell get no answer; . . .

> *Therefore:*
> The people across the street are away on a trip.

Or, consider this one:

In his article in *La Chronique Médicale*, Paris, November, 1905, Dr. J. Barraut examined Mozart's medical history in detail: Mozart had scarlatina when he was young. In the last six months of his life he felt very weak, became emaciated, had difficulty breathing, was subject to fainting spells. He also had paresis, and some swelling of the legs and hands. Dr. Barraut concluded that Mozart died of nephritis, or Bright's disease.

The logical structure of these two arguments is just the same, despite superficial differences. In each case the conclusion is that something has happened. And the evidence for this conclusion consists in a number of supposedly true statements about certain other events, situations, or states-of-affairs. It is evident that these arguments are very different from deductive arguments. Even if we accept all the statements about the house across the street, it does not follow *necessarily* that the people are away on a trip; they may merely be pretending to be; or they may all have died of poisoned food. And even if we accept all the reports about Mozart's physical condition, we can't say Dr. Barraut's diagnosis is *necessarily* true, though it is more likely to be true than any other we can think of.

Moreover, the argument for a hypothesis is very different from the argument for a generalization. That Mozart died of nephritis is not a generalization; and the fact that he sometimes fainted is not an *instance* of any generalization stated here, though, of course, it *could* be an instance of a generalization. The logical connection between hypothesis and evidence is that of *accounting* for, or *explaining*. That the people have gone away on a trip is a reasonable conclusion to draw from the facts about the sodden newspapers and uncut grass because it is one way of explaining why the newspapers *are* on the front steps and why the grass *is* uncut. You could explain these facts in other ways, that is, you could draw other conclusions, but any hypothesis you try to prove will be a plausible one only if it explains the facts that are offered as evidence for it.

The statement "Mozart had nephritis" is a hypothesis that accounts in a sensible way for all the observed symptoms. We reason this way: *if* the hypothesis is true, then those symptoms are just what we should expect on the basis of what we already know about this disease. Again: if our neighbors have gone off (and *if*—here's where other "ifs" have to come in—they forgot to notify the paper boy, and didn't engage someone to keep their lawn cropped), then what we should expect to see across the street is what we do see. A **hypothesis**, then, is a conclusion of an inductive argument supported by statements about matters of fact that can be accounted for by that conclusion. And the principle according to which we are reasoning in such an argument is this:

> *Every known fact that can be accounted for by a hypothesis is positive evidence that the hypothesis is true.*

As we go on in the present chapter, we shall have to consider each of these types of argument more carefully. At this stage of the discussion, it is only important to notice how they differ from each other, and how they still *both* differ from deductive arguments. When you want to know whether you're justified in believing a generalization, your problem is whether you have enough, and the right sort of, instances. When you want to know whether you're justified in believing a hypothesis, your problem is whether you have enough, and the right sort of, conditions that it can account for. But in neither case can you expect to get evidence that will enable you to *deduce* the conclusion. Induction has its own goals, and its own rules of the game.

A CHECK-UP QUIZ. Is the conclusion in each of the following inductive arguments a *generalization* or a *hypothesis*?

1. After reading half a dozen whodunnits by the noted author, John Dick Carson, I'm convinced that you can count on him to tell a good story, and I look forward to his next.

2. I guess it's no use trying to get grass to grow in that corner of the yard: I've tried for four years, with no success.

3. The senselessness and brutality of the crime strongly suggest that it is the work of someone who is insane.

4. In 1948 Truman got 50.1 per cent of the vote in Ohio, and in 1950 Taft got 57.5 per cent. It has been assumed by some that 200,000 just switched to Taft, but the truth would seem to be that in 1950, 200,000 of the Truman supporters stayed at home on election day, while the Republicans got out 200,000 more of their voters.

5. I keep seeing advertisements showing pictures of people who have switched to Juicymint Chewing Gum: it looks like most people are.

6. I have noticed several times that when my child is irritable and hard to handle, he comes down with a cold or a virus the next day. In his case, at least, these behavior patterns seem to be a fairly dependable symptom of illness.

7. The young couple got out of the car at a busy intersection, elegantly dressed, and gravely set up a little stand, with a sign reading, "$1 bills for fifty cents; today only." They had rolls of dollar bills, which they offered to passers-by, but hardly anybody would bite. I guess most people thought they were nuts, but I figured they were from one of those crazy television programs that go in for such stunts.

8. Of those who returned the *Firebird's* questionnaire (about one-third of the student body did so), about 78 per cent, or five out of seven, were in favor of enlarging the student council. This is evidently the prevailing student opinion.

9. We are sure that our candidate will win. Precinct workers send in confident reports; our candidate gets good turnouts for his speeches; there is general discontent about farm prices and unemployment, and this favors the party that is out of power. Also, our opponents show in various ways that they are running scared.

10. Every time we try to save money, something goes wrong; illness, or the car breaking down, or the children needing something, or what not. I guess we'll never be able to save anything.

FURTHER READING: Max Black, *Critical Thinking*. New York: Prentice-Hall, Inc., 2d ed. 1952, chs. 13, 14. M. C. Beardsley, *Practical Logic*. New York: Prentice-Hall, Inc., 1950, ch. 7.

§7. DEPENDABLE GENERALIZATIONS

A generalization is launched from experience, but it allows you to anticipate things you *haven't* yet experienced. No matter how sleepy and ready to purr that next tiger you see appears to be, you won't put your hand through the bars to pet him. You know enough about tigers *in general* to have serious doubts about that tiger *in particular*. And whether or not you are conscious of it, your reasoning runs on these lines:

> All tigers are unfriendly.
> That is a tiger.
> _____
> That is unfriendly.

It is evident right off that *this* argument is a deductive argument. When you already *know* a generalization, or are prepared to rely on its truth, and apply it to a new instance, you are arguing deductively. If the generalization holds for all members of a class, then it must hold for every individual member. But the question we have to consider now is not how you *apply* a generalization once you've got it, but how you get it in the first place. In short, what is the *inductive* argument of which the generalization is a conclusion?

Presumably it is something of this sort:

> That Indian tiger I read about yesterday was unfriendly.
> The tiger someone told me about last year was unfriendly.
> The tiger I saw in the Bronx Zoo was unfriendly.
>
> .
> .
> .
>
> ---
>
> ALL tigers are unfriendly.

The broken line here represents a "therefore" but an inductive sort of "therefore"; it may be read: "hence it is probable that ..." The argument mentions some unfriendly tigers of which you know by acquaintance or report, and presents these as reasonable grounds for suspecting that their characteristics are to be found in the entire species.

Even if there are other instances of unfriendly tigers that you can think of (and the dots leave room for them), there probably won't be many. Yet you aren't going to take any chances on the nth tiger when he comes along. More Americans have been bitten by dogs than by tigers. But more Americans pet strange dogs than pet strange tigers.

Evidently part of what is involved here is the *risk* you take if the generalization turns out to be mistaken. Tigers (in general) bite harder than dogs. They also scratch. When we are asked to trust a generalization of any sort, and to act on it. ("Bridges of this type will support 5 tons"; "the annual accident death rate in the United States is about 57 per 100,000 people"; "This operation is successful in 95 per cent of all cases"), then the greater the trouble we would have if the generalization turned out to be false, the more assurance we want that the generalization is *not* false. We want it to be a *dependable* generalization. "Tigers bite" is highly dependable; "Dogs bite" is not highly dependable, or, if you like, "Dogs *don't* bite" is fairly dependable, but "Most dogs brought up in urban and suburban families don't bite" is even better.

What makes a generalization dependable? This question is a rather large order, and the attempt to give an exact answer would lead pretty far. But even if we must stay close to the level of common sense, there are certain principles that can be roughly stated, kept in mind, and often used. Many of the generalizations that we have to rely on in the ordinary affairs of life—about people, politics, social institutions—have to be made without the help of precise scientific methods. We have to face the fact that until such methods are applied, these generalizations simply cannot be made as dependable as we would like them to be. But that doesn't mean that we can't make them better or worse, more sound or less, by thinking clearly or by refusing to think at all. There is, in fact, a good deal we can do to guard against the worst errors.

When you are confronted with an argument for a generalization, your first care must be to sort out its ingredients carefully, so that you know exactly what the generalization *is*, and what it is a generalization *about*. "The study of Latin disciplines the mind," according to one theory. The first question is: What class of things is the generalization supposed to apply to? Presumably, in this case, people; it could be restated in the form: "People who study Latin have their minds disciplined by this study." The class of *people who study Latin* is the class generalized about: let's call it the **class under investigation**. Sometimes it may be obscured by the use of abstract terms. "Science is not antireligious"; does this mean that *scientists* are not antireligious?

The second question is: How *much* of the class under investigation is covered by the generalization? *All* people who study Latin? *Some* of them? *Most*? There is not much hope that we can test the generalization unless we fix its range a little more firmly. Perhaps it means "all"; at least, it must mean "more than half." The third question is: What is actually being asserted about this portion of the class under investigation? How do you tell when someone's mind gets more disciplined than it was before? Surely the term "disciplined" can refer to some very important characteristics. Surely, too, it is in need of clarification. For example, what is meant might be something like this: If a person gets a score of 85 per cent on a standardized logic examination, studies Latin for a year, and then gets 90 per cent on an examination of the same degree of difficulty, we might take that as *some* evidence that his mind has been disciplined to some extent. Then *one* test of mental discipline would be success with logic examinations. This may not be a good test of mental discipline, but *some* test would presumably have to be used.

The fourth question is: What instances are offered as evidence of the generalization? In every such argument, there are *two* classes involved: the class under investigation (which is the class the argument aims to get *to*), and the class of known instances (which is the class the argument takes off *from*). This second class is always part of the first one, that is, a subclass of it. It is a **sample** of the class under investigation.

The term "sample" is familiar, but perhaps not in quite the broad sense in which we shall use it. You may think chiefly of samples that we are free to pick. A cannery inspector grading apricots that are ready for canning might dip several times into a large vat, stirring each time, and examine several of the apricots that he scoops up before pronouncing them to be of grade *B* quality. He doesn't examine every apricot, in fact only a small percentage, but he generalizes about the whole batch. Now the principle is the same in cases where we have to take the sample that comes along, as with the weather man's data. The difference is that the cannery inspector *has* to produce a generalization because he's paid to, and his practical problem is to get a sample that will make his generalization dependable, whereas in many common affairs of life we can only get a certain amount of evidence, and our practical problem is whether to generalize or *not* to generalize from the sample we have.

A generalization is dependable if the predictions we make by depending on it are actually borne out by our future experience. But how do we decide *now* whether the generalization is dependable? The problem of generalizing is the problem of choosing a sample that will give us the right picture of the whole class under investigation. In other words, our generalization will be dependable if our sample is typical of the class under investigation.

It's easy to see what, in theory, a good sample would be. If you wanted to know, by polling 1,000 men, what percentage of American men wear garters (and you might, if you were a manufacturer or retail seller of garters), you would want to pick your 1,000 men in such a way that the percentage of garter wearers in the sample would be close to the percentage of garter wearers in the whole population. If every one of your sample men wore garters, or if none of them did, though in the general population the percentage was half-and-half, you would be badly misled.

Now, we can never be *certain* that a sample we choose is typical of the class under investigation. But there is something we can do—and can ask that others do before we put much stock in their generalizations, however glittering—to make it *likely*, or make it *more* likely than it would otherwise be, that the sample is the kind of sample we're after. We can take pains to choose our sample in such a way as to cancel out factors that might prevent the sample from being typical.

Suppose, in your experience, there are certain characteristics that always seem to go together: say, every cat you have ever seen that has white fur and pink eyes is also deaf. Is this true of *all* cats, or is it just a coincidence in your sample? Now, to get a sample that would justify this generalization, you would want to make sure that it isn't just Pekinese cats that are always deaf when they have white fur and pink eyes; or not just elderly cats, or cats that have had certain diseases. So you would want your sample class of white-furred, pink-eyed cats to include cats of more than one breed, young and old, long-haired and short-haired, and so on. For then it would be clear that the connection between fur, eyes, and deafness doesn't depend on these other conditions. You can pick your sample one by one so that it includes the greatest variety of cats that you can find. Or you can take a *random* sample, letting chance do the picking for you, in the expectation that the random sample will give an unbiased picture of the whole cat-population.

When the famous Salk poliomyelitis vaccine was to be tested a few years ago, the method of sampling was carried out with brilliant success. The problem was to find out, by trying the vaccine on *some* school children, what percentage of immunizations for the different kinds of polio could be expected if *all* school children were vaccinated. To make sure that various kinds of children would be included in the sample, and under various health conditions, certain typical cities were carefully selected; but within those cities the children who received the vaccine were selected at random. To make sure that psychological factors would not affect the results, some children were given "dummy" shots, containing no vaccine at all, and the records were kept secret. Moreover, other groups of children who received no shots at all were kept under observation for comparison with the test group, for when the polio rate for the vaccinated children went down drastically, the testers wanted to be sure that it was due to the vaccine and did not happen with unvaccinated children too.

Whenever, then, you are considering an argument for a generalization, once you understand what the argument is, there is always this final question to ask: *Is there any reason to believe that the sample is not typical of the class under investigation?* If there is such a reason, you are right to mistrust the generalization; if there is not, it may be dependable.

Suppose a young man gives up three jobs because he feels he has been unfairly treated by his boss each time, and all three bosses have red hair, so he resolves never to work for anyone with red hair again. This is an important decision, for, if his generalization is wrong, he may turn down a very fine job for a bad reason. Will his sample support the generalization?

Are there any other characteristics the three bosses had in common, besides the color of their hair, that might be the real cause of their behavior? Perhaps they were all advertising executives, and the young man is just not temperamentally equipped for that sort of job; the redness of the hair would then be merely a coincidence. Were they very different in *other* respects—educational background, business experience, personality, habits of work? But in this case, no matter how different they were, it is clear that the sample is too small to count on. We know from experience that the fairness of human behavior is adversely affected by many things: ulcers, high blood pressure, indigestion, insomnia, financial worries, domestic difficulties, and so forth; and we know that human beings differ from each other in an extraordinary variety of ways. If we wanted to be sure that having red hair was always a defect in a boss, we would have to have a large enough sample to include bosses with various common ailments, from various sections of the country, in various types of jobs, and so on. It would take hundreds of bosses to get a sample adequate for a dependable generalization. And so we may say that this young man has committed the **fallacy of hasty generalization.**

The most startling type of hasty generalization is that which is launched from a single instance. When we stop to think about it, it is plain that one instance is never sufficient to make a generalization dependable. For a single instance is always an instance of, and equally good evidence for, a *number* of generalizations, and it's not until you get more instances that you can decide which generalization to choose. The back cover of a national magazine reports that "Doris Droop, star of stage and screen, likes Nibelung, the *dry* beer." We are expected to generalize from this. Now, if it is a fact, it is an instance of all of the following (and countless other) generalizations, some of which are quite untrue:

> All actresses like Nibelung beer.
> One-tenth of one per cent of all actresses like Nibelung beer.
> All actresses whose names begin with "D" like Nibelung beer.
> Most screen stars like Nibelung beer.
> All women like Nibelung beer.
> Everybody likes Nibelung beer.

We would need quite a few more testimonials to make a reasonable choice among these generalizations.

Yet the single-instance generalization is surprisingly common—and particularly with those generalizations that are called *causal laws*. It is well known that arsenic is poisonous—that is, the ingestion of a certain quantity of it, by any human being, *causes* death. It was once *thought* that tomatoes are poisonous. There doesn't seem to be any clear record of how this rumor got started, but perhaps it got started the way many other superstitions did. Someone ate a tomato and soon died of a heart attack. As long as nothing was known about the chemistry of tomatoes or the mechanism of the heart, it was easy to jump to the conclusion that eating the tomato was the *cause* of death. And as long as everyone took this seriously and kept away from tomatoes, there was no way they could find out that their generalization was false.

This sort of argument is known as the **post hoc, ergo propter hoc** ("after this, therefore because of this") argument; the fallacy consists in observing that, for example, George Smith recovered from his illness after doses of Prester John's Patent Medicine, and inferring that *therefore* he owes his recovery to the medicine. Or, to take another example, you may have heard speeches on this theme:

And I urge you to look again at the record of the Administration since it was swept back into power and responsibility. Immediately on gaining office, the President issued his famous order to the Navy to unleash Chiang Kai Chek's troops in Formosa, leaving them free to attack the Communists on the mainland. The chain reaction was tremendous. The Communists made peace in Korea; Stalin died; the French began to take the offensive in Indochina . . .

Think what an enormous amount of evidence it would take to establish causal connections among these events. So far as this paragraph goes, the argument is simple: B followed A, therefore B was the result of A. What follows an action is sometimes an effect of it, but you cannot know that it is an effect until you see that exactly the same sort of thing happens several times, under different conditions.

A CHECK-UP QUIZ. Here are some generalizations and the samples on which they are based. In each case, give a reason why the sample may not be typical of the class under investigation.

1. *Generalization*: Allowing children to play with guns encourages their criminal tendencies, and makes them more likely to become juvenile delinquents. *Sample*: Jack O'Gorman, 14, arrested for armed robbery, confessed that when he was three or four years old, the six-shooters he carried all the time, and slept with, were his most precious possessions.

2. *Generalization*: Child prodigies usually crack up or turn out to be mediocre when they grow up. *Sample*: A Sunday supplement writer, urging mothers not to be distressed if their children show no special talents, mentioned five cases of people who scored at the "genius" level when they were children, and either became mentally ill or failed to become outstanding successes.

3. *Generalization*: Lobster always makes me ill. *Sample*: On two occasions I ate lobster at late-evening celebrations, and each time I was sick the next day.

4. *Generalization*: 86.83 per cent of the people in this city are against the proposed increase in the entertainment and luxury tax. *Sample*: 1,800 people were interviewed on their way into the Palace Theatre during the month of June and 1563 of them said they were against the proposed increase.

5. *Generalization*: There is a much higher proportion of divorces among wealthy and famous people than among ordinary people.

Sample: Divorces prominently reported in newspapers in the last few years.

See also Exercise 5, pp. 78-80.

FURTHER READING: Harold Larrabee, *Reliable Knowledge*. Boston: Houghton Mifflin Co., 1945, ch. 12. M. C. Beardsley, *Practical Logic*. New York: Prentice-Hall, Inc., 1950, ch. 12, §§ 58, 59, and chs. 13, 14.

§8. CLASSIFICATION

The more we learn about the general features of the world, by generalization, the better able we are to organize our knowledge. And the more orderly our knowledge becomes, the more efficiently we can set about increasing it. The fundamental way of organizing knowledge is that which consists in sorting things out—that is, thinking of them as belonging to different *classes* of things. We observe differences between things—between reds and blues, between men and women, between wood and metal, between mushrooms and toadstools—and assign them to different classes by marking them with different names. And we observe similarities between things—between scarlet and crimson, between Americans and Africans, between oak and birch, between one species of mushroom and another—and assign them to the same class by marking them with the same name.

When we draw attention to a distinction, by breaking a class down into some of its subclasses, we are *subdividing* the class. For instance, life insurance policies are sometimes subdivided this way:

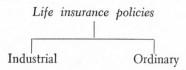

When we draw attention to a similarity by grouping a class together with other classes, we are *subordinating* the class to a larger class. For instance, we might ask, of what class are life insurance policies a subclass? This sort of question is often hard to answer: is a policy a thing, an event, an experience, an activity, or what? Well, it is at least a form of contract. It is a mutual pledge of performance between two parties: this is what it has in common with other kinds of contract. And the *difference* between this kind and all other kinds lies in what

is promised: by one party, to pay regular sums; by the other to pay a
forfeit if you lose your life. Thus we get:

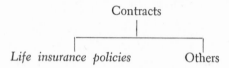

Each of these diagrams shows one class broken down into two
subclasses, or, if you like, two classes combined into a superclass. The
diagrams are really pictures of statements; for example, "Life insurance policies can be subdivided into (a) industrial and (b) ordinary."
Such a statement about relations among classes we shall call a
classification. And the classes and subclasses it involves we shall call
its **categories**.

These diagrams are not very extensive classifications, but they have
the essential ingredients. There are two levels, or **ranks**, one subsumed
under the other. In order to subdivide a class, we must select some
characteristic that will make a distinction between some of its members and others. In the first diagram, this distinguishing characteristic
is *face value*. The industrial policies are those whose face value is less
than $1,000; the ordinary policies are those whose face value is $1,000
or over. This characteristic is called the **basis of division**.

In a more elaborate classification, there will be several ranks, and
each will have its own basis of division. Consider, for example, this
partial classification of arguments:

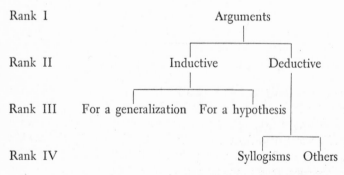

In Rank II, arguments are classified according to whether or not
they make a claim that their conclusions follow necessarily from

their reasons. In Rank III the basis of division is *type of conclusion*; in Rank IV it is, as we shall see, *logical form*. "Others" is a miscellaneous category, which could, of course, be broken down farther. The classification, with this catch-all section, is not as tidy as it might be, but classifications, like budgets, can be useful even if they are not figured out to the last detail.

In judging a classification, whether your own or someone else's, there are two sorts of question to keep in mind. First, there are certain logical conditions a classification *has* to satisfy or it cannot be considered a success at all, for it is likely to confuse your thinking more than it helps. But second, even if a classification is logically impeccable, it may still not be of much use if it is not a *significant* classification.

Consider the minimal conditions first. The fundamental rule here is that *in each rank of a classification the subdivision must be made in terms of a single basis of division*. It won't do to subdivide pickles into sour pickles and small pickles; there are two bases of division here, *taste* and *size*. Or suppose someone said, "Insurance policies may be divided into several classes: fire, collision, accident, industrial, liability, group, marine, life, and theft." This is a hopeless logical jumble. The term "industrial" refers to the *amount* of the policy, and it indicates a subclass of life insurance. The term "group" refers to the rules for obtaining such a policy. And so on. There are several different bases of division that need to be sorted out.

Of course, you could make a classification of insurance policies that would take care of all these categories. On the first rank, for example, you might distinguish "individual" and "group" policies; on the second, subdivide according to the type of thing insured, and so on. "Men, women, and children" is a muddled classification as it stands, but it doesn't confuse us because we readily supply the two ranks, and straighten it out in our minds:

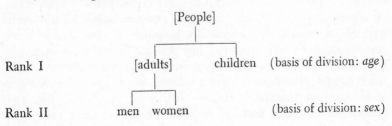

	[People]		
Rank I	[adults] children	(basis of division: *age*)
Rank II	men women	(basis of division: *sex*)

Any attempted classification, no matter how defective, can be put to rights by inserting enough missing categories and redistributing the categories through several ranks. But the first thing is to realize that it *is* defective. And you find this out by checking each subdivision to see whether it is done on one basis of division or more. Consider again the usual subdivision of prose writings into four categories: description, narration, explanation, argument. Surely there are at least three different bases of division here. Again, the social sciences are sometimes subdivided into economics, political science, sociology, and history. As a matter of fact, it is a knotty problem to decide how many bases of division there are here, and just what they are, but there is surely more than one. In both of these cases, it would help our thinking considerably to get clearer about the bases of division involved.

When a classification proceeds at some rank by more than one principle of division, it commits the **fallacy of cross-ranking**. It telescopes two or more ranks into one, and throws into confusion the real logical relationships between the categories. Such a classification entangles the categories so that they may overlap—some things get into more than one category—and they may be insufficient—some things get left out because there is no category at all for them. Like having someone else sort out the papers on your desk for you, to *mis*classify is sometimes worse than not to classify at all.

A classification groups some things together, and it also distinguishes them from other groups. A classification is said to be *significant* if its categories put things together that belong together, and if its distinctions are worth making. Evidently significance, considered in this way, is relative to some purpose. For the purpose of staying alive, the distinction between mushrooms and toadstools is very important, but the distinction between one kind of mushroom and another is not. For the purposes of cooking, however, the second distinction may be noteworthy. Or consider our partial classification of insurance policies. The distinction between industrial and ordinary life is important for some life insurance companies, but most companies don't sell industrial life policies. If we were writing a treatise on life insurance in general, we should have to choose a more fundamental classification. For example, we might subdivide life insurance into four basic classes: (1) term, (2) whole life, (3) limited payment life, and (4) endowment. To get these categories, we should use two bases of division: *length of time of premium payments* and *point at which proceeds are paid*. So our classification would have two ranks.

Grouping things and separating things are two aspects of the same process, like the inside and outside of a curve. And once we are clear what the purpose at hand is to be, we must ask what classification is the most significant for that purpose. Such a classification will make the most fundamental distinctions (for that purpose) in the first rank, the less fundamental distinctions in the lower ranks. The grocer classifies his produce into fruits and vegetables in a common sense way. The botanist classifies the same objects in a very different way. He classifies cherries, tomatoes, oats and acorns as *fruits*, but not apples and strawberries. Nor does he classify strawberries as berries, but he *does* classify bananas and oranges as berries. This seems whimsical and arbitrary to anyone who hasn't studied botany. But the botanist knows a great many generalizations about these things, and he knows that acorns and cherries have more fundamental characteristics in common than strawberries and cherries.

What the word "fundamental" means here can be roughly indicated in this way: When you know that something is red, you can't infer much more about it from that alone because there are not many true generalizations like "All red things are...." But when you know that something is the product of the fertilized ovule of the flower (and that's the botanists' definition of "fruit"), you can infer quite a lot more about it if you know some well-established biological laws. Thus *being the product of the fertilized ovule of a flower* is a more fundamental characteristic of parts of plants than *redness* for the purpose of the botanist. It depends on what generalizations are already known. A classification is not a generalization, but a *good* classification is made with generalizations in mind.

Thus, if you take the trouble, you can think of thousands of possible bases of division for human beings: sex, income, color of hair, waistline, place of residence, favorite color, size of thumb, average number of words uttered per week, date of first arrival of ancestor in Western Hemisphere, occupation of maternal grandfather—you could go on indefinitely. Now, if you have a limited concern, such as manufacturing gloves, thumb-size may be important to you. But if you are a sociologist you will look for more fundamental bases of division; that is, characteristics that will be better clues to the nature of the people in each category. The sociologist knows more generalizations about the relation between a person's income and his other character-istics (his tastes, his type of job, his interests, his education) than about the relationships between a person's thumb-size and his other characteristics.

You face a similar problem whenever you classify—for example, when you make an outline of a paper you're going to write, or a speech you're going to give, for an outline is a classification of the ideas you plan to use. Not that you choose the ideas and then classify them; your decision about what ideas to use or reject will be modified while you are arranging them because in order to work out good categories you will have to think out more clearly the connections between the ideas, and you may discover that some of them aren't connected at all, or not in the way you first thought. You can start with small groups of ideas and build up the major groups, or start with the major groups and work down. But in either case you aim at a final outline that will mark by its main headings the important distinctions in your paper, considering the point of your argument or the central theme of your exposition, and relegate the subordinate distinctions to sub-sub-headings.

Sometimes people object to classification, and like to think they themselves defy classification. They quote Dean Inge to the effect that "all labels are libels," and say that putting things, or people, into categories distorts the truth about them. For instance, they object to calling people "introverts" and "extroverts." Or they insist it is misleading to try to distinguish contemporary religious and theo-logical views, like "liberal theology," "neo-orthodoxy," and "funda-mentalism." It is even said that a certain modernist clergyman, when asked, "Do you believe in God?" replied, "I dislike these hard and fast distinctions."

These objections are either objections to bad classifications, or else they are misunderstandings. A classification with vaguely-defined categories will be misleading if the distinctions in fact are clear-cut; and a classification with clear-cut categories may be misleading if it suggests that the differences in things are sharper than they really are. A classification that puts trivial distinctions in its first rank will over-stress their importance. But to put a person in a category does not need to suggest that there is any other like him (he may be unique, the only one of his kind). Indeed, to make a category, like *purple cow*, does not assert that it necessarily has any members at all. And if X, Y, and Z are classed together, this does not deny that there are important differences between them (say, between one neo-orthodox theologian and another); the differences can be made clear by subdividing further. Man is an animal, but it doesn't follow that he is *nothing but* an animal. Like most tools of thought, classifications can be wittingly or unwittingly misused. But it is hard to see how, unless we sometimes use them well, we could get a good grip on the world at all.

A CHECK-UP QUIZ. Which of the following subdivisions commit the fallacy of cross-ranking?

1. shoes *into* leather shoes, wooden shoes, cloth shoes, paper shoes, metal shoes.

2. trucks *into* delivery trucks, pick-up trucks, dump trucks, trailer trucks, sand trucks.

3. trains *into* steam, electric, diesel-electric, atomic-steam.

4. canned goods *into* fruits, juices, vegetables, meats, desserts.

5. swimming strokes *into* sidestroke, crawl, backstroke.

6. pies *into* mince pies, apple pies, one-crust pies, lemon meringue pies.

7. popular songs *into* ballads, hillbilly songs, funny songs, waltzes, show tunes.

8. arts *into* painting, drawing, sculpture, music, poetry, drama, the novel, ballet, architecture.

9. discourses *into* verse, novels, plays, short stories, essays.

10. clouds *into* cumulus, stratus, nimbus, cirrus, cirro-stratus, cirro-cumulus, and cumulo-stratus.

See also Exercise 6, p. 81.

FURTHER READING: Morris Cohen and Ernest Nagel, *Introduction to Logic and Scientific Method*. New York: Harcourt, Brace and Co., 1934, ch. 12, sec. 5.   M. C. Beardsley, *Practical Logic*. New York: Prentice-Hall, Inc., 1950, ch. 12, §§ 56, 57.

§9. THE ARGUMENT FROM ANALOGY

When you point out that two different things (say, a marshmallow and a meat-ax) have some characteristic in common (they both have weight), you are placing them in the same category with respect to this similarity (the category of physical objects). Now, when you point out that two things have a number of characteristics in common, you are drawing an analogy between them. For example:

> A family budget and the budget of the United States Government are alike in many respects. They both list income and outgo; some of the expenses are for the same sort of thing; when the budget is unbalanced, the deficit has to be made up by borrowing.

There is an analogy between a map and the territory of which it is a map: only here the correspondence is not a correspondence of qualities (Idaho is not blue, though the patch representing Idaho on the map may be blue), but of *structure* (the shape of the Idaho-patch, and its position in relation to the New Jersey-patch, are the same as the actual shape of Idaho and its geographical relation to New Jersey). A good map has a very close analogy to its territory. George Washington once compared the Senate of the United States to a saucer in which the legislative tea is poured to cool it off before drinking. This analogy is a rather remote one, though not without some element of truth.

Analogies can be very helpful to our thinking, so long as we know what to do with them. We can use them to illustrate and clarify general principles. It helps us to understand the nature and function of the blood stream to think of it as the "internal environment," the bit of ocean (which it is chemically so much like) that the early creatures carried with them when they first undertook to live on land. When we use analogies this way, of course, we have to be careful not to push them too far, for they all break down at some point. Comparison with ocean waves will take the beginner a little way in a study of sound waves (for example, in making clear what resonance is); comparison with sound waves will take him a little way in the study of radio waves (for example, in explaining reflection). But if pressed too far, the analogy will be misleading. The "ether" is not an ocean.

Analogies can also be very fruitful for suggesting working hypotheses that may lead to important discoveries. In the early part of this century, when Nils Bohr constructed his model of the atom as a miniature solar system, with the electrons revolving around the nucleus, this picture led atomic scientists to think of many ideas that they could test experimentally. Some of these turned out to be true, and important, and perhaps they would not have been thought of, or not so soon, without the analogy, though we now know that the analogy is a rather over-simple and far-fetched one. The analogy between the growth of the embryo and the course of evolution, between electro-magnetic fields and gravitational fields, between the universe and a machine—these, and many others, have been very useful in the history of science. Not because they are thought to *prove* anything, but because they call to mind possibilities that the investigator can go on to explore, to find out whether they *are* provable.

When you draw an analogy between two different things, and use this analogy as a reason for inferring something about one of those things, then you are making an **argument from analogy**. For example:

> A family budget and the budget of the United States Government are alike in many respects. They both list income and outgo; some of the expenses are for the same sort of thing; when the budget is unbalanced, the deficit has to be made up by borrowing. Now, it is obvious that if a family budget remains unbalanced very long, the family will lose its credit, and go bankrupt. It follows that the same is true of the government. As the great Adam Smith wrote, "What is prudence in the conduct of every private family can scarce be folly in that of a great nation."

In this passage a *conclusion* is drawn from the fact that the two kinds of budget have certain common features.

The pattern of inference at the center of this argument can be summarized abstractly in this way:

> X and Y both have certain characteristics a, b, c, ... And it is known that Y also has another characteristic q. *Therefore*: X has the characteristic q.

There are two things, then: X (the national budget) and Y (a family budget). There are certain *assumed resemblances* (having income and outgo, etc.), and the underlying principle is that if X and Y have a number of characteristics in common, then any further characteristics found in Y will also be found in X.

This underlying principle, once we state it clearly and think about it, is plainly false. If two things have a good deal in common, it is a sensible guess that they *might* have more in common; the guess is good enough to justify further investigation to see whether they actually *do* have more in common. But it remains a guess until it is tested; we are not justified in believing that they have more in common *without* the investigation. This is because, no matter how many characteristics a pair of things share, there may be any number of other ways, as yet unknown, in which they are different. You cannot even say that the more known resemblances there are between X and Y, the more likely it is that X will have any further characteristic found in Y. No matter that a national budget can be compared in many ways with a family budget; it by no means follows that it is like it in *all* ways, or in any other particular way. Of course, we should not conclude that the national budget *can* remain unbalanced: whether it can or not is an important, difficult, and debatable question. The point is that the argument from analogy does not settle it.

Earlier in this chapter it was said that there are only two kinds of inductive argument, that is, only two ways of giving reasons for an inductive conclusion. The argument from analogy might be considered a third kind, for it is different from the other two. But it is not a *successful* kind of inductive argument at all. No argument having this pattern, and based on this principle, can give us a *good* reason for believing anything. The argument from analogy is fallacious.

When arguments from analogy seem plausible, it is usually because they are vaguely stated and easily confused with other kinds of argument. Suppose I say, "John's parents both have blue eyes, and so do Jim's; John has blue eyes; therefore, Jim must have blue eyes." Now, taken as it stands, this is an argument from analogy, and evidently a very feeble one. The conclusion may be true, but it is wildly jumped to. This is easy to see if we substitute another argument based on exactly the same principle: "John's parents both read Greek, and so do Jim's; John likes horseradish; therefore, Jim must like horseradish."

Now, the difference between these two arguments is this: in the first case, but not in the second, we know a true generalization that would justify the inference, and we assume this generalization without stating it. When we supply it, we get:

All people whose parents both have blue eyes are people with blue eyes.
Jim's parents both have blue eyes.

Jim has blue eyes.

But this is not an inductive argument at all: it is a deductive one, and of a simple type, in which a previously-tested generalization is applied to a new instance. This argument is a good one, but it is not an argument from analogy.

Note that in this argument, you don't need to refer to John at all. In fact, the only way you can work him in is as evidence for the generalization itself:

John's parents both have blue eyes, and John has blue eyes.

All people whose parents both have blue eyes are people with blue eyes.

This is a generalization, to be sure, but it doesn't contain very much evidence. Surely we would want to know about quite a few more instances than John before we were ready to draw this broad conclusion.

In short, the argument from analogy looks a little like a deductive argument and also a little like an induction of a generalization, but it is neither one nor the other. If it were the former, it would be sound, but you would already have to know the relevant generalization before you could use it. If it were the latter, it would not assume the generalization, but it would not prove it either. There may be a general truth that *all* budgets will produce bankruptcy if not balanced in a limited time. This can be investigated. But if we were investigating it, we would want to examine a large number and variety of budgets, *including* some national ones. And before we undertake that investigation, we ought not to draw any conclusion.

Now, when you are confronted with an argument from analogy (and they turn up very often in ordinary discourse), you know at once that it is unsound. But that doesn't always mean that you can show someone else that it is unsound. In the course of a dispute, you may not have the chance to explain why arguments from analogy are weak in general; what you need is a method of puncturing the particular analogy at hand. Usually the most effective way of answering an argument from analogy is to force it into a different form, where it clearly depends upon a generalization, and then to discuss the truth of the generalization. This is also the most fruitful way of going after the argument, for it turns everybody's attention to the important question, and may lead to the discovery of a new generalization.

Let's take a simple and crude example first. One old gambit of the temperance orator was to say: "The delicate membranes of the stomach are like the delicate membranes of the eye; if you want to see what alcohol does to your stomach, just pour some gin in your eye." Now we may grant that there are *some* resemblances between eye tissue and stomach tissue: the question is whether these are *relevant* resemblances. In other words, the question is whether there is some true generalization like "Everything that hurts the eye will hurt the stomach" that will allow us to infer that if gin hurts the eye it will also hurt the stomach.

So we might reply to him, "Do you mean that *everything* that hurts the eye will also hurt the stomach?" He may wish to narrow the suggested generalization from "everything" to "every liquid," or in some other way. But unless he is willing to subscribe to *some* relevant generalization, he simply hasn't got what it takes to draw the conclusion he wants. We are therefore justified in saying to him, "If your argument proved anything, it would prove just as well that lemonade, vinegar, and hot coffee are bad for the stomach because they will hurt the eye. Doesn't that show that there must be important *differences* between the eye and stomach, so that what is true of one is not necessarily true of the other?"

The person who argues from analogy has his own tactic: he must focus attention upon a single pair of examples, and he may seem plausible as long as you keep your eye on what he shows you. But the person who doesn't want to be misled by an analogical argument has his tactic, too: he can place the examples in a wider perspective; he can question the closeness of the analogy; he can show that if it proved anything, it would prove something that is obviously false; he can insist that the conclusion cannot be drawn unless a certain generalization is true. Of course, the generalization may *be* true, once it is tested: then it will be worth knowing. This doesn't justify the argument from analogy, but it forces the argument into a different and logically dependable form, where its force is clear.

Thus, to take one more example, suppose the officials of a public school argue that parents should have nothing to say about how the schools are run because teachers and principals are experts in education, like doctors and lawyers, and a layman doesn't tell a doctor how to cure diseases or a lawyer how to win cases. This argument from analogy can set off a lot of discussion, and that discussion can be futile or fruitful. The question is, in what respects are educational experts like medical experts, and are these respects relevant here? Some are, and some aren't. Surely the teachers and principals know *some* things that they can speak with authority about (for example, the best way to teach arithmetic); surely there are other questions that arise, about educational *policy* and the more ultimate *goals* of education, that all citizens have to make up their minds about and help decide. It is no good to wrangle about the analogy itself; that proves nothing. But if the right questions are asked about the *difference* between the things that teachers are experts on and the things they are *not* experts on, much light may come from the dispute, and to all of the parties concerned.

A CHECK-UP QUIZ. Which of the following passages contain *arguments from analogy?*

1. The situation facing the democracies in 1955 is very similar to the situation facing the Greek city-states in the time of Philip of Macedon: there is the same threat of domination by a militaristic power, the same mutual suspicion among the threatened countries, the same pervasive fatalism. It is evident that we are destined to be overcome and overrun.

2. One great advantage of the American federal system is that the separate states can operate like laboratories of government, in which various ways of doing things (for example, different laws about voting age, divorce, automobile licenses, birth control; and different types of legislature, county court system, party primary) can be tried out on a small scale, and tested to see whether they ought to be adopted by the Federal Government for the country as a whole.

3. People in the upper income brackets are like the upper streams and springs in a watershed, for their spending and saving (investments) give life and health to the whole economy. That is why it is important to give tax relief to them, so that their prosperity will trickle down to the less wealthy, since we know that water always flows downhill, never up.

4. Senator Stuart Symington in a Senate speech: "One of the dreams that lulls us into this hopeful make-believe is the theory of the so-called atomic standoff. This is the argument that, when both we and the Communists have plenty of atomic weapons, neither of us will use them. To gamble on such a miracle is like

betting that two men armed with loaded pistols will merely wrestle until one of them is thrown to the ground and kicked to death."

5. The social and political institutions of the bee are characterized by a remarkable degree of selflessness in subordinating the individual to the hive. Each bee seems to know his place and to fulfill it to the best of his ability—and in so doing, he appears content. It is possible that the success and permanence of these arrangements can teach us lessons of great value in our own political thinking on the human level. For example, our government might be much more stable if we took greater pains to discover everyone's abilities and needs, and give him the right job—a proposition I recommend to the social scientist for further serious study.

FURTHER READING: L. S. Stebbing, *Thinking to Some Purpose*. Pelican Books, 1939, ch. 9. Irving M. Copi, *Introduction to Logic*. New York: The Macmillan Co., 1953, ch. 11.

§10. APPRAISING A HYPOTHESIS

Any argument for a hypothesis, whether trivial ("A mosquito has bitten me") or momentous ("The Russians have exploded a hydrogen bomb"), is first of all a report of a set of facts, and second an attempt to show that the hypothesis is the best available way of accounting for those facts. As new facts turn up, hypotheses may have to be mended or discarded in favor of others. Or we may be able to think of a better way of accounting for the same facts. Thus an argument for a hypothesis is a sort of cross section of an inquiry at a particular stage.

The term "inquiry" has a rather broad sense here; it takes in any very persistent attempt to answer a question. An inquiry, or investigation, begins when someone finds himself confronted with a problem. It may be immediate: "Why doesn't the car start this morning?" "Why does my house get cold whenever I turn on the television set?" Or it may be more far-reaching: "Who was responsible for the defeat at Pearl Harbor?" "Would a different wartime policy toward China have prevented it from going Communist?" When you really want to know the answer, and when you tackle the question like a good mechanic or historian, your thinking will follow a familiar pattern. First, you think of possible answers to the question; these might be called "*working hypotheses*." Second, you look for facts that will help you choose between these working hypotheses—facts, in other words, that will eliminate some of them, and build up strong evidence for others. Third, you choose the hypothesis that you find most acceptable. When you put this hypothesis into words, and set forth the evidence that you have collected and organized, you are making an inductive *argument* for it.

The situation is not fundamentally different when someone else attempts to convince you that his hypothesis, or theory, is true in view of the facts he offers. In this case, your task is to appraise his hypothesis, in other words, to decide how much confidence to place in it. Sometimes you may be interested in the satisfaction of scientific curiosity—about the Indian rope trick, or the cause of the aurora borealis, or whether ancient South Americans could have been wafted across the Pacific Ocean on balsa rafts. More often, however, you are after some reliable knowledge that you can use to make vital, practical decisions.

The main features of an argument for a hypothesis can be studied in the following argument:

> An overturned skiff was found drifting in the Sound early this morning, and brought in by fishermen. Inquiry revealed that the skiff had been taken out yesterday noon by a Mr. John Smith, who said he was going fishing all afternoon. A heavy storm came up suddenly about four o'clock in the afternoon, and it has been ascertained that Mr. Smith was unable to swim. It is presumed that he met death by drowning

We can probably agree that the conclusion here is a reasonable one to draw in view of the evidence at hand.

Now, the first thing to note about the argument—and in this respect it is typical of arguments for a hypothesis—is that, however convincing it may be, it could be made even more convincing by adding further evidence. If Mr. Smith's body should be washed ashore, we would be more confident of the hypothesis. The hypothesis still would not be certain, for Mr. Smith could have died by poison or in a heart attack, but it would be more likely to be true. And if we found water in his lungs, and no known poison in his system or other signs of violence, we would perhaps be justified in feeling what is called a "moral certainty," and accepting it as true beyond a reasonable doubt.

The second thing to note is that we can also think of still other facts that would, if discovered, make the hypothesis *less* convincing. If Mr. Smith turned up alive and well, with a story of having been rescued by a passing launch, this would destroy our confidence in the hypothesis, for it would conflict with it. We should then have to say that the "presumption" that he was dead was a mistake. So with hypotheses in general: no matter how convincing one may be, a discovery made tomorrow or the following day may conceivably weaken or destroy it. Thus a hypothesis always wears a tentative, provisional air, so to speak: we accept it, and we act upon it, only until a better one comes along.

Nevertheless, it is also true that a hypothesis may be so convincing that we do not expect a better one to come along. And so we speak of "proving" a hypothesis (proving the guilt of a defendant, or proving a historical hypothesis, or proving a scientific theory). We mean, not deductive demonstration, of course, but something looser: we call a hypothesis "proved" when we have such strong evidence for it that we no longer fear (or hope for) any further evidence that would refute it. The practical question in appraising a hypothesis is, then: At what point are we justified in regarding it as "proved"?

It would be very handy if a simple and universal reply could be given to this question. Unfortunately it cannot, for many reasons. There are no mechanical rules for appraising hypotheses, but, as with precious stones and real estate, there is a skill that can be developed. And some people are better at this than others. We shall discuss two important principles that are to be taken into account in appraising a hypothesis.

Go back for a moment to the case of the overturned boat. Suppose you and a friend both read the newspaper account, and you said you agreed with its conclusion. And suppose your friend replied, "I don't agree at all. I believe Mr. Smith rowed out in the Sound, met someone in another boat by prearrangement, overturned the skiff himself, and went off with his fellow conspirator." Now this second hypothesis (let's call it Hypothesis B) accounts for the known facts just as yours (Hypothesis A) does. But until more facts come along (for example, evidence that Mr. Smith committed a robbery two days after his "drowning") that can be accounted for by Hypothesis B, but *not* by Hypothesis A, you are surely right to think that your hypothesis is more likely to be true than your friend's. And for a fairly plain reason.

Some kinds of things (like weddings, sunrises, twins, automobile accidents) happen quite frequently: other kinds of things (like double weddings, eclipses of the sun, quintuplets, and bus accidents) are rather rare. When someone explains a set of facts by saying that such-and-such an event happened, we ought to consider how often that sort of event has happened before. Of course, *new* kinds of things (like hydrogen bomb explosions and the appearance of mankind on the earth) happen, too. And if the facts are such that the only very satisfactory way we can explain them is by supposing that something utterly new and strange has happened, then we must (tentatively) accept that explanation. But if we can explain the very same facts in terms of some far more common occurrence, that is evidently the sensible thing to do. The **frequency** of a hypothesis, then, is the number of times events of the sort it describes have occurred. And the principle we apply is this: Other things being equal, if we have two or more hypotheses that account for the known facts in a particular case, the one with the greatest frequency is the most probable.

You would say to your friend, then, that being overturned and drowned is something that has probably happened much more often than *pretending* to have been overturned and drowned. You are of course appealing to a generalization here, for which you must have adequate evidence, and perhaps your friend will not agree with this assumption. But if it *is* true that A-type things are more frequent than B-type things, why then, in the absence of evidence against it, Hypothesis A is more likely to be true than Hypothesis B. We see this principle used very often in criminal cases, where there are usually questions about what a person would "naturally" do—that is, what he would most *commonly* do—under the circumstances. If the hypothesis that the defendant is guilty involves the supposition that he did something that would be, not perhaps impossible for such a person, but highly unusual and unexpected from one of his character or personality, that will take something away from the plausibility of the hypothesis. "Is he the sort of person who would tell a lie? keep a secret for years? doublecross an old friend?"—these are questions about the frequency of the hypothesis. And the answers must be sought in terms of dependable generalizations already discovered.

Now go back once more to the case of the overturned boat. There is another objection you might bring against your friend's Hypothesis B. Your hypothesis takes care of the facts by telling a story of what you suppose has happened: Mr. Smith was fishing, or rowing home; the storm came up; a wave overturned the boat; he was drowned. No one else is involved; no deep-laid plot; no elaborate skulduggery and deception. Hypothesis B, on the other hand, involves *two* people, Mr. Smith and his unknown co-worker; it involves a plan, a pre-arranged meeting, a deliberate overturning of the skiff, and then the disappearance and subsequent concealment of Mr. Smith. This story is a good deal more complicated than the story told by Hypothesis A. Of course, as before, if further evidence turns up that Mr. Smith is still alive, Hypothesis A will be out, and that will be the time to consider Hypothesis B. But in the meantime, it would be unreasonable to choose to believe Hypothesis B instead of Hypothesis A (even if it makes a better story) because it is unnecessarily complicated.

It is not possible to give a precise measure of the difference, but quite often we can say with some assurance, though vaguely, that one story is simpler than another. It may involve fewer persons or things, a shorter series of episodes, or a more symmetrical central structure. The story of "The Three Little Pigs" is simpler than *War and Peace*; whether or not it is simpler than "The Gingerbread Man" is a harder question. The **simplicity** of a hypothesis, then, is the fewness of things, people, and events it describes. And the principle we apply is this: Other things being equal, if we have two or more hypotheses that account for the known facts in a particular case, the simplest one is the most probable.

This principle, in Mr. Smith's case, gives us the same result as the first principle. But we can apply this one in other cases where we have little or no evidence about the frequency of the hypothesis. There is a (probably made-up) story about Lysenko, the Soviet biologist. In the course of a lecture, he put a flea on his desk and said, "Jump!" Presently the flea jumped. He then removed the flea's hind legs, and said, "Jump!" again. This time the flea did not jump. "Observe, gentlemen," said Lysenko; "This proves that when you remove the flea's hind legs, its hearing is impaired." The conclusion could be true, but there is no reason to believe it when a much simpler explanation is so easy to think of. Similarly with the rule that people are to be presumed innocent until proved guilty; this is not only a right that a constitutional system confers upon them, it is also the simpler hypothesis.

The principles of frequency and simplicity will not guarantee the right judgment in all cases, nor can they be applied mechanically. But they help to keep us from jumping to conclusions without stopping to think that there may be other conclusions much safer to stand on. Seizing upon one hypothesis when a simpler or more frequent one would do the same job of explanation might be called the **fallacy of forced hypothesis**. The forced hypothesis is the far-fetched one—the one with unnecessary frills, or the long arm of coincidence. None of us can escape this fallacy all the time, but if we bear it in mind we can learn faster from our inevitable mistakes.

An inductive argument for a hypothesis may be a brief paragraph, or an elaborately drawn-out book. To appraise it accurately, and make a good judgment of it, may require a considerable background of information on our part. And it may also require a skillful management of many of the principles of language and logic that we shall be discussing throughout this book.

When you are presented with such an argument, your first step will be to sort out clearly in your mind the ingredients of the argument. What *is* the hypothesis? And what is the evidence offered for it?

There are many questions that you might want to ask about the hypothesis, even before you consider the evidence. For if it is faulty in certain ways, *no* evidence will help it. Is it clear? There is no telling what evidence it needs to be supported by until you know what it asserts. Are there terms in it that need to be defined or made more precise? We shall return to these questions in Chapter 4.

When it comes to the evidence, and its bearing upon the hypothesis, the question to ask is fundamentally this: *Can you think of any other hypothesis that would explain the same facts with greater simplicity or frequency?* When you read a report of a scientific study, a thoughtful magazine article, or a book on a much-debated historical question, you'll find that much of this work is done for you. The author himself will list a number of hypotheses that have been invented to solve the problem, and he will show why he thinks that one of them is to be preferred. But many of the arguments that come to you in the public press are not so fair. Often only one hypothesis is put forth, and that's the one you're asked to accept. The rule of caution here is not to accept that hypothesis (if the matter is important) until you have stopped to think of at least one alternative hypothesis to compare with it. Perhaps you will decide in the end that the hypothesis presented is indeed the best one available. On the other hand, perhaps you can think of a better one yourself; or at least one good enough to make you wonder whether it has been considered and tested. That is your insurance against one of the most compelling and disastrous forms of bad argument: the fallacy of forced hypothesis.

Suppose, for example, you read an editorial about the recent dismissal by a federal judge of some counts in an indictment of a man suspected of subversive activities: the editorial says that it is clear that the judge was prejudiced in favor of the defendant, and should be disqualified from the case. This hypothesis *would* explain the court's decision, but you shouldn't accept it until you ask yourself whether faulty indictments are rarer than prejudiced federal judges. And if the defendant's actions themselves, as reported in the newspapers, can be explained innocently, without inventing an elaborate secret plot, you should not presume him guilty until facts are brought forth that cannot, or cannot very easily, be explained if he is innocent. Frequency and simplicity are always to be considered in comparing and appraising hypotheses—though it must be admitted that they are not a perfect substitute for charitableness.

In cases like these we may, indeed, have to make the hardest choice of all—to reserve judgment. If we can think of two or more hypotheses to explain a certain set of facts, and no one of them seems very probable, it is reasonable to be skeptical of them all—to keep an open (which is not the same as an empty) mind until we can find more evidence to decide the issue. It takes imagination and quickness of wit to invent hypotheses; it takes perseverance and hardheadedness to test them. Few of us can combine both sets of qualities to a high degree —which is why the process of inquiry usually takes a team. But all of us can try to keep the distinction clear—between making up a hypothesis and proving that it is true—and we can bear in mind that, however entertaining, humorous, or emotionally satisfying a hypothesis may be, the proof is in the evidence that can be got for it.

A CHECK-UP QUIZ. A hypothesis (say, 1. "A hurricane is on the way") that explains certain facts (say, 2. "The barometer is falling" and, 3. "The radio announcers are advising people to stay indoors") may itself be explained by another hypothesis (say, 4. "Certain con-ditions have been existing in the Caribbean"). Letting the squiggly arrow stand for "explains," the relation between these statements is then:

Here is a list of ten statements about a particular situation. Referring to them by number, use squiggly arrows to show which are explained by which.

1. Mr. Snitkin saw flames in the cellar of the house at 10:20 P.M.
2. Several empty kerosene cans were found in the cellar.
3. The house is two stories high.
4. Arson was committed.
5. It was a cold night.
6. The house was on fire at 10:00 P.M.
7. The labor union leader who owns the house has made some enemies in a rival union.
8. A man was seen running away from the house at 9:55 P.M.
9. There was smoke coming from the house at 10:00 P.M.
10. Mr. Snitkin called the Fire Department to report a fire at 10:22 P.M.

See also Exercises 8 and 9, pp. 84-91.

FURTHER READING: Morris Cohen and Ernest Nagel, *Intro-duction to Logic and Scientific Method*. New York: Harcourt, Brace and Co., 1934, ch. 11. Harold A. Larrabee, *Reliable Knowledge*. Boston: Houghton, Mifflin and Co., 1945, chs. 5, 6, 14, 15. M. C. Beardsley, *Practical Logic*. New York: Prentice-Hall, Inc., 1950, ch. 15.

Outline-Summary of Chapter 2

There are two kinds of inductive argument:

(A) In the first kind, the conclusion is a *generalization*—a statement that all or some of the members of a certain class of things have a certain characteristic ("Most glass is brittle"). The evidence for the generalization consists of statements that there are known instances of it (brittle pieces of glass). These instances are a *sample* of the whole class (or *class under investigation*). For a sample to be probably typical of the whole class, the sample (1) should contain instances that are very different from one another as regards characteristics that are likely to be relevant, and (2) should, as regards other characteristics, be randomly selected. An argument in which little or no care is taken to get a fair sample commits the *fallacy of hasty generalization*, a special case of which is the *post hoc, ergo propter hoc fallacy*.

(B) In the second kind, the conclusion is a *hypothesis*—a statement that something has happened, or is the case ("Johnny has the measles"). The evidence for the hypothesis consists of statements describing observed facts ("Johnny has a rash"; "Johnny has a temperature"; "Johnny is irritable"; etc.) that can best be *explained by* that hypothesis. To be a good explanation, a hypothesis (1) should have a greater *frequency* than alternative explanations (say, that Johnny has a rare tropical disease), in that the event or situation it describes happens more often than that described by the alternative explanation; or (2) should have a greater *simplicity* than alternative explanations (say, that Johnny's friend has painted on the spots, and Johnny has only a mild cold but is pretending to be sick so he won't have to go to school), in that it involves fewer people, objects or events. An argument in which a hypothesis is accepted as true and an apparently simpler or more frequent hypothesis is rejected, commits the *fallacy of forced hypothesis*.

A *classification* exhibits the logical relationship between a set of classes, or categories (that, for example, *sharps* and *flats* are both subclasses of *accidentals*). At each rank, or level of subdivision, the distinction between one class and another should be made on a single *basis of division* (the basis of division between odd and even numbers is *divisibility by the number 2*). The most significant classification of a class, at a given time, is that which groups together those things with the greatest number of characteristics that tend to go together, according to generalizations known at that time.

The *argument from analogy* is a fallacious form of argument in which it is supposed that two objects, X and Y, have a certain number of characteristics in common, and it is concluded that some further characteristic found in X will therefore also be found in Y.

Exercise 5

Discuss the dependability of the following generalizations. In each case begin by distinguishing the class under investigation from the sample:

then examine the sample carefully, and say why you think it is, or is not, likely to be typical.

1. A local opinion-pollster has discovered that three-quarters of the citizens of Centerville are opposed to flexible price supports of farm products. He learned this by personal interviews with over three hundred adults whose names were selected in the following manner: He went through the city directory, picking out each 25th name, and writing each name on a slip of paper. The slips of paper were then put into a barrel and thoroughly stirred up. Three hundred and fifty were then picked out by a blindfolded person, and the interviewer went to see every person who was available.

2. A study of the sporting preferences of past and present Presidents of the United States, some of whom have been ardent golfers, tennis players, etc., shows that none of them has ever been a softball player. It seems clear that softball players do not become Presidents.

3. A comparative test of the efficacy of two insecticides, DDT and Compound X, was made in the following way: The inside of a container was sprayed with DDT, and some flies put into it for a time. They all died. The container was rinsed out, and sprayed with Compound X. Again the flies died, and in approximately the same time. It was concluded that that two insecticides were equal in their effect upon flies.

4. Television definitely has a bad effect upon many children. A breakdown of television programs over a six-month period shows that while TV drama programs average 9.8 acts of violence per hour, children's dramatic programs during the prebedtime hours average 22.4 acts or threats of violence per hour, and the acts of violence are more than twice as frequent as in adult programs. In a study of hundreds of children aged 5 to 10 selected from various schools in the city, it has been shown that the regular TV viewers are 35 per cent less healthy than those who see it not at all or only occasionally; that 85 per cent of these children show sleep disturbances; and that 54 per cent have eating disturbances.

5. To get public opinion on a proposed increase in tax exemption for children, interviewers were sent with questionnaires from door to door. Certain neighborhoods were selected, each having a different degree of prosperity, and the interviewers went to every home in each neighborhood. When no one answered the doorbell, the name was crossed off the list. The interviewers went out at nine in the morning, and returned at noon, Monday through Saturday, during the first three weeks in January. The results showed overwhelming support of the proposed increase.

6. A college newspaper that was conducting a campaign to persuade the faculty to give shorter assignments wanted to discover student opinion on this point. Ballots were printed in the newspaper, and students were asked to bring them to the newspaper office, which was in the basement of an astronomical observatory in a far corner of the campus. About one-fourth of the students replied, and it was found that, of these, almost four-fifths said that they were in favor of shorter assignments because they were having great difficulty in keeping up with their classwork and were consequently failing in one or more subjects.

7. More than 400 American communities are now employing the drunkometer to test drivers who may be under the influence of alcohol, and to obtain convictions of those whom the drunkometer shows to have an unsafe concentration of alcohol in the blood stream. A drunkometer reading of .15 per cent will be considered *prima facie* evidence of guilt. The drunkometer was recently tested by a research committee on some hundreds of men who volunteered for the test in response to a public appeal; in all but a very few cases it was found that the driver's vision, re-action time, and general capacity to judge distances were seriously impaired when the drunkometer reading was .15 per cent or over.

8. Dr. Wynder cited data from twelve studies covering 6,000 lung cancer patients in various countries, and listed these eleven reasons for concluding that cigarette smoking is a direct cause of cancer: (1) Cancer of the lung is rare in nonsmokers. (2) Heavy smokers are a much higher percentage of lung cancer patients than they are of the general population. (3) There is a direct correlation between the amount smoked and the incidence of cancer. (4) There has been a definite increase in the lung cancer death rate in countries where there has been a marked increase in tobacco consumption. (5) The increase in lung cancer is greater among men than among women, and men are more frequently heavy smokers. (6) There has been a slight increase in lung cancer among women that parallels an increase in smoking by women. (7) The incidence of the disease is greater in cities than in the country, corresponding to a greater cigarette consumption in cities. (8) Most lung cancers are of a type usually caused by irritants. (9) Similar cancers have been produced on the skin of animals by the application of the condensate from cigarette smoke. (10) Nonsmokers who get lung cancer are those exposed to other irritants, for example, in industrial jobs. (11) Lung cancer among non-smokers not exposed to other irritants generally is not the epidermoid type that smokers get. Dr. Wynder said that smoking did not always produce lung cancer, but that it increased the likelihood of it.

Exercise 6

A

Make a systematic classification of one of the following classes, from the point of view suggested, and carry it out to several ranks. Write a short essay justifying your choice of the basic categories, and making clear the generalizations you had in mind in choosing those categories as basic.

1. Sports (from the point of view of a student of American culture who is interested in the reasons for human behavior in this field).
2. Card games (from the point of view of someone writing a book explaining the rules of card games).
3. Foods (from the point of view of a person who has to plan and cook meals).
4. Movies (from the point of view of someone interested in principles of aesthetic criticism in this field).
5. Sources of evidence (from the point of view of a student of logic and the law).

B

Reorganize the categories in some items of the Quiz for §8, page 63, supplying missing categories to make logical classifications.

Exercise 7

Analyze the following arguments from analogy, and write brief attacks on five of them. In each case, (1) make explicit the assumed resemblances, (2) state the conclusion, and (3) expose the fallaciousness of the argument as clearly as you can.

1. A left-wing member of Parliament has stated in the House of Commons that the only reason the Soviet Union would ever attack England is that it permits the United States to maintain a dozen bomber bases. Maybe so. On the other hand, a wise second story man rarely climbs in a window where there's a hornet's nest under the sill.

2. You can't argue that evidence from wire tapping should be excluded from the Federal Courts on the ground that it might lead to abuses. You might just as well argue that policemen shouldn't be allowed to carry revolvers because they might shoot everybody.

3. Look at the tremendous benefits that have come to all of us as a result of not having tariff barriers between the states of the Union.

Evidently the states of Europe would benefit in the same way from the removal of tariff barriers.

4. You can't expect a person to solve mathematical problems without special training in mathematics. No more, then, can you expect people to think logically without special training in logic.

5. Objections that the more conservative parishioners raised to the Rev. Mr. Goldthwaite's pulpit oratory seem to us unfounded and beside the point. They thought he was "beneath the dignity of his position" in singing songs, showing moving pictures, and telling jokes. But a sermon is, after all, essentially a sales talk aimed to get the widest possible market for salvation, and so whatever will work to increase the demand is clearly justified.

6. The history of such countries as Poland, Czechoslovakia, and Hungary shows that Communism, once its virus is injected into the bloodstream of a nation, is like a fatal disease. If allowed to run its course, it spreads from cell to cell, it paralyzes various functions of the body politic, and in a final paroxysm of fever it destroys the national sovereignty. The only way to deal with it, then, is to cut out the infected part as soon as it is discovered, before it can spread the cancer. And that means passing a law to take away the citizenship of all Communists among us.

7. (a) An interviewer from *U.S. News and World Report*, speaking to Lewis Strauss, chairman of the Atomic Energy Commission (arguing that it is not the "function" of atomic scientists to enter into discussion of questions about the moral and political wisdom of using atomic weapons): "But it seems quite simple. If you have a plumber to your house to install some plumbing, he may say it's crazy for you to have a bath in five different rooms . . . he's there to furnish the plumbing. But these scientists come in and say, 'We don't think we should develop the H-bomb. We think it's immoral.' Well, what business is it of theirs if it is immoral?" (b) Mr. Strauss, in reply: "Well, go back to this plumber. He comes and sees you have a television set. There's a program that your children are looking at, and he disapproves of it and he disconnects the set. If he does that, he has stepped out of his role." (c) Comment by the American Association of Scientific Workers *Newsletter*: "If any 'plumber' analogy is to be made at all, it might be more pertinent to put that much-maligned artisan in the position of being asked to install a water heater which he knew might kill the whole family with CO [carbon monoxide] gas."

8. No body can be healthful without exercise, neither body natural nor politic; and, certainly, to a kingdom, or estate, a just and honourable war is the true exercise. A civil war, indeed, is like the heat of a fever;

but a foreign war is like the heat of exercise, and serveth to keep the body
in health; for in a slothful peace, both courages will effeminate and
manners corrupt. (Bacon)

9.   What if the foot, ordain'd the dust to tread,
        Or hand, to toil, aspired to be the head?
        What if the head, the eye, or ear repin'd
        To serve mere engines to the ruling Mind?
        Just as absurd for any part to claim
        To be another, in this gen'ral frame:
        Just as absurd, to mourn the tasks or pains,
        The great directing Mind of All ordains.

                                    (Pope, *Essay on Man*)

10. Senator Wayne Morse, speaking in the Senate on S.3706, a bill
to amend the Subversive Activities Control Act of 1950 (Section 13A of
the bill provided that whenever the Attorney General has reason to
believe that any labor union is a "Communist-infiltrated organization,"
he may ask the Subversive Activities Control Board for a finding to that
effect. Senator Morse objected that the Attorney General's very charge
that the union was Communistic would be taken by the public as proof,
so that an Attorney General would have the power to harm a particular
union greatly merely by making the charge):

What is my alternative? My alternative is that, by law, we ought to
make Communism in a labor organization an unfair labor practice, and
authorize industry to appear before the Board that has jurisdiction over
labor disputes and make the charge there, and then let the Government
proceed on the basis of the charge made by an employer.

Let me tell my colleagues of a weakness in my argument, because I
hope I am a good enough lawyer to recognize that the first thing a lawyer
ought to do in preparing a case is satisfy himself that he understands the
arguments that can be used against him as well as the arguments he can
use against those who differ with him. By way of argument by analogy, it
can be said, "Yes, but the Attorney General or the Department of Justice
does go before a grand jury in a criminal case and files charges and asks
for an indictment." If one wanted to make an argument by analogy by
way of crime indictments, something could be said for this section of
the bill.

However, let us not forget what the objective is in proposed legislation
such as this. There really is an effort being made to remove from the
labor relations field—from employer-employee relationships—the unfair
labor practice that is engaged in by Communist labor leaders. That is
what we are after. We are dealing not with matters of crime, but with

techniques that are used by the Communists in the economic field. (*Congressional Record*, August 11, 1954, p. 13462.)

11. A *magazine advertisement said*:

How would you like to play football if the referee was on the other team? He would make *your* team live up to the rules. But *he* could grab the ball whenever he wanted to, *he* could get away with clipping, and *he* could be offside. What kind of a game is that?

This may sound funny to you, but it's no joke to us—*your* producers of electric power, owned by *you* stockholders, and providing cheap electricity to *you* consumers, to keep *your* radios and lights and refrigerators going.

Because that's the hole we're in. The government makes the rules for all power companies—*and* the government is in the power business for itself! The catch is that in this game the officials make two different sets of rules. The government can get its capital at very low interest rates—it pays no taxes—and if it can't make ends meet because of poor management, it can dip into the U.S. Treasury for some of *your* taxes to bail itself out! We can't do that.

Of course the government can win *that* kind of a game—if you let it. Of course it can be a Rose Bowl champion, with that kind of setup. The business-managed, taxpaying electric light and power companies, who have given America the best electric service in the world, are in there bucking the line. But *look out!* That referee is running with the ball!

Exercise 8

Make an appraisal of the following arguments. In each case, write out the hypothesis; think of an alternative hypothesis that would account for the facts offered in evidence; explain why you think the hypothesis offered is more satisfactory, or less satisfactory, than the alternative; think of other evidence that you would want to look for to test the hypothesis further.

1. A few days before Christmas, Bobby accidentally turned up in the back of a closet an Erector set that later appeared under the Christmas tree. He had told his father and mother that he was writing Santa Claus to bring him a stamp album, but though he didn't get around to mailing the letter, he got the stamp album for Christmas. One of the little toys in his stocking was stamped "Made in Japan," not "Made in Santa's Workshop." And neither on his presents nor on the floor was there any sign of chimney soot. Bobby decided then that the Christmas presents came from his father and mother, not, as they claimed, from Santa Claus.

2. We too easily forget that certain kinds of knowledge equal or greater

than ours may have died with the wise men of long-gone cultures. We now know, for example, that the ancient Inca priests more than 1,500 years ago could somehow raise themselves in the air, or fly through it, though their secret was well kept. In the Nasca Valley of Peru, in the sand of the desert there are enormous figures, drawn with deep, long lines, of birds (one more than 500 feet long), spiders, a whale with a harpoon driven through its eye. These were drawn by the ancient Incas, and have not been touched since. But the astounding thing about them is that the pictures can only be seen and recognized for what they are from an airplane flying about 1000 feet above them. From the ground they are just broad marks in the sand; from the high-flying airliners they cannot be seen. We do not know why these mysterious pictures were drawn, but evidently those who made them must somehow have been able to hover in the air above them and look down.

3. Since Russia abandoned its athletic isolationism at the 1952 Olympics, its athletes and teams have been stacking up an impressive series of victories. In 1954 alone, the speed skater Shikov won the world championship in Japan; their skiers took the biggest events in Sweden; their runners, men and women, were first-rate; their hockey team beat the Canadians in Sweden; they took home three out of five prizes from the famed Henley Regatta in England. Many more examples could be cited. But what is the explanation? It seems clear that the Western nations, lulled into laziness by their mechanical gadgets, cars, and television sets have become soft from lack of exercise, and are in a physical decline.

4. If there is no evidence in Shakespeare's life that he was cultivated enough to write the dramas bearing his name, what about the case of Bernard Shaw? asks R. C. Marsh in a letter to the *Harvard Alumni Bulletin*. His letter is in answer to a previous *Bulletin* letter that urged the faculty to expose the myth of Shakespeare:

Mr. Ogburn's letter [Oct. 23] points up an even more shocking negligence of the Harvard English faculty—their inability to find the author of the plays and other writings attributed to one Bernard Shaw.

Surely it is clear that Shaw, that Irish adventurer, that unsuccessful popular novelist living in London on the proceeds of hack journalism, that irregular synthesis of an amateur mezzo-soprano and a day-dreaming wholesale corn merchant, lacking even the qualification of education at one of the provincial universities, could never have composed the lines of "Saint Joan" and "Pygmalion."

What evidence have we for this, save that they were published under his name and that, clever fraud that he was, he was able to hoodwink people of judgment into regarding them as his work?

Who then is the personage shielded by this pretentious pixie? Is not the clue found in Shaw's own aversion to his solid, Christian name? The plays of Bernard Shaw were written by George, Prince of Wales, later King George V. Does not this explain the decline in the powers of this "Shaw" after the death of that worthy monarch in 1936? Undoubtedly all efforts will be made to preserve this deep and well-kept secret, but Harvard scholarship can fetch it out of the murk. I call upon Howard Mumford Jones to set himself to it with no further delay.

The New York Times, Feb. 6, 1955

5. In 1892, there were living at 92 Second St., in Fall River, Mass., Mr. Andrew Jackson Borden, a wealthy but thrifty man of 70; his second wife, Abby, aged 64; his two daughters by his first marriage, Emma and Lizzie; and a servant named Bridget Sullivan. On Tuesday, August 2, Mr. and Mrs. Borden were violently ill during the night; Lizzie too, by her own report, but not as bad. Emma had gone out of town on a visit. The following day, a Mr. Morse came to the house for a short stay. On that day, Lizzie told a friend of hers, Miss Russell, that her family had been made ill, that the milk must have been poisoned, and that she was afraid her father had an enemy who was trying to kill him.

Thursday, August 4, was a scorching day. Mr. Morse left the house at 7:45, after breakfast; Mr. Borden locked the screen door after him. Bridget, who started work at 6:00, was sick after breakfast, but felt well enough to do some window washing—a proceeding that involved several trips to and from the barn for equipment and water. Mr. Borden left the house around 9:00; Mrs. Borden worked upstairs; Lizzie had some cookies and coffee. Just before 11:00, Mr. Borden returned to the house and found the doors bolted in front and at the side of the house; Bridget, however, let him in. At that moment Lizzie appeared and said that her stepmother had received a message that someone was sick, and had gone out. Mr. Borden went to the sitting room. Bridget presently went upstairs to rest before lunch.

About 11:15, Lizzie called to Bridget that she had found her father murdered; she had been out in the yard, she said, and heard a groan. Mr. Borden lay on a sofa, his head savagely beaten in by a number of blows. Shortly afterward, Mrs. Borden was found in her room upstairs, on the floor, also hacked and battered beyond recognition. Mr. Morse's movements that morning were fully accounted for. There was no sign of robbery. The wounds showed that the murder instrument must have had a sharp cutting edge like an axe or hatchet. Lizzie said she had spent twenty minutes or so, just before finding her father, in the loft of the barn, eating pears and looking for lead to make sinkers, though the barn loft was the hottest place in the vicinity. Further investigation showed that Mrs. Borden had been killed at least one hour, and perhaps two, before Mr. Borden. Mrs. Borden was still in her house-cleaning clothes, and no trace was ever found of the supposed note or the messenger who was said to have brought it. A druggist, supported by two other witnesses, identified Lizzie as the woman who had tried to buy prussic acid from him to kill moths the day before the murders; Lizzie denied that she had done so. Tests failed to reveal traces of blood on the household axes and hatchet, or on the clothes worn by Lizzie Borden. She was indicted, tried, and acquitted. But surely it is evident that she is the one who committed the crimes.

6. Here are the facts on fluoridation. Sodium fluoride is a deadly poison. The American Medical Association admits it has not been absolutely proved that fluorides prevent tooth decay in children. But a small knot of fluoridaters, without taking the general public into their confidence, is already experimenting on us and our children in a dangerous illegal mass-medication deal by putting fluorides in the drinking water of many communities.

Now according to the *American Review of Soviet Medicine*, August, 1945, (p. 543), an article by I. Lukonski says, concerning experiments with fluorine, "More advanced work was being pursued in Russian laboratories." Rena M. Vale, a leading ex-Communist informant, has stated that in Communist circles the fluoridation of drinking water is a well-known weapon for reducing the mentality and will power of the American people. Laboratory tests show that fluorine can produce a lessened mental reaction in mice. Grand Rapids, Mich., which is fluoridated, reports a felony a day, and newspapers say an unusually large percentage of the elementary school pupils failed to pass last June. The most active proponents of fluoridation are the recent graduates of dental schools. It is widely known that Communists begin their work with education, and recent exposures have shown that there are secret Marxist teachers in many schools.

What more proof do you want that you are in deadly peril from a Marxist plot?

7. Anthropologists of the British Natural History Museum have concluded that the remains of the "Piltdown Man," long regarded as the earliest known specimen of *homo sapiens,* are a deliberate hoax. The remains were unearthed in a gravel pit in Piltdown, Sussex, in 1911, by workmen who found the cap of a heavy skull, which they broke into many pieces before realizing that it might have scientific value. The fragments were taken to Charles Dawson, a lawyer and amateur geologist, who later took them to the Museum, along with a jawbone also found at the same site. After working five years to piece them together, Sir Arthur Keith,

famous British paleontologist, pronounced them to be 500,000 years old. Piltdown man was called Eoanthropus, or Dawn Man.

Suspicions of this conclusion were aroused some years ago. The other bones taken from the site were not particularly old. Dr. Franz Weidenreich, German paleontologist, pointed out before his death in 1948 that in all mammals there is a correlation between the size and form of the brain case and the size and form of the jaws—the larger the former, the smaller the latter. The Piltdown man was the sole exception to this law, and Dr. Weidenreich said that the jawbone was the jawbone of a modern ape. Recent study has shown that the jawbone is very much like that of an orangutan. Chemical tests showed that the bones have absorbed less fluorine from the soil than would be expected in hundreds of thousands of years. They have also shown that the jaws were treated with potassium bichromate and iron salt, apparently to make them appear aged. The teeth of the jaws seem to have been pared down.

The experts did not express any opinion as to the probable identity or motives of the person who fooled a large part of the anthropological world for forty years.

8. Excerpt from the trial of the Knave of Hearts, in *Alice's Adventures in Wonderland*:

"There's more evidence to come yet, please your Majesty," said the White Rabbit...: "This paper has just been picked up...I haven't opened it yet,...but it seems to be a letter, written by the prisoner to–to somebody."

..."Who is it directed to?" said one of the jurymen.

"It isn't directed at all," said the White Rabbit: "in fact, there's nothing written on the *outside*." He unfolded the paper as he spoke, and added, "It isn't a letter, after all: it's a set of verses."

"Are they in the prisoner's handwriting?" asked another of the jurymen.

"No, they're not," said the White Rabbit, "and that's the queerest thing about it."...

"He must have imitated somebody else's hand," said the King....

"Please, your Majesty," said the Knave, "I didn't write it, and they can't prove that I did: there's no name signed at the end."

"If you didn't sign it," said the King, "that only makes matters worse. You *must* have meant some mischief, or else you'd have signed your name like an honest man."...

"That *proves* his guilt, of course," said the Queen: "so, off with..."

9. Brief excerpts from the printed transcript of the hearing on April 24, 1953, of the Permanent Subcommittee on Investigations of the Senate Committee on Government Operations, Senator McCarthy pre-

siding, and Mr. James A. Wechsler, editor of the *New York Post*, testifying:

THE CHAIRMAN: I asked you whether you consistently criticized at all times the various heads of the Un-American Activities Committee. Have you ever in the past or can you now think of a single chairman of one of those committees who, in your opinion, was a good man and did a good job? ... (p. 261)

MR. WECHSLER: ... I am unable to present any documents suggesting that I praised a chairman of the House Un-American Activities Committee.

THE CHAIRMAN: The principal villains in your book are those in the Congress who have gone about the job of exposing Communists. ...

MR. WECHSLER: No, ... we have repeatedly taken the position that the *New York Post* is as bitterly opposed to Joe Stalin as it is to Joe McCarthy. ...

THE CHAIRMAN: ... Your position is that both you and your wife are now anti-Communist? ...

MR. WECHSLER: Emphatically and strongly. (p. 265) ... I joined the Young Communist League in April 1934. I was going to be 19 in October. I left in 1937. (p. 268) ... My position on the Russian-German pact of 1939 was one of bitter denunciation. (p. 269) ... I was ... extremely active in the anti-Communist wing of the American Newspaper Guild. (p. 270) ... I was a vigorous supporter editorially of the Marshall plan. I was a vigorous supporter of the Truman doctrine. (p. 271) ... I was ... one of the founders of Americans for Democratic Action. (p. 277). ...

THE CHAIRMAN: ... I may say ... I am convinced you have done exactly what you would do if you were a member of the Communist Party, if you wanted to have a phony break and then use that phony break to the advantage of the Communist Party. ...

MR. WECHSLER: ... The only way I could in your view prove my devotion to America and the validity of my break with Communism would be to come out in support of Senator McCarthy. This I do not plan to do.

THE CHAIRMAN: That I am not asking you to do. If you ever did that, I would be worried about myself. (p. 276)

Exercise 9

Each of the passages below describes a situation that is puzzling in some way, and raises a problem that calls for a solution. In each case, first, think of at least two hypotheses that would solve the problem; second, think of certain other information *not* contained in the paragraph that would help to confirm or to refute each hypothesis; third, turn the page upside down to see whether the further information given in the second paragraph helps you to decide between the two hypotheses you have invented.

A

The car, wrecked beyond repair, with a dead man inside, was found by an early-morning driver on Route 30, up against a large tree just off the road, beyond a curve. The driver had apparently been dead for a few hours. There were no skid marks on the road, and no earlier report had been turned in.

(1) It was found that he had been driving prettily steadily all day and most of the night. (2) The radio was turned on in the car, though it had ceased to work. (3) The proprietor of an all-night diner a few miles back on the road identified the driver as a man who had been in and drunk two cups of black coffee at about 3:30 that morning.

B

During the six months since Wilkins became a clerk in the store, there has been a shortage of $1,743. Suspicions have been aroused by a report from a fellow employee, Jenkins, that other employees have observed that Wilkins often has not rung up a purchase on the cash register until a customer's attention was occupied elsewhere. Like other employees, Wilkins has had his own register, and has always turned in at the end of a day an amount equal to that rung up during the day.

On February 16 a surprise check on his register, in the middle of the afternoon, showed that it contained $7 more than had been rung up. There was a pile of wooden matches beside the register. When searched, Wilkins was found to have some of the same matches in a pants pocket, though a few minutes before, when asked for a match, he had said he had none with him, and had gone over to the register and taken some from the pile there to give to the employee who had asked him. *The Problem*: Is Wilkins guilty, and if so, by what method did he work?

Further information: (1) Jenkins' statement was supported by other employees, when questioned. (2) Wilkins was once observed to ring up $2.98 on a $3.98 purchase, and when this was pointed out, he said his finger slipped. (3) The number of matches in his pocket was the same as the number of extra dollars in the register: 7. (4) A further inquiry revealed that the amount he was paying in installments was very large for his salary.

C

The good-looking man and the very attractive woman, both in their thirties, arrived at the Florida motel one evening in April, saying they would probably stay two days. They stayed four months, which pleased the proprietor, for his motel was off the beaten track and in that season his customers were especially rare. They took adjoining cabins, but called themselves "Mr. and Mrs. Johnson." Each day they would sun themselves for an hour after breakfast, then disappear into one of the cabins until noon with all the shades pulled down, then they would take a walk or one of them would drive out for groceries. After lunch they would lie in the sun for an hour again, and then shut themselves indoors until five o'clock, when they would emerge with tall drinks. Anyone who passed close by during these sessions would hear the low, steady murmur of voices. Several briefcases that were always locked were in the cabins, and sometimes carried back and forth. They never went out in the evening, and though they were pleasant to the few people about, they did not volunteer any information about themselves. During their stay at the motel, they both got very tan; the woman did not change otherwise, but the man grew a moustache, and let his hair grow longer.

(1) The woman who cleaned the cabins one day found a piece of paper that had slipped behind a table; it had the name "Gerald A. Arrowroot" written on every line. (2) A passerby once happened to notice, when one of the briefcases was opened outdoors, that it contained what looked like old newspaper clippings. (3) Though for the most part the couple had no apparent communication with the outside world, there was one telephone call late at night to New York, and one of the attendants at the motel thought he heard the woman say, "This is Sylvia Arrowroot." (4) A few weeks after the couple left, the manager of the motel saw in a New York paper a picture of "Mr. Johnson," and the caption: "Long missing Arrowroot heir is found in Newark. Amnesia victim identified as Gerald A. Arrowroot."

3

Premises and Their Implications

The difference between induction and deduction is a difference in what we can hope to accomplish by way of proving something. When we argue inductively, we must be content to support the conclusion with sufficiently strong evidence to place it beyond reasonable doubt. When we argue deductively, however, we are insisting that anyone who accepts the premises upon which we base the argument *must* accept the conclusion because the conclusion necessarily follows from the premises.

One of the key questions we are going to have to ask about any deductive argument, then, is: Does the conclusion follow? Suppose someone were to argue this way:

> He must be a good worker, for good workers are scarce, and whenever I need him to do a job he certainly makes himself scarce.

This argument is so full of holes that no one is likely to offer it. But suppose an editorial writer argues this way:

> Only fuzzy-minded do-good America-last one-worlders would want to see other nations impose their alien laws and customs on the United States. And obviously anyone who supports the principles of the Bricker Amendment stands firmly against such foreign domination. So we can be sure that the leading members of the American Bar Association are not one-worlders, now they have come out publicly for the Amendment.

Once we break through to the heart of this argument, we see that it is a deductive argument of a rather simple sort. But is it a *good* one? That is the kind of question we shall deal with in this chapter.

§11. THE NATURE OF DEDUCTION

The simplest sort of deductive argument—indeed, the absolute minimum—would be an argument with one premise and one conclusion:

No large stockholders are members of the Cabinet.
———
No members of the Cabinet are large stockholders.

(The horizontal line separates premise from conclusion, and may be read "therefore" or "it necessarily follows that.") Let us begin by using some small-scale models like this one to make clear an important distinction. There are two things we can, and must, ask about any deductive argument that has an interesting and worth-while conclusion: We can ask about the *truth* of the premises, and we can ask about the *validity* of the argument. That is, we can ask whether in fact no large stockholders *are* members of the Cabinet. And we can ask whether *if* the premise is true the conclusion *has* to be true.

The question of validity (to take that first) is a question about the *relationship* between the premise (or premises) and the conclusion. It is a question of *logical connection*. When the conclusion does in fact follow necessarily from the premises—as we would all agree that it does in the example above—then we may say that the premises **imply** the conclusion. And when we recognize that there is an implication of this kind, we can deduce the implied statement from the statements that imply it. But, of course, this isn't enough to give us assurance that the conclusion is true. It only permits us to say, hypothetically, that *if* the premises are all true, *then* the conclusion must be true. *If* Susie is the sister of Tim, and Ruth is the daughter of Susie, *then* Tim is the uncle of Ruth. As soon as you understand what is being said, and think it through with care, you see that it must be so. *If* the bill is in the wallet, and the wallet is in the pocket, *then* the bill must be in the pocket.

Statements like these, that begin with "if," can give you interesting and important information about what is implied by a set of premises, but they aren't fullfledged deductive arguments. For they don't assert that the "if" part is true. A deductive argument not only claims that its conclusion follows from its premises; it also claims that its premises are, so to speak, *worth* following from. And a deductive argument cannot be regarded as a success unless its premises are true. Now, though truth and validity must be kept distinct, there is an important relationship between them. When you know that an argument is valid, you may not know whether any of the statements in it are true, but you *do* know that *if* all the premises are true, then the conclusion is true. And you know that if the conclusion is *false*, then at least one of the premises must be false.

But that is all you know, from validity alone. In a valid argument, for example, you *don't* know that if the premises are false, then the conclusion must be false. A valid argument can have true premises and a true conclusion; it can have false premises and a false conclusion; and it can have false premises and a true conclusion. The only thing it *can't* have, if it's valid, are true premises and a false conclusion. In an invalid argument, of course, anything can happen: true premises and true conclusion; false premises and false conclusion; false premises and true conclusion; *and* true premises and false conclusion. So, incidentally, if you are sure that the premises of an argument are true and the conclusion false, you can be just as sure that the argument is invalid.

Here, for example, is an invalid argument with a true premise and a false conclusion:

All Senators are members of Congress.
All members of Congress are Senators.

And here is a valid argument with a false premise and a true conclusion:

Bannister and Landy ran the mile in less than three minutes.
Bannister and Landy ran the mile in less than four minutes.

You can see this must be valid, for *if* they ran the mile in less than three minutes, they necessarily ran it in less than four minutes. Of course they *didn't* run it in less than three minutes, but they *did* run it in less than four. You can easily make up examples of the other possible combinations of truth and falsity with validity and invalidity.

How are we to know whether a particular deductive argument is valid or invalid? This question is one that can be answered in every case definitely and conclusively. If the argument is not very elaborate, we can see directly whether or not its conclusion follows. But often we cannot do this. However, every deductive argument has a *logical structure* that it shares with other deductive arguments; and every structure has a set of rules to say what kind of conclusion can follow and what cannot. If you recognize the structure, and apply the rules, you can determine its validity exactly.

At this point we need another model—one with a few more complications. As a deductive argument, there is not much to it, but you can learn a lot about deductive arguments in general from studying this one. And you will find later that there are a good many uses to which you can put this form of argument.

(1) No Rosicrucians are skeptics.
(2) Murgatroyd is a skeptic.
_____
(3) Murgatroyd is not a Rosicrucian.

You don't have to concern yourself with the *meaning* of these words, for the time being. We are interested, not in what the argument is *about* (Rosicrucians, Rotarians, vegetarians, or members of the Foreign Legion), but in its structure.

The first point to note about its structure is that it consists of three, and only three, statements, two of which are premises, and one the conclusion. Second, these statements are statements that in turn have a certain structure. And, third, they are related to each other in a special way.

When we examine the structure of the individual statements, we can consider them all as having certain features in common. Each of them contains some form of the verb "to be": "is" or "are." And on either side of the verb are the words that make up the *logical* subjects and predicates of the statements. The first statement, for example, contains two words, each of which refers to certain classes of people: "Rosicrucians" and "skeptics." These words are called "terms," and in the sort of statement we are now considering there are always two terms. We shall call them **two-term statements.**

Terms can consist of more than one word. The statement, "No well-read Rosicrucians over the age of 90 who have been born in Rhode Island are good-natured skeptics who can speak six languages," is a two-term statement too, for besides the verb and the word "No," there is the term "well-read Rosicrucians over the age of 90 who have been born in Rhode Island" (this is a special class of people) and the term "good-natured skeptics who can speak six languages" (this is another class). The left-hand term in a two-term statement is called the **subject-term;** the right-hand term is called the **predicate-term.**

Look at the first statement more carefully. Suppose we take the whole class of people and subdivide them according to whether they are or are not Rosicrucians and/or skeptics. We would get four sub-classes: (a) those who are Rosicrucians, but not skeptics; (b) those who are *both* Rosicrucians and skeptics (that is, skeptical Rosicrucians); (c) those who are skeptics but not Rosicrucians; (d) those who are *neither* Rosicrucians nor skeptics. These four subclasses we can represent by overlapping circles, labelled R and S.

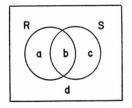

Now, statement 1 above ("No Rosicrucians are skeptics") says that there *are* no skeptical Rosicrucians, in other words, that subclass *b* on the diagram is empty. We can represent this statement by shading out subclass *b*, to show that it has no members.

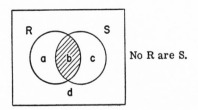

A statement that one class is completely excluded from another, is called a **Universal Negative statement,** or *UN*-statement. It is universal because it applies to *all* Rosicrucians; it is negative because it *excludes* one class from another. Any *UN*-statement ("No cats are animals that bark," "No fish are animals that talk,") can be diagrammed by two overlapping circles with the overlapping part shaded out.

Next, consider the third statement in our example, the conclusion: "Murgatroyd is not a Rosicrucian." For present purposes, we can interpret this statement as a UN-statement, too. This interpretation would not be wholly satisfactory at a more advanced level of logic study, but it will serve us well here. Murgatroyd is, of course, not a class in the usual sense; he is an individual. But let us think of him as a class of one. We can have classes of thousands (skeptics), and classes with no members (skeptical Rosicrucians); why not then allow classes with only one member (the class consisting solely of Murgatroyd)? Of course, the class of people *named* "Murgatroyd" may be a class with more than one member (though it's probably not numerous). But we are not thinking of this class; we are referring to a single person, Clarence Q. Murgatroyd, of 17 Crumbling Thatches Road, East Hempswitch, Long Island. And we put him in a class by himself.

From that point of view, the statement "Murgatroyd is not a Rosicrucian," excludes the class consisting solely of Murgatroyd from the class of Rosicrucians, and so it is a Universal Negative statement.

Suppose our first premise had been "*All* Rosicrucians are skeptics"? This is also a two-term statement. But it says that the class of Rosicrucians is *included in* the class of skeptics. In other words, it says that there are no *non*skeptical Rosicrucians, or that the subclass consisting of Rosicrucians who are *not* skeptics is a class without any members. This statement can easily be represented by shading out a different area on the diagram:

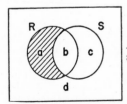

All Rosicrucians are skeptics.

Shading out the area *a* pushes the Rosicrucians who remain, if there are any, over into area *b*, and so inside the S-circle. The diagram shows that what remains of R is completely included in S.

A statement that one class is completely included in another is called a **Universal Affirmative statement** or UA-statement. It is universal because it applies to *all* Rosicrucians; it is affirmative because it *includes* one class in another. Any UA-statement ("All cats are animals that meow," "All fish are animals that swim") can be diagrammed by two overlapping circles, with the nonoverlapping part of one circle shaded out.

Statement 2 in our example, "Murgatroyd is a skeptic," will also be treated here as a Universal Affirmative statement. It says that the whole class consisting solely of Murgatroyd is included in the class of skeptics.

So far, in considering the logical relations between any two classes, we have had only two cases: either the first class was completely inside, or completely outside, the other. But of course it might be *partly* inside, and/or it might be partly outside. This gives us two more kinds of two-term statement to put into our list. But to get examples of these we must take a different argument:

> No Rosicrucians are skeptics.
> Some logical positivists are skeptics.
> _____
> Some logical positivists are not Rosicrucians.

Consider the second premise. It says that there actually are some (it doesn't say how many; at least one) skeptical logical positivists. And we can represent this statement by drawing two overlapping circles again, and putting an asterisk in the subclass consisting of logical positivists that are skeptics:

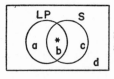

Some logical positivists are skeptics.

The asterisk means that subclass *b* has some members. Now the statement, "Some logical positivists are skeptics," is an Affirmative statement, because it says that part of the class of logical positivists is *included* in the class of skeptics. But it is not a Universal statement, for it applies to only *part* of the class of logical positivists. Statements of this sort ("Some cats are tree-climbers," "Some fish are flying animals") are called **Particular Affirmative statements** or PA-statements.

To diagram the conclusion, "Some logical positivists are not Rosi-crucians," we draw an *LP*-circle and an *R*-circle, and put an asterisk in that part of the *LP*-circle that is *outside* the R-circle.

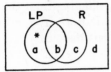

Some logical positivists are not Rosicrucians.

Statements of this sort ("Some cats are not tree-climbers," "Some fish are not flying animals") are called **Particular Negative statements** or *PN*-statements.

We have distinguished, then, four kinds of structure that a two-term statement can have. It can be:

Universal Affirmative
("All taxes are beneficial")

Universal Negative
("No taxes are beneficial")

Particular Affirmative
("Some taxes are beneficial")

Particular Negative
("Some taxes are not beneficial")

Now we can say exactly what it is that our two model deductive arguments have in common. Each consists of three, and only three, two-term statements. Two of the statements are premises, and one the conclusion. Each statement belongs to one of the four types we have distinguished. Among them, the statements contain three, and only three, *terms*. Each of the terms appears twice in the course of the argument. One of the terms appears in both premises. In the last example, the term "Rosicrucians" appears in the first premise and in the conclusion, the term "logical positivists" appears in the second premise and in the conclusion, and the term "skeptics" appears in both premises. Any deductive argument that satisfies these two conditions—containing three two-term statements and three terms, arranged in the manner described—is a **syllogism.**

When we speak of a "syllogism," we mean a deductive argument that has a certain type of structure, differing from the structures of other kinds of deductive arguments. It is a very common structure, one that turns up constantly in ordinary discourse, and that is one of the reasons for considering it with some care. For example, a syllogism always has to have at least one Universal premise, stating a general truth that is either itself inductively derived from particular data or deduced from some other truth that it so derived. Hence we are thinking syllogistically whenever we conclude that what is true of a whole class of things must be true of some part of the class, or of some particular member of the class. If we know that in all radioactive substances, without exception, the intensity of radioactivity diminishes according to a definite physical law, and we discover that the fall-out from a hydrogen bomb explosion is radioactive, we deduce syllogistically that the radioactivity in the fall-out will diminish according to the same law.

Again, we use syllogisms, whether we know it or not, when we argue that a certain action should be performed, or a certain policy should be followed, by applying some general principle to the particular case.

> No territories that are noncontiguous with the continental United States are territories that should be admitted to the Union as states.
>
> Hawaii and Alaska are noncontiguous with the continental United States.
> _____
> Hawaii and Alaska are not territories that should be admitted to the Union as states.

This argument, which has been advanced (though one cautious legislator was careful to say he was advancing it only "at this time"), shows that if the general principle is followed, it must be followed in these two cases, but of course it will take *another* argument to defend the principle itself. One syllogism can't do everything. But when we defend trading with Iron Curtain countries on the ground that it will open up communications with them and help to bring their peoples news of the outside world, or oppose trading with them on the ground that it will help them economically—in either case, the argument is a syllogism.

A classic example of a very powerful syllogism is the Supreme Court's decision in the school segregation cases in 1954. The logical structure of the court's opinion is a simple syllogism:

> Unequal school facilities are unconstitutional.
> Segregated school facilities are unequal.
> _____
> Segregated school facilities are unconstitutional.

Critics of that decision sometimes argue that the court acted improperly because the decision was based on psychological and sociological considerations about the effects of segregated schools upon Negro and white children. It is true, of course, that much of the document was concerned with the inductive evidence for the second premise, that segregation inevitably produces inequality. But it is clear that the conclusion could not be drawn from the second premise alone, without the help of the first premise; and the first premise is a legal principle—one, moreover, that both sides accepted.

The next question is this: How do we decide whether or not a syllogism is valid? This question we come to in the following section.

A CHECK-UP QUIZ. Which of the following deductive arguments are syllogisms according to the definition given in this section?

1. Henrietta has a daughter; *therefore*, Henrietta's sister has a niece.

2. All owls are birds; my pet owl, Marilyn, is a wise owl; *therefore*, my pet owl, Marilyn, is a wise bird.

3. All recent appointees are slow workers, but Hesketh is not a slow worker; *therefore*, Hesketh is not a recent appointee.

4. Some pieces of advice are gratuitous remarks, and all gratuitous remarks are ill-advised remarks; *therefore*, some ill-advised remarks are pieces of advice.

5. Some people were promised money by Marley for goods already shipped; Marley has not yet paid; *therefore*, Marley owes them money.

6. The sun is a body larger than the earth, and any body larger than the earth is a body larger than the moon; *therefore*, the sun is a body larger than the moon.

7. Burbo weighs more than Finny and Lily put together; *therefore*, Burbo weighs more than Finny by himself.

8. All friends of Joe are friends of Johnny; Harry is a friend of a friend of Joe; *therefore*, Harry is a friend of a friend of Johnny.

9. All friends of Joe are friends of Johnny; Harry is a friend of Joe; *therefore*, Harry is a friend of Johnny.

10. Harry is no friend of Johnny; but all friends of Joe are friends of Johnny; *therefore*, Harry is no friend of Joe.

FURTHER READING: Henry W. Johnstone, Jr., *Elementary Deductive Logic*. New York: Thomas Y. Crowell Co., 1954, ch. 12. M. C. Beardsley, *Practical Logic*. New York: Prentice-Hall, Inc., 1950, ch. 7, §§32-33; ch. 8, §39. Max Black, *Critical Thinking*. New York: Prentice-Hall, Inc., rev. ed., 1952, ch. 3.

§12. TESTING A SYLLOGISM

The model syllogisms we have been using so far are pretty streamlined examples. You might think it's no help to have rules for testing *their* validity, since that is evident to the meanest intelligence. But in studying matters of some complexity, whether turbines, nuclear fission, Gothic architecture, or Finnish grammar, it is often a good idea to begin with such artificial models before branching out into a direct study of the examples you actually expect to encounter.

Still using simplified examples, then, we shall see how to decide, clearly and unquestionably, whether a syllogism is valid or invalid. Putting aside some refinements, we can state four *rules of inference* that syllogisms must obey, and we can say that any syllogism that violates one or more of these rules is invalid.

The first two rules are plain enough:

Rule 1: *At least one of the premises must be affirmative.* It is easy to make up syllogisms with two negative premises, but no conclusion will follow from the premises:

No prosperous countries are countries that go Communist.
No countries in Southeast Asia are prosperous countries.

?

Whatever you write here by way of conclusion, you can see at once that it won't do. Any syllogism with two negative premises, then, violates Rule 1, and commits the fallacy of two negative premises.

Rule 2: *If one premise is negative, the conclusion must be negative.* If one of the premises excludes part or all of one class from another, the conclusion will have to be an exclusion-statement, too. If not, the results will look like this:

> No acts of cruelty are morally justified acts.
> Some deliberate lies are morally justified acts.
> ―――――――――――――――――――――――
> Some deliberate lies are acts of cruelty.

All these statements may conceivably be true, but the argument is not valid. The conclusion, "Some deliberate lies are not acts of cruelty," could be drawn, but that is different. Syllogisms that violate Rule 2 commit a fallacy we can call "the fallacy of negative premise and affirmative conclusion." Fortunately we shall have little use for this awkward name, for syllogisms that committed this fallacy would in nearly all cases be obviously fallacious, so this fallacy is seldom committed.

The other two rules involve a further distinction about the terms that appear in two-term statements. In some games of cards there are what might be called "strong" cards and "weak" cards, and the rules say that certain things can be done with the strong cards that can't be done with the weak ones. The strong cards may be trumps, for example. But which cards are trumps may vary from hand to hand, and may depend on how the bidding goes before the play begins; thus, hearts are not *inherently* trumps, but are made so by the bidding. Now, similarly, in a syllogism there are certain terms that are strong, and others that are weak. This has nothing to do with the terms themselves: the term "babies" is not necessarily weaker than the term "wrestlers"; it depends on which kind of two-term statement it appears in, and on whether it is the subject or the predicate. In order to be valid, a syllogism must obey certain rules about the strength and weakness of its terms.

It is customary to speak of the strong terms as "distributed," and the weak ones as "undistributed"; other words would do as well, and it is best not to be concerned about the words themselves, though they are so common that we shall continue to use them here. Think of the matter in this way: Subject-terms in Universal statements and predicate-terms in Negative statements are strong terms; other terms are weak. And when we say that a term is **distributed** we shall mean that it is one of these strong terms. Whenever the question arises, then, as it will shortly, whether or not a certain term is distributed, all you have to do is see whether it is the subject of a Universal statement or the predicate of a Negative statement. If it is, it is distributed; if not, not; and if it is the subject of a Universal statement in one premise but the subject of a Particular statement in a second premise, then it is distributed in the first premise but not in the second.

The distribution of terms may be summarized in another way:

In a UA-statement, the subject is distributed, the predicate not.
In a PA-statement, neither the subject nor the predicate is distributed.
In a UN-statement, both the subject and the predicate are distributed.
In a PN-statement, the subject is not distributed, but the predicate is.

This makes it all very symmetrical: four types of two-term statement, four possibilities as regards distribution of terms, and each type takes one of the possibilities.

Now, the terms that appear in a syllogism differ according to the position in which they appear. There is one term that appears in both premises; it is the common element that connects the two premises so that they can combine to yield a conclusion. It is the hinge of the argument, and it is called the **middle term.** Each of the other two terms appears once in a premise and again in the conclusion; they are the **end-terms.** The next rule of syllogistic inference, then, is stated this way:

Rule 3. *The middle term must be distributed at least once.* If anyone should write:

Some operations of the Federal Government are operations that compete with private business.
Some operations of the Federal Government are inefficient operations.

?

it is clear that he would be stumped for a conclusion. From these premises you can't deduce anything new at all.

The crudeness of this example should not, however, make this rule seem trivial. For the fallacy that consists in the violation of this rule, that is, the **fallacy of undistributed middle,** is actually a rather fertile source of crooked thinking. It often appears in this form:

> All Communists are people who believe that China should be admitted to the United Nations.
> Some advisers to the State Department are people who believe that China should be admitted to the United Nations.
> ___
> Some advisers to the State Department are Communists.

The middle term in this syllogism is "people who believe that China should be admitted to the United Nations"; in the first premise it is the predicate-term in a *UA*-statement, in the second premise it is the predicate-term in a *PA*-statement. In neither position is it distributed, and so, to speak in terms of a game, there is no play.

The same fallacy is often the root-principle of guilt by association. Consider, for example:

> All friends of Sam are friends of Mack.
> Murgatroyd is a friend of Mack.
> ___
> Murgatroyd is a friend of Sam.

—where "friend(s) of Mack" is the undistributed middle term. If Sam is a despicable character, this inference could do Murgatroyd a lot of harm.

The last rule depends upon another point about deduction. The conclusion of a deductive argument makes explicit, and shows clearly, something that was only implicit and unnoticed in the premises. But it cannot go beyond what the premises imply, or there will be no necessity about it. This is what could happen if an end-term were in a stronger position in the conclusion than in its premise. Hence

Rule 4: *An end-term that is undistributed in a premise cannot be distributed in the conclusion.* And the violation of this rule we might call **"the fallacy of unwarranted distribution."**

This too is a fairly frequent and deceptive fallacy. Take first a simple example, which might almost be called the principle of "innocence by disassociation":

> All friends of Sam are friends of Mack.
> Murgatroyd is not a friend of Sam.
> ___
> Murgatroyd is not a friend of Mack.

The conclusion is a UN-statement, so its predicate-term "friend(s) of Mack" is distributed in the conclusion; but in the first premise, the same term is the predicate of a UA-statement, and in that position it is undistributed. In short, it moves from an undistributed to a distributed state, and this move is forbidden by the rules of the syllogistic game.

One more example may be helpful for comparison:

> No aggressive nations are nations that are eligible to join the United Nations.
> Some recently-formed nations are nations that are eligible to join the United Nations.
> _____
> Some aggressive nations are not recently-formed nations.

The predicate-term in the conclusion, "recently-formed nations" is distributed there because it is the predicate-term in a PN-statement; but in the second premise, where it is the subject-term in a PA-statement, it is undistributed.

With these four rules, you can tell whether a syllogism is valid or not as soon as you are clear about the statements in it and about the terms in those statements. But of course, like all rules, they can be wrongly applied. And therefore it is sometimes convenient to have a way of checking your results by means of a diagram. It appeared earlier that to diagram a single two-term statement we would need two overlapping circles; to diagram a three-term *argument*, which is what a syllogism is, we need three overlapping circles, and we have to overlap them so that all possible combinations of classes and subclasses can be represented:

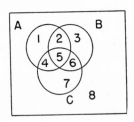

If we let A, B, and C be the three terms, we can combine them in eight different ways. For instance, area 1 contains those things that are in A but not in either B or C; area 6 contains those things that are not in A, but are in both B and C; areas 4 and 5 together contain all the things that are in both A and C, whether or not they are in B. For one diagram, let us go back to our earlier model:

No Rosicrucians are skeptics.
Murgatroyd is a skeptic.
_____
Murgatroyd is not a Rosicrucian.

The steps in diagramming a syllogism are simply these: (1) Draw the three-ring map, and label the circles with appropriate letters (say, R for "Rosicrucians," S for "skeptics," M for "Murgatroyd"). (2) Diagram the two premises, just as we were doing earlier. (3) See whether the conclusion can be read off the diagram of the premises.

Here is the diagram of the premises in our example (the shading goes in different directions to keep the premises distinct, but you need not bother with this once you get used to the diagrams):

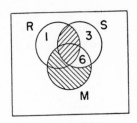

Areas 2 and 5 are shaded out by the first premise, which says that the class of Rosicrusian-skeptics is empty; areas 4 and 7 are shaded out by the second premise, which says that the class of Murgatroyd-non-skeptics is empty. Now if we were to diagram the conclusion on the same map, we would find that it shades out areas 4 and 5 (the class of Murgatroyd-Rosicrusians). But areas 4 and 5 have *already* been shaded out by the premises. To add the conclusion to this diagram, in short, would add nothing to it; the conclusion is already there. And that shows that the syllogism is valid: the conclusion can be read off the diagram of the premises.

The situation is very different when we diagram an argument like our "guilt by association" syllogism. Here we have the three terms "friends of Sam" *FS*, "friends of Mack" *FM*, and "Murgatroyd" *M* again, and when we diagram the premises they look like this:

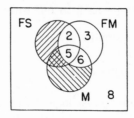

We can see right away that these two premises have something wrong with them, for together they only shade out three of the eight areas on our map. Area 4 is shaded out twice, which is a mere repetition. The conclusion, "Murgatroyd is a friend of Sam" calls for shading out areas 6 and 7, but when we try to read this conclusion off the diagram, we can't do it: area 6 has not been shaded out; the conclusion does not follow.

When it comes to syllogisms with Particular statements in them, the same steps in diagramming can be used, but there is one extra twist. We shall begin with a valid syllogism to see what ought to happen in this kind of diagram. Our second model syllogism was:

> No Rosicrucians are skeptics.
> Some logical positivists are skeptics.
> _____
> Some logical positivists are not Rosicrucians.

The letters *R*, *S*, and *LP* will do, as before, for our abbreviations When one of the premises is a Particular statement, there is some convenience in diagramming it first:

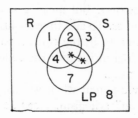

The second premise tells us that there are logical positivist skeptics, so we know there is something in area 5 or 6 or maybe both. But we can't be *sure* it is both, and so when we put an asterisk in each, we draw a line between the asterisks, to remind ourselves that we are not sure which one belongs. If the syllogism is valid, the other premise will tell us:

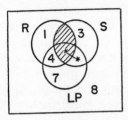

The universal premise, that is, tells us that area 5 is empty, and so we know that the asterisk definitely goes into area 6. And now it is possible to read the conclusion off the diagram, for according to that conclusion there should be an asterisk definitely in that part of the LP-circle that is outside the R-circle. And so there is.

The diagram of an invalid syllogism will show instantly that no conclusion can be drawn, or that some conclusion can be drawn but not the one that *was* drawn. Let's take our other example of an undistributed middle, which, in abbreviated form, was:

All C are P.
Some A are P.
———————
Some A are C.

The diagram of the two premises is this:

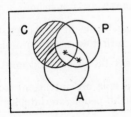

The asterisks and the shading never connect with each other, and they generate no inference. The conclusion calls for an asterisk definitely in areas 4 or 5, where C and A overlap. But though there is an asterisk in 5, it is only a tentative one. We don't know that it is in 5, but only that it is in *either* 5 or 6. If we had some further information that it is not in 6, we could be sure it is in 5. But these premises give us no such information.

It is not necessary to be handy with these diagrams in order to understand the syllogism. They are only maps, or analogies, that some will find helpful and some will not. If they strike you as convenient, you should try them out on a number of syllogisms until you feel familiar with them. If you find them difficult, but understand the rules of syllogistic inference, you have all you really need to test a syllogism—at least, once the syllogism is in good shape. But that raises another question for the following section.

A CHECK-UP QUIZ. Which of the following fallacies, *if any*, is committed by the following syllogisms: (1) the fallacy of two negative premises; (2) the fallacy of negative premise and affirmative conclusion; (3) the fallacy of undistributed middle; (4) the fallacy of unwarranted distribution?

1. All awkward creatures are amusing creatures.
   All babies are awkward creatures.

   All babies are amusing creatures.

2. All comic books are books worth reading.
   Some comics are not comic books.

   Some comics are not books worth reading.

3. No ranch houses are houses with cellars.
   Some houses with cellars are not damp houses.

   Some damp houses are ranch houses.

4. All airfields near towns are dangerous things.
   Some airfields near towns are convenient things.

   Some convenient things are dangerous things.

5. All scholarly people are intelligent people.
   All brachycephalic people are intelligent people.

   All brachycephalic people are scholarly people.

6. Some bromides are true statements.
Some true statements are not interesting statements.

Some bromides are not interesting statements.

7. All Cypriots are Greeks.
No Cypriots are unpatriotic.

No Greeks are unpatriotic.

8. No chewinks are unmusical birds.
Some chewinks are shy birds.

Some shy birds are unmusical birds.

9. Some vocal music is contrapuntal music.
No contrapuntal music is shapeless music.

Some shapeless music is not vocal music.

10. Some willowy women are wimple-wearers.
All wimple-wearers are fashionable dressers.

Some fashionable dressers are willowy women.

FURTHER READING: Henry W. Johnstone, Jr., *Elementary Deductive Logic*. New York: Thomas Y. Crowell Co., 1954, chs. 13-15. M. C. Beardsley, *Practical Logic*. New York: Prentice-Hall, Inc., 1950, ch. 10, §§46-48. Max Black, *Critical Thinking*. New York: Prentice-Hall, Inc., 2d ed. 1952, ch. 8.

§13. PUTTING A SYLLOGISM IN ORDER

Once you know the rules, or learn the diagram-check, there is no great difficulty about deciding whether or not a syllogism is valid—providing it is set up like the ones we have been considering, with all the terms and statements in good shape. But our examples have been artificially clean and neat; the syllogisms that we encounter in everyday life are very seldom set out so clearly. Their logical structure is disguised, so that a large part of the problem of testing their validity consists in getting them ready to have the rules applied.

We shall say that a syllogism is in proper form—not proper for ordinary speech, but for logical testing—when it satisfies the following conditions: (1) the premises are listed first, then the conclusion; (2) within each statement the terms are plainly indicated; (3) each statement is clearly recognizable as Universal or Particular, Affirmative or Negative. There are many ways in which a syllogism in ordinary language, before this logical pruning, can deviate from its proper form. The three most important ways we must consider in this section.

(1) The premises and conclusion may be in the wrong order. For example:

> Only reasonably well-paid civil servants can be counted on to do their best, so you can't expect the Post Office workers to do their best, when, as we all know, they are never well paid.

The three statements here are given in this order: first, a premise; second, a conclusion (we know it is the conclusion from the word "so"); third, another premise (as the word "when" indicates in this context). The first thing to do, then, in getting this syllogism in shape, is to straighten out its general structure:

> Only well-paid civil servants can be counted on to do their best.
> They are never well paid.
> _____
> You can't expect the Post Office workers to do their best.

This helps to make the argument clearer, but don't throw away the original paragraph yet; there is more to be done.

(2) The three terms may not be clearly indicated. There are several steps that may have to be taken at this stage. First, there may be elliptical expressions and cross references to fill in. For example, "they" in our example refers to "Post Office workers," and that term should be substituted for "they" in the second premise. Second, the statements of a syllogism are always about the inclusion of one class in, or its exclusion from, another. Every statement in a syllogism can in principle be put in a form that makes clear exactly what the classes are, and how they are related. This may involve some rather delicate manipulation, and may lose *part* of the meaning of the original statement. But it is perfectly legitimate, provided it preserves that part of the original meaning that the deductive inference in the syllogism depends on.

For example, suppose someone says "John works at the G.E." If this is a two-term statement, and if it is going to be used in a deductive argument of some kind, then we ought to be able to name the two classes and restate the sentence so that the names of the two classes explicitly appear as such. The names of classes are nouns, either proper nouns or general nouns, and these will be the subject-terms and predicate-terms in our two-term statements. In this example, one class is evidently the class consisting solely of *John*; the other class is the class of *workers at the G.E.* (or *persons who work at the G.E.*). So this statement can be restated in the form: "John is a person who works at the G.E." This does not mean exactly what the original statement meant, but it keeps that part of the meaning that is needed for a syllogism in which the statement is to appear as a premise. The point about the translation is that, however awkward, it makes explicit the two classes that are involved.

This point is important to stress. You don't really understand a two-term statement until you know clearly what the two terms are. Sometimes this takes a little thought. Suppose you read in a newspaper, "It is illegal to sell so-called 'fair-trade' articles below the prices set by their manufacturers." One class is the class of *so-called 'fair-trade' articles*; the other is the class of *articles that it is illegal to sell below the manufacturers' prices*. And the statement says that the former class is wholly contained in the latter.

Now, in our syllogism, we must look for three classes, get them named properly, and make sure that the same class has the same name throughout the argument. It is helpful to ask first what is the very general class within which the three classes of the syllogism are distinguished. What is the syllogism *about* in the broadest sense? It is about people, but, more narrowly, it is about civil servants. Now, within this general class of civil servants, the three terms of the syllogism refer to these three classes:

> *civil servants who are well paid* (or, *well-paid civil servants*).
> *civil servants who can be counted on to do their best* (or, *who can be expected to do their best*).
> *Post Office workers.*

(We shall assume that "can be counted on to" and "can be expected to" mean the same thing here.)

With the help of these more standardized terms, we can now rewrite the three statements of the syllogism so as to clarify them a good deal (and where, as in this case, the terms are rather long, it is often helpful to separate them in some way from the rest of the statement).

Only/well-paid civil servants/are/civil servants who can be counted on to do their best.

Post Office workers/are never/well-paid civil servants.

Post Office workers/are not/civil servants who can be counted on to do their best.

(3) Finally, the structure of some of the statements may not be plain. For the purposes of deductive inference, it is vital to know what type of statement you have before you—for its structure determines what you can deduce from it, and what you can deduce it from. And you save yourself a good deal of trouble if you put each statement into a form that shows clearly which type it is.

For ordinary purposes, you don't have to be very fussy about this. When we were talking about Universal Affirmative statements, we wrote them in the form "All ... are ..."; for example, "All squares are rectangles." But there are several other forms that would do as well, or almost as well; we could write "Every square is a rectangle," "Any plane figure that is a square is also a rectangle," or "The class of squares is included in the class of rectangles." There are some differences in meaning, but the meaning they have in common is what we are interested in here. Logicians generally prefer the "All ... are ..." form because it is short, plain, and least likely to be misleading.

There are other forms that are not so easy to work with because they tend to obscure the logical structure rather than call attention to it. Instead of "All squares are rectangles," we could write "Only rectangles are squares." This makes the same statement, for it asserts the same relation between the same two classes. But "only" is a somewhat tricky word, and if this statement were going to appear in a deductive argument, it would be better to recast it. Similarly, in the syllogism we are working on, the first statement, "Only/well-paid civil servants/are/civil servants who can be counted on to do their best," is better put in the form: "All/civil servants who can be counted on to do their best/are/well-paid civil servants." The general rule is that "Only A is B" can always be recast as "All B is A."

There are other words that it is better to get rid of, if you can, when you want to put a statement in its best shape for deductive inference. One of them is "except." Take the statement, "All civil servants except Post Office workers are well paid." This is the same as saying that all of the civil servants who are *not* Post Office workers are well paid, and can therefore be written as: "All/civil servants who are not Post Office workers/are/well-paid civil servants." The Universal Negative statement, "No civil servants except Post Office workers are well paid," can be rewritten as: "No/civil servants who are not Post Office workers/are/well-paid civil servants."

In our example, the second premise is evidently a UN-statement that excludes the class of Post Office workers from the class of well-paid civil servants. The word "never" has the same force here as "no." The conclusion, too, appears to be a UN-statement, and so the whole syllogism, at last in its proper form, will look like this:

> All/civil servants who can be counted on to do their best/are/well-paid civil servants.
> No/Post Office workers/are/well-paid civil servants.
> ___
> No/Post Office workers/are/civil servants who can be counted on to do their best.

Now it is easy to apply the four rules: the syllogism has at least one affirmative premise (the first); it has a negative premise, but also a negative conclusion; the middle term ("well-paid civil servants") is distributed in the second premise, where it is the predicate of a UN-statement; and both end-terms, though distributed in the conclusion, are distributed also in the premises, where one of them ("civil servants who can be counted on to do their best") is the subject of a UA-statement, and the other ("Post Office workers") is the subject of a UN-statement. The diagram also shows its validity:

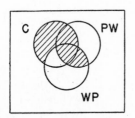

The only question that remains is whether the premises are true. But this question would involve another argument.

To sum up, let us run over the procedure for determining the validity of any syllogism in ordinary discourse. Here is a final example:

Step 1. Read it carefully.

> There must be some Executive Agreements that the President doesn't think Congress would approve because not all of them are submitted to Congress, but surely all agreements the President submits are ones that he thinks Congress would approve.

Step 2. Pick out the conclusion, write it below a horizontal line, and then put down the two premises. This is a good point at which to take out the pronouns and substitute their antecedents.

> Not all Executive Agreements are submitted to Congress.
>
> All agreements the President submits to Congress are Executive Agreements that he thinks Congress would approve.
> _____
> There are some Executive Agreements that the President doesn't think Congress would approve.

Step 3. Find the three classes and the general class of which they are a part. The general class seems to be something like *agreements with other nations* (a fuller context would help us be more sure). The three terms of the syllogism would then be "Executive Agreements" *Ex*, "agreements submitted to Congress (by the President)" *S*, and "agreements that the President thinks Congress would approve" *W*.

Step 4. Notice the structure of each of the statements in the syllogism, and, if necessary, recast them to make the structure apparent. The first premise has the general form "Not all *A*'s are *B*'s," and when we try out our four patterns of two-term statements on it, we see that it is a *PN*-statement, for "Not all *A*'s are *B*'s" is the same as "Some *A*'s are not *B*'s." "Not all Executive Agreements are submitted to Congress" can be written "Some/Executive Agreements/are not/agreements submitted to Congress." The second premise is clearly a *UA*-statement: "All/agreements submitted to Congress/are/agreements the President thinks Congress would approve." The conclusion has the general form, "There are some things that are *A* but not *B*." Now, if you say, for example, "There are hot red things," this is like saying, "Some hot things are red things." And so the statement, "There are some Executive Agreements that the President doesn't think Congress would approve" can be written as a *PN*-statement: "Some/Executive Agreements/are not/agreements that the President thinks Congress would approve." It *could* have been recast differently, putting the "not" into the predicate-term instead: "Some/Executive Agreements/are/agreements that the President does *not* think Congress would approve." This is just as good a translation, but it is not what is wanted in this context, for if we are going to treat this argument as a syllogism in order to see whether it works, we must have the same term in the predicate of the conclusion as we had earlier in the second premise.

Now we can rewrite the whole syllogism:

> Some/Executive Agreements/are not/agreements submitted to Congress.
> All/agreements submitted to Congress/are/agreements the President thinks Congress would approve.
> _____
> Some/Executive Agreements/are not/agreements the President thinks Congress would approve.

When we go through every step slowly this way, it may seem too much trouble to take for an argument consisting of only three statements. This argument does have some puzzling features. But the main point is to learn what you *can* do, in a hard case, when it is important to be sure about validity. And the more often you run through the steps with examples like this, the more skillful you get at spotting the structure of a syllogistic argument, its statements and terms, and seeing whether it is valid or invalid without going through each step separately.

Step 5. Test the syllogism by the rules. When you go down the list, you see that this syllogism passes all tests but the last: the predicate term in the conclusion is distributed there, but that term is not distributed in the second premise. This syllogism commits the Fallacy of Unwarranted Distribution.

Step 6. If you wish, recheck by means of a diagram. In this case, our decision is backed up by the diagram:

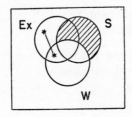

Evidently no inference can be drawn (by the syllogistic rules at least) from these two premises.

> A CHECK-UP QUIZ. Recast each of the following statements into one of the four forms of two-term statement:
>
> > "All . . . are . . ." (Universal Affirmative)
> > "Some . . . are . . ." (Particular Affirmative)
> > "No . . . are . . ." (Universal Negative)
> > "Some . . . are not . . ." (Particular Negative)
>
> 1. There are people who collect both coins and postage stamps.
> 2. Cherry trees never grow over a hundred feet tall.
> 3. Only people who know which fork to use are welcomed in polite society.
> 4. Tigers make docile pets unless they are hungry.
> 5. Not all of Beethoven's string quartets are in the key of F major.
> 6. Everyone can understand the message except those who will not try.
> 7. Nobody is both a poet and a politician.
> 8. Wishes do not always come true.
> 9. Occasionally his jokes are amusing.
> 10. You can be sure it's tasty if it's Theobald's.
>
> See also Exercise 10, pp. 142-44.
>
> FURTHER READING: M. C. Beardsley, *Practical Logic*. New York: Prentice-Hall, Inc., 1950, ch. 8 and §50 of ch. 10.

§14. BASIC LOGICAL CONNECTIONS

When the truth or falsity of one statement (or group of statements) is bound up intimately with the truth or falsity of another statement (or group of statements), the two statements (or groups of statements) are said to be **logically connected.** Take, for example, this pair of statements:

> (1) Enid is Edward's aunt.
> (2) Edward is Enid's uncle.

If the first statement is true, the second one *cannot* be true; and vice versa. Or take this pair of statements:

> (1) Enid is Edward's cousin.
> (2) Edward is Enid's cousin.

If the first statement is true, the second one *has* to be true; and again vice versa.

On the other hand, it is obvious that the following two statements have nothing to do with each other as far as their truth or falsity is concerned:

(1) Enid likes Roquefort cheese.
(2) Edward is a good swimmer.

Well, if you use your imagination, you may be able to think of some weird hypothesis for which both of these facts (as we shall assume they are) might be evidence, and then they *would* be logically connected in a roundabout way. But taking them just by themselves for the moment, it is clear that if the first one is true, the second one can be true or false; and if the second one is true, the first one can be true or false. There is no necessary connection; they are **logically independent** of each other.

The most direct sort of logical connection that one statement can have with another is the same connection that holds between the premises and the conclusion of a valid syllogism: the first may *imply* the second one.

The statement "Enid is Edward's aunt" *implies* the statement "Enid is a female."

The statement "Enid is tall and blonde" *implies* the statement "Enid is tall."

The statement "Fourteen people are taller than Edward" *implies* the statement "At least six people are taller than Edward."

In all these examples, implication is a one-way affair: if the first statement is true, the second must be true, but *not* vice versa. If, for example, Enid is both tall and blonde, she is certainly tall, but if she is tall, it doesn't follow that she is necessarily blonde.

But implication can also go both ways. If Enid is a cousin of Edward, then Edward must be a cousin of Enid, *and* if Edward is a cousin of Enid, then Enid must be a cousin of Edward. Two statements that imply each other are said to be **logically equivalent.**

"Enid is a cousin of Edward" *is logically equivalent to* "Edward is a cousin of Enid."

"No Senators are ministers" *is logically equivalent to* "No ministers are Senators."

"Gunshot Gulch is north of Rustler's Valley" *is logically equivalent to* "Rustler's Valley is south of Gunshot Gulch."

In all these cases, the first statement implies, and is implied by, the second. If Gunshot Gulch is north of Rustler's Valley, then Rustler's Valley *must* be south of Gunshot Gulch; and vice versa.

There are many problems that arise in the ordinary course of business where we want to know, and where it is quite important to know accurately, whether or not two statements are logically equivalent. For if they are equivalent, then, of course, any statement implied by either of them is also implied by the other, and any statement that implies either of them also implies the other.

Here are two insurance policies; are their provisions exactly the same, or are they not? Here are two proposed amendments to a law, or changes in managerial procedure; do they amount to the same thing, or would they have different consequences in practice? Of course this isn't going to take much thinking as long as the statements are short. If yesterday was Monday, then tomorrow is Wednesday; there can be no question about it. But compare these two statements:

(1) Every employee entitled to benefits under Article 3, Section 8, who has been employed at least ten years, will register in Age Group I and pay a registration fee of $10.
(2) No one who has been employed at least ten years is entitled to benefits under Article 3, Section 8, unless he registers in Age Group I and pays a registration fee of $10.

It may take a certain amount of careful reflecting to determine whether these are equivalent, and such reflection can be helped considerably by logical rules.

There are many common types of logical equivalence that will repay careful inspection. We shall have room for only a few examples here: let's choose them from among the four types of two-term statements we have been working with.

Take the Universal Affirmative statement, "All oysters are bivalves." The diagram of this statement shows that what this statement says is that the subclass consisting of oysters-that-are-not-bivalves is empty: in other words, "No oysters are nonbivalves." Notice how we got this equivalent statement. We changed the "All ...are ..." form to the "No ... are ..." form (that is, we changed the statement from one quality—affirmative or negative—to the other). And we changed the predicate-term from "bivalves" to "non-bivalves" (that is, we changed the predicate-term from one quality —positive or negative—to the other). You can do the same thing with any of the four types of two-term statement; in every case you will come out with a logically equivalent one.

Or take the Universal Negative statement, "No martens are non-weasels." If you switch the two terms around, without changing anything else, you again get a statement that is equivalent to the original one: "No nonweasels are martens." The same thing can be done with Particular Affirmative statements, but not with the other two kinds. For example, from "All martens are weasels" is doesn't follow that "All weasels are martens." These are logically independent of each other.

Two statements that are equivalent to each other are, so to speak, inseparable companions. From either, you can infer the other. But there are also pairs of statements that don't get along at all, and in fact repel each other, so that they can only be put into the same discourse by forcefully overcoming their natural repugnance. Suppose you have two statements, and they are logically connected in this way: if either one is true, the other is necessarily false, and if either is false, the other is necessarily true. They are then **contradictories** of one another.

> "All oysters are bivalves" *contradicts* (and *is contradicted by*) "Some oysters are not bivalves."
>
> "Leslie is a male" *contradicts* (and *is contradicted by*) "Leslie is not a male."
>
> "Bacon wrote *Hamlet*" *contradicts* (and *is contradicted by*) "Bacon did not write *Hamlet*."

Each of these pairs is evidently a pair of strict contradictories. Either Bacon wrote *Hamlet* or he did not (there is no third possibility), and he didn't both do it and not do it (the two possibilities are mutually exclusive). There are other pairs that are in opposition to each other, however, not because they are themselves strict contradictories, but because they imply contradictory statements. For example, the statement "Enid is Edward's aunt" implies that Enid has a brother or brother-in-law who is Edward's father, whereas the statement "Edward is Enid's uncle" implies that Enid does *not* have a brother or brother-in-law who is Edward's father. Two statements that imply contradictory statements are said to be **logically incompatible.**

> "Enid is Edward's aunt" *is incompatible with* "Edward is Enid's uncle."
>
> "Samuel Butler died in the 18th century" *is incompatible with* "Samuel Butler died in the 19th century" (provided you are talking about the same Samuel Butler).
>
> "The house on the corner is red all over" *is incompatible with* "The house on the corner is green all over."

And when you are talking about actual things, and not merely imaginary ones, the Universal Affirmative statement and the Universal Negative statement are incompatible with each other. If it is true that "All human beings are selfish," then it is false that "No human beings are selfish," assuming that the term "selfish" is given the same sense in both statements. These two statements are not *contradictories* of each other, however, for if one of them is false, it doesn't follow that the other must be true. Perhaps not all people are selfish, and not all people are unselfish; that is, some are selfish and some not. A pair of statements having the form "All A's are B's" and "No A's are B's" are said to be **contraries** of each other. And it is very important not to get contraries confused with contradictories. They behave in different ways. If you know that a statement is false, you can be sure its contradictory is true, but you *cannot* be sure its contrary is true, though it may be. But contraries *are* logically incompatible with each other: if one is true, the other must be false.

If a person believes two incompatible statements, whether he knows it or not (and presumably he wouldn't believe them both if he *knew* they were incompatible), there is something seriously wrong with his thinking. For it amounts to believing and disbelieving the same statement without being aware of it. And that is like placing the same bets on all the horses in a race. Anyone who believes two incompatible statements is guilty of *self-contradiction;* he takes back in one breath what he puts forth in another.

To describe this sort of situation in a slightly different way, let's suppose someone is making a speech, or writing an article, or merely setting forth his views informally. When such a discourse contains two statements that are logically incompatible with each other, the discourse is **inconsistent** with itself. Of course, a man can change his mind without inconsistency: he may get evidence on Wednesday that shows his Tuesday belief was mistaken. But if under the same circumstances, and in the same discourse, he asserts two incompatible statements, he is guilty of inconsistent thinking. And this is a fallacy.

Inconsistency is easier to fall into than it may appear from the examples given so far. Naturally, if you catch yourself saying that you are both working and out of a job, you will have no trouble spotting and avoiding the inconsistency. No danger here. But what of the man who says, "Teachers should avoid controversial issues in the classroom"? As Robert Hutchins has pointed out, the phrase "*non*controversial issue" is a contradiction in terms, for if there is no disagreement, there is no issue. What of the political party leaders who said a few years ago that they were about to launch a "top-level grass-roots drive" for getting support? Perhaps these terms are not clear enough so that we can be certain this phrase is self-contradictory, but in general a "top-level" drive would go in the opposite direction from a "grass-roots" one. Again, "dynamic conservatism" sounds a bit like Oscar Wilde's remark about the man who lived in "ostentatious obscurity."

As you can see in this example, inconsistency often comes from wanting to hold on to two conflicting things, to have your cake and to eat it. Those party leaders wanted the movement to be spontaneous and yet carefully managed. Perhaps they should have said (what is not self-contradictory) that they wanted to *combine* them in some degree. There are also those who like to give this parting advice to the Secretary of State as he flies off to another international conference: "We are of course ready at all times to negotiate with other nations—but we should make it clear right now that we do not intend to give in on the slightest point."

Inconsistency is harder to see, of course, when it appears in a longer discourse. Consider this paragraph from a book on Mozart:

> What is the function of art? It is nothing else at bottom but to express the relationship between an individual and his universe. This being so, it is clear that all arts—music, drama, literature, painting, sculpture—have essentially the same function. It is only their means that seem different. Kierkegaard himself, in his essay on Mozart's *Don Giovanni*, seems to agree with this, but he goes on to make a dubious distinction between what he calls "concrete"

mediums (language or speech) and "abstract" mediums (music), and thus, like all philosophers, lets his ideas run away with him. His distinction is dogmatic and empty, as is shown by the fact that in his essay he never attempts to define "concrete." Actually, his distinction involves a division between the medium and the content of a work of art, a division which he elsewhere wisely repudiates. For there is no such thing in art as a material or a medium in itself, separated from the idea of which it is the form. The material and the idea are one and inseparable.

This passage is complicated enough to raise many questions beside the one we are concerned with here, the question whether it is consistent with itself.

Note that the writer criticizes Kierkegaard for making a distinction between the *medium* of a work of art and its *content,* as he calls it. The writer appears to hold that there is no such distinction. But earlier in the passage, he has said that the various arts differ only in their *means* (that is, *medium*) and have "essentially the same *function.*" Now, "function" does not usually mean the same thing as "content," so you might say the author is quite consistent: he objects to the distinction between "medium" and "content"; he does *not* object to the distinction between "medium" and "function," which he in fact uses. But what is the function of which he speaks? It is to "express the relationship between an individual and his universe"— that is, to express a certain idea. And what is the content of which he speaks? It is an "idea," which in the last sentence is said to be "inseparable" from the "material." So it looks as though the author is both *asserting* that different mediums can express the same idea and *denying* that different mediums can express the same idea. If he cannot be decisively convicted of inconsistency, there are surely enough grounds of suspicion to make a fuller explanation desirable. And that is perhaps the judgment we should come to in this case.

This passage poses a difficult, but not untypical, reading problem. Being able to detect inconsistency, or to show where a passage verges upon inconsistency, is evidently an important part of logical skill. But it is even more important to apply to your own thinking.

A CHECK-UP QUIZ. In each of the following pairs, say whether the two statements are (1) logically equivalent, (2) logically incompatible, or (3) neither.

1. (a) Milton was a greater poet than Chaucer.
   (b) Chaucer was a greater poet than Milton.

2. (a) Some automobile accidents are due to carelessness.
   (b) Some automobile accidents are due to defective cars.

3. (a) Those who are in favor of Dior's new styles have good taste.
   (b) Those who are in favor of Dior's new styles have poor taste.

4. (a) Some Brussels sprouts are grown on Long Island.
   (b) Among the vegetables grown on Long Island are Brussels sprouts.

5. (a) No Agriculture Department officials below Grade 15 are permitted to have rugs in their offices.
   (b) Officials of the Agriculture Department who have not reached Grade 15 are ineligible for office rugs.

6. (a) Anyone who runs for political office must be highly ambitious.
   (b) People who run for political office always have a strong sense of duty.

7. (a) Any European defense organization that excludes Germany is doomed to failure.
   (b) Any European defense organization that has a chance of success will have to include Germany.

8. (a) Only well-adjusted people make good writers.
   (b) Only ill-adjusted people make good writers.

9. (a) No other international organization would be more effective in keeping peace than the United Nations.
   (b) A World Government would be more effective in keeping peace than the United Nations.

10. (a) People who go in for exotic foods are always clever at interpreting modern art.
    (b) Everyone who is clever at interpreting modern art also goes in for exotic foods.

See Exercise 11, pp. 144-45.

FURTHER READING: M. C. Beardsley, *Practical Logic*. New York: Prentice-Hall, Inc., 1950, ch. 9. Irving M. Copi, *Introduction to Logic*. New York: The Macmillan Co., 1953, ch. 5.

§15. REASONING WITH "IF" AND "OR"

Although we can't expect to consider in this one chapter more than a few of the simplest and commonest types of deductive argument, there is much to be said for glancing briefly at two types besides the syllogism. As we saw, a great many statements that occur in ordinary discourse can be treated as two-term statements, and can be classified as having one of the four structures possible for two-term statements. And when you have two such statements of the right sort, you can deduce a conclusion from them. But there are many statements that have other logical structures, and these enter into other kinds of deductive argument. Two of the other structures are quite familiar; they are based on two of the most important words in our language.

A statement that is built on the pattern "Either ... or ..." is called a **disjunctive statement**; for example: "*Either* Congress will modify the bill when it goes to conference *or* the President will veto it." A statement like this is really a *compound* statement, for it combines two two-term statements ("Congress will modify the bill when it goes to conference" and "The President will veto it") into a larger statement by means of the small but logically significant word "or." When you utter a disjunctive statement like this one, you are saying that *at least one* of the statements inside the disjunction is true, but you are *not* saying that *only* one is true. You might be sure that the President will veto the bill unless Congress modifies it, but even if Congress modifies it, the President may still veto it.

It is true that the word "or" is sometimes used to mean "either this or that, *but not both.*" For logical purposes, it is convenient to decide on one meaning of "or" and stick to it. The usual interpretation, which we shall follow, is to let "or" mean the same as "and/or" —that is, "either this or that, and perhaps both."

It follows that if we want to base a deductive argument upon a disjunction, we can do it only by *contradicting* one of the two-term statements inside the disjunction. The basic pattern of thought is this: we first come to believe that either statement A or statement B is true; we then discover, let's say, that statement A is *not* true; we can then deduce that statement B is true. For if at least one is true, but the first is not, then the second has to be. For example:

Either that noise is thunder *or* it is due to blasting.
[There is no construction going on nearby so] it is not due to blasting.

That noise is thunder.

The part in brackets here doesn't really belong to this argument, but it gives a reason for the second, or minor, premise. That's why it's in brackets; it could have been left out. The important thing about the minor premise is that it contradicts one of the two-term statements inside the first (disjunctive) premise. Thus the conclusion can be drawn. An argument of this kind is called a **"disjunctive argument."**

To get a good disjunctive argument, evidently at least two things are called for. First, you must be confident that the first, or major, premise is really true: that the alternatives it describes are really exhaustive. The noise *might* be due to a subway or fireworks. The truth of the major premise doesn't affect the *validity* of the argument, of course, but whenever you are using disjunctive statements you have to take special pains not to oversimplify by arbitrarily limiting the possibilities. Second, the minor premise must really contradict one of the alternatives in the major premise. If they merely *seem* to be incompatible, without really being so, then no confusion can follow:

Either some of the things he told me were false *or* I misunderstood him.
Some of the things he told me were not false.

I misunderstood him.

This argument breaks down because the statement "Some of the things he told me were not false" is not in any way incompatible with the statement it purports to deny: "Some of the things he told me were false."

The second point is especially important, for it warns us against another form of disjunctive argument which is quite similar to the one we have been discussing, but is invalid. Suppose we assert a disjunctive major premise and then a minor premise that *affirms*, instead of denying, one of the two-term statements in the disjunction:

Either controls will be instituted *or* there will be a slight recession.
Controls will be instituted.

There will not be a slight recession.

The way we are using the word "or," this conclusion cannot be drawn. Even if controls *are* instituted, something else may still cause the recession. This argument commits the **fallacy of false disjunction**. Of course, with a different major premise we can get the conclusion. Suppose we write:

> *Either* controls will not be instituted *or* there will not be a slight recession.
> Controls will be instituted.
> ——————————————————————————
> There will not be a slight recession.

Here there is no fallacy, for the minor premise contradicts one of the statements inside the disjunction, and the other statement inside the disjunction is brought down into the conclusion without any change.

A single disjunctive argument is very simple and not very illuminating when put in compact form. But the principle of it is far reaching. For a large and important discourse may be based on just this structure, only expanded and developed to encompass subordinate arguments of various kinds. Imagine a long essay or book based upon this general plan: there is a problem; three major solutions are possible; the first solution won't work for the following reasons; the second solution won't work, for the following reasons; therefore, let us try the third solution. Many kinds of arguments, inductive and deductive, may be involved, but the over-all pattern is that of the disjunctive argument.

A statement that is built on the pattern "If ... then ..." is called a **conditional statement;** for example: "*If* factory inventories of television sets continue to increase, *then* prices of television sets will be lowered." When you utter a statement like this, you mean to assert that something will happen *on condition that,* or *provided that,* something else happens. You don't commit yourself to saying what will happen to the prices of television sets if factory inventories do *not* continue to increase—that is simply left open. You're only saying that they will go down *if* the inventories increase.

There are a great many ways of asserting conditional statements. For example, "I will stay with you *unless* she comes" makes the same statement as "*If* she does not come, *then* I will stay with you." The "If ... then ..." form is favored by logicians because it is least suggestive and most easily understood.

It is convenient to give different names to the two statements that are inside a conditional statement. This wasn't necessary in disjunctive statements because there the inside statements are on the same level, so to speak: "*Either* you go *or* I go" is logically equivalent to "*Either* I go *or* you go" (apart from what they suggest). But "*If* you go, *then* I stay" is not at all equivalent to "*If* I stay, *then* you go." In any conditional statement, we shall call the statement that comes after the "*if*" the **antecedent** of the conditional, and we shall call the statement that comes after the "*then*" the **consequent** of the conditional. In the conditional mentioned above,

"*If* factory inventories of television sets continue to increase, *then* prices of television sets will be lowered,"

the antecedent is "factory inventories of television sets (will) continue to increase," and the consequent is "prices of television sets will be lowered." (The word "will" in the antecedent is not necessary; sometimes slight adjustments have to be made in the tense of a statement when it is put into or taken out of a conditional.)

Now, there are at least two fundamental ways we can get valid deductive arguments out of a conditional statement. Indeed, as soon as we mention these, it is apparent that there is no limit to the number of possible forms that we can get by combining and recombining. But we shall consider only the basic models here.

The first way is by combining two or more conditional statements. The easiest way to do this would be simply to string them together:

If factory inventories of television sets continue to increase, *then* prices of television sets will be lowered.

If prices of television sets are lowered, *then* people will buy more television sets.

If people buy more television sets, *then* factory inventories of television sets will decrease.

If factory inventories of television sets continue to increase, *then* factory inventories of television sets will decrease.

The conclusion here looks like a contradiction at first glance, but of course it is not really one, for the consequent refers to a later time (perhaps a much later time) than the antecedent. An argument that consists of a chain of conditionals, each linked to the one before, and with a conditional statement as a conclusion, is called a **conditional syllogism.**

But there is another familiar way of getting a conclusion out of a conditional statement, and that is by affirming or denying one or the other of the two-term statements that are inside the conditional. An argument of this sort is called simply a **conditional argument.** There are four possibilities for minor premises: you can affirm (or deny) the antecedent (or consequent). Two of these yield conclusions; two of them do not.

Consider first this example:

> *If* Hawaii is ready for statehood, *then* Alaska is ready for statehood.
> Hawaii is ready for statehood.
> _____
> Alaska is ready for statehood.

Remember that we aren't concerned here with the truth or falsity of the first, or major, premise, which is of course much debated. We are concerned with the structure of the argument. And it is simple enough. First we assert a conditional statement. Next we assert that the antecedent of the conditional is true (that is, we affirm the antecedent), and we deduce that the consequent is true. Not a very surprising conclusion, perhaps, but a very sound one.

Now suppose we try affirming the consequent instead of the antecedent.

> *If* Hawaii is ready for statehood, *then* Alaska is ready for statehood.
> Alaska is ready for statehood.
> _____
> Hawaii is ready for statehood.

This is surely invalid. Some people who agree with both premises refuse to accept the conclusion, and there is nothing inconsistent about this position. The argument commits a fallacy known as the **fallacy of affirming the consequent.** You can affirm the antecedent and derive the consequent; if you affirm the consequent, nothing follows.

On the other hand, you *do* get a conclusion if you *contradict* the consequent.

> *If* Hawaii is ready for statehood, *then* Alaska is ready for statehood.
> Alaska is not ready for statehood.
> _____
> Hawaii is not ready for statehood.

Here the minor premise denies the consequent. Anyone who agrees with both premises is *bound* to accept the conclusion on pain of inconsistency. Assuming that the conditional statement is true as a whole, why then, if its consequent is false, its antecedent must also be false. Or, to put it another way, "*If* you go, *then* I go" is logically equivalent to "*If* I don't go, *then* you don't go."

Now suppose we try contradicting the antecedent, instead of the consequent:

> *If* Hawaii is ready for statehood, *then* Alaska is ready for statehood.
> Hawaii is not ready for statehood.
> _____
> Alaska is not ready for statehood.

This conclusion does not follow at all. You can deny the consequent, and derive the contradictory of the antecedent; if you deny the antecedent, nothing follows. And an argument like this one commits the **fallacy of denying the antecedent.**

When you spot a conditional argument, then, you can test its validity very easily. First, make sure you know what the conditional, or major, premise is, and in which direction it goes. Second, see whether the minor premise affirms or denies the antecedent or consequent in the major premise. If it affirms the antecedent or denies the consequent, a conclusion can be drawn; otherwise not.

Often, of course, conditional reasoning will be exemplified not in a single sentence or paragraph, but as the large framework of a broader argument. One way argument can move on is first to establish some statements of the "If ... then ..." form (and it may require several arguments to establish them), and next to establish the antecedents so that the consequents can be deduced. A spread-out conditional argument is not always easy to get the hang of, but if you think of it in terms of our simpler models, you can trace its general plan. And no matter how large or small, it must stand or fall by the same basic rules.

A CHECK-UP QUIZ. Which of the following arguments commit the fallacy of False Disjunction? Affirming the Consequent? Denying the Antecedent?

1. If experience is the best teacher, then it is important to be a good observer. Experience *is* the best teacher. Therefore, it is important to be a good observer.

2. If God intended women to wear pants, he would make them two-legged. And he did make them two-legged. Therefore, he intended them to wear pants.

3. If human nature is inherently good, then laws would not be necessary for human beings. But they are necessary. Therefore, human nature is not inherently good.

4. Either the letter will be returned by the Post Office or there will be a Postage Due stamp on it. It will not be returned. Therefore, there will be a Postage Due stamp on it.

5. If we build the house near the swimming pool, it will be noisy. We will not build the house near the swimming pool. Therefore, it will not be noisy.

6. Either she is a vegetarian or she believes in boycotting her butcher. She *is* a vegetarian. Therefore, she does not believe in boycotting her butcher.

7. Either he is suffering a relapse or he has become infected with a new disease. He apparently has not become infected with a new disease. Therefore, he must be suffering a relapse.

8. If all home run hitters are infielders, then Willie Mays is an infielder. Which he is not. Therefore, some home run hitters are not infielders.

9. If every man has a wife, some women would lack husbands. Some women *do* lack husbands. Therefore, not every man has a wife.

10. If some Euclidian triangles have the sum of their angles greater than 180 degrees, then some Euclidian rectangles must have the sum of their angles greater than 360 degrees. But no Euclidian triangles have the sum of their angles greater than 180 degrees. Therefore, no Euclidian rectangles have the sum of their angles greater than 360 degrees.

See Exercise 12, pp. 145-47.

FURTHER READING: M. C. Beardsley, *Practical Logic*. New York: Prentice-Hall, Inc., 1950, ch. 11, §§51-54. Henry W. Johnstone, Jr., *Elementary Deductive Logic*. New York: Thomas Y. Crowell, Co., 1954, chs. 7-10. Max Black, *Critical Thinking*. New York: Prentice-Hall, Inc., rev. ed., 1952, chs. 4-6.

§16. THE USES OF DEDUCTION

Making logical deductions is at bottom nothing but seeing that certain statements follow necessarily from others. This is something that we are called upon to do every day—and we can't think efficiently without doing it correctly. For when we know that a given statement is true, we can be sure that whatever follows from it is also true. But if we did not recognize this, we should have to take each statement as it comes and consider it by itself. And perhaps we could never know any very important statement to be true unless we could get help from other statements that either imply it or are implied by it.

Besides the basic employment of deductive logic in deciding whether a given deductive argument is valid or invalid, there are three different, but closely related, applications of it. In this section we shall consider these other uses briefly.

A. *Hidden Premises.* Many of the arguments that we encounter in newspapers or magazines or radio and television programs like *Meet the Press* come to us in more or less fragmentary, or elliptical, form. Though people reason deductively (well or ill) very often, they usually do not take pains to make their arguments perfectly explicit, as we did with the syllogisms we examined earlier. They may, for example, leave out some of their premises, either because they are not exactly sure what their premises *are*, or because they assume that we shall quickly recognize their premises and assent to them, or (sometimes) because their premises are rather shaky and they do not wish to call our attention to the weaknesses of their arguments.

The basic premises of an argument are the underlying assumptions that the arguer makes, and when you are deciding whether to accept his conclusion, you must find out whether his assumptions are true. But you cannot find this out until you know what his assumptions *are.* So you need a method for getting at the hidden premises of a deductive argument—the premises that are not stated but implicitly taken for granted. And this you can do by using the rules of deductive logic.

Suppose someone says, "College students should not be permitted to study the *Communist Manifesto* because it may give them some false ideas." This looks like a deductive argument; indeed, it is clearly two-thirds of a syllogism. The conclusion is there, and one of the necessary premises; the question is: what *other* premise would have to be assumed in order to let the conclusion follow? It will generally be a help to recast the argument in a little more formal way, so you can get a good look at it:

> The *Communist Manifesto* is a book that may give students some false ideas.
> *Therefore:* The *Communist Manifesto* is not a book that college students should be permitted to study.

This is what you are given. What you are after is the premise that will complete this argument so that it will be a valid syllogism. If the problem were very difficult, you could bring in the rules of the syllogism: for example, you would say: well, it must be a negative premise, because the conclusion is negative here but the given premise is affirmative. But in this case the answer is fairly easy. The hidden assumption is:

> [No/books that may give students some false ideas/are/books that students should be permitted to study.]

It is a good idea to put this statement in brackets to show that you are supplying it yourself. Now the jigsaw puzzle is complete; you know what must be true if the conclusion is to follow. Whether the assumption *is* true—that, of course, is another question.

Consider one more example, where it is more difficult to bring the hidden premise into the light of day. People have argued that:

> Only where there is economic freedom is there freedom of religion; therefore, there can be no freedom of religion without political freedom.

Once you recognize this as an incomplete syllogism, you can see that the missing premise has something to do with the relationship between places with economic freedom and places without political freedom, for these are the two terms that are only used once. But to determine what *is* the relationship requires a certain amount of figuring.

Suppose we recast the given statements so that they are clearer:

> All/places where there is freedom of religion/are/places where there is economic freedom. (*explicit premise*)
> No/places where there is freedom of religion/are/ places without political freedom. (*conclusion*)

The missing premise has got to be a Universal Negative statement in which one term is "places with economic freedom" and the other term is "places without political freedom," that is:

> [No/places with economic freedom/are/places without political freedom.] (*implicit premise*)

The critical reader keeps a wary eye out for underlying assumptions, especially when they are not even mentioned. And this holds also for the writer. When you set out to present a deductive argument, and you want to make it really convincing, you have to discover your own assumptions. Not that you must always *present* all your premises; some of them will be obvious and harmless. But you can ask yourself such questions as these: "What am I taking for granted here? Am I sure of the truth of all my premises? Have I given the reader enough of them so that he can see my point?" Whether or not you succeed in making your point may well depend on how well you answer these questions.

B. *Syllogism-chains.* Sometimes we want to discover the hidden implications of a set of statements that we accept, or are about to accept. Suppose the statements are true: what would follow? If the statements are just a pair that can be made the premises of a single syllogism, the answer is right at hand. But there may be several statements.

A single syllogism sometimes seems like a trivial sort of argument, not because of any mistakes in it, but because it doesn't take us very far in our thinking. But a *series* of syllogisms (together, perhaps, with arguments of other types, including conditional and disjunctive arguments) may take us very far, and even to a conclusion which would be hard to foresee just from looking at the premises alone. Consider this reasoning:

> Deepening the Delaware River channel will admittedly benefit U.S. Steel's vast new plant at Morrisville because it will make available to it the shipping that comes through the Port of Philadelphia. This project is consequently a help to national defense and should be subsidized by the Federal Government.

There are four statements here, all having the same subject-term, "deepening the Delaware River channel." The ultimate conclusion is that this project should be subsidized by the Federal government. So much is plain.

But if we try to get this conclusion out of the premises we are given, we discover two things. First, we discover that some of the premises we need are left out. Second, we discover that there is not one syllogism here, but, in fact, three. Syllogism One is this:

> [Anything that makes shipping available to the U.S. Steel plant at Morrisville will benefit the plant.]
> Deepening the Delaware River channel will make shipping available to the U.S. Steel plant at Morrisville.
>
> ―――――――――――――――――――――――――――――――
>
> Deepening the Delaware River channel will benefit the U.S. Steel plant at Morrisville.

The conclusion of Syllogism One becomes the second premise of Syllogism Two:

> [Anything that benefits the U.S. Steel plant at Morrisville is a help to national defense.]
> Deepening the Delaware River channel will benefit the U.S. Steel plant at Morrisville.
>
> ―――――――――――――――――――――――――――――――
>
> [Deepening the Delaware River channel is a help to national defense.]

And Syllogism Two's conclusion (which is not explicitly stated) becomes the second premise of Syllogism Three:

> [Anything that is a help to national defense is something that should be subsidized by the Federal government.]
> [Deepening the Delaware River channel is a help to national defense.]
>
> ―――――――――――――――――――――――――――――――
>
> Deepening the Delaware River channel is something that should be subsidized by the Federal government.

Now we know exactly how the conclusion was obtained, and what assumptions are made. We have a series of syllogisms in which the conclusion of one becomes a premise of the following one; an argument like this is called a **syllogism-chain**. This one is valid, of course, though you might want to question the truth of some of the premises, for example, the first premise of Syllogism Three.

Now, suppose you start with a handful of premises (a collection of facts obtained, perhaps, from various sources), and you want to know whether any conclusion can be logically deduced from them. Take, for example, the following statements:

(1) Children who are inoculated against whooping cough never get it.
(2) Every child with parents in the PTA goes to P.S.13.
(3) Any child who goes to P.S.13 has been inoculated against whooping cough.
(4) Some children at the party came down with whooping cough.

From these four premises it follows that:

Some children at the party are not children whose parents are in the PTA.

We get this conclusion by turning the four premises into a syllogism-chain. Take any two of them that have a usable common term: say 1 and 3. Put these together in a syllogism, and you can deduce from them that:

No children who go to P.S.13 are children who get whooping cough.

Put this conclusion with statement 2, and you can deduce that:

No children with parents in the PTA are children who get whooping cough.

Put *this* conclusion with statement 4, and you can deduce the final conclusion. This can go on forever—that is, until you run out of premises.

Of course, from a small set of simple premises, nothing very surprising can be deduced. It's not as startling as deducing from the premises of Euclid's geometry that every triangle can be inscribed on one and only one circle, or that there are exactly five regular solids. But the principle is the same. And the application to ordinary life is the same as in science. On many important subjects, we carry around with us whole clusters of beliefs, of which we may be more or less clearly aware, and for which we have more or less adequate reasons. Sometimes it may be vital to discover the implications of what we believe. Perhaps we believe inconsistent things without knowing it, and are frustrating ourselves by unwittingly undoing one day what we did the day before: supporting incompatible causes, or adopting conflicting plans. We can expose the inconsistency, and correct it, if we explore the statements implied by the statements we accept. And this is one of the things deductive logic teaches us how to do.

C. Circular reasoning. There is still another way, which as yet has not been mentioned, in which a deductive argument can go astray, though without being in the least invalid. Suppose someone argues this way: "Miracles can't happen because miracles are impossible, and impossible things can't happen." You have the feeling that this conclusion follows all right—it makes a good syllogism—but that something is wrong with it. Suppose we set it out in stricter shape:

> All impossible things are things that can't happen.
> All miracles are impossible things.
> _____
> All miracles are things that can't happen.

The trouble is that the conclusion and the second premise really say the same thing in different words, since "impossible things" and "things that can't happen" have the same meaning here. To all intents and purposes, the second premise and the conclusion are the same statement in different words.

A deductive argument in which the conclusion turns up explicitly or implicitly (in the same or synonymous words) as one of the premises, is a **circular argument**. It is not crooked, like an invalid one, but it has its own sort of futility. For, in effect, it gives the conclusion as a reason for the conclusion, and anyone would have to accept the conclusion already before accepting the argument. Such an argument commits the **fallacy of begging the question**.

Question-begging arguments are harmless when you see them for what they are. The trouble is that the question-begging can be disguised so that sometimes these arguments seem to give you a real reason when in fact they don't. Here is a case, for example, where someone is appointed Superintendent of Schools in a small town by unanimous vote of the School Board. Then one of the citizens discovers, or thinks he has discovered, some objection to the Superintendent: perhaps that he is a member of the American Veterans Committee or the Civil Liberties Union. The objector spreads this word around, but nobody gets excited about it. Then he thinks of another idea. He writes letters to the paper and to the School Board saying that he objects to the appointment, and since he objects, that makes the new Superintendent a "controversial figure," and contro versial figures ought never to be School Superintendents, so the appointment should be withdrawn.

The gist of this argument is (a) I object to him because he is controversial; (b) he is controversial because I object to him. What could be more circular? Either some other reason must be found for objecting to him, or some other reason must be found for saying he is controversial. If not, the question at issue is merely begged. The situation is too much like that of the mother saying to her child, "Eat your spinach, so you'll grow up strong enough to make *your* children eat theirs."

There are many terms that are quite often used for question-begging dodges. For example, there is the term "essentially." This is useful for defending a universal statement against conflicting evidence. "All Republicans are isolationist (or reactionary, or something else)," says A. "By no means," replies B. "What about So-and-so? He's a Republican, but not an isolationist." "Oh, you can't count *him*," says A; "He voted against Taft at the Convention in 1952, so he's not *essentially* a Republican." But if the word "essentially" (or "really," or "genuinely," or "truly," or "at heart," or "in the last analysis") is not handy, any word that is very vague will do. "We shall always welcome *constructive* criticism," says the office boss, with just the slightest warning emphasis on the word "constructive." This is enough to remind the wary listener that any criticism the boss doesn't want to hear may be rejected as "not constructive." The word is loose enough so that he can write his own ticket, and no doubt some months later he will be heard proclaiming that "Despite our policy of free discussion, there has been no constructive criticism."

There is not much you can do with a circular argument except to point out that it leaves things where they stood before. A deductive argument is supposed to be a bridge from one set of statements to another. Even if it's only a small footbridge, it takes you somewhere. But a circular argument never gets off the ground. This is something to keep in mind as a reader and as a writer too. For there are few temptations more constant than the temptation to think you have a reason for a belief when you have no reason at all. And circular arguments are the fruit of yielding to this temptation: they allow us to present to others, and, worse, to ourselves, the verbal husk of a "reason," which is after all only the conclusion itself in a thin disguise.

A CHECK-UP QUIZ. Write out missing statements (premises or conclusions) for each of the following incomplete syllogisms: do this in such a way as to make them all valid.

1. . . . .
   Some human sounds don't have any meaning.
   Some human sounds are not words.

2. Well-cooked dinners are never unpalatable.
   . . . .
   Some hurriedly-cooked dinners are not unpalatable.

3. Every government worker is valuable to society.
   No one who is valuable to society deserves to be underpaid.
   . . . .

4. Without someone to love, a person cannot be well adjusted.
   Only well-adjusted people can be bus drivers.
   . . . .

5. Every friend of yours is a friend of mine.
   . . . .
   Henry is no friend of yours.

6. Anyone who is to become a doctor must take organic chemistry.
   Gwendolyn will not take organic chemistry.
   . . . .

7. . . . .
   Some of these documents are marked "secret."
   Some of these documents are not to be taken out of the office.

8. Those who filed their returns late have been fined.
   . . . .
   Not one of our employees filed his returns late.

9. . . . .
   All of those about whom some question was raised have been
     investigated and cleared.
   Some of those who have been investigated and cleared have not
     yet returned to work.

10. Congress's foreign policy legislation was more heavily supported by Democrats than by Republicans.

. . . .

The Administration cannot take credit for the foreign policy legislation passed by Congress.

See Exercises 13, 14, and 15, pp. 147-50.

FURTHER READING: M. C. Beardsley, *Practical Logic*. New York: Prentice-Hall, Inc., 1950, ch. 10, §49; ch. 11, §55.

Outline-Summary of Chapter 3

In a *valid* deductive argument, the premises *imply* the conclusion: in other words, if the premises are all true, then the conclusion must be true. There are many kinds of deductive argument, differing from one another in their structure; among these are:

A. *The syllogism* ("All harps are stringed instruments; all lyres are harps; therefore, all lyres are stringed instruments").

1. A syllogism consists of three two-term statements (that is, statements with a subject-term and a predicate-term), each of these being one of the following four types:
   a. Universal Affirmative statements ("All lyres are harps");
   b. Particular Affirmative statements ("Some harps are lyres");
   c. Universal Negative statements ("No lyres are wind instruments");
   d. Particular Negative statements ("Some harps are not lyres");
2. A syllogism contains three terms:
   a. a *middle term* that appears in both premises ("harps" in the example above); and
   b. two *end-terms*, each of which appears in one premise and in the conclusion ("lyres" and "stringed instruments" in the example above).

In order for a syllogism to be valid, it must conform to four rules, the violation of any of which is a fallacy:

Rule 1: At least one of the premises must be affirmative.

Rule 2: If one premise is negative, the conclusion must be negative.

Rule 3: The middle term must be distributed (that is, it must be either the subject-term in a Universal statement or the predicate-term in a Negative statement) at least once.

Rule 4: If an end-term is distributed in the conclusion, it must also be distributed in the premise.

B. *The conditional argument,* which has as its major (first) premise a conditional statement ("If it rained last night, then the grass is wet") containing an *antecedent* ("It rained last night") and a *consequent* ("the grass is wet"), has exactly two valid forms:

1. affirming the antecedent ("If it rained last night, then the grass is wet; it did rain last night; therefore, the grass is wet"),
2. denying the consequent ("If it rained last night, then the grass is wet; the grass is not wet; therefore, it did not rain last night").

C. *The disjunctive argument,* which has as its major premise a disjunctive statement ("Either it is raining or it is snowing"), has one valid form, in which the minor (second) premise denies one or the other of the alternatives ("Either it is raining or it is snowing; it is not snowing; therefore, it is raining").

If in a pair of statements the truth or falsity of either of them implies the truth or falsity of the other, the two statements are *logically connected;* if not, they are *logically independent.*

Two types of logical connection are particularly noteworthy:

1. Two statements are *logically equivalent* if they imply each other (as "All garter snakes are harmless snakes" implies, and is implied by, "All harmful snakes are nongarter snakes");

2. Two statements are *logically incompatible* if they imply *contradictory* statements (two statements, such as, "All garter snakes are harmless" and "Some garter snakes are not harmless", being contradictory when, if either is true, the other must be false, and if either is false the other must be true): A discourse that contains two incompatible statements ("All murderers should be executed" and "No murderers should be executed") is *inconsistent,* or self-contradictory.

A deductive argument in which the conclusion appears as one of the premises, either in the same words or in synonymous words, either explicitly or implicitly, is a *circular,* or question-begging argument. ("I am convinced that news commentators are truthful, for my favorite news commentator says so"—where the truthfulness of the commentator has to be assumed *before* taking his word, and therefore cannot be *based* on his word).

Exercise 10

Analyze the following syllogisms and determine whether they are valid or invalid.

1. Only die-hard liberals in the Senate were responsible for carrying on the disgusting filibuster against the new Atomic Energy Act. The

liberals, therefore, are the ones who ought to be censured by the Senate, for anyone responsible for that filibuster surely ought to be censured.

2. Some friends of the management are able to pay their bills. Only people who are able to pay their bills are admitted to the restaurant. Therefore some of those who are admitted are not friends of the management.

3. As is pretty generally agreed (at least in the case of the so-called "basic crops": corn, cotton, wheat, peanuts, and rice), agricultural products that play a vital role as food should be protected by flexible price supports. Since beef is also an important food, it is clear that it, too, should be supported.

4. Some of the "Anzus" nations in the Pacific will sign the pact, but none of the "Columbo" nations in Southeast Asia are "Anzus" nations. Therefore, some of the "Columbo" nations will not sign the pact.

5. Objects that are sold at auctions must sometimes bring discord into the families that buy them, for some of them are regarded with more favor by one party than by another, and objects that are so regarded sometimes bring discord.

6. Some government documents that are classified as "secret" would be embarrassing to those who classified them, but none of them are permitted to be published. It is clear, then, that some documents that one is permitted to publish do not cause embarrassment to those who classified them.

7. New power-producing plants built by Federal funds must be approved by vote of Congress, and they should not be allowed to give preferred treatment to private utilities. It follows that no plants that should be allowed to give preferred treatment to private utilities are plants that must be approved by vote of Congress.

8. No maritime nation can be secure in time of war without a strong merchant marine, and no such nation can have a strong merchant marine without government building subsidies; it is obvious, therefore, that only with government building subsidies for merchant shipping can we be secure in time of war.

9. Some blind people can read any book printed in Braille, so some books on economics can be read by some blind people, for there are books on economics printed in Braille.

10. Devices for artificial rain-making are contrary to nature and to the Will of God because they are not in keeping with the normal course of events, and what is in keeping with the normal course of events is according to nature and to the Will of God.

11. In segregated schools there is no opportunity for pupils of different races to come into conflict with one another, and schools in which this is the case are the kind of schools America needs. Therefore, segregated schools are the kind America needs.

12. It is impossible to have freedom of scientific inquiry without free enterprise in the economic sphere, for scientists are free to inquire only in countries where there is financial support for research, and free enterprise systems always provide such support.

13. The state laws prohibit games played for money in which chance plays a predominant role in determining the outcome. This is surely the case with Bingo, which is therefore prohibited by the state laws.

14. Any nation that attacks another nation without provocation is an aggressor nation, and such unprovoked attackers surely ought not to be admitted to the U.N. It follows that aggressor nations should not be admitted to the U.N.

15. Those who believe that peace is a more desirable thing than war should be encouraged to persuade others that they are right. Now, this is exactly what is believed by pacifists, who consequently should be encouraged to persuade others that they are right.

Exercise 11

Examine the following pairs of statements and determine in each case whether one of the statements implies the other, or whether they are logically equivalent, or incompatible, or independent.

1. (a) Only icosahedra can have twenty exactly similar plane faces.
   (b) Only a polyhedron with twenty exactly similar plane faces can be an icosahedron.

2. (a) The snout of a pipefish is the snout of a thin fish.
   (b) Pipefish are thin fish.

3. (a) Nobody in the town likes Murgatroyd.
   (b) There is someone in the town who likes everybody.

4. (a) All atonal music is written by gloomy composers.
   (b) All tonal music is written by cheerful composers.

5. (a) Some delusions are not hallucinations.
   (b) Hallucinations and delusions are exactly the same thing.

6. (a) Bills passed by Congress for which there is a considerable popular support should never be given a pocket veto.
   (b) Bills passed by Congress for which there is a considerable popular support should never be vetoed at all.

7. (a) Rooms that are too small will seem larger if the walls and woodwork are painted the same color throughout.
   (b) Rooms that are too small will seem even smaller if the walls and woodwork are painted the same color throughout.

8. (a) Murgatroyd is the first dark-haired man she has married.
   (b) None of the men she married before Murgatroyd, if any, were dark haired.

9. (a) That town is called South Fulton, Tennessee.
   (b) That town is south of Fulton, Tennessee.

10. (a) No Congressional committee hearings that are concerned with the judgment of particular individuals should be permitted to be televised.
    (b) All Congressional committee hearings that should be permitted to be televised are those that are not concerned with the judgment of particular individuals.

11. (a) There are professional criminals who aren't unpleasant people.
    (b) There are unpleasant people who aren't professional criminals.

12. (a) It has been reported that some of the nations who were not invited to participate in the conversations are not among those unwilling to sign the pact.
    (b) It has been reported that some of the nations who are willing to sign the pact were not invited to participate in the conversations.

13. (a) All parties to the dispute have agreed to the compromise, with the exception of those who have strong Communist minority parties.
    (b) At least one party to the dispute that has not agreed to the compromise is one that has a strong Communist minority party.

14. (a) No longer supported by the rank and file of his party, ill, and discredited by his recent diplomatic fiasco, it is clear that he will soon be out of office.
    (b) He has been losing support both within the party and outside; and though he is still well and healthy, he will soon be out of office.

15. (a) All the red books in his library are philosophical works except the ones that are paper bound.
    (b) All the red books in his library are paper bound except the philosophical works.

Exercise 12

Analyze the following disjunctive and conditional arguments and determine whether they are valid or invalid.

1. If the public schools were to be improved, a change in their basic philosophy was needed. The newer education movements introduced a change in their basic philosophy. Hence, the newer education movements improved the schools.

2. If the Republican Party is permitted to make political appeals on television, then by Section 315 of the Communications Act of 1934, the American Vegetarian and Constitution Parties also have a right to equal time. But these parties surely do not have a right to equal time with the Republican Party, and therefore the Republican Party is not permitted to make political appeals on television.

3. Either the United States will have to treat its allies with understanding and respect, or it will have to go it alone in foreign relations. But it cannot go it alone, so it will have to treat its allies with understanding and respect.

4. If there are any ethical absolutes in human experience, it is important to study Latin so that one can read Cicero's moral exhortations in the original language. However, we now know that there are no such ethical absolutes, and it follows that it is not important to study Latin.

5. Either the California Indians should be given a share of State relief funds, or they should be voted special help by the Federal Government. Because of their specially unfortunate position, these Indians should indeed be voted special help by the Federal Government. Therefore, they need not be given a share of State relief funds.

6. The alliance between politics and crime in a corrupt city can be broken up, provided the party in power can be removed from office. The party machine can be wrecked, provided the alliance between politics and crime can be broken up. The party in power can be removed from office, provided the party machine can be wrecked. Therefore, the party in power can be removed from office, provided it can be removed from office.

7. Under the existing circumstances, their choice is limited to the following alternatives: (1) to continue to plead their cause before the court of international public opinion; (2) to attempt to gain their end by war. It is clear that they will not choose the second alternative, so they must choose the first.

8. In order to get from Ashville to Newkirk by the time the train left, he would have to average forty-five miles per hour on that rough mountain

road, which is quite impossible. It follows that he was not in fact on that train.

9. It was reported that the syndicate is prepared to sell the ball club on condition that the group who buys it will keep it in the city. The group has now agreed to this condition, so the sale may be expected to go through.

10. Of course there should be a rigorously-enforced Federal Fair Employment Practices law *if* the majority of people all over the country' are psychologically and morally ready to agree that employers have no right to decide what kind of people they want to hire. But obviously people are not ready to accept this everywhere, from which it follows that there should not be any such law.

Exercise 13

In syllogisms 1-10 below, a premise is missing; write out the premise required in each case if the conclusion is to follow. In syllogisms 11-15, more than one premise is missing, and when all the required premises are supplied, the result will be a syllogism-chain.

1. German property in the United States that was seized during World War II should be returned to its owners, for this would promote German friendship toward the United States.

2. Soil that is loosened by a disc harrow holds moisture better than soil that is turned over by a plow, so it must give a greater yield in crops.

3. All literary descriptions of the past that do not inspire an ardent hatred of oppression fail to live up to the highest ideals of the People's Democracy, hence novels written and published under capitalistic conditions fail to live up to these ideals.

4. Treaties and executive agreements that affect the internal affairs of the nation should be prohibited by a new amendment to the Constitution, for they are clearly unconstitutional.

5. High-school students should have courses on how to drive a car—after all, this is a very important thing for them to know.

6. It is certainly within the power of Congress to pass laws that will equalize educational opportunities for all, since such laws undoubtedly "promote the general welfare."

7. It is not true that all human beings are selfish, for some human beings sacrifice themselves for others.

8. There must be unhappy people, for there are certainly wicked ones

9. It cannot be true that wealth is undesirable, for this opinion runs counter to the opinion of the majority.

10. Not every argument that philosophers have invented to prove the existence of God is a sound argument, for among them are some circular arguments.

11. There is no Commandment against gambling, so Bingo is not immoral.

12. Federally-financed highway construction will not be approved by the Hoover Commission, for Socialistic schemes always tend to keep the budget unbalanced.

13. Nineteenth-century American music and painting is not of the highest quality; after all, music and painting that is largely an imitation of foreign work can hardly be very original.

14. People who think too much are likely to raise inconvenient questions about the wisdom of some government policies, and therefore highly educated people should not be elected to public office, since they will tend to encourage subversion.

15. Anyone who is willing to defend an unpopular opinion, and who is therefore intellectually courageous, is performing a public service. That is why I believe that the most extreme conservatives and radicals should be accorded respect and gratitude.

Exercise 14

What conclusion, if any, can be drawn from each of the following sets of premises?

1. All the houses on *P* street are either one-story or two-story houses. The one-story houses are all made of brick; none of the two-story houses have green roofs; some of the nonbrick houses are new; all the expensive houses have green roofs.

2. People who have an equity in the Government should not be disenfranchised, provided they are otherwise qualified to vote. People who are required to pay taxes have an equity in the Government, and citizens residing in the District of Columbia are required to pay taxes.

3. No objects that exhibit a unified design are ugly. Objects that fulfill a function are organized for a purpose. Objects whose parts are ordered in relation to a specific end are unified in design. Objects that are organized for a purpose have their parts ordered in relation to a specific end.

4. All members of the debating team are majors in English. Some editors of the *Firebird* are against organized sports. All editors of the *Firebird* are on the debating team. No English majors are in favor of the Honor System. All those who are against organized sports are in favor of the Honor System.

5. Works of literature that give us a sense of heightened consciousness are bound to enrich our lives. Some good poems contain sharp and vivid imagery. Whatever increases our sensitivity to the world around us also makes us better citizens of that world. Literature that is marked by sharp and vivid imagery creates a sense of heightened consciousness. Anything that enriches our lives will increase our sensitivity to the world around us.

Exercise 15

Read the following passages carefully. Point out, and explain clearly, all *inconsistencies* and all examples of *circular reasoning*.

1. A long-time resident of Delaware County, Mr. Henrickson was married twice, the second time to his widow's sister, by whom he had one child, Albert, now an office manager in the Bala Cynwyd Brick Works.

2. Only short poems can be good; not long ones. Of course, many so-called poems, like *Paradise Lost*, take up a large number of pages. But, as Edgar Allan Poe said, if they are good it must be because they are really collections of short poems, which only goes to prove my point.

3. If you don't believe that atheists are dishonest, read what that atheist has written—for the article is certainly dishonest, and you can tell he's an atheist from what he says.

4. Well, here's the way the new administration has cleaned things up. We have quietly, but finally, removed the old members of the military planning boards who were responsible for giving Asia to the Communists and involving us in a hopeless foreign war in Korea. Second, we have freed the military from the position of being mere lackeys, with no authority, as they were under the former administration. Third, we have brought the Korean war to a victorious conclusion for the democratic powers of the world.

5. I support the principle of states' rights, and by that I mean every state should be left alone to stand on its own feet and handle its affairs in its own way, with no interference from Washington. That is the old and original principle of the Constitution. But it follows that the states must be strengthened and made to flourish, and that is why I ask the Federal Government to give our state help when there is a drought, or a flood, or when we cannot support adequate schools, or when there is land to be reclaimed from erosion.

6. All that we know of history goes to show that planned economies discourage initiative. For, consider: Economies that discourage initiative are inevitably wasteful, and centralized economies discourage initiative,

since they are planned. But planned economies are always centralized. It follows, as I have said, that planned economies discourage initiative.

7. Get the U.N. out of the U.S. and the U.S. out of the U.N.! As everyone knows, the U.N. is too feeble to preserve peace—it didn't preserve peace in Israel, in Korea, in Indochina, in Guatemala, in Pakistan. What good is the U.N. if it can't do that? But what is worse is its gradual encroachment upon the sovereignty of our nation. Insidious forces working within the U.N. have helped it to grow so that it threatens the very independence and existence of the U.S.

8. It is clear that U.S. District Judge Luther W. Youngdahl, who some months ago dismissed four counts in the Government's original indictment of Professor Lattimore, is prejudiced in favor of the defendant and holds a fixed opinion of his innocence, and should therefore voluntarily disqualify himself from the case when the new indictment is brought up, as it will be in the near future. For his decision shows that his bias will prevent him from conducting a fair trial of Professor Lattimore's guilt.

9. To judge a poem, we must look for the intention of the author. How can you tell whether it is good or not unless you know what the author intended? We must know the extent to which he was able to carry out what he proposed to do; that is the measure of his success and his skill. When we cannot tell from the poem itself exactly what was the intention, we must go beyond and back of it, to the writer himself—to study his letters, diaries, and notebooks, in order to discover what he had in mind. But of course we must use these methods very carefully. Authors sometimes change their minds while they are writing, and have been known to forget their original intention. When we speak of "intention," what we are really after is the author's intention *just at the moment he wrote the poem*, not before or after. And of course the best evidence for this lies in the poem itself.

10. Although our great Administration has been working hard, the Calamity Janes, Dismal Desmonds, and other defeatists and knockers have been saying we were in a horrible Recession that would soon swallow us up. All the time they were talking, the facts and figures showed that there was no Recession at all—they made it up out of whole cloth to discredit us. The truth is we were in a *dynamic doldrums*—that is, the overall level of business was excellent by almost any standard, though economic barometers were static or moving slightly downward. But this is only one of the ways our opponents have distorted and misrepresented the truth. They refuse to give us any credit for what we have done. Here we have been threatened with a serious economic situation, calling for action, and the Administration has taken prompt and effective measures to turn back the tide.

4

Some Ways of Words

When you approach a discourse with practical purposes in mind, you want to understand what it asserts, if anything, and whether the assertions are backed up by good reasons. The task of interpretation evidently comes first, for unless you know *what* the conclusions and the reasons are, you can't know whether they are acceptable ones. But it happens all too often that we think an argument is a good one because we don't see clearly what the argument *is*. If we had been a little more careful and patient in interpreting it, we would never have been misled.

Of course the problem of interpretation—that is, discovering what a discourse means—arises for any discourse that isn't fairly simple and instantly plain. Thus the principles of interpretation that will be discussed in this and the following chapters apply to discourses of all sorts—not only to editorials and articles, and speeches in the *Congressional Record*. For dealing with the finest subleties of rich and highly condensed poetry, the tools we shall provide need more sharpening than we shall give them, but they will be sharp enough for most ordinary practical purposes.

When we interpret a discourse we must always keep in mind that words, like grocery stores and buses, are objects (sounds or marks on paper) that get their importance from the way they function in a social setting, that is, in the endlessly varied ways in which people act toward, and together with, each other: building, quarreling, trading, helping, scheming, or making love. When a word, or phrase, or sentence is uttered, it is always part of a human situation and has some relation to the concerns and interests of the people involved. Hence, when we try to interpret an utterance of any sort, we may find that the *circumstances* under which it is uttered afford clues that help us to understand its meaning. It may be that we must know, or would be helped by knowing, who the speaker is, where he is speaking, what he does for a living, or what is going on in the world about him.

Now, there is a good deal of difference between one discourse and another as regards the amount you need to know about the author (or speaker) and his social and economic and political situation in order to interpret the discourse. A thrifty telegram offers very little information to someone who does not know who sent it and what previous message it replies to. A passage studded with words like "here," "yesterday," "on this occasion," and "the institution which I have the honor to represent" clearly depends on a good deal of knowledge about the circumstances if it is to be fully understood. On the other hand, you can read Euclid's *Elements* or a lyric poem by Sappho even if you know nothing, or almost nothing, about these authors or when they lived.

No doubt when you interpret a discourse you should use all the relevant clues you can lay your hands on. But the discourse itself is the thing to keep your eye on. And in a very large number of cases there aren't many clues outside the discourse. You read an editorial, but you don't know who wrote it (though, of course, you probably have read the news columns for the past few days). You can understand an article written by someone who is only a name to you. You can follow a Congressman's speech even if you have no other evidence about his ulterior motives. And even after you have all the information you can get about the circumstances of the discourse, you still have to *read* it; you have to grasp the meanings of the words and the connections among them.

For this purpose it is essential to know something of the normal behavior of words, and of their occasional misbehavior too. In this chapter we shall make some basic distinctions about words and their meanings, and introduce some useful terms to preserve these distinctions. As we go along, we shall take note of some of the pitfalls that can trip us when we don't keep these distinctions in mind or fail to apply them to what we read or hear. Not that we must learn to go about with a suspicious air, sniffing dubiously at each harmless-looking discourse, supposing that it is guilty until we have proved it innocent. Moreover, analyzing words won't solve all our problems; it won't stop people who *want* to misuse words, and thrive by it, from going ahead. But you can find out whether people *are* misusing words whenever you want to know, and you can also do a great deal to keep yourself from misusing words and thereby confusing other people and yourself.

§17. MEANING AND CONTEXT

One of the fundamental facts about words is that the most useful ones in our language have many meanings. That is partly why they are so useful: they work overtime (but, as we shall see, not for nothing). Think of all the various things we mean by the word "foot" on different occasions: one of the lower extremities of the human body, a measure of verse, the ground about a tree, twelve inches, the floor in front of the stairs. The same is true of nearly every common noun or verb. The editors of *The American College Dictionary,* in their preliminary investigation of words most frequently used, found 55 distinct senses of the word "point" in 1,100 occurrences of the word, and they distinguished 109 different senses of the word "run."

Considering the number of ways of taking a particular word, the task of speaking clearly and being understood would seem pretty hopeless if it were not for another very important fact about language. Though a word may have many senses, these senses can be controlled, up to a point, by the *context* in which the word is used. When we find the word in a particular verbal setting—that is, take it with the words that come before and after it in a discourse—we can usually decide quite definitely which of the many senses of the word is relevant. If a poet says his verse has three feet, it doesn't occur to you that he could mean it's a yard long or is three-legged (unless perhaps you are a critic planning to puncture the poet with a pun about his "limping verse"). The context rules out these maverick senses quite decisively.

We might be puzzled if we read in a newspaper that "in the suicide's pocket the police found a large envelope full of bills." In this sentence, as it stands, the word "bills" can easily be taken in two very different senses. But if the context were expanded so as to read, "The police were surprised to find in the suicide's pocket a large envelope full of bills of various denominations," we should understand that "bills" meant *paper money*, and we might wonder whether it was indeed suicide or accident. Or if the context were expanded differently, so as to read, "The police were surprised to find in the suicide's pocket a large envelope full of unpaid bills," we should understand that "bills" meant *requests for payment of a debt*, and we might wonder whether that explains the suicide.

This is a rather simple illustration of the way in which the context of a word helps to pick out one of its senses and fix that sense. But of course "context" is used broadly here: it may be the rest of a sentence (the *immediate* context), a page, a whole book, or a newspaper file. A "shady street" is one thing; a "shady neighborhood" is something else. The word "strike" means one action on the front page of a paper and another action on the sports page; the words "liberal" and "patriotic" mean certain attitudes in *The New York Times* and mostly different ones in *The Chicago Tribune*. When some time ago a British physicist announced with pleasure that the hydrogen bomb is "safe," his statement caused gasps of surprise; in the technical talk of atomic scientists, "safe" apparently means that it couldn't set off a chain reaction that might destroy the earth itself. This is not the way the man in the street uses the word.

Many common words like "line," "pipe," "base," "stock," and "head," have acquired many serviceable meanings in different occupational contexts—say, in the shoptalk of plumbers, pitchers, or plastic engineers. Think of what the word "wing" means to a birdwatcher, an airman, a stagehand, a general, or an architect. But just because these meanings are so completely distinct—no one can confuse the wing of an airplane with the wing of a house—it is easy to control them by very light contextual pressure. A word or two makes it clear that it is the airman's wing rather than the architect's that is referred to. But when the differences between the senses of a word are slighter and subtler (they may be even more important, however), the most careful management of the context may be required to get and keep one sense in focus. The exact meaning of a word like "middle class" or "evolution" or "justice" may depend upon the whole book in which it appears.

That is why it is often easy to misrepresent what someone has said by quoting some of his remarks out of their context. The words may not, strictly speaking, be *mis*quoted, but their meaning has been changed. The political candidate's promise to obtain peace or balance the budget is echoed and attacked by his opponent—who is careful to leave out the conditions and qualifications that originally surrounded it. Even if a writer is scrupulous enough to put in dots to indicate that something has been left out, he may not be *quite* scrupulous enough to stick to the original meaning. You have seen advertisements of a new play, with a few words from a review. The phrase "... emotional subtlety ... (Bridgeport *Post*)" may be from a sentence that goes: "It has all the emotional subtlety of a barroom brawl." The phrase "... great drama ... (New Haven *Register*)" may be from a sentence that goes: "No doubt it was considered a great drama when it first appeared in 1927, but ..." And this is nothing to what a professional wiretapper can do if he records a telephone conversation and picks out words to rerecord on a new tape.

Representative Wayne L. Hays, a member of the Special House Committee set up by the 83rd Congress to investigate tax-exempt foundations, frequently argued during the committee's hearings that the "research directors" of the committee were willing to make judgments on passages torn out of contexts that might change their meaning considerably. He finally made a dramatic demonstration of this by producing three paragraphs which the associate research director testified were "closely comparable" with, and parallel to, Communist literature that he had read. They were excerpts from two papal encyclicals.

A loose and sloppy writer lays himself open particularly to accidental misquotation, but any writer would find it very hard to write a paragraph that is proof against a deliberate and skillful excerpt-lifter. Dean Sturges of the Yale Law School perhaps came as close as anyone can when, in 1949, the Harvard Law School *Record* asked him for an appropriate comment on the Harvard Law School's decision to admit women students for the first time. Dean Sturges is reported to have sent the following telegram:

YALE LAW FACULTY AND STUDENT BODY DEEPLY MOVED. FEEL IT QUITE POSSIBLE HARVARD MAY MAKE CONTRIBUTION TO WOMANHOOD. DOUBT MANY ADVERSE CONSEQUENCES HARVARD FACULTY OR STUDENT BODY. WE HAVE ALWAYS FOLLOWED WITH GENUINE INTEREST LONG STRUGGLE HARVARD LIBERALS IN THIS MATTER. OUR MANY GENERATIONS OF WOMEN GRADUATES ARE OF COURSE A PRIDE AND JOY. BEST WISHES.

Try digging a quotable compliment out of that.

The importance of context in the interpretation of meaning varies from one discourse to another. In a technical article on mathematics or physics, most sentences can stand pretty much on their own feet and be well understood apart from their context. Scientific terms are designed to resist the influence of context so that they can pass from one context to another without changing their meaning. But sentences in ordinary discourse that contain pronouns often lean on other sentences that contain the antecedents of those pronouns. Moreover, some words in our language—and they are among the most useful, but the trickiest, ones—are so adaptable to their context, like chameleons, that they take most of their character from it, and when they are considered apart from any context, they have only the most indefinite meaning. Words like "efficient," "dangerous," "internal," "successful," "free," tell us very little unless we are told, for example, the *purpose* for which it is efficient, or the *standards* in terms of which the success is judged. Contexts like "freehanded," "free lunch," "free love," "free will," "freeborn," "free association," help to limit the word "free" to a somewhat more definite range of meaning, but even in such cases we often feel that we don't know exactly what the word "free" means unless the context provides answers to the questions: "Free *from* what?" "Free *for* what?" "Free *to do* what?"

Another thing that shows the importance of context is the fact that when people use the wrong word we sometimes know what word should have been used. When Mrs. Malaprop says, "I would by no means wish a daughter of mine to be a progeny of learning . . . I would have her instructed in geometry, that she might know something of the contagious countries," we understand what she thought she was saying because the context so clearly tells us what words are called for if the sentences are to make sense. A malapropism is a word that is wrongly used in a sentence in place of another word that sounds somewhat like it. And if we couldn't tell from the context what the appropriate word would be, we could never recognize a malapropism.

But of course it would be a mistake to overemphasize contextual influence and say that a word *never* has the same meaning in two different contexts. If this were true, language would be even more difficult to manage than it is now. A person who says, "I believe in the dictionary" and later "I believe in the Bible" is presumably using the word "believe" in the same sense in both contexts. Perhaps sometimes when we say that a word is used twice in the same sense we ignore slight differences that could be important for one purpose or another. It is a good idea to keep in mind that a change in context *may* make a change in the sense, but it doesn't seem that it *must*. In the present paragraph the word "context" has, up to this point, been used three times, in three slightly different (immediate) contexts; but it has about the same meaning each time.

It is only when the context is considerably different that the meaning is likely to change. A person who says, "I believe in the dictionary," and, later, "I don't believe in ghosts," is using the word "believe" in two very different senses. But in each of these contexts it can have only one possible meaning, and when the whole context is taken into account there *may* be no question what that meaning is. "I believe in a federal world government" means about the same as "I believe *there should be* a federal world government." "I believe in extrasensory perception" means about the same as "I believe *there is such a thing as* extrasensory perception." "I believe in woman's intuition" means about the same as "I believe *that some of the things that* women intuit *are true.*"

When a word can have different meanings in different kinds of context, we can say that it has **variable meaning.** Its meaning *varies*, and it therefore has a variety of senses when it appears in the dictionary. Some words are more variable than others. But the variable meaning of words doesn't ordinarily give us any trouble so long as there is enough contextual control. The trouble arises when the context is not complete enough to rule out all but one possible meaning. If I say, "Henry rents the house," there is no way for you to tell from the sentence itself whether Henry rents the house *from* someone or *to* someone. When a word can have one (but not both) of two (or more) meanings in a certain context, we shall say that the word is **ambiguous** *in that context.*

The ambiguity of a word is always relative to a context: no word is ambiguous *in itself*. Some words like "freedom," "religion," "democracy," are ambiguous in quite a few contexts, and that is why you have to be careful in interpreting and in using them. Sometimes such words are said to be "meaningless," but the trouble with them is just the opposite: they have so many subtly different meanings that it takes a good deal of skill—more than most writers command—to keep their meanings well under control. And when the writer fails in this task, it is up to the reader. Other words, such as the common nouns, are variable in meaning but are hardly ever ambiguous. It takes a good deal of ingenuity to write a medium-sized sentence in which the word "foot" is ambiguous.

A case of ambiguity, as we have defined it, is a case where there is some *doubt* about the way a discourse is to be interpreted, and you have to choose between alternative readings. Unfortunately, this is not the way the word "ambiguity" is always used. When A. E. Housman, in his poem "To an Athlete Dying Young," writes,

> Home they brought him, shoulder high,
> Townsman of a stiller town,

the word "town" has at least two meanings: the young man's village is quieter for the funeral than it was on the day everyone cheered his victory, and also he is now among the noiseless dead. But "town" is not ambiguous here. It has *both* meanings at once, and there is no uncertainty about them at all.

This sort of double meaning, or **multiple meaning** as it may be called, is also characteristic of one type of pun. There is the old pun, for example, about the two women leaning out of their windows across an alley and shouting at each other angrily: they can never come to an agreement because they are arguing from different premises. Another type of pun is built on *homonyms*, that is, words that have the same sound but different senses ("boy," "buoy"; "recede," "reseed"; "bier," "beer"; "air," "heir"). If you want to call homonyms the same word because they have the same sound, you would then have to say that such words have an even more variable meaning than we supposed. On the whole, we may as well call them different words if they are spelt differently, and then we shall not need to say any more about homonyms, except to note that they can give rise to the sort of pun made by Macbeth when he says he will plant circumstantial evidence on the grooms:

> "If he do bleed,
> I'll *gild* the faces of the grooms withal,
> For it must seem their *guilt*."

This sort of double entendre, whether in pun or poem, is sometimes called "ambiguity," but it is a very different thing from ambiguity in the sense in which we are using the term. The distinction can be clarified by means of some terms that come up later (in

Chapter 6). The important thing at the moment is to note that there is a difference. The high-pressure context of a poem can squeeze many senses, all at once, out of some of its words; this is the multiple meaning of poetic discourse. But we have ambiguity, in the strict sense, when the context is too loose and flabby to hold the words steadily to *any* definite sense. The poet has managed to say several things at once; the ambiguous writer has not quite succeeded in saying anything.

A CHECK-UP QUIZ. Consider carefully each of the following pairs of sentences. Does the italicized word or phrase have the *same* meaning, or a *different* meaning, in both sentences in the pair?

1. (a) All *men* are created equal.
   (b) The industry made a practice of hiring only *men*.

2. (a) The proper study of mankind is *man*.
   (b) *Man* is the only animal that laughs.

3. (a) Officers and *men* traveled on the same ship.
   (b) Peace on earth, good will to *men*.

4. (a) He told me his *plans* for the future.
   (b) He showed me the *plans* for his new house.

5. (a) The *construction* of the house has already begun.
   (b) He goes up every day to see how the *construction* is coming along.

6. (a) I have some *money* in my pocket.
   (b) It takes *money* to build a house.

7. (a) I *believe in* life after death.
   (b) I *believe in* water fluoridation.

8. (a) I don't *believe in* coddling children.
   (b) I don't *believe in* having long engagements.

9. (a) I don't *believe in* child labor.
   (b) I don't *believe in* sea monsters.

10. (a) I *believe in* the Gallup poll.
    (b) I *believe in* Santa Claus.

FURTHER READING: Simeon Potter, *Our Language*. Penguin Books, 1950, chs. 7, 9. Charlton Laird, *The Miracle of Language*. Cleveland and New York: The World Publishing Co., 1953, especially ch. 4. Hugh R. Walpole, *Semantics*. New York: W. W. Norton, Inc., 1941, chs. 1, 5.

§18. THE TWO TYPES OF AMBIGUITY

When you notice that a discourse contains an ambiguity, you have made an important discovery about it. But that is still an early step in critical reading. For if there are two meanings, the next thing is to find out what the two meanings are. Maybe the word only *seems* ambiguous, and when you distinguish the two senses clearly you find that there is, after all, something in the context, or perhaps in the circumstances surrounding the discourse, that rules out one of the possible senses. If there really *is* no way to decide on a single sense, at least you know which are the possible ones.

To explore ambiguity further, to distinguish its two basic types, and to show how it can be dealt with by readers and writers, we shall need a pair of useful terms. A word can be considered from two points of view: we can speak of its relationship to the things in the world or of its relationship to other words. When we say that a word *means* something, we are saying that it refers to something beyond itself: this is the **semantical** aspect of the word. So far, in this chapter, it is this semantical aspect of words that we have been talking about. But we also speak of the grammatical properties of the word, as when we say that it is a noun or adverb, or that it is a transitive or intransitive verb, or that it occurs as a direct or indirect object in a certain sentence. This is the **syntactical** aspect of the word.

Every word in a language has both a semantical and a syntactical aspect, and there is no difficulty about distinguishing them. For example, when we say that the word "kudos" means a combination of praise and acclaim, we are talking about its semantical aspect; when we say that it is a singular (not plural) noun, we are talking about its syntactical aspect.

We can be in doubt about either of these aspects of a word, and so there is semantical ambiguity (or ambiguity of reference) and there is syntactical ambiguity (or ambiguity of syntactical construction).

A word is **semantically ambiguous** in a certain context if it can have more than one meaning in that context. When the possible meanings are very different, the ambiguity is easy to detect and is likely to be silly. "Authorities are puzzled by the case of whisky left in front of the Center Church last night. No one has turned up to claim it, but Chief Brockton is working on the case." The difference between a *case of whiskey* and a *police case* is too great to lead to any confusion. When the meanings are closer they are harder to distinguish, though the difference may be no less important. When we read that someone's testimony confirmed a cabinet official's statement, the context may not make it clear whether "confirm" here means (as it can) *prove conclusively* or only *provide further evidence for*. Conversely, when the newspaper reports that "Mr. Jones refuted the Secretary's statement," "refuted" may mean *disproved*, or only *denied*—which is quite a different thing.

A *sentence* may be said to be ambiguous if it contains either a semantically ambiguous *word* or a syntactically ambiguous phrase or clause.

A phrase or clause is **syntactically ambiguous** if its parts are not clearly and definitely fitted together; if, in other words, there is more than one way of interpreting the grammatical relationships between the words. This can happen in several ways. For example, there are relative pronouns with more than one available antecedent: "A moment after Mrs. Birchard christened the ship, she was afloat on the river." There are misplaced modifiers: "The house was built as a present for Mrs. Driscoll, who married Dr. Driscoll in 1946, at a cost of $50,000." There are colloquial short cuts of speech, that is, elliptical constructions: "Henry liked pudding better than his wife." Or, "Feed a cold and starve a fever," which can mean that *if* you feed a cold you'll find yourself starving a fever, but which can also mean (and is sometimes thought to mean) that you *should* eat heartily when you have a cold.

There are certain adverbs that often cause syntactical ambiguity by turning up at just that point in a sentence where their function is uncertain. "Businessmen who are afraid to take risks frequently lose out to their competitors" is ambiguous because "frequently" can modify either "take" or "lose." "Employees only may use the service elevators" can be read as "*Only* employees may use the service elevators" or as "Employees may use *only* the service elevators." The distinction between a restrictive and a nonrestrictive clause is usually marked by a comma, but if the sentence is set up in such a way that there has to be a comma anyway, then we can't tell whether the clause is restrictive or nonrestrictive. If a man writes in his will, "I leave my money to be divided among my servants, and also among my relatives, who have visited me during my final illness," he may be taken to mean (1) that his relatives have in fact visited him or (2) that the money is to go only to the relatives who have. Another sort of syntactical ambiguity turns up in enumerations that are mingled with fuller identifications. If "Those present were the Assistant Director of the Budget, Morgan MacGruder, and William Carmichael," you can't tell whether there were three people or only two.

Though an ingenious quibbler can discover ambiguity in the most unlikely places, we need not, for practical purposes, bother to count a sentence as ambiguous when one of the possible senses is so absurd that it would never occur to anyone to take that as the *only* sense. Everyone, at first glance, would understand that the phrase "square dance records" means *square-dance records*, not *square dance-records*, for whoever heard of a square record? Thus "square dance records" isn't really syntactically ambiguous, though "Russian dance records" might be *records of Russian dances* or *Russian records of dances* Again, in "square dance records," the word "records" clearly means *recordings*: square dance records are not *documents that record the history of various square dances*, though in the sentence, "The library keeps its irreplaceable records in a special vault," "records" *might* be semantically ambiguous.

The best way to decide whether the ambiguity of a sentence is semantical or syntactical is to examine its syntax first. You ask such questions as: Is there any word that could be either of two different parts of speech? Is there a pronoun with a doubtful antecedent? Is there a modifier that could modify either of two different words? If you can find any of these types of wobbly syntax, the sentence is syntactically ambiguous. And you can clear up the syntactical ambiguity by rewriting the sentence in two different ways. "Henry liked pudding better than his wife *did*" and "Henry liked pudding better than *he liked* his wife" are no longer ambiguous.

After you are sure that the syntax of a sentence is straight, you are ready to examine the individual words. And there are two methods of clearing up semantical ambiguity: (1) filling out the sentence in two different ways so that the context controls the sense, or (2) substituting two different words or phrases for the ambiguous one. The first method gives you: "Chief Brockton is working on the case of whiskey" and "Chief Brockton is working on the mysterious case of the abandoned whiskey." "Case" is not ambiguous in either of these statements. The second way gives you: "Chief Brockton is trying to drink all the whiskey" and "Chief Brockton is trying to solve the mystery."

A sentence *can* have both kinds of ambiguity at once, though perhaps such sentences are not very common. Suppose someone said, "We read about the Johnsons' new baby in the evening paper, a few hours after it was delivered." The pronoun "it" has two possible antecedents (syntactical ambiguity), and the word "delivered" has two possible senses (semantical ambiguity). But in this example, the semantical ambiguity disappears as soon as the syntax is cleared up to show whether "it" is the paper or the baby. The important point about the distinction between the two kinds of ambiguity is not to become expert at deciding exactly which is which in every case; it is to help you keep in mind the right questions to ask about any discourse that might be dangerously ambiguous.

The trouble with ambiguity is that it may disrupt communication without either party knowing that communication has broken down. If two people on the long-distance telephone *know* that they aren't understanding each other, they can wait until the circuit is improved. But if they *don't* know it, the consequences can be serious. When a message can be interpreted in two different ways, the sender may interpret it one way, without realizing that it has another meaning, and the receiver may interpret it the other way, without realizing that it could have the first meaning as well. A news story reporting a new medicine to alleviate ulcers may be headlined:

DUODENAL ULCER
DRUG ON MARKET

The reader may think: What's news about that? Naturally ulcers are a drug on the market. But what is silly in this case becomes pretty serious when the discourse involved is a military order, a business agreement, a diplomatic report, a mail-order catalogue, or a love letter.

As an example, take the Constitution of the United States. In Section 8 of Article 1, it says that "Congress shall have power ... to regulate commerce with foreign nations, and among the several states ..." What does "among" mean? The traditional interpretation has been that "among" means *between*, and on this interpretation Congress has had the power to regulate interstate, but not intrastate, commerce. This interpretation has in recent years been challenged by serious and impressive arguments. "Among" can also mean *between and within,* and there is evidence that in fact the framers of the Constitution wanted it to have this broader sense. The same sort of question has been raised about the word "commerce," which apparently was used in a much broader way in the 18th century than today. You can see that a good deal hinges on the meanings of these words.

It is useful to think of an ambiguous statement as being not *one,* but *several* statements—one for each of its possible meanings. A statement, as we have already defined it, is either true or false; it is convenient also to restrict the term "statement" so that a statement cannot be *both* true and false. An ambiguous statement *could* be both true and false, true in one sense and false in the other. Instead of speaking in this confusing way, however, we shall simply say that when a statement is ambiguous it could be *this* statement or *that* one; if it is this, then it is true, and if it is that, it is false. In a similar way, we shall say that an ambiguous *question* is really two questions, for it may have two different answers. Can a man be in two places at the same time? Yes and No. If "same time" means *simultaneously,* the answer is No. If "same time" means *at moments having the same name,* the answer is Yes: he can be at two places at 12:00 noon on July 4, 1955, if one is a city on daylight saving time and the other is a nearby village on standard time; or if he crosses the International Date Line in between.

It is a peculiarity of ambiguous statements, then, that we do not know whether they are true or false until we get rid of the ambiguity. If such a statement appears as the conclusion of an argument, we really have not one, but two or more conclusions. We must separate them from each other before we can decide which of them, if any, is well supported by the reasons given. And if the ambiguous statement appears as the reason in an argument, the same problem arises: we can't find out what the reason is *good for* until we know exactly what the reason *is.*

As a reader, then, your weapon against ambiguity is always to *distinguish.* Ambiguity paralyzes or befuddles our thinking only so long as we don't spot it or can't discern the relevant senses. But for clear thinking you shouldn't be satisfied merely to protect yourself against *other* people's slippery meanings: you can fool yourself just as well as they can fool you. That's why you have to apply to your own writing (when you read it over) the same principles you apply to other discourses: you check to see whether it is ambiguous, and if it is, you pin down the meaning you really want so that your reader can't mistake it.

The best help in avoiding *syntactical* ambiguity is a good grasp of some parts of grammar. This is not to say that violating the rules of grammar always leads to ambiguity. "I is hungry" is no more ambiguous than "I am hungry"; to use a verb in the wrong person or number is not ordinarily a mistake in thinking. There is a *conventional* element in grammar; some rules of grammar rest upon a sort of arbitrary tacit agreement to put words together in certain ways, and other rules might have done as well.

Nevertheless, it is important to realize that many of the conventions of grammar—even some of the ones it seems safe to disobey occasionally—are themselves based on the conditions of clear thinking and communication. They may be compared with the "rules of the road" that govern the flow of traffic. It is a matter of convention that we drive on the right side of the road rather than on the left side as is done in England. Given cars with a right-hand drive, the British convention is just as good as ours, and no doubt we could get as accustomed to it as we are to our own. But it is *not* just a matter of convention that everyone should drive on the *same* side of the road: it is a matter of the greatest importance.

In the same way, it is a matter of convention that we require nonrestrictive clauses to be set off by commas and leave restrictive clauses without commas. We might have done it the other way. But it is plainly a great advantage to have *some* rule about clauses; wherever it is followed, one sort of syntactical ambiguity is eliminated. It is true that 18th century writers had no such rule, and generally used commas for all clauses, but that doesn't mean they got along as well without it: some of their sentences are incurably ambiguous because there is no way of knowing whether the clauses are restrictive or nonrestrictive.

Thus it is a matter of convention, if you like, that we normally put the verb between the subject and the object, and say "I saw him" instead of "I him saw," as in German. But it is *not* a matter of convention that we *have* a convention. And though languages differ enormously in their working rules, we are all born into a language that is already a going concern, and to communicate, so we can cooperate, with others, we have to get some grip on its working conventions. The principal points to keep in mind, as far as syntactical ambiguity is concerned, are these: (1) Put all modifiers as close as you can to the words they are to modify, and keep them away from other words you don't want them to modify. Instead of "Jane only lets John kiss her," put the "only" where it belongs: say, in front of "Jane," or in front of "John." (2) Use commas to keep parallel parts of a sentence in order, and to set off interpolations (like "I think") within a clause. Instead of, "He robbed banks and served terms in jail for many years," make it clear whether "many years" covers the bank robbing or only the time spent in jail. (3) Don't take grammatical short cuts unless you know the way: make sure your context will guide the reader to fill in just the words you left out, not a quite different set. Instead of "Somebody loves everybody," write "There is at least one person who loves everybody else," or "Everybody is loved by at least one other person." This last example is a hard one; if you can manage this, you have little to worry about.

There are two general ways of guarding against *semantical* ambiguity. One way is to build up the context by adding a qualifying phrase or by supplying examples of what you have in mind, so that the word with a tendency toward sideslipping is always under firm control. When you get on really familiar terms with a word, you become sensitive to the ways it is likely to be affected by certain contexts, and it will have a hard time slipping away from you. The other way is to stiffen the word, so to speak, by holding it explicitly to a single sense: you do this by providing a *definition* of it. But that is the subject of the next chapter.

A CHECK-UP QUIZ. Which of these sentences are *semantically* ambiguous, and which are *syntactically* ambiguous?

1. The gorilla is more like a man than a chimpanzee.
2. No one in the family cared for the white mice.
3. He said, saddle me the ass. And they saddled him.
4. The boat was fast.
5. Advertisement: "PET HOSPITAL. Dogs called for, bathed, fleas removed, and returned to you for $1.00."
6. SISTERS MARRIED BROTHERS;
   HAVE BABY SAME DAY
7. She is a rather common type.
8. Advertisement: "Why ruin your hair with an amateur home

permanent, when it can be done for $5 by professionals at the Venus Beauty Parlor?"

9. The next issue will be devoted to criticism of recent novels.

10. The photographer dusted the table.

See also Exercises 16 and 17, pp. 182-83.

FURTHER READING: A. M. Frye and A. W. Levi, *Rational Belief*. New York: Harcourt, Brace and Co., 1941, ch. 5. L. M. Myers, *American English*. New York: Prentice-Hall, Inc., 1952, chs. 15, 16, 19. M. M. Bryant and J. R. Aiken, *Psychology of English*. New York: Columbia University Press, 1940, chs. 19, 20.

§19. VAGUENESS

A statement is either true or false; it can't be half-and-half. (A "half-truth" is false.) And an object is either an airplane or it is not; it can't be more or less an airplane. "True" and "airplane" are *either-or* words, but many other words in our language are not either-or words, but *more-or-less* words. A piece of bread can be more or less stale, an argument more or less convincing, a person more or less rich, tired, or bald. These words refer to qualities that vary in degree or amount. They are terms of comparison, or *comparative terms*. Under this label we shall include all words about which it makes sense to ask: How much? or How many? You can ask, "How rich is the Aga Khan?" or "How stale is the bread?" You can't ask, "How airplane is this object?" and when people ask, as they occasionally do, "How true is this statement?" this seems to be a loose colloquial way of asking, not how *true* it is, but how much *evidence* there is for it—which is quite a different thing.

Most of our common comparative terms are also used to classify things. We speak of bread as being more or less stale; but also, in terms of its degree of staleness, we divide bread into *stale* bread and *fresh* bread. If a person is rich enough, we call him "rich," and make a threefold division here between the rich, the poor, and the ones who are neither. If a person loses enough hair, we call him "bald"; if a tire loses enough air, we call it "flat"; and if a driver has enough accidents, we call him "unsafe."

The word "enough" is a key word here, for it leads us to ask questions like this: Exactly *how* dry must bread be in order to be stale? How much money must a man have in order to be rich? How many hairs must a man lose in order to be bald? How many accidents must a driver have, and how serious must they be, if he is to be considered unsafe?

* These are all natural questions, and the important point about language that we want to be clear about here is just that *they have no answers*. We have never come to any agreement, tacit or explicit, about these words; there is simply no general rule according to which anyone with less than 196 hairs is bald, or anyone with more than $17,412.35 is rich. How old is middle-aged? Where does red leave off and orange begin? How cold is a cold shoulder? We have never drawn a line at any particular place, and so there is no definite line: this is what we mean when we say that a word is *vague*.

A vague word refers to a certain range of variation in intensity or quantity. Think of a sort of scale, ranging, say, from people with no money to the person who has the most, or from people with no hair to people with bushy tresses, or from bread right out of the oven to bread that has been around for months. In the case of a vague word, there is always a certain part of the scale to which the word definitely, and by universal agreement, applies: anyone who has twenty millions is surely rich, anyone with nothing but a slight fringe of hair is bald, and bread that has begun to mold is definitely stale. Moreover, there is always a certain part of the scale to which the word definitely does *not* apply: a person with only forty-five dollars is *not* rich; a person with hair covering the top of his head is certainly *not* bald; and bread that is only an hour old is *not* stale.

But in between these two parts of the scale there is a *doubtful area* where we have not decided whether to apply the word or not. There will be borderline savings accounts, heads of hair, and loaves of bread that you can describe either way, just as there are people you don't know whether to call "middle-aged" or not. If the word were *precise*, it would be defined so as to draw a sharp line. It is just the nature of a vague word that the line it draws is fuzzy.

As you can see, vagueness is a very different sort of thing from ambiguity. In ambiguity you have a choice between two distinct senses of a word, which may be as unrelated as plane geometry and marital disorders (as in two senses of "triangle"), only there is no way to decide how to choose. In vagueness, you know what the sense is all right, but you don't know *how much* there is of the quality referred to. Thus a word that has several meanings may be vague in some senses but not in others (compare "cold war" and "cold shoulder," "hot jazz" and "hot air"). And even when there is no question about the sense of a word, its doubtful area may shift from context to context. A large child is not the same as a large elephant; in both of these contexts the word is vague, but the doubtful area for children would be in pounds, and for elephants in hundreds of pounds. Compare "hot day," "hot bath," "hot oven" and "hot star." In each of these contexts "hot" means a different degree of temperature, and some of these "hot"s are fuzzier than others: "It's a hot day" is very loosely used, but when the cook book advises a "hot oven" for popovers, this has a pretty definite agreed-upon meaning.

So far, we have defined the word "vague" in such a way that only comparative terms are vague. But it is useful to broaden this a little further. Some words that are not comparative words themselves are defined in terms of other words that *are* comparative words. "Explosion" means "a rapid combustion"; thus, so long as there is no general rule that specifies *how* rapid a combustion must be before it is to be called an explosion, the word "explosion" is vague in *one* respect. Similarly, "democracy," in some of its senses, is vague in some respects. When you want to know whether a given word is vague, then, ask yourself, first, whether there is any question of *degree* involved in applying the word, and second, whether the degree involved is anywhere precisely specified.

It is important to realize that vague words can be very useful. In fact, some of them are useful *because* they are vague: it is handy to be able to report that the room was "crowded," without having to calculate the number of people per square foot; it is equally handy for us to be able to speak of the "context" of a word, without having to specify exactly and for all cases exactly how many words before and after a given word we shall include in its context. As for most other vague words, if we haven't bothered to make them precise it may be simply that we haven't needed to do so. A vague word is useful so long as it marks *some* distinction: that is, as long as we can point out something to which the word surely applies (the New England town meeting is definitely a democracy, in one sense of this word) and something to which the word surely does not apply (the Franco government in Spain is definitely *not* a democracy, in the same sense of this word).

Or take another example. The words "good taste" and "bad taste" are vague: how bad does taste have to be before it is "bad"? When the Senate Judiciary Subcommittee on Juvenile Delinquency was investigating comic books, in the spring of 1954, it was struck by a comic book whose cover showed a man with a bloody axe in one hand, holding up a severed woman's head in the other. The publisher of this comic book, who was testifying, cited it as an example of "good taste." Senator Kefauver, somewhat taken aback, asked the logically correct question to discover whether the publisher really meant anything by this description: how would the cover have to look if it were in *bad* taste? "It would be in bad taste," replied the publisher, "if the head were held a little higher, with the blood dripping out." This showed that he was drawing *some* line, though perhaps a rather odd one, and hence that "good taste" at least meant *something* to him.

Vague words get us into trouble only when we don't notice that they are vague. We expect too much of them, and they let us down. We think there must be a sharp line between "neutrality" and "involvement," when in fact there is just a blurry no man's land. Sheep and goats, chairs and tables, males and females can be separated from each other in a way that will satisfy nearly everyone, for these words have highly determinate meanings. Moreover, nature and human workmanship have provided us with easily distinguishable things instead of borderline cases. But two heads of hair may differ by a single hair, two bank accounts by less than a dollar, and the ages of two people by a few minutes. In such cases, there will be heads of hair, bank accounts, and people's ages that we won't have any generally agreed upon way of describing.

And this is why it is essential for words to be reasonably precise when questions of truth and falsity arise. The main counts of the Government's indictment of Professor Owen Lattimore accused him of "following the Communist line" and being a "promoter of Communist interests." These counts were thrown out by the Court of Appeals on the ground of vagueness, in keeping with the Sixth Amendment, which specifies that a person has a right to know what crime he is accused of before he can be tried. If the words used to describe the crime are not clear, how can he know what he is being tried for, and how can he defend himself? And how can the jury be expected to decide objectively whether he is guilty of it or not?

But of course, no matter how vague a word may be, we can always make it as precise as we wish for particular purposes and in particular contexts. We *can* draw a sharp line when we want to. A herring is a large sardine; that is a vague way of talking. For its convenience, however, the Food and Drug Administration calls a sardine a "herring" only when it is at least nine inches long. That is fairly precise. In common speech, the words "urban" and "rural" are vague. But the United States Census makes a sharper distinction: if a town has a population of 2,500 or more it is "urban," if not, it is "rural." "High-income group" is vague, but Congress, in a particular act, may arbitrarily draw the line at $25,000. This is a perfectly sensible procedure. Of course, it will always sound odd to say that a person making $25,000 a year is in a "high-income group," whereas a person making $24,999.99 is not. But you have to draw the line *somewhere* if you draw it at all. Where the scale is in terms of pennies, any particular place to draw the line will seem arbitrary.

Sometimes the line drawn may, in fact, be *too* arbitrary for the purpose at hand. If a great deal hinges on the distinction, it may be more than the such a slight difference will bear. It doesn't seem fair to pass a student who gets 60 and fail a student who gets 59; we don't feel sure enough about the accuracy of tests and grades to make such an important result depend upon such a minute difference. This is why some educators prefer to use a vaguer scale, such as A, B, C, or Pass, High Pass, Honors, for grading students. Precision is always relative to what we want to do with it. Unnecessary precision is pedantic and fussy, like honing a razor to cut butter. Still, to develop skill in careful thinking, it is sometimes useful to practice a little pedantry. If you know how to make precise distinctions, you are free to decide, in a given case, just how far you ought to go. Each case is different, and only by studying it carefully can you determine what degree of vagueness is probably safe and perhaps desirable.

We would have little trouble in handling vague words, once we understood their habits, if it were not for one ingenious way of misusing them that may impose upon our thinking when we are off guard. It consists in arguing that there is no difference, or no important difference, between two things because the apparent difference is made up of a whole series of small differences. It doesn't matter much whether you smoke ten cigarettes a day or eleven, it doesn't matter much whether you smoke eleven or twelve, and so on. Someone might argue that therefore it doesn't matter whether you smoke ten or forty:

there is no difference between heavy smoking and light smoking because any attempt to draw the line, say between thirteen and fourteen, is arbitrary. The amount of freedom you enjoy in one country only differs in degree from the amount of freedom you enjoy in another country; sometimes people argue that since it is only a difference of degree, it is therefore not much of a difference at all: "they are both about the same."

This sort of argument commits the **black-or-white fallacy.** It is a subtle attempt to paralyze choice by belittling an important difference. It is especially plausible when the distinctions are vague. The prefix "crypto-" has in recent years been used to great advantage in muddling people's thinking about political attitudes. As it is sometimes loosely used, a man can apparently be a disguised, or "crypto-" Communist without knowing it, or, indeed, without doing anything about it. According to this line of thought, a Democrat is a "crypto-liberal," a liberal is a "crypto-socialist," a socialist is a "crypto-communist," and a communist is a traitor; therefore Democrats are traitors, or practically traitors. When put in such a bare form, without any fancy trimmings, this argument doesn't look as though it would fool anyone. But it has been a staple commodity with some rabble rousers, who have done their best to make it appear that there is no important difference between both ends of their equation.

The same method of reasoning sometimes turns up in discussions of the degree of economic difficulty the United States economy may be undergoing at a certain time. There is "inventory correction," "rolling adjustment," "recession," and "depression," and (because the black-or-white fallacy works both ways) there may be an attempt to play down the differences by those who want to show that current troubles are *worse* than they really are (hardly distinguishable from a small depression) and at the same time by those who want to show that current troubles are *not as bad* as they really are (merely a sizeable inventory correction). The only way to get a proper perspective on the situation, and escape both fallacious arguments, is to insist on some definite distinctions between these various ills. For example, let's not call it a depression unless it involves a downward movement on the part of nearly every economic index, and unemployment of at least five million over a period of at least two years. If that seems *too* fine a line, it is easy enough to relax it. But at least we can keep the discussion from bogging down in a mushy terminology like "crypto-depression."

The black-or-white argument is a favorite with extremists, who are blind to the differences between shades of gray because to them the only "real" difference is between black and white. On a scale of cigarette smoking or civil liberty the *big* differences are made up of many *small* differences, but that doesn't make the big difference any less big. There are differences in *kind* and there are differences in *degree*, but some differences in degree are, from a practical point of view, just as crucial as differences in kind. We succeed only in drugging our thinking when we allow these differences to be smudged over by verbal trickery.

A CHECK-UP QUIZ. Which of the following arguments commit the *Black-or-White Fallacy?*

1. If we were to lower the tariff barriers and let foreign countries, with their lower wages, undersell some of our essential industries, they would gradually be driven out of business. Then we would become dependent on other countries for these goods, and, if war came, we would be that much weaker.

2. As far as the American Indians are concerned, the problem is hopeless. Even if we helped them preserve their tribal ways, we could not do it *forever*. Even if we give them more freedom, they will still be largely ignorant. Even if we help them go to schools, they will still not have jobs. Even if we help them get jobs, they will be discriminated against by their neighbors. Obviously there is no use whatever in trying to do *anything* for them.

3. It is my opinion that we have gone far enough in exploring the secrets of nature, but we are still desperately ignorant of ourselves. Step by step our natural scientists have pushed back the barriers, distinguishing and classifying the elements, analyzing distant stars, peering into the nucleus of the atom, and explaining the workings of living matter. But our social scientists have only begun to understand human behavior and its laws.

4. Yes indeed, I am against the United States Post Office. It's the thin edge of socialism. If the Government is in the business of carrying mail, then why not electric power? Then it's only a short step to owning telephone and telegraph lines; next, steel mills and coal mines—until everything is swallowed up in creeping socialism. There's no logical stopping place once you start; the

only thing to do is keep the Government completely out of everything.

5. Those who support the Committee's proposal are sincere but misguided. We must continue to govern this convention by majority rule, as we have long done. That is the democratic way. Those who want to change the rule so that we can nominate Presidents and Vice-Presidents only by a two-thirds vote do not realize that this is utterly arbitrary. There is no magic in two-thirds. If you demand a two-thirds rule, why not three-fourths, or seven-eighths? You might as well do what the dictators do, and make everybody vote yes.

6. A: "There are too many billboards cluttering up the scenery. There should be a law to limit them." B: "That would be unjust. If a man has something to sell (and what is so immoral about that?), it is natural that he should put up a sign to let people know. One sign doesn't spoil the scenery and neither will two. If somebody else adds a third, the difference is negligible, and the next man has just as much right as he does; there is no fair place to make them stop."

7. Of course, if we negotiate with our enemies, or potential enemies, we cannot expect to get concessions from them on matters that are important to us unless we are willing to make concessions to them on matters that are less important to us but much desired by them. This is always the problem of negotiation: to make delicate adjustments and bargain effectively. But we must be careful not to concede too much for too little.

8. As Dr. Nicholas Murray Butler said, in a letter to the *Times* on July 15, 1947, "to admit one or more of these distant territories to statehood would be the beginning of the end of our historic United States of America. We should soon be pressed to admit the Phillipine Islands, Cuba and possibly even Australia." He was speaking about the proposal, that keeps turning up in every Congress, to admit Hawaii and Alaska as states. His argument is still crushing and irrefutable. The admission of noncontiguous territories violates the classic pattern of our country, and if we let in Hawaii and Alaska there is no reason why other noncontiguous commonwealths and possessions should not petition for statehood. To be sure, there is the precedent that only incorporated territories have heretofore been admitted as states, but this is not a constitutional provision, and if the precedent of contiguity is abandoned in favor of Hawaii and Alaska, then

Puerto Rico, the Virgin Islands, Guam and Samoa could well maintain that they would be discriminated against if denied statehood. Indeed, it is not at all certain that future petitions for statehood would be confined to areas now under the United States flag.

FURTHER READING: L. Susan Stebbing, *Thinking to Some Purpose*. Pelican Books, 1938, ch. 12.

§20. VERBAL SHIFTS AND DODGES

As we have said, a word with variable meaning has to take its cue from its context if it is not to be ambiguous. When a word appears and reappears in a long discourse, its *immediate* context is constantly changing. In most cases, it will probably keep to the same meaning nevertheless. But its meaning *may* change with the context, even in the same discourse. The closer the senses of the word and the longer the discourse the more smoothly the word shifts from one sense to another, and the more easily the shift escapes notice. A word can change its meaning even in the same sentence: In "Business is business," the first "business" means *buying and selling,* but the second "business" means something like *cutthroat competition*. But there is no danger when the shift is as plain as this.

Now, consider two rather similar bits of reasoning. First:

Every car that my neighbor buys, he turns in after two years.
Today he bought a sedan.
Therefore: in two years he will turn in a sedan.

We would all agree that this is a sound deductive inference: if the premises are true, the conclusion has to follow. But compare the second one:

Every car that my neighbor buys, he turns in after two years.
Today he bought a new car.
Therefore: in two years he will turn in a new car.

In this example, the premises might be true, but the conclusion is obviously false. Yet the two arguments are exactly the same except that one contains the word "sedan" and the other contains the phrase "new car." Apparently the word "new" doesn't behave like the word "sedan."

It isn't hard to see what has gone wrong. "New" is an elliptical word with an implicit reference to a certain time: it always means *new at such-and-such* a time, and the time referred to has to be supplied by the context. So in the second premise, "Today he bought a new car," "new" has to mean *new when he bought it*, but in the conclusion, it has to mean *new when he turns it in*. The word "new" has shifted in midstream, so that there are really two "new"s involved, both hiding under the same label. As soon as we make the distinction, the mistake is evident.

When a word shifts from one sense to another in the course of an argument, we shall call it **equivocation.** An equivocal argument has the general *look* of a good argument because the use of the same word throughout helps to disguise the difference in meaning. Thus the conclusion may *seem* to follow from the premises, though in fact it does not. An equivocal argument is therefore a fallacious argument; it commits the **fallacy of equivocation.** Whether or not a writer is aware of what is going on, it is still a fallacy. He may be fooling himself as well as us. But equivocation can't impose upon us unless we take it for granted that whenever the same *word* turns up in an argument it must automatically have the same *meaning*. Most of the time it will, but sometimes it will not, and those are the times we have to be on the watch.

The cases of equivocation that are really hard to cope with are the ones that take whole pages or chapters to work themselves out—for with that much room a word can slide from one sense to another almost undetectably. Or it can slip from a context in which it has one meaning to a context in which it is ambiguous and then to a third context in which it has a second meaning while the unwary reader's attention is kept on something else. You can't often equivocate successfully in a single paragraph, but sometimes it is done. Let's consider a more serious example:

> There is much talk of planning ahead for an "intelligent long-range use of our natural resources" and for "increasing cooperation between labor, business, and agriculture." But those who talk like this don't realize the essential evil of a Planned Society, in which everything is worked out by the bureaucrats and every man's life is regimented in every detail. Planning is wrong, and I'm against it; let us deal with the problems of today and let tomorrow take care of itself.

This is sufficiently muddled so that its basic structure is not evident at first glance. But it can be worked out. The conclusion is that it is wrong to plan for the future of the United States economy; the reason is that a planned society is evil. Now, in the reason, the word "planned," as we can see in the second sentence of the paragraph, means, in effect, *decided by the government and imposed upon the citizens*; that's what the writer objects to. But in the conclusion, the word has shifted to another sense, for, as we can see by examining the first and third sentences, the writer there means by "planning" something like *foreseeing and preparing for future contingencies*. His argument, then, looks like this (in abbreviated form):

A planned society is evil;
Therefore: planning is wrong.

But, in fact, when we substitute two other phrases for the two different senses of "plan," it turns out to be really like this:

A society in which measures are decided by the government and imposed upon the citizens is evil;
Therefore: It is wrong to attempt to foresee the future and prepare for its contingencies.

When we make the substitution, it now *looks* as silly as it is, and what is left is as harmless and obvious a non sequitur as the argument: "Anything that goes up must come down. The moon is made of green cheese. Therefore, the moon must come down."

To deal with the fallacy of equivocation, then, you first put your finger on the word or phrase or syntactical construction that has shifted its meaning, and you next mark the different meanings by different words. Then the equivocation disappears, and you can see how the argument fares without the help of the fallacy. It might still be a good argument, or it might be a worthless one; anyway, you can't be sure until you penetrate its disguise. An authority on modern art wrote:

People who attack abstraction in modern paintings are blind to the facts of Nature. For Nature always creates geometrical shapes, though in infinite variety: how could she do otherwise, when all shapes are geometrical, strictly speaking? And that is why the nonrepresentational painter fills his canvas with rectangles, triangles, cubes, cones, etc.—for these are the true geometrical shapes.

You wouldn't think offhand that a word like "geometrical" could be used as the pivot of an equivocation, but this writer has done it. When he says that Nature creates "geometrical shapes," he has to admit that *all* shapes are geometrical: "geometrical" here means just "having a shape," for "geometrical shape" is redundant. But when he explains why some nonrepresentational painters have used geometrical shapes, the meaning of "geometrical shape" has narrowed to "simple figures studied in plane geometry." You can't defend cubistic and other abstract paintings in this way, for if all shapes are equally geometrical, then pyramids are no more geometrical than annunciations, picnics on the grass, or bathing beauties. We must not conclude, of course, that nonrepresentational painting cannot be explained or justified. All we can say is that this particular attempt is a failure, for the connection between the premise and the conclusion is only an illusion.

There is a special kind of equivocation that involves two people. A *dispute* between two people is a conversation in which one of them argues for, and the other argues against, a certain conclusion. Now, suppose A gives a reason for a certain statement, using a certain word in one sense, and B gives a reason against the same statement, using the same word in a different sense. For example:

> A *says:* "In my opinion, the United States Supreme Court was correct in ruling that the censorship boards of New York and Ohio had no right to prevent the showing of *La Ronde* and *M* on the ground that these movies were 'immoral' and 'tended to incite crime.' As the Court declared, terms like 'immoral' and 'harmful to the public,' and similar terms, are too indefinite to be used as standards for censoring moving pictures, and cannot be consistently and fairly applied."
> B *says:* "On the contrary, the Supreme Court's ruling strikes at the very heart of Americanism. There was nothing indefinite about morality for Washington, Lincoln, and Calvin Coolidge. The American tradition is built on the conception of an absolute and unalterable moral law."

Now, when A says the word "immoral" in the censorship statute is too "indefinite," he seems to be using the word "indefinite" to mean *vague.* But in his reply, B changes the meaning of the word "indefinite" to *relative,* or *variable in meaning.* Thus the gist of the dispute is this:

A *says* the Court's decision was correct because the word "immoral" is too vague for a statute.

B *replies* that the Court's decision was incorrect because the word "immoral" doesn't shift its meaning from context to context.

Since B is objecting to something that A never said, his reply is beside the point. Whether or not B knows what he is doing, he is dodging the issue, and the dispute is merely verbal.

But this kind of equivocation doesn't *always* make the dispute a merely verbal one. Consider another example:

A *says:* "I believe in free enterprise; no government interference with business should be permitted. Steel companies should be allowed to fix their rates on the basing-point system, and railroads should be allowed to set up differential freight rates if they want to."

B *says:* "I believe in free enterprise too; I conclude that the government should prohibit combinations in restraint of trade, and conspiracies by one part of industry directed at other parts, for these combinations, as in the practices you mention, dry up free enterprise."

The merits of the two arguments don't concern us here—you don't even have to know what the "basing-point system" is. The important thing for our present purpose is that, although it seems as though A and B disagree about the proper way to secure free enterprise, actually they are using the phrase "free enterprise" in two different senses. For A, it means *the absence of any laws regulating private industry*; but B has shifted its meaning to *conditions of maximum competition in industry*.

Now, perhaps A and B really want to discuss the question whether or not the basing-point system and differential freight rates are for the good of the general public in the long run. But to carry on this discussion effectively, they must first agree to use their words in the same sense throughout the whole discussion. If they don't, they will merely frustrate and irritate each other, making verbal passes that never strike home, instead of coming to grips with the issue. B could say:

"I understand that by 'free enterprise' you mean the complete absence of government regulation. I will use these words in the same way you do in this discussion. But then I don't believe in free enterprise *in this sense*; I believe in capitalism and competition. And I think we cannot have competition between industries unless the government steps in to prevent monopolistic practices, such as the basing-point system and differential freight rates."

This doesn't settle the dispute, of course; it only gets it back on the track. *B* is now making his point clearly, and without dodging the issue. And his point is surely relevant.

Indeed, it is very seldom that an argument can be dismissed as utterly worthless simply because it is found to involve some verbal misbehavior—ambiguity, or extreme vagueness, or equivocation. Of course, if it turns out that two heated debaters are really talking about entirely different things, we can see there really isn't any dispute at all as soon as we find out what they *are* talking about. It is as though one accused the other of stealing a horse, and the other replied indignantly that he never stole a hearse in his life. But ordinarily even a pretty defective argument may have some point to it, or may help us to see how a more reasonable case could be made. Impatience in verbal analysis is as bad as gullibility. The purpose of straightening out the meaning of a passage is to clear away the brush so that we can see where, if anywhere, the path leads.

A CHECK-UP QUIZ. Which of the following arguments involve *equivocation?* Point out the words or phrases that shift their meaning.

1. Man is the highest being on the evolutionary ladder, according to biology. That's why women are inferior—because they are not men.

2. Anyone who puts productive machines out of commission is committing sabotage—and therefore anyone who goes on strike is committing sabotage, for he is shutting off his machine, and that puts it out of commission.

3. We don't need another holiday a week after Christmas, but a holiday in March would be a boon to business and a morale builder. New Year's Day should come on the first day of Spring.

4. *Alice:* Would you—be very good enough—to stop a minute—just to get—one's breath again? *White King:* I'm *good* enough, only I'm not *strong* enough. You see, a minute goes by so fearfully quick. You might as well try to stop a Bandersnatch.

5. If you work for a living, then you are in business. Therefore, what helps business helps you.

See Exercises 18, 19, 20, pp. 183-88.

FURTHER READING: Robert H. Thouless, *Straight and Crooked Thinking*. New York: Simon and Schuster, Inc., 1932, chs. 9, 10.

Outline-Summary of Chapter 4

It is important to distinguish four ways in which words behave; though these types of behavior are often confused, their consequences are very different.

1. A word can have one sense in some contexts and different senses in other contexts ("He *passed* the examination," "He *passed* the football," "He *passed* the house") though its meaning in *each* context may be perfectly definite and plain. Such a word is said to have *variable meaning*.

2. A word can appear in a context in which it might have either (but not both) of two senses (In "The boat was *fast*," "fast" can mean either *speedy* or *tied up*). Such a word is said to be *ambiguous* in that context. If a sentence contains an ambiguous word, it is *semantically ambiguous*; if it contains a grammatical construction that can be understood in more than one way (a "big boys' club" may be a big club for boys or a club for big boys) it is *syntactically ambiguous*.

3. A word can have several senses at once in the same context (to say, "my love is like a red red rose" is to say she is beautiful and blooming, but her beauty will not last forever; and more besides—see Chapter 6). Such a word is said to have *multiple meaning* in that context.

4. A word can mark off a certain range in the variation of some quality, but without being so precisely defined that it draws a sharp line (there is no sharp line between "dirty" and "clean"). Such a word is said to be *vague* in that context.

There are two especially noteworthy kinds of fallacious argument in which these characteristics of words are taken advantage of.

1. An argument can get a spurious plausibility from the fact that one of its key words shifts from one sense to another in the course of the argument ("He believes in studying the *liberal* arts; therefore, he is a political *liberal*."). Such an argument commits the *fallacy of equivocation*.

2. An argument can get a spurious plausibility by making a difference of degree appear less important than the evidence would actually warrant by showing that the difference of degree is made up of a series of minute or vague distinctions ("It doesn't matter whether we do it now or a little

later, and it doesn't matter whether we do it a little later or a little later than that. . . ; therefore, it doesn't matter whether we do it now or next month"). Such an argument commits the *black-or-white* fallacy.

Exercise 16

Rewrite each of the following ambiguous sentences in two (or more) ways to make clear the distinct meanings involved.

1. Our dog has a hearty appetite. He is very fond of children.

2. You have been listening to William L. Shirer, who will return at this same time next Sunday with more important news.

3. The skies are not cloudy all day.

4. There is a job for everyone to do.

5. The Reverend Mr. Jones's sermon was entitled "Enduring Americanism."

6. According to Washington reports, changes in the bill introduced by Republicans have improved it considerably.

7. We propose to admit all intelligent and interested people, whatever their race, color, creed, or sex, who are clearly needed for the work of the party.

8. Advertisement: "FOR RENT. Modern 3-room apartment, ideal for two. Married couple preferred."

9. The present Act applies to those newspapers competing with other newspapers which are not members of a press service.

10. ILLINOIS LEGION REJECTS GIRL SCOUT SUPPORT AFTER HANDBOOK FUROR.

11. Today, James Goldsmith filed kidnapping charges against his in-laws, Bolivian tin magnate Antenor Patino and his wife.

12. Listen to WPQ's early morning disc-jockey show with Doc Harroway, who offers his own cures for insomnia, singing commercials, and shaggy dog stories.

13. In the reorganization, Assistant Vice President Jones replaced Director Jackson.

14. More people are buying Fords.

15. In reference to the dispute between Senator Malarky and the Chairman of the Senate Committee on Scientific Methods of Inquiry, Senator Macarony, the Chairman of the Senate Committee on Unconstitutional Cerebration, commented: "It is a hurricane in a coffee-pot."

16. Lost: one dirty child's mitten.

Exercise 17

Show how the following ambiguous questions could be answered Yes or No, depending on the way they are interpreted.

1. Does three times two plus one equal nine?
2. Is Jones the oldest member of the local Lions Club?
3. Does the compass needle point north?
4. Is it possible to see music?
5. Does a person who takes a sport seriously turn his play into work?
6. Does the exception prove the rule?
7. Is the life of a private in the United States Army Communistic?
8. Is it natural for people to try to accumulate wealth?
9. Is it possible for a person to step into the same river twice?
10. Did Shakespeare say, "The evil men do lives after them"?

Exercise 18

Expose the equivocation in the following arguments: point out in each case the shifty word or phrase, and explain how its sense changes in the course of the argument.

1. The management of an industry has the sole responsibility for keeping its plant and means of production in repair, and the health of the workers is certainly an indispensable means of production. It follows that the management has the sole responsibility for preserving the health of the workers.

2. No one who has the slightest acquaintance with science can reasonably doubt that the miracles in the Bible actually took place. Every year we witness new miracles of modern science, like television, jet planes, antibiotics, heart operations, and heat-resistant plastics.

3. A *popular writer argued*: It is horrible to read about the Russian purges. We know that people were liquidated by the Soviet Government simply because they didn't agree with the commissars in power. I abhor these purges, and I shall never cease to. But we must not let our emotions run away with us. How can we condemn the Communists without hypocrisy? Don't we have our own purges? We purge the government of people who are "subversive," we purge the labor unions of "Reds"—and Hollywood, and the schools, and what not. But if purges are evil in Russia, they are no less evil in America.

4. *An essayist wrote*: Poverty is ineradicable, as the proverb says. The poor are always with us, and they always will be. As long as anyone

is free to accumulate a little more of the world's goods than others, there will always be some people at the bottom of the scale: these are the poor. Even if you move them up the scale of wealth by charity, they will only leave someone else at the bottom.

What conclusion may be drawn from this? That all this talk of raising the standard of living is utopian folly—and utter nonsense. For it follows that some people must always be poor—that is, on the brink of starvation and despair. And however we may bewail this fact, as humanitarians, not all the wisdom of Solomon can change it.

5. It is very important for schools to drill children in spelling. For a good speller is one who pays close attention to words, and anyone who pays close attention to words must be a clear thinker, since he sees the difference between subtly different meanings.

6. Anyone who talks too much, while drunk or sober, and thus betrays his country's secrets, is a security risk. Such a person is guilty of betraying his country to the enemy, and is therefore a spy and a traitor.

7. I am suing him for breach of contract. I let him borrow my dog a week ago, and now he says he will give it back. But he promised to give me the *same* dog I lent him, and since the dog has grown, he is not the same, but different.

8. A complete vacuum, or empty space, is impossible. For suppose you had a box with empty space between its sides; then there would be nothing between the sides. But when two things have nothing between them, they are next to each other, so the box would be no box at all.

Exercise 19

In the following passages you are to think of B and C as each replying to what A has said. Either B or C (and perhaps both) may be using one of A's words in a different sense. Underline the shifting words and then rewrite each equivocal reply so that the speaker says the same thing without equivocating.

I

A: "I will never vote for Jones. His record is highly conservative, for he always opposes any bills which are intended to improve the lot of the working man."

B: "He is not conservative at all. A genuine conservative wants to conserve—that is, to keep everything as it is. But Jones has voted for many changes in our laws."

C: "Well, Jones is not wholly conservative, for he has voted for some bills to reform the labor laws—especially laws to keep labor leaders from tyrannizing over union members."

II

A: "... And I think we have made some achievement in bringing our educational system much closer to the ideal of a truly progressive education. We have made the schools, through their activities programs and their cooperation with the community, a real place for children to grow in independence, intelligence, and happiness. This is education at its best."

B: "Progressive education is a false and materialistic goal; it may make children happier, it may make them better citizens, and for all I know it may be the best way to fill the world with sane, healthy, and creative men and women. But what will it do to their *souls*? Progressive as it is, it will not teach children humility before the Eternal, sorrow for their sins, and preparation for the Other World to come."

C: "Progressive education has been a dead-end street in American education—from which we are at last returning to the highroad. To educate means to lead out of darkness and ignorance. Letting children make up their own minds about some of the things they do in school; teaching them arithmetic the easy way by playing games or visiting the grocery—this is not *leading*. In fact, progressive education is not really education at all."

III

A: "We have no business meddling in foreign affairs. We should be absolutely neutral in all civil wars abroad. That is, we must give no aid to either side; we must send them nothing. Let them strictly alone."

B: "This is nonsense. We can't possibly be neutral. If we don't help either side we are really favoring the stronger side. But it's not neutrality to favor one side over the other. Neutrality is impossible."

C: "This is nonsense. We can't possibly be neutral. If we refuse to sell goods to either side—arms and ammunition—we are refusing to help the side we want to win. This encourages the side we *don't* want to win; and encouraging the *wrong* side is certainly not neutrality. It is folly."

IV

A: "Anyone can see from the history of Communism in Russia that Communism is unalterably opposed to religion and aims to stamp it out."

B: "No, it is not. Look at the Constitution of Soviet Russia, and the

C: "No, it is not. In fact, when you talk with Communists, and see pronouncements of Stalin during recent years, and you will see that the government is quite tolerant of religion."

how passionate they are; and when you consider their celebrations in Red Square, so full of pageantry, you find that Communism is *itself* a religion to its followers. How can it be opposed to religion?"

V

A: "In my opinion, Congress should pass the Housing Bill, and the Aid for Education Bill, and other pending bills to help the underprivileged. According to the Constitution, it is the duty of Congress to promote the 'general welfare'."

B: "But in the long run the welfare of all will be better promoted by encouraging them to stand on their own feet than by transforming the Federal Government into a charitable institution."

C: "This is one of the few points where we are able to improve upon the Constitution because we have had more experience than the Founding Fathers. It is not the business of Congress to concern itself with the general welfare, but to help our citizens to be free, independent, mutually respectful, and happy."

Exercise 20

Discuss the key words italicized in each of the following passages. Distinguish some of their senses that could be relevant to the passage; show how some of these senses are ruled out by the context; point out semantical or syntactical ambiguities that still remain; note where words are excessively vague; describe any cases of equivocation; and suggest ways of clarifying the meanings of terms where that seems desirable.

1. We must now discuss the *form* of poetry, as distinct from its *subject matter*, or *content*. When we say that the poem is a "sonnet," or a "rondo," we are talking about its *form*: that is, the pattern of its sound, including meter and rhyme. Thus *form* is opposed, for example, to its being a love poem, or a poem about birds. All that is *expressed* in poetry, or what the writer intends to *embody* in the *medium* he chooses, is *expressed* by means of *form*, and therefore there can obviously be no *form* without *content*, or *content* without *form*. *Content* is *what* is done; form is *how* it is done. Thus there can be two love poems, one cheerful, one sad, and they differ in *form*, though not in *content*, at least in the *essential content*. But a reader who merely grasps the *content* of a poem, without

fully understanding its *form*, is obviously missing the most important thing.

2. We confuse ourselves with bad semantics when we speak about the relations between one *nation* and another. It is partly a misuse of words with exact shades of meaning. For example, I have heard Russia referred to as an "*ally*" of the United States and Great Britain during World War II. She was never an *ally*. Great Britain and the United States were *allies*, but Russia was merely *a nation with a common enemy*. She shared the work and the glory of victory. She was an unwilling *cobelligerent*, not a *cooperator*. But we must also guard against the personification of *nations*, as if they were people come to dinner, or salesmen in a shop, or children at a party. We should beware of saying "The Republic of Korea won't play ball with us," or "Communist China wants to muscle in on the United Nations"; these statements may be true of the *rulers* of a *state*, but not of the *state* itself.

3. It is usually the case that *unorthodox* opinions on any important subject are unpopular, and unpopular opinions are hard for the social group to tolerate unless it restrains itself with an effort of will. But scholars and teachers have to hold some views that are off the beaten track in order to think *freely* and constructively. A scientist's hypothesis may be false, but how can he *prove* that it's false unless he can propose it, deduce its consequences, and test them? We must make every effort to encourage this kind of intellectual *heresy*, even when people propose *unacceptable* solutions of social problems like euthanasia or sterilization of the feeble-minded. As long as they don't combine secretly to carry out their proposals illegally, by force—as long as they refrain from *overt* acts, and confine themselves to the merits of the issue—they are doing no wrong. *Heresy*, yes; *conspiracy*, no!

4. Man's religious struggle to discern a supernatural power and meaning beyond his physical environment has a long *history*. Before the dawn of *history*, he was no doubt trying to puzzle this out, as he is today. The *history* of this struggle has never fully been written, and perhaps never will be, though parts of the story have been told. Part of the difficulty lies in the mass of facts. We know about various primitive practices, for example, which, in the strict sense, are not part of the *history* of religion at all, though they have been recorded by assiduous scholars.

5. We hold these truths to be *self-evident*, that all men are created *equal*, that they are *endowed* by their Creator with certain *unalienable* Rights, that among these are *Life*, *Liberty* and the pursuit of *Happiness*. That to *secure* these rights, *Governments* are *instituted* among Men, deriving their just powers from the *consent* of the governed. That when-

ever any form of *Government* becomes destructive of these ends, it is the *Right* of the *People* to alter or to abolish it, and to institute new *Government*, laying its foundation on such principles and organizing its powers in such form, as to them shall seem most likely to effect their *Safety* and *Happiness*.

5

Defining Your Terms

When the meaning of a discourse is shaky or shifty, it has a fine chance of confusing somebody—if not the reader, then the writer. For when a discourse is ambiguous or equivocal or excessively vague, it is hard for anyone, including the author, to tell whether the reasoning is sound or unsound. And it is easy to think it less sound, or more sound, than it really is.

But it isn't fair to blame this on language itself, as though words were naturally mischievous or tyrannical, and always up to tricks. They have their ways, but the habits that sometimes make them ornery are the same habits that make them so handy, versatile, and expressive. In themselves, they are neutral. Your problem, as a writer, or speaker, is always to keep *control* over them and steer them clear of confusion, first, by seeing that your audience picks out the sense that you require for the purpose at hand, and, second, by seeing that the word sticks to the same sense as long as you need it to.

Clear writing is in good part just this matter of control over the words we use. When we relax control, our words go their own way, following their natural bent, and they seem absent minded, or obstinate, or mean. As Humpty Dumpty said, "The question is, which is to be master—that's all. . . . When I use a word," he boasted to Alice, "it means just what I choose it to mean—neither more or less." Now, we can't all achieve such a complete mastery over words as Humpty Dumpty, who makes "glory" mean "a nice knock-down argument." But with a certain amount of care we can persuade them to do the jobs we want them to do; we can make their meaning, in a particular argument, as clear and constant as it needs to be.

Mostly our control over words might be called "remote control." Without giving the matter much deliberate thought, we learn to manage the contexts of words so as to fix their meaning adequately; that is, we choose them so that they keep each other's variability of meaning in check. But sometimes this isn't enough. When a word has many closely-connected senses that are nevertheless important to distinguish, or when it has a tendency to slip easily from one sense to another, or when the sense we want it to carry is a new or unusual one—in such cases as these, we have to exercise *direct* control by making explicit exactly how we are using, or are proposing to use, the word. Some very important words, like "happiness," "freedom," "science," "religion," are hardly ever safe to use without some clarification of their relevant meaning. Other words need this only on special occasions.

The most effective sort of direct control over a word is to give a *definition*. The purpose of definitions is to make communication possible where it would break down without them, or to make communication clear where it would be fuzzy without them. Suppose you are writing an essay or a letter, and you find yourself using the words "identical twins" and "fraternal twins." Is your reader likely to know what you mean? If you happen to know that he has never read anything about genetics, these words may mean nothing to him. Or, what is worse, he may *think* he knows what they mean when he doesn't. Thus the word "fraternal" may mislead him into thinking that fraternal twins are twin brothers, and that identical twins are twins of the same sex. We are sometimes misled by grammatical analogies: an "actress" is a female actor, but a "pythoness" is not a female python. This is the sort of case in which a definition may be called for.

Clear thinking depends pretty heavily upon aptness in making and keeping *distinctions*—not just *any* distinction, but the one relevant to a particular argument. When an earnest discussion turns out to have been futile, it is often because one party does not grasp, or cannot hold on to, the distinctions that the other party thinks are the ones on which the whole issue turns. The main force of an argument may rest on the distinction between two senses of a word—"revolution," "appeasement," "right"—or between two closely related words

—"revolt" and "revolution," "appeasement" and "compromise," "contemporary" and "contemporaneous," "presently" and "at present."

Thus, generally speaking, there are two things you need definitions for:

1. A definition is a way of *supplying* the meaning of a word that a reader or listener would otherwise not understand. In this book, for example, the words "syntactical ambiguity," "*ad hominem* argument," and "syllogism" may be new to you, and that is why they have to be defined. When you write about a field in which you have some special knowledge (the stock market, nonobjective painting, mushrooms, bebop, or the principles of color television), you will want to use words that are unfamiliar to most people. In that case, your reader, unless he happens to be a fellow expert, needs the help of definitions.

2. A definition is a way of *restricting* the meaning of a word whose meaning is variable. For example, such words as "argument," "ambiguity," "comprehension," and, indeed, "definition," have other senses than the ones we are adopting in this book. The definition of "connotation," later, makes explicit one way of using the word so that we can agree upon it and helps to fix that chosen meaning for the rest of the book. Of course, you can't foresee all the mistakes a careless reader will make, but by defining your key words, you can ensure that a reasonably attentive reader will get your point. When in doubt, define!

§21. THE DEFINITION OF "DEFINITION"

When you are having a conversation with someone and he doesn't understand what you are saying, he can always ask, "What do you mean?" or look blank or puzzled, and you will know that he needs a fuller explanation. But suppose you are speaking on the radio or writing a report for someone who will read it when you are not around. He can't ask you what you mean. But you can ask *yourself* whether at any point you are saying something that might be obscure: you can at least make sure that *you* know what you mean.

There are three chief ways of clarifying the meaning of a word when that meaning is in doubt.

The first method is to *give examples*. If you use a word like "cerise," and discover that the person you are talking to doesn't know what this word means, you could easily make it clear by producing a sample of this color. If that is impractical, you could try to think of cerise-colored objects that he might have seen: "Have you ever seen a really ripe red cherry? That's the color called 'cerise'." This method works well for words that name specific colors, or tastes, or smells, or touch qualities, or sound qualities; and it can be used for words like "shillelagh," "farandole," and "tachistoscope" too, but if the thing is complicated, an example won't be very satisfactory unless you also talk about the example. If someone wants to know what "passacaglia" means, you can play him a recording of one, but you'd better also tell him how it differs from a chaconne.

The second method is to *explain usage*. Suppose you are talking with someone who is learning English, and he says, "The climate is delightful this afternoon, isn't it?" He looks at you questioningly, as usual, to learn what mistakes he has made, and you reply, "In English, we don't speak of the 'climate' today or this afternoon, but only of the '*weather*.' The way we use these two words, it's correct to speak of the weather as changing from day to day or from morning to afternoon, but the climate is the weather over a long stretch of time. It's like the difference between a *battle* and a *war*." This reply describes the way people in English use the words "weather" and "climate." Similarly, if your friend says, "Yesterday I heard a man say 'Ouch!' Now what did he mean by that?", you might say, "English-speaking people often utter that sound when they feel a sudden, sharp, but not severe, pain."

The third method is to *substitute other words*. If you use the word "crepitation," and someone says, "Huh?", you can say, "In other words, 'crackling.' " This third way of clarifying the meaning of a word, then, consists in offering another word that has the same meaning in the situation at hand,—and to do this is to *define* the word whose meaning is in doubt.

It is rather important to get a clear idea of definition, what it involves, and how it is different from the other ways of clarifying meaning. This will involve a few new distinctions, which will in fact be very useful throughout the remainder of this book.

When you apply a term to a thing, you ascribe to that thing certain *characteristics*. For example, when you say, "that is a bird," you assert that it has such characteristics as being warm blooded, being a vertebrate, and having feathers. In one sense of the word "meaning," we would sometimes say that the term "bird" *means* these character-

istics. For our purposes it will be best to take no chances on ambiguity here, and to have a special name for this sense of "meaning."
We shall say that a term signifies certain characteristics; the **signification** of a term, then, will be the set of characteristics that we attribute
to anything in applying the term to it. Of course, the signification of
a term may be different in one context from what it is in another;
perhaps there are some characteristics it signifies in most, or all, types
of context, but usually there are others that it signifies in only a few
types of context. In any context, however, we can ask of any term,
whether noun, adjective, verb, or complex phrase, what characteristics it signifies in that context. When we speak, as it is sometimes
convenient to do here, of the signification of a term, without any
reference to the context, this is just a loose way of referring to one of
its familiar significations: in a great many contexts, "bird" signifies
the characteristic of having warm blood, among others, but clay
pigeons are also called "birds."

Now, when you use a term and there is some doubt whether others
will know what it signifies, you must define that term. And to do this
you must find *another* term, already familiar to your audience, that
signifies the same characteristics as the term you want to define. You
will say, in the terminology we have introduced,

> "Identical twins" *has the same signification as* "twins that develop
> from the same egg."
> "Fraternal twins" *has the same signification as* "twins that develop
> from different eggs."

These statements are definitions. In each one, there is a term on the
left side, the meaning of which, in its context, is doubtful in some
way: this is the **term-to-be-defined**; and there is a term on the right
side, the meaning of which is supposed to be understood: this is the
defining term. The **definition** is a statement that these two terms
have the same signification.

In ordinary language we have a number of different ways of introducing definitions. For example:

(1) "Hairsplitting" *means* making unnecessarily subtle distinctions.
(2) Making unnecessarily subtle distinctions *is called* "hairsplitting."
(3) The word "hairsplitting" *is used to refer to* the act of making
unnecessarily subtle distinctions.

(4) The word "hairsplitting" *is often applied to* the act of making unnecessarily subtle distinctions.

(5) "Hairsplitting" *is a colloquial term for* making unnecessarily subtle distinctions.

For most purposes, these and similar phrases are perfectly adequate. Indeed, the definitions in this book are for the most part presented in an informal manner. But when you must be very clear in your own mind about the exact elements of the definition, you will find it useful to write out your definition, at least for your own benefit if not for your reader's, in a more rigorous way. This is where our formula comes in:

"Hairsplitting" *has the same signification as* "making unnecessarily subtle distinctions."

The advantages of this formula are plain: first, it makes perfectly clear that the statement *is* a definition, and not something else; second, it shows which term is the term-to-be-defined and which is the defining term; and third, it forces us to put the defining term in a complete form, parallel in grammar to the term-to-be-defined, and thus helps to call our attention sharply to any inaccuracies in the definition.

This third point is worth noting especially. The statement, "An accident is when something happens that nobody intended," might be offered as a definition, but it is not in proper shape. Nor is the trouble merely a minor lapse in grammatical tidiness. Whenever possible, the term-to-be-defined and the defining term should be able to be substituted for each other in the context at hand. Obviously we can't substitute "when something happens that nobody intended" for the term "accident" in such a statement as, "The police decided that his death was an accident." Nouns are to be defined in terms of nouns (or noun phrases), adjectives in terms of adjectives, verbs in terms of verbs. You can write,

"Accident" *has the same signification as* "event not deliberately caused by anyone."

or,

"Accidental" *has the same signification as* "not deliberately caused by anyone."

Sometimes it is difficult to stick to this rule, for it requires us to be clear and explicit about what *kind* of thing the term-to-be-defined stands for; whether it is an event, an action, a state of affairs, an object, or whatever. But a definition is not orderly and complete unless the two terms are *coordinate* in this way.

It would be awkward to write out the whole phrase, "has the same signification as" each time we give examples of definitions. Let us use the equals-sign as an abbreviation:

"Hairsplitting"="making unnecessarily subtle distinctions."

Notice that in this fairly formal way of writing out definitions, the two terms are always put between quotation marks. That is because a definition is a statement about *words*, not a statement about *things*. This distinction is obvious enough, yet it is often overlooked, and overlooking it sometimes leads to sloppy thinking and sloppy writing. Compare these two statements:

Love is blind.
"Love" has four letters.

Evidently, when we say "Love is blind," we are using the word "love" to refer to *love*. When we say " 'Love' has four letters," we are not talking about love any more, but about the *word* "love." Unfortunately, there is no universal rule in English for marking this distinction. Many writers put a word in italics when they are speaking about it, but there are various other uses for italics, and it seems much better to follow the practice of logicians and philosophers by using quotation marks instead. Quotation marks have other uses, too, but there is much less likelihood of confusion.

It is one thing, then, to *mention* a word, and another thing to *use* the word for mentioning something else. Consider carefully the difference between these two statements:

(1) There are two kinds of argument: inductive and deductive.
(2) There are two meanings of "argument": (a) an asserted discourse that contains reasons; (b) a dispute between two or more people.

In the first statement, the word "argument" is used to refer to arguments, so it is not in quotation marks; in the second statement, the word "argument" is *itself* referred to, so it is in quotation marks. In

a definition, the terms are not used, but mentioned; it is highly misleading to speak of "defining horses," as though it were something
like driving horses or shoeing horses; it is not horses but the *word*
"horse" that we define. A statement is not a definition unless it can be
expressed in the formula

$$\text{"X"}=\text{"Y"}$$

Here, then, is the definition of "definition":

> "Definition"="statement that one term has the same signification
> as another term."

You can see now why not every way of clarifying the meaning of a
term is a definition, though some that are not are often loosely called
"definitions."

To give *examples* is not to define a term. A person who doesn't
know what the term "philosopher" means can be helped by examples;
we might say to him, "Plato, Aristotle, Spinoza, Hume, Kant, Bertrand Russell, and John Dewey are philosophers," and if we give him a
large and varied enough list he may form a fairly good idea of the
signification of the term. But to make sure it is accurate, we have to
give him a definition.

To give a *description* is not to define a term. By comparing philosophers with scientists or poets, we might be able to convey a rough
notion of the way the term "philosopher" is used. Or we could say,
"Well, many philosophers are interested in questions like whether
there is free will," but, however helpful it may be, such a statement
about philosophers is no substitute for a definition of the *term*.

To give a *figure of speech* is not to define a term. "A philosopher
may be defined as a blind man looking in a dark cellar for a black cat
that isn't there" (sometimes people add: "—and finding it!"). This
statement pokes fun, but it doesn't really tell us anything about the
signification of the term "philosopher." In *The Devil's Dictionary*,
by Ambrose Bierce, there are many such "definitions": "*Positive*:
mistaken at the top of one's voice," "*Prejudice*: a vagrant opinion
without visible means of support." It is true that figurative language
can sometimes help us to understand words, but it is not equipped to
perform the tasks we require of definitions. Architecture may *not* be
defined as "frozen music," nor music as "liquid architecture."

Of course, we must keep these word-clarifying devices in our reper-toire for occasions when some explanation, or partial explanation, of a term's signification is in order, but a full definition is not needed. And there are other cases where a definition, however desirable, is simply impracticable. First, there are the terms that signify simple sensory qualities ("chartreuse," "acrid," "smooth," "soft"); the only really satisfactory way of clarifying such terms is to point to some-thing. Second, there are the terms that are so very general that our language affords no adequate equivalents for them ("thing," "event," "being"); when there is any question about the way we are using such terms, we can explain our usage, but perhaps not provide full defini-tions.

Except for these two types of term, there is probably none that completely resists definition for *all* contexts. But there are some that we would be hard put to it to define, and it is lucky that they are the ones whose usefulness in ordinary speech doesn't depend on their being precisely definable. Try to define "knick-knacks," "phony," or "snafu." "Knick-knacks" is pretty vague in any context, and you would have considerable difficulty in finding another term, no matter how carefully qualified, that would capture exactly its degree of vagueness. But it is a handy word just because it is vague, and, like the word "whatd'yecallit," it can be used on many occasions when we haven't the time to be more precise.

You can certainly *understand* a word without being able to furnish a definition of it on request. But you can't always be sure you under-stand it *clearly* unless you try to define it. You may have a fair enough conception of the meaning of "democracy" for many purposes, but when it comes to a difficult question (let's say, about the extent to which a democracy can afford to go in withholding information about the hydrogen bomb or the Department of Justice from its own citi-zens) then you may have to decide whether you do or do not include majority decision about basic policies in the signification of the term "democracy." Perhaps you know *some* of the characteristics it sig-nifies, but when the situation calls for exactness about what it sig-nifies and what it *doesn't* signify, then you need a *complete* record of its signification. And this complete list will then be the defining term in a definition of "democracy."

A CHECK-UP QUIZ. Which of the following statements are definitions?

1. Humanities are such subjects as English literature, Greek, history, and literary criticism.

2. The philosophy taught by Plato, and philosophical systems derived from, and closely similar to, that philosophy, are often called "Platonism."

3. True gratitude may be defined as the lively expectation of benefits to come.

4. "Concrete" is the opposite of "abstract."

5. A "sonata" is a musical composition, usually in three or four movements, in which the first movement is nearly always an allegro in exposition-development-recapitulation form, followed by a slow movement, and often with a lively finale.

6. A symphony is a sonata for orchestra.

7. When insurance policies refer to "catastrophies," they mean accidents in which five or more persons are killed.

8. Well, "slithy" means "lithe and slimy."

9. Well, "toves" are something like badgers—they're something like lizards—and they're something like corkscrews.... Also they make their nests under sundials—also they live on cheese.

10. Well, "outgribing" is something between bellowing and whistling, with a kind of sneeze in the middle: However, you'll hear it done, maybe—down in the wood yonder—and, when you've once heard it, you'll be *quite* content.

FURTHER READING: Hugh R. Walpole, *Semantics*. New York: W. W. Norton, Inc., 1941, ch. 6. L. S. Stebbing, *A Modern Introduction to Logic*. London: Methuen & Co., 1930, ch. 22.

§22. THE TWO DIMENSIONS OF MEANING

Our interest throughout this chapter is not in the theoretical but in the practical aspect of definitions; that is, we want to see what can be expected of them and how they are most efficiently handled. But even for practical purposes, we have to understand what sort of thing a definition is, and so we have to be clear about what we mean when we speak of the "signification" of a term. This technical term can be sharpened if we introduce another important term that contrasts with it.

It is convenient to think of the distinction we are about to make as a distinction between two *dimensions* of meaning, a horizontal and a vertical dimension. But, first, this is perhaps the place to agree on a few ground rules for our use of the word "meaning" itself. It is certainly one of the hazards of our discussion that the word "meaning" has such a variable meaning. Fortunately many of the meanings of "meaning" do not concern us here, and we can quickly lay them aside. In common speech, we say:

Clouds mean (*are a sign of*) rain.
When he says that, he means (*is thinking of*) me.
He says that he will do it, but he doesn't mean (*intend*) to.
If you do that, it means (*will cause*) trouble.
If x equals 3, that means (*implies that*) 2x equals 6.
What is the meaning (*purpose*) of life?

In this book the verb "to mean" will not be used in any of these senses, but only as applied to words: thus it will be said that a *word* means something, but not that *physical objects* or *events* or *people* mean something.

But even after we resolve to limit the word "meaning" to words, there are still, as we shall see, some further distinctions that need to be made. And the basic one is the distinction between two directions, so to speak, in which a term can point, or between two axes of reference: it can direct our attention to *things*, and it can also tell us what *sort* of things they are.

To start with, let's take a simple common noun, say "widow." In the first place, this term is a general name of a number of individual people: it includes, or comprehends, all the widows who ever lived, or ever will live. The class of people who are correctly named by the term "widow" we shall call the **comprehension** of the term. And we shall say that the term "widow" **comprehends** Queen Victoria, Xanthippe, Calpurnia, Constanze Mozart, Mrs. Roosevelt, and so forth.

But, in the second place, the class of widows is marked out from all other things in the world by the fact that all the members of this class have a certain set of *characteristics*: they are human, they are female, they have been married, and their husbands have died. The term "widow" also stands for these characteristics, and calls them to the attention of anyone who understands the word. It is this set of characteristics that we are calling the "signification" of the term. The term "widow" signifies the characteristics of being human, being female, having been married, and being one whose husband is dead. To this we have to add, "generally speaking," because in a particular context the exact signification of the term *in that context* may not be exactly as we have listed it.

Thus what a term comprehends is always a *thing*, or many things, (including physical objects, people, events, states of affairs, processes, and actions). It comprehends this typewriter, that dog, those people working in the next room, all revolutions. And what a term signifies is always a *characteristic*, or several characteristics, of things (including qualities and relationships). It signifies whiteness, four-leggedness, having died, being a descendant of Roger Sherman. When a salesman presents you with a sample of his soap, you have an object that is comprehended under the brand-name; when you look up a word in the dictionary, what you get is usually information about its signification.

Perhaps the essential difference involved in this distinction can be sharpened by considering alternative ways of putting it. The comprehension of a term is sometimes called its *"extension"*—the class of things over which the term, so to speak, extends. And the signification is sometimes called its *"intension."* Or you could contrast the *implications* of a term with its *applications:* the comprehension consists of those things that the term applies *to*; and the signification consists of those characteristics that the term implies *about*, or attributes *to*, the things it comprehends. Or you could say that in a sentence like "Bring me the green book," the term "green" helps to *indicate* which book is wanted (this is its comprehending dimension), and it also *predicates* a characteristic of that book (this is its signifying dimension).

The distinction between comprehension and signification holds for all terms, of whatever sort. There is a difference, very significant for some purposes, between terms that refer to *observable* things or actions (that is, what can be perceived by the senses: apples, houses, moons, llamas, dancing, whistling), and terms that refer to things or actions that cannot be sensed (a state, government, souls, economic depressions, electrons). A baseball game you can watch, but the game of baseball you can't—though you can talk about it, and in fact if you didn't understand it, you couldn't watch a baseball game with much enjoyment.

There are no good labels for these two sorts of terms: those that comprehend observable things are sometimes called *concrete* terms; those that comprehend unobservable things are sometimes called *abstract* terms. Both of these labels are somewhat misleading, but we need not choose them here. The point is that a term like "government," just as much as a term like "apple," has both a comprehension and a signification. It comprehends individual governments, such as the governments of the United States, Thailand, and Ethiopia; it signifies a complex of interlocking human relationships that are the common features of all governments, though they would be quite difficult to specify exactly.

It would be simpler if we could get along without making this distinction. But it turns out to be indispensable if we are to understand the most important principles for using words well, and for thinking clearly *in* words. There are three particularly noteworthy features of the relation between signification and comprehension; to overlook them is the source of pretty serious confusions, and yet they cannot even be clearly described unless we make the distinction.

For, first, it must be observed that two terms can have the *same* comprehension but *different* significations. You can see that if two terms have the same signification, in a certain context, then they are bound to have the same comprehension, but it doesn't work the other way around. The term "President of the United States" comprehends the same person as the term "Commander-in-Chief of the United States Army," but these two terms do not signify the same characteristics. "Three-sided plane figure" and "three-angled plane figure" comprehend the same figures, though "side" doesn't comprehend the same things as "angle." It may be that every two-legged creature without fur or feathers is an animal that uses language, and every animal that uses language is a two-legged creature without fur or feathers. If so, then the two terms "two-legged creature without fur or feathers" and "animal that uses language" have exactly the same comprehension, but obviously their significations are utterly different. Do they *mean* the same thing? This question is ambiguous, for if "mean" means "comprehend," they do, and if "mean" means "signify," they do not.

Second, a term can have a signification and yet comprehend nothing at all. There never were any harpies (in the literal sense), and there can't possibly be any four-sided triangles, so "harpy" and "four-sided triangle" comprehend no things: there is nothing for them to apply to. But "harpy" signifies the characteristics of being a bird, having a woman's head, making horrid shrieks, and so forth. And "four-sided triangle" signifies the characteristics of being a plane figure, having three sides, and having four sides. No doubt these particular terms aren't likely to turn up in ordinary discourse, but we are often working with terms like "spies in the Signal Corps" and "nuclear-powered locomotives," and the odd thing about such terms is that we don't know, until we investigate, whether or not there are, or can be, such things. But *before* we investigate we have to know what the terms signify, or we wouldn't know what we were looking for. Is the word "chimera" *meaningless*? This question is ambiguous, for if "meaningless" means "lacking in comprehension," it is, but if "meaningless" means "lacking in signification," it is not.

Third, a term can comprehend something, and yet have no signification at all. Terms like

> Dr. Samuel Johnson
> Philadelphia
> *Uncle Tom's Cabin*
> Arcturus
> The Red Cross

are called *proper names*. They are distinguished from *general terms* because they refer to one and only one thing (or person), whereas general terms can be applied to a number of things. There are many *ships*; there is only one *Queen Mary*. Or, in other words, the comprehension of "ship" has many members, but the comprehension of "the *Queen Mary*" has only one member.

When you know the proper name of a person, you have a label by which you can refer to him, but you don't know, from the name alone, anything about him. The name "Napoleon Bonaparte" names a certain historical figure, but it does not signify any characteristics of Napoleon, such as being a general, being short in stature, or being an emperor. Proper names are tags that may be attached at will to particular things merely for reference purposes, like the call numbers of a library book or the numbers on an automobile license plate. Perhaps if a man's name is "O'Higgins," the chances are he's Irish (or South American); in that case, "O'Higgins" is more than a proper name.

Some terms that are occasionally called "names" do have a signification: *"The Decline of the West"* and *"The Adventures of Tom Sawyer"* tell us something about the books on whose title pages they appear. But these are, logically speaking, *descriptions* rather than names. It may be hard to draw a sharp and firm line between names and descriptions, and fortunately it isn't necessary for our purposes. The main point here is that it is possible for a term to comprehend without signifying.

Hence it is misleading to say, as we sometimes do, that, for example, "Theophilus" means *beloved by the gods*, or that "Peter" means *rock*. In such cases we are speaking of the *etymological derivation* of the term, that is, its *original* signification but not its present signification, for it has none. When we name a child "Peter" we are not stating that he is a rock, any more than calling a girl "Patience" or "Prudence" implies that she actually has these admirable virtues (though we may hope she will have them). This is just the difference between *naming* her "Prudence" (which we do even though she may turn out to be very imprudent) and *asserting* that she is prudent.

The three points we have been considering about the connection between signification and comprehension show how important it is to distinguish them. For, if we do not distinguish, we might think, for example, that two terms have the same meaning (signification) merely because they name the same thing: for example, "the team that finished first in the National League in 1927" and "the team that finished last in the National League in 1953." Or we might think that a word refers to nothing because it has no signification, as when Humpty Dumpty is disgusted because Alice's name doesn't "mean" anything. Or we might think that a word has no meaning (signification) because it has no comprehension ("Nothing is perfect, so how can the word 'perfect' mean anything?").

Finally, by means of this distinction we can say very clearly what a definition does and what it does not do. When you explain a word by giving examples, you call attention to part of its comprehension, and this is often quite helpful. But when it is necessary to make explicit the complete signification of the word, you must *define* it; that is, you must offer *another* term that has the same signification and is already understood.

A CHECK-UP QUIZ. In which of the following sentences does the term "mean" mean "signify," and in which of them does it mean "comprehend"? (In some of them it doesn't mean either of these things.)

1. "Xylophone" *means* a musical instrument with wooden bars of various lengths that emit distinct tones when struck with wooden hammers.

2. In this book, "ambiguity" *means* undecidability of meaning.

3. Keep out! This *means* you!

4. For people living on low wages, being out of a job even for a short time *means* a great deal of suffering.

5. In Browning's poem, "The Lost Leader" *means* Wordsworth.

6. This *means* war!

7. "Gottlieb" in Leibniz's name *means* the same as "Amadeus" in Mozart's name.

8. Whizz Fizz Soap Flakes *mean* easy dishwashing and sparkling dishes.

9. In some books, the term "sign" is used to *mean* the word "go," the song of the nightingale, Beethoven's *Pastoral Symphony*, measles spots, and I don't know what, as well as the object marked "New York 123 miles."

10. For the purposes of this Act, "redeeming stock" shall *mean* acquiring stock (by a corporation) from a shareholder in exchange for property (whether or not the stock so acquired is canceled, retired, or held as treasury stock).

FURTHER READING: Irving M. Copi, *Introduction to Logic*. New York: The Macmillan Co., 1953, ch. 4, sec. 3.

§23. TESTING A DEFINITION

For the most part, when you need to give a definition, either to get around a possible ambiguity or to help someone with an unfamiliar word, you are singling out one of the customary ways of using the term, that is, one of its ordinary significations. Under these circumstances, your definition is a statement that on some occasions people who use the term-to-be-defined attach to it the same signification as the term you use to define it. "Credulity" sometimes signifies the same as "tendency to believe upon insufficient evidence."

One of the things we want to know about such a definition as this is whether it is *true*, that is, whether people actually do use the two terms in the same sense. But this question is going to be ambiguous unless we sharpen it a little. Consider the definition:

"Bonnet"="hood."

If we take these terms as they would appear, say, in the fashion pages of *The Ladies' Home Journal*, the definition is evidently wrong, for, in the lingo of milliners, "bonnet" does *not* have the same signification as "hood." Yet it is true that what Americans call the "hood" of a car, the British call the "bonnet." So we can make the definition a true one if we put it in this way:

"Bonnet" as it appears in British writings and conversations about cars has the same signification as "hood" does in American writings and conversations about cars.

These rather cumbersome qualifications can be abbreviated and put between parentheses:

"Bonnet" (in British writings and conversations about cars)="hood" (in American writings and conversations about cars).

As we have seen, a term may signify one set of characteristics in certain kinds of discourse (in union contracts, in chess manuals, in the shop talk of actors or acrobats) and a different set of characteristics in other kinds of discourse (in Supreme Court decisions, in the *Publications of the Modern Language Association*, on bubble-gum wrappers). Every special study, like logic or the law, and every special art and craft, like oil painting or plumbing, develops its own vocabulary, sometimes inventing new terms but just as often giving new senses to terms borrowed from common speech. Logicians and plumbers can't do their work without making a number of distinctions that aren't needed by other people, and the terms they use to mark these distinctions are the *technical terms* of their fields. Thus we get such terms as "Oedipus complex" (in psychiatry), "bend sinister" (in heraldry), "entropy" (in thermodynamics), "floor joists" (in carpentry), and "pencil" (in optics).

When you want to furnish one of the significations of a term like "bourgeois" you may have to indicate the *range of contexts* you have in mind: in the files of *Life* magazine, in conversations at the Union League, in the later works of Marx, in last Sunday's editorial, in last night's news broadcast. Or, to take a simpler example, you might distinguish:

> "Pencil" (in discourses about art)="fine brush of hair or bristles" (in ordinary language).
> "Pencil" (in discourses about medicine)="small medicated stick" (in ordinary language).
> "Pencil" (in optics)="class of converging rays" (in ordinary language).
> "Pencil" (in ordinary language)="cylinder of black lead or colored chalk encased in wood or paper" (in ordinary language).

These parenthetical phrases indicate the **scope** of the definition, or rather the scope of each of its terms. Every definition has an implicit scope, though its scope may be very vaguely indicated. A dictionary, for example, does not specify the scope of each of its definitions, but it is published in a certain year and claims to report common usage current in that year. And when important meanings of a particular word are limited to a single region, or a single profession, or a single social group, a good dictionary will indicate the scope of these special senses as "medical," "nautical," "military," "law," "heraldry," "criminology." And of course some dictionaries are limited to a particular scope: they are dictionaries of slang or chemistry, or business dictionaries, or philatelic dictionaries.

Where it is important to be very precise in defining a term, or where there is some danger that a definition may be thought to be wrong because its scope is not clear, you can always be as definite about the scope as you wish to be. You can show that you are talking about the meaning the word has in the Constitution of the United States, in the works of Vilfredo Pareto, or even in Act V, Scene 2, of *Antony and Cleopatra*. But in this chapter, to save space, we shall leave out the scope of our definitions whenever it seems safe to do so.

Any two terms that have the same signification must also have the same comprehension. In a correct definition, therefore, the term-to-be-defined and the defining term apply to, or name, exactly the same things. Every person who is a widow, in the ordinary sense, is also a previously married woman whose husband has died—and vice versa. This fact provides us with a useful method for testing definitions.

Suppose we represent the comprehension of a term by a plane figure of some sort, say a circle: we can think of all the things the term refers to as being inside the circle, and all the things the term does *not* refer to as being excluded from it. Let the comprehension of the term-to-be-defined be pictured by a circular line, and let the comprehension of the defining term be pictured by a circle of crosses:

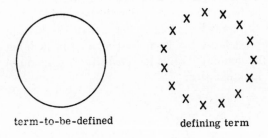

term-to-be-defined   defining term

Then in a correct definition, the two circles will exactly coincide:

The circle picturing the class of things called "dodecahedrons" (in geometry) will enclose exactly the *same* things as the circle picturing the class of things called "solids having twelve plane faces" (in geometry).

Now, you can see that there are two ways in which a definition could go wrong. The circle of the defining term might bulge out beyond the other circle, or it might fall short of it. Or it might do both: being too wide on one side and too narrow on the other. Thus there are two questions to ask about a definition when you want to know whether or not it is correct.

First, can you think of something to which the defining term applies, but to which the term-to-be-defined does not apply? Suppose someone wanted to explain the technical meaning of the word "hit"

in baseball language, and suppose you heard him propose the following definition:

> "Hit" (in baseball)="fair batted ball that enables the batter to
> reach base."

Is every fair batted ball that enables the batter to reach base a hit,
in the strict sense? No, not if someone in the field makes an error
that helps the batter to get on base when he wouldn't have been able
to do so if the error hadn't been made. Part of the signification of
the term-to-be-defined has been left out of the defining term, and
as a result the defining term is too *inclusive*. A diagram of the definition would look like this:

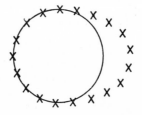

A definition is incorrect if it is too inclusive, that is, if the defining
term takes in some things that are not in the comprehension of the
term-to-be-defined.

In this case (though not always), as soon as we think of enough
examples to test the definition thoroughly, we can see how to make
it better. Suppose now that a ball is batted fair and the batter reaches
base without the benefit of an error. It is necessarily a hit? No, not if
it forces out another runner. We must add this further characteristic
to the defining term to make the definition correct:

> "Hit" (in baseball)="fair batted ball that enables the batter to
> reach base without the help of an error and without the force-out of
> another runner."

In order to be correct, then, a definition has to supply in the defining term *every* characteristic signified by the term-to-be-defined; otherwise, it will be too inclusive. In a celebrated trial some years back the
judge recommended to the jury the following definition of "perjury."

It is, he said, "the *willful* giving of *false* testimony as to a *material* matter before a *competent* tribunal *while under oath.*" Every one of the italicized words is necessary to make the definition complete.

The second question is this: can you think of something to which the term-to-be-defined applies, but to which the defining term does not apply? Consider this definition of another baseball term:

> "Run batted in" (baseball)="score made possible for a base runner by the hit of another player who is at bat."

Is batting in a runner already on base the only way a batter can get credited with an RBI? No, he can hit a home run, that is, bat himself in, and that counts as an RBI too. In short, the defining term in this example is too *exclusive*, for it leaves out some of the events covered by the term-to-be-defined, and its diagram would look like this:

A definition is incorrect if it is too exclusive, that is, if the defining term fails to take in everything that is comprehended by the term-to-be-defined.

To revise a definition that is too exclusive, we have to cut out part of the defining term. In the definition of "RBI" we easily cut out the requirement that the hit must be made by "another player." Would that fix the definition? Well, does it have to be a *hit* at all? Suppose it is an outfield fly that is caught, so the batter is out, but a runner on third gets home safe; the batter will get credit for a run batted in provided there was no error involved. Of course, there are other complications too, but we need not consider them all here. The problem is clear in any case: it is to broaden the comprehension of the defining term so that it coincides with that of the term-to-be-defined.

When the defining term is too inclusive in one respect, taking in things that don't belong, and also too exclusive in another respect, leaving out things that *do* belong, it is doubly incorrect. For example:

"Canned goods" (in United States) = "things sold in cans."

Evidently these two terms do not coincide:

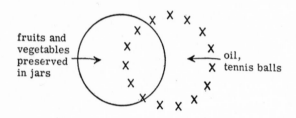

Some canned goods are things sold in cans, all right; the two circles overlap. But when you put something in a can you aren't *canning* it unless you process it in some way to preserve it from spoiling; and you *are* canning something if you preserve it by sealing it in a jar.

If a definition is either too inclusive, or too exclusive, or both, then it is incorrect. But even if two terms do have the same comprehension, they might still have different significations, so a definition that passes both of our tests might still be wrong. If it happens that every animal with pink ears and a curly tail is also an animal that eats daisies and barks, and every animal that eats daisies and barks is also an animal with pink ears and a curly tail, then the circles picturing the comprehensions of these two terms would coincide, but still the term "animal with pink ears and curly tail" would not have the same signification as "animal that eats daisies and barks." Nevertheless, comparing the two classes is a convenient *negative* check upon a definition.

You can use these tests in dealing with other people's definitions, and you can apply them to your own. When you make up a definition, it is convenient to have a method that will insure, as far as possible, that the definition will pass those tests. There is a fairly simple method in general use, and though it comes with no money back guarantee of success, it is bound to help you avoid the worst mistakes. It consists in classifying the comprehension of the term-to-be-defined.

Suppose you want to define the term "sonnet," as it is used by literary critics and literary historians. The *first* thing to do is select a class of things that you are sure is broad enough to contain all sonnets. What kind of thing is a sonnet? Well, it is a kind of *verse*. At least you are sure that all sonnets are verses—and, of course, equally sure that *not* all verses are sonnets. There are various classes you might have picked: for example, the class of *discourses*, or the class of *discourses containing less than five hundred words*. It doesn't matter very much where you start, so long as you pick a class that contains all sonnets; the larger the class, the safer you are, but the smaller the class, the sooner you'll arrive at your definition.

For the *second* part of the task consists of a series of steps by which you narrow down the defining term until its comprehension fits that of the term-to-be-defined. You have part of the defining term "... verse ..."; you must now fill in the rest of it. How do sonnets differ from all other members of the class of verse? Think of other kinds of verse, and see what needs to be added to your defining term in order to rule them out. Well, surely a sonnet always has to have fourteen lines; the defining term then becomes: "verse consisting of fourteen lines...." That's still too broad, for it includes, for example, Browning's "Misconceptions," which consists of two seven-line stanzas and is in dactylic meter. It's easy to take care of "Misconceptions"—just add the requirement that sonnets must be in iambic pentameter. Then the defining term will be: "verse in iambic pentameter consisting of fourteen lines."

Have we gone too far? It is true that some poets have applied the name "sonnet" to fourteen-line verses not in iambic pentameter, but this is very rare and somewhat perverse, and, as long as we know what we're doing, we can set their verses aside as, in fact, *misuses* of the word. But even so, we still haven't narrowed things down far enough: a fourteen-line fragment of blank verse would certainly not be a sonnet. Something about the rhyme scheme has to get into the defining term. Here we are faced with a choice. There are two things we could do, either of them legitimate and useful for certain purposes. We might abandon the project of defining "sonnet," and instead break this term down into "Shakespearean sonnet" and "Petrarchan sonnet," and perhaps invent other terms for other types of rhyme schemes. Certainly if we were to define "sonnet" as "verse in iambic pentameter consisting of fourteen lines, with the rhyme scheme *a, b, b, a, a, b, b, a, c, d, e, c, d, e,*" we would be leaving out a large number of fine sonnets.

If we insist on going ahead with our plan to define "sonnet," then we shall have to find some way of qualifying the defining term so that it is loose enough to cover various possible rhyme schemes, but at the same time tight enough to eliminate verses that are nothing but a series of couplets or have no rhymes at all. It's not easy to draw a satisfactory line here, but let's try this one:

> "Sonnet"="verse in iambic pentameter, consisting of fourteen lines, each of which rhymes with at least one other line, and some of which rhyme with nonadjacent lines."

Perhaps this will seem a bit pedantic, but it is about right: it gives a fairly close *approximate* report of the way the term "sonnet" is customarily used. Have we left out anything that might leave a loophole for error? Think of various other aspects of sonnets that could be mentioned in the defining term. Subject matter? No, sonnets are about all sorts of things, including sonnets, and no matter what it is about, we would still want to call it a sonnet if it satisfied our other conditions. The definition seems to be complete. Perhaps it can be improved upon; but only by a more thorough and careful use of the same method.

A CHECK-UP QUIZ. Are the following definitions too inclusive, too exclusive, or just right?

1. "Square" (in geometry)="equilateral rectangle."

2. "Square" (in geometry)="Parallelogram with four right angles and four equal sides."

3. "Aunt" (in ordinary language)="parent's sister."

4. "Aunt" (in ordinary language)="female relative of same generation as parents."

5. "Kite" (in talk of children)="triangular object made of wood and paper to be borne in air by wind at the end of a string."

6. "Postage stamp" (in ordinary language)="piece of paper for affixing to letters, issued by a government that promises to carry and deliver letters to which it is affixed."

7. "Moon" (in astronomy)="body revolving around a planet."

8. "Soufflé" (in cookery)="a spongy, puffed-up food."

9. "Puzzle" (in ordinary language)="a set of pieces designed to be fitted together into some prearranged pattern."

10. "Forward pass" (in football)="a play in which a player throws the ball to a teammate."

See also Exercise 21, pp. 222-23.

FURTHER READING: Morris Cohen and Ernest Nagel, *An Introduction to Logic and Scientific Method.* New York: Harcourt, Brace, and Co., 1934, ch. 2, sec. 2.

§24. EFFICIENT AND DEFICIENT DEFINITIONS

The correctness or incorrectness of a definition is one aspect of it that needs to be considered by a reader or writer, for an incorrect definition is likely to cause confusion. But there are other important aspects of definitions that affect their usefulness in the process of communication.

The whole point of giving a definition is to clarify the meaning of a discourse, that is, to make it more understandable. It is a bridge between a way of speaking that is, at least for the moment, puzzling and another way of saying the same thing that is more familiar, or less ambiguous, under the circumstances. If it doesn't succeed in guiding the reader, or listener, to language that is clearer to him, it might as well not be offered at all, for even if it is correct, it is not useful.

Now, quite often, you have a choice between two or more possible ways of defining a term. You can define "equilateral triangle" as "triangle with equal angles" or "triangle with equal sides," and for most purposes either of these will serve very well. In this example the choice is not very important because each of these defining terms is about as likely to be understandable as the other. But you can define "ankle" as "region about the joint between the foot and the leg" or as "tarsus," and in this case it might make a difference to whom you are talking. Some people don't know that "the first metatarsophalangeal joint" has the same signification as "the big toe."

When you define one term by means of another, you suppose that the second one is more understandable than the first. Of course, if you are talking with someone, and he says he doesn't understand your defining term any better than the term-to-be-defined, you can easily help him out—in two ways. You can offer an alternative definition, or you can pick out the part of the defining term that puzzles him, and define *that* too. If you are explaining, for example, some technical terms you have learned in economics, you might say "wealth" means "material things that have utility." If he doesn't understand the special sense that "utility" has in this definition, you can add that "utility" means "the capacity of a thing to satisfy some desire."

But when you are writing to an audience that can't talk back, you have to make an estimate of its linguistic equipment. Since you can't define *all* the terms you use, you have to take care that the ones you leave *un*defined will be reasonably clear. And this is where one of the common deficiencies of definition comes in.

If a person unfamiliar with American speech asked you what "black eye" means, you might give its definition accurately in this way:

> "Black eye"="ecchymosis of the flesh below the eye, produced by extravasation of blood beneath the cuticle."

If he happens to have a reading knowledge of English medical books, but not a speaking knowledge of everyday English, this definition may suit his needs nicely. Otherwise, he will be no better off than he was before, and you will have to go on and give further definitions to clarify the first one, for example:

> "Ecchymosis"="bluish discoloration."

The definition of "black eye," taken by itself, then, violates the first rule for constructing useful definitions, that is, the rule that in a definition the defining term should be at least as understandable as the term-to-be-defined to the person receiving it. For most people, the definition:

> "Tarsus" (medical)="ankle" (common speech).

is likely to be a more helpful definition than:

> "Ankle" (common speech)="tarsus" (medical).

In these two definitions, both the term-to-be-defined and the defining term are single words. They are one-word *synonyms*. Any two terms that have the same signification in *some* contexts may be called synonyms; perhaps they have other senses that are different, but they have at least one sense in common. Thus, in a correct definition the term-to-be-defined and the defining term are synonyms. Now a definition *may* be a useful one for some purposes if it points out, say, that "deglutition" is another word for "swallowing." But in general, a definition is more useful if its defining term is *not* a single word but a phrase that breaks down the signification of the term-to-be-defined, and separates out the characteristics it contains. To define "liberty" as "freedom" doesn't take us far in an understanding of the meaning of the word "liberty," and it doesn't serve to fix the particular sense that is wanted in a particular context. It is more helpful to say, for example,

> "Liberty" (political)="absence of government interference in personal conduct."

or,

> "Liberty" (political)="range of individual choices not prohibited by government."

There is a second way in which a definition can be useless even though it is formally correct. When a term is defined by means of itself (that is, when the term-to-be-defined appears in its own defining term), the definition evidently cannot do what it is supposed to do: either we don't know what the term means, in which case we can't understand the defining term, or we *do* know what it means, in which case we don't need the definition in the first place.

> "Liberty" (political)="the right to do anything that does not interfere with the *liberty* of others."

No doubt this tells us a little about the term "liberty," but it does not really define it; it only pretends to be a definition.

A definition of this sort is said to be a **circular definition.** A definition is circular when the whole of the term-to-be-defined is contained in the defining term. But note that a definition is not circular unless the *whole* term-to-be-defined appears in the defining term.

> "Freedom of speech"="freedom to speak, write, or publish any discourse that is neither (a) libelous, (b) treasonable, nor (c) obscene."

This definition is not circular, even though the word "freedom" appears in both terms. It is not "freedom" that is being defined here, but the whole term "freedom of speech," and it is quite conceivable that a person may know, in general, what "freedom" means in this context without knowing what the term "freedom of speech" means, say, to United States citizens. This definition is far from precise, but at least it is *not* circular.

Few definitions are circular by themselves. Unless a definition is pretty long and complicated, its circularity is easy to spot and likely to be corrected. But some of the definitions we encounter do not stand by themselves; they belong to *sets* of definitions. Any discourse that is fairly long and informative will turn around certain *key terms*. These terms will be used often because they mark the most important ideas in that discourse. Some of these terms will be defined by means of others; some will be left undefined. Take, for example, this book. The term "fallacy" is used in several places, and it is defined. The term "argument" is used in defining "fallacy"; the term "discourse" is used in defining "argument"; the term "word" is used in defining "discourse." But "word" is not defined in this book; it is assumed that you know well enough for our purposes what "word" means, and that there will be no serious trouble if we take care as we go along to keep out possible ambiguities.

In this way, the definitions that are used in a serious discourse— an economics book, a physics book, a cookbook, a treatise on major league baseball, or a manual for Hi-Fi fans—will arrange themselves in *chains of definitions,* one building upon the other. And though, in such a definition-chain, each of the definitions taken by itself is perfectly all right, the chain *as a whole* may be circular. Consider, for example, this trio of definitions:

> *Def. 1*: "Government"="group of people having political authority."
>
> *Def. 2*: "Political authority"="the acknowledged right to make laws and punish violations of them."
>
> *Def.3*: "Law"="regulation issued in the name of a government."

You might want to question the correctness of these definitions, but that's not the point here. The set is circular because the term "government" is used in defining "law," "law" is used in defining "political authority," and "political authority" is used in defining "government." Thus "government" is indirectly used to define itself.

There is a *third* important practical aspect of definitions, another fairly common way of misusing them. But in order to understand it we must go back a little.

There is a kind of unwritten contract between reader and writer, according to which a writer, in choosing his terms, engages himself to stick as closely as he can to common usage. This arrangement is evidently practical and convenient. But suppose there just is not available in English a word or short phrase that signifies exactly that set of characteristics you want to talk about. If for some special reason (hard to imagine, but conceivable) you wanted to write a book about the class of objects that are *pink, brittle, lighter than water, inedible, smooth,* and *combustible,* it would certainly be handy to have a name for those objects (say, "piblwiscs"). Or suppose there is a word in English for what you want to talk about, but that word has become so slippery, or so bound up with strong feelings, that you are afraid you can't control it. For example, it's almost impossible to make people understand clearly what you want to mean in a given context by the word "beauty" without such a great deal of explanation that you might often do better to find, or invent, some other word.

In these circumstances, there are two things you can do. (1) You can take an English word and extend its meaning in a new way, that is, give it a special meaning that it has never had before. How far this takes you from ordinary usage is, to be sure, a matter of degree. In this book, for example, the terms "suggestion" and "slanting" are given special senses not very different from some of the senses they already have, though sharper and more restricted. The special sense assigned to the term "comprehension" is quite different from its most familiar meaning, but the logician's term for it ("denotation") is more widely used in a different sense, and is easily misunderstood. (2) You can coin a new term. It may be an etymological derivation ("ferroequinology," "cruxverbalist"), a combination of existing words ("smaze," "smog"), someone's name ("macintosh," "micky finn"), or the first letters of a phrase ("NATO," "SHAPE"). It may be a new combination of familiar words ("definition-chain") or an arbitrary noise ("glop").

When you do either of these things—give an old word new meaning, or make up a new word—you are no longer claiming to describe other people's way of using words. You are saying, in effect, "Never mind how other people use these words (if they do at all); this is the way I propose to use them." A definition of this sort is, so to speak, an *extempore* use of words, and it may be called an **Impromptu Definition.**

In an Impromptu Definition the term-to-be-defined has a peculiarly limited scope. Its scope is not "in English" or "in Logic books," but "in *this* book," "in *this* essay," or, to put it generally, "in the *present* discourse." An Act of Congress generally contains such phrases as: "For the purpose of this Section, the term 'subversive organization' shall mean . . ." That is an Impromptu Definition.

Now let's say you are writing an essay on some contemporary novelists who are preoccupied with crime, war, and poverty. You want to distinguish between novels that merely picture these conditions and novels that appear to urge the reader to change these conditions through political action. If you plan to discuss the second type in some detail, you will find it convenient to have a term for them. You might invent a new term: "program novel." And to explain this term, you would give an Impromptu Definition:

> "Program novel" (in the present essay)="novel in which the nar-
> rator describes bad social conditions and urges political measures to
> remedy them."

This is tailormade, so to speak; cut to the particular requirements of the essay.

Though a writer is free to make his own rules and define his terms in any sense he likes, provided he can make it clear to his readers, still, he must stick to his own rules after he has made them. An Impromptu Definition is also a promise, and this is one promise a writer has an obligation to keep. Now, suppose someone writes:

> The old distinction between "luxuries" and "necessities" must be
> revised in the light of modern conditions. We must include among
> necessities what I shall call *"psychic necessities,"* under which I
> include anything that is so widely possessed in a given community
> that the deprivation of it is felt as a social handicap.

This new term, "psychic necessity," is properly introduced here by an Impromptu Definition, and, though vague, it might be an extremely useful one for marking an idea the writer wishes to call attention to and discuss. The definition, of course, considerably stretches the usual meaning of the term "necessity": under the new rule, all sorts of things, like television sets, diamond rings, whitewall tires, and expensive clothes, might be necessities in some communities, though ordinarily they would be called "luxuries." Still, as long as the writer clings to his own special usage, and takes care to help his reader follow suit, there is no logical mistake, and there is no threat to clear thinking.

Suppose, however, he introduces his term in a new sense, and then gradually shifts back into one of the old senses, so that he seems to be proving something that he really isn't proving. This would be a special kind of equivocation. He might begin, for example, by saying that only luxuries (in the usual sense of this term) should be heavily taxed. Then he might redefine the term "necessity" in this broader way, so that television sets, which were luxuries in the old sense, are necessities in *his* sense. Then he might argue that television sets should not be taxed because they are not luxuries. But this conclusion doesn't follow. If we put the argument baldly:

> Necessities [in the old narrow sense] should not be taxed;
> *therefore:*
> Necessities [in the new broad sense] should not be taxed;

it is clearly fallacious.

A **Question-begging Definition**, then, is an Impromptu Definition introduced to make a statement appear true in some ordinary sense by assigning it an arbitrary sense in which it *is* true. Consider the following dispute:

> A: "The intelligent students are the best leaders."
> B: "But look at the Alpha Alpha Alpha Honor Society; all those students have grades over 88, and only one out of fifty is a leader among the undergraduates."
> A: "Oh, you can't count *them*—they're just *grinds*. They get high grades, but I don't call them really intelligent, in my sense of the term, because they're not well rounded."

Here A starts out by using the term "intelligent" in what looks like one of its normal senses, but when B gives evidence against his statement, instead of admitting he is wrong, he shifts to an Impromptu Definition of "intelligent" so that B's objection no longer applies. But of course A has not proved that intelligent students in the *ordinary* sense of the term are leaders; he has merely changed the subject. In fact, if A is pressed to explain *his* sense of the term, he will probably have to admit that he includes being a leader ("well-rounded") as part of the definition of "intelligent." In this way he begs the question at issue, or takes for granted what he is supposed to be proving, by *defining* "intelligent" so that it becomes *true by definition* that intelligent students are leaders. You can "prove" anything that way.

Similarly, a writer is free, if he wishes, to introduce such a term as "Communist-connected organization," and define it as "organization containing at least one member who is, or has been at some time, a member of some organization containing at least one person who is also a member of an organization cited on the Attorney General's list of left-wing subversive organizations." This is a pretty useless definition since it defines the term so broadly that practically every organization in the country, including Students for America, the Attorney General's legal staff, and the DAR will be "Communist-connected" according to this definition. The connection is too thin to be worth much notice. But, as a reader, you need to keep an eye on such Impromptu Definitions that seem at first rather harmless and inane: sometimes they are brought in for the purpose of begging a question, and later in the discourse you find, if you are paying close attention, that the writer is trying to get back into his term some of the important things it ordinarily means, even though he has begun by renouncing ordinary usage.

A well-executed Question-begging Definition is, it must be admitted, one of the slickest of all verbal ploys. Nor need it be conscious and deliberate. But, in any case, it is something to watch out for. We can redefine our terms as much as we like; but by doing so we can neither change the facts nor come close to finding out what they are.

A CHECK-UP QUIZ. Which of the following definitions are *circular*? Which are *question-begging definitions*?

1. A "boss" is a person you can tell to go to the devil—behind his back.

2. A "boss" is one who orders around all other workmen except his own boss.

3. By "civil rights" I mean "freedoms that are guaranteed by the Constitution and that it is right for the government to protect."

4. A "filibusterer" is one who filibusters.

5. To filibuster is to delay legislation by making long and irrelevant speeches.

6. I propose to use the word "play" to cover all activities that are enjoyed for their own sake, whether useful or not. In this sense

art is a form of play. But obviously play is not as important as work, and therefore it follows that art is not a significant part of human life.

7. According to the usual definition, "censorship," as applied to movies, would consist in prohibiting people from showing movies after they have been made. But it doesn't seem to me to make a great deal of difference whether movies are mutilated *after* they are made or *before* they are made—that is, by imposing a childish "decency" code upon the script writers. In the end, it comes to much the same thing. Therefore, when I use the word "censorship," I mean to include all forms of restriction upon the form and substance of motion pictures.

8. A "second cousin" is the cousin of one's parent or child.

9. A "means" may be defined as something employed for the achievement of any end, or for producing something that is in turn a means for some end.

10. According to my way of using the term, an action can be called "selfish" if it results in any benefit for the person who does it, or if he *thinks* it will result in any benefit. Many gullible people talk glibly about "unselfishness," and praise others for their "unselfish acts." But from my definition it is clear that they are entirely wrong; there is no such thing as an unselfish action.

See Exercises 22, 23, 24, pp. 223-27.

FURTHER READING: James MacKaye, *The Logic of Language*. Hanover, N. H.: Dartmouth College Publications, 1939. Max Black, *Critical Thinking*. New York: Prentice-Hall, Inc., 2d ed., 1952, ch. 11.

Outline-Summary of Chapter 5

The *comprehension* of a term is the class of individual persons, places, things, or events that the term can be correctly applied to (the term "city" comprehends New York, London, Philadelphia, Tokyo, etc.). The *signification* of a term is a set of characteristics that are attributed to something when the term is applied to it (the term "city" signifies the characteristics of being a populated place, having more than 25,000 inhabitants, and having its own government). A *definition* is a statement that one term, appearing in a certain discourse or class of discourses, has the same signification as a second term, appearing in a certain discourse or class of discourses. A definition can be set forth in this form:

"City" (in U.S. census reports)="self-governing area containing more than 25,000 inhabitants" (in ordinary speech).

Some definitions are descriptions of the way a term is commonly, or customarily, used. For such a definition to be *correct*, its term-to-be-defined and its defining term must comprehend the same things. Thus a definition is incorrect:

(a) if its defining term is too *inclusive* (it would not do to define "city" as "a populated place," since some populated places are not cities but towns or villages.); or

(b) if its defining term is too *exclusive* (it would not do to define "city" as "a populated place governed by a mayor," since some cities have a city manager).

For a definition to be *useful*:

(a) its defining term should be no *less* familiar (to the reader or listener) than the term-to-be-defined (it would not ordinarily be helpful to give Dr. Johnson's definition of "to wipe" as "to take away by tersion");

(b) it must not be circular, in other words, it must not define the term by means of itself (for example, " 'a tracing' means 'an exact copy of something, made by putting thin paper over it, or over another tracing of it, and following the lines' ");

(c) it must not be a Question-begging Definition. This is an Impromptu Definition (that is, a definition that assigns a new meaning to a word) introduced into an argument in such a way as to make a debatable conclusion true by definition (for example, proving that all cows are purple by defining "cow" as "purple quadruped").

Exercise 21

Rewrite the following definitions in proper form, with "=" between the terms, and the scope indicated where it is unusual. Then test the definitions to determine whether the defining term is too inclusive, too exclusive, or both.

1. In theatre terminology, a "concert" is a public performance of music in which various instrumentalists play together.

2. To sterilize, medically speaking, is to kill bacteria by exposing them to a high temperature.

3. In the legal sense, a marriage is said to be "annulled" when it is officially declared not to be a marriage.

4. A work of literature, according to English scholars, is anonymous if it has no author.

5. A "strike" is a situation in which employees refuse to work, but do not cease to be employees.

6. A "lockout" is a situation in which an employer refuses to allow his employees to work, but does not fire them.

7. Iconoclasts are people who go around attacking things that most people believe in.

8. When two people with conflicting desires reconcile their conflict by making mutual concessions, this is called a "compromise."

9. A sacrifice is what you make when you incur some sort of loss that results in good for somebody else.

10. People who are paid to influence the votes of Senators are called "lobbyists."

Exercise 22

Criticize the following definitions, and point out, where they occur, such faults as these: (a) the defining term is too exclusive; (b) the defining term is too inclusive; (c) the defining term is too vague; (d) the defining term is ambiguous; (e) the definition is circular.

1. "Bipartisan foreign policy" means "foreign policy decided upon by the Administration after consultation with legislators of the opposing party."

2. "Symphonic poem" means "musical composition used to illustrate a story."

3. "Abstract painting" means "painting in which there is nothing similar to anything in the real world."

4. "Security risk" means "a person who might do something that would be harmful to the government's efforts to keep certain things secret."

5. "Production goods" (in economics) means "material objects used in the manufacture of consumer goods or other production goods."

6. "Professional" (in sports) means "person who supports himself entirely by funds derived from participating in sporting events."

7. "Amateur" (in sports) means "person who is not a professional."

8. "Race" (in sports) means "event in which two or more people or animals attempt to move over a certain course as rapidly as possible, in order to determine who can reach the goal first."

9. "Insult" means "remark designed to hurt someone's feelings if possible."

10. "Junto" means "group of men voluntarily combined to exercise jointly the executive powers in a party or state."

11. "Descendants" means "people descended from a person's children, or from their descendants."

12. "Slum" means "area having high population density and low average income."

13. "Christianity" means "set of beliefs and practices derived from the teachings of Jesus Christ."

14. "Ibsenism" means "set of beliefs and concepts derived from the plays of Henrik Ibsen."

15. "Illusion" means "visual perception that gives a false or misleading impression of an object or event."

Exercise 23

The following passages involve Impromptu Definitions that are introduced to make distinctions for certain purposes. Discuss the passages carefully, pointing out any mistakes in the way the definitions are given, and suggesting improvements where you can.

1. The difficulty in defining "aggression" for the purposes of international law has bothered United Nations committees for a long time. One difficulty is that, if the definition is vague, or is stated in terms of who made the first move, it will be impossible to determine definitely who is the aggressor when a clash occurs, and impossible to pin the label on one of the countries involved so that the world will acknowledge its guilt. When one country attacks another, it usually claims that the other country made threatening remarks, was secretly planning an attack, or at least looked dangerous, and there is no way to settle the matter. Now Jugoslavia's representatives on the General Assembly's Political and Security Committee have proposed a very clear and exact definition. The proposal provides (1) that within 24 hours after an attack each party announce its willingness to cease fire and withdraw on condition the other party does likewise; and (2) that the nation failing to make this announcement, or abide by it when made, be branded the aggressor. Tito evidently fears a sneak attack by one of the four Soviet satellites on his border, and he expects that such an attack would be justified by a propaganda campaign claiming that he is the guilty party; his proposal provides a clear-cut test that would take care of such a situation in advance.

2. *To the Screen Editor,* New York Times:
I have seen neither "About Mrs. Leslie" nor "Indiscretion of an American Wife" and they may be soap opera as is said in *The Times* of

Sunday, July 11. But to call them so merely because of their heroines' "ability to suffer with amazing fortitude the slings and arrows of emotional misfortune" is a mistake. Fortitude in adversity is a profound fact of life and has been expressed in literature and art (movies included), and to them, those who must endure adversity often turn to find inspiration for fortitude. What distinguishes soap opera is the use of tragedy for maudlin ends. . . . If that is kept in mind there will be less confusion between what is soap opera and what is genuine drama.

3. It is not Communism, Socialism, New Dealism, Left-Wingism, ADA-ism, or any of these, as such, that we have to fear; it is the virus that lurks equally within them all; I call it "*statism.*" Statism is opposed to Individualism; and it is the real enemy. But we cannot fight it unless we are perfectly clear about what we are fighting against. As soon as a government goes one step beyond protecting people's lives and livelihood, and begins to take *away* their lives and livelihood, that is statism. A confiscatory income tax, for example, deprives the wage earner of what he has earned by his own sweat, and a highway built at public expense deprives people of the discipline and initiative that they would experience if they had to figure how to get it built without making the government do it. Statism is leaning on the state, instead of on oneself; it is giving up one's freedom, or some part of it, for security and protection. Gestapos, price controls, concentration camps, income taxes, stock market regulations, government subsidies, a controlled press, and welfare handouts, are examples of statism.

4. *By a Philadelphia Lawyer* (*Philadelphia* Evening Bulletin):
The question to be decided here is, therefore: Is the filing of a fraudulent income tax return an offense involving moral turpitude?

Moral turpitude has been defined by the courts on thousands of occasions. One of the best definitions, in Bouvier's Law Dictionary, which is a classic in the legal profession, is that moral depravity is "an act of baseness, vileness or depravity in the private and social duties which a man owes to his fellowmen or to society in general, contrary to the accepted and customary rule of right and duty between man and man." The test, as established by legal interpretation, is the degree of baseness or vileness of principle, word or action.

There is no case exactly in point on record in Pennsylvania, but in Maryland, where the same law relating to the right to practice medicine is on the books, the court recently held that a doctor could NOT be stricken from the medical rolls because he filed a false income tax return. The reasoning of the court is quite interesting.

"We are not prepared to rule," said the Circuit Court for Prince Georges County, "that an attempt to evade the payment of a tax due the nation, or the commonwealth, or the city, or the school district, wrong as it is, unlawful as it is, immoral as it is, is an act evidencing baseness, vileness, or depravity of moral character. The number of men who have at some time sought to evade the payment of a tax or some part of a tax to some taxing authority is legion. Any man who does that should be punished civilly or by criminal sentence, but to say that he is base or vile or depraved is to misuse words."

A doctor, it would therefore seem, may lose his liberty for evading income tax, but he doesn't lose his license.

5. The editor of a new sports magazine advises prospective contributors: "On articles, the magazine is interested in the field of sport, spectator or participant. We define the field as including all sporting endeavors that involve competition, whether between human beings or between human beings and natural forces. Thus, baseball is a sport by our definition, but so is mountain climbing, cave crawling, hiking, and—of course—hunting and fishing. We would consider an Eskimo seal hunt outside our province since it is motivated by economic rather than sporting reasons. We consider exhibitions in which there is no element of competition (ice extravaganzas, gymnastic demonstrations) as entertainment, not sport." How would you state this definition in compact form? How would it apply to contract bridge? stamp-collecting? crapshooting? juggling? birthday party games like Pin the Tail on the Donkey?

6. Everyone who has reflected upon art will agree that there is a special emotion, a kind of ecstasy, difficult to describe, but unmistakable to the connoisseur which all good works of fine art arouse in us. This aesthetic emotion, as we may call it, must be caused by something in these works, something they have in common: let us describe the emotion as an experience of "*significant form*." Our question is, then, What is significant form? Consider a painting—say, El Greco's painting of Jesus in Gethsemane—and examine it attentively. It is not that it has colors, and lines, and shapes, and masses—even poor paintings have those—but that they are arranged in some special way, in a way that moves and exalts and thrills us. This is what I mean by "significant form": aesthetically moving lines and colors.

7. The new editor-in-chief of *True Confessions* has written a memorandum to writers explaining the needs of his magazine, and specifying the sense he attaches to the term "confession." "The confession story," he says, "has provided us with some of the greatest realistic, revealing, personal literature of the ages—Cellini's *Autobiography*, The *Confessions* of Jean Jacques Rousseau, De Quincey's *Opium Eater*. Boil down, to its essence, any of the great enduring fiction classics and you will find—a

confession. *Anna Karenina, Madame Bovary, Tess of the D'Urbervilles, Sister Carrie, Of Human Bondage*—these are all confession stories—all based on human emotional problems, personal conflict, human desire, human greed, human passion."

8. The United Nations is specifically ordered by Article 2, Paragraph 7, of its Charter not to "intervene in matters which are essentially within the domestic jurisdiction of any state." The problem is to define "domestic." South Africa is forcefully making its point that her treatment of Negroes is an internal affair, and no business of the United Nations. But on the other hand it can be argued that this issue, and others like it (for example, the Cyprus problem, the nationalistic revolts against France in Tunisia and Morocco, the native uprisings against the Dutch in West New Guinea), have international implications and constitute a "threat to the peace," which Chapter VII of the U.N. Charter gives it a right to deal with. But until the Charter is revised so that it lays down more exact criteria for determining when a matter is "essentially within the domestic jurisdiction of any state," there will be no agreement on these important cases, and politics and power rather than reason and law will prevail.

Exercise 24

Select three or four of the following groups of related terms. Define each term in the group, then give examples of its comprehension, if you can, and show how your definitions apply to the examples. For each group there is a note about the purpose or occasion to be kept in mind in making the distinctions.

1. "College," "junior college," "university" (for a pamphlet advising high-school seniors about going to college).

2. "Game of chance," "game of skill" (for a law regulating gambling).

3. "Lie," "white lie," "misrepresentation" (for an essay on the ethics of advertising).

4. "Mystery story," "detective story," "suspense story" (for an article on escape literature).

5. "Communist organization," "Communist-controlled organization," "Communist-front organization" (for a law about "subversive activities").

6. "Discover," "invent," "create" (for a patent or copyright law).

6

The Uses of Connotation

There must be very few comedy routines older than the double-take, which is still funny when it's well timed. A double take is a delayed response to a message of some sort: the victim hears the message, perhaps part of it registers, but he doesn't get the full meaning of it at first.

Some people rarely do double takes because they get so much meaning from what they hear or read the first time; other people, because they never do get any more of the meaning than the scrap they pick up at first glance. They read the headlines in a newspaper but not the news stories, and they don't linger over the headlines either for fear they may be missing something on the next page. They read the last chapter of the detective story first so they will get the vital part in case somebody takes it back to the library. And when it comes to poetry, they are almost completely baffled. They are, in short, so fearful of missing something that they have no idea how much they are missing.

Now, for some purposes we don't need to concern ourselves about the full meaning of a discourse. It's enough to know that the house is on fire, or that your sweetheart has jilted you. This is the *gist* of the message, and it's plenty to cope with. You aren't interested in refine-ments: that the fire started at 5:19 A.M. in the cellar, or that your sweetheart sincerely hopes you will always be friends. The ability to get the gist of an oral report, or an article, or a book in a hurry is a valuable ability. To borrow a phrase from music, it might be called "sight-reading," and sometimes it's a good thing for survival.

But when you read a newspaper report, or an article, or a book as a basis for forming opinions and making decisions about political or social or economic matters it's *not* enough to get the general idea that so-and-so is apparently a "security risk," or that those British are getting stubborn again about China, or that negotiations at a conference of Foreign Ministers have "bogged down." Here our survival, in the long run, depends on getting a much more precise and clear grasp of what is being said. Sight-reading is risky. In fact, it would be better if some people never read newspapers at all than to read them the way they do now—picking out here and there a vague and distorted half-truth, and making up their minds rapidly and unchangeably about the world, with only the foggiest notion of what is actually going on.

No doubt in the ordinary course of events we need not try to grasp all that a passage can mean, as we do in reading poems. But we often need to understand meanings that take some skill to see: the precise shade that a word has in its context, the subtle hints conveyed by a metaphor or simile. And as we get better at understanding these things, we become able to deal better with another important aspect of words—their effects upon our feelings.

In the present chapter we ought to consider, then, some of the distinctions and principles involved in interpreting the less obvious aspects of verbal meaning.

§25. DESIGNATION AND CONNOTATION

The signification of a term in a particular context is the whole set of characteristics it refers to in that context. But some of these characteristics are more closely bound up with the word than others are; they become part of its signification in a variety of contexts, they get recorded in dictionaries, and speakers of English come to regard them as the central, or core, meaning of the word. And as this meaning is more widely established and stabilized, the other meanings become more variable, more responsive to the control of context, and more easy to overlook. The interplay between these two branches of the signification makes possible some of the most vital and useful, but also some of the most tricky and deceptive, ways of using language.

The distinction between these two levels of meaning, so to speak, needs to be well marked; its importance will become clear. We shall use the terms "designation" and "connotation" to make the distinction.

When we speak, in this book, of the **designation** of a term, we shall mean a set of characteristics that has become a fairly standard or common signification of the term. If there are several standard senses, then the term has several designations. But lay that complication aside for the time being. When a term acquires a fairly fixed conventional meaning, it applies to a distinct set of things, and these things are its *comprehension*. They are grouped together in a class. But on what grounds? Well, ordinarily such a group is like a club or organization of some sort—there are rules of membership, or qualifications that each thing has to possess in order to be admitted. The class of *cots*, for example, includes all lightweight beds; in other words, to be included in this class, an object must be (1) a bed, or something you can sleep on, and (2) light in weight. This pair of characteristics marks off the class of cots from all other classes in the world, and we shall say that the term "cot" *designates* these two characteristics. The designation is *part* of its signification.

Of course, individual cots have a lot of other characteristics besides being light in weight and being a bed: some are wooden, some metal; some are stretched with canvas, some with wire mesh; some fold up, some don't; some are comfortable, some are not. But being light in weight and being a bed are the *indispensable* characteristics of cots, and only these two characteristics are involved in the standard, or customary, meaning of the term "cot." Even if it turned out that every cot that ever existed happened to be painted purple, we would probably not include this characteristic in the designation of "cot," for if someone decided to paint his cot yellow, we would still be willing to call it a "cot"; but if he boarded up the sides, filled it with dirt, and planted petunias, we would no doubt say that he had transformed it into something else.

It may at first give you a little trouble to find that in a number of books on English composition and rhetoric, the word "denotation" is used for what we have here called the "designation" of a term. This use of the word "denotation" is a shift from the sense universally assigned to it in logic books—just as the word "presently" in ordinary speech is gradually being shifted from its original meaning "shortly afterward" to "at present." In this book we shall avoid the term "denotation" because of its variability of meaning. Whenever, in another book, you find the term "denotation" used in the sense of "dictionary meaning," you have only to substitute the term "designation," to translate its terminology into the one used here.

But over and above the standard signification of a term (that is, its designation), there may be certain nuances of meaning that are more difficult to describe because they are less obtrusive or more dependent upon context than designation. Because cots are always, and by definition, light in weight, they are *generally*, though not always, readily portable; hence they tend to be moved about, and to be a relatively impermanent place to sleep. They are *likely* to be less expensive, less impressive, less handsome than fullfledged beds; a cot is therefore often thought of as the sort of bed slept in by a poor man, or a humble and unpretentious man, or a servant, or a man who does not expect to stay long. These characteristics are not part of the designation of the term, but some of them *are* part of its full signification in some contexts. We shall consider them, then, as part of the **connotation** of the term "cot," and we shall say that a term *connotes* those characteristics which, in one context or another, are part of its full signification but not part of its designation.

To make the notion of connotation as clear as possible, we have to draw two lines here, and neither of them can be very sharp.

Connotation, as just indicated, is bounded on one side by designation. It may be very difficult to tell on some occasions whether a characteristic belongs to the designation or the connotation of a word. But if the distinction can't be made with perfect precision, fortunately it does not need to be. What happens is that we find a pair of terms ("hurt" and "offended") or a whole set of them ("irritated," "annoyed," "cross," "mildly angry," "put out," "slightly burned up") whose significations overlap almost completely, but not quite. In some contexts you could substitute one for the other without doing any damage. But there are other contexts in which the difference, however subtle, might be tremendous. And this difference we are calling a difference in "connotation," to call attention to its importance.

Connotation is bounded on the other side by what we may call the *personal associations* that each one of us individually may come to attach to certain words. Some people are irrationally disturbed by snakes, or spiders, or cats; others are not. Individual childhood experiences or unconscious fears may give to certain words, because of the objects they refer to, certain special associations. But these are private association; connotations are public in the sense that they can be recognized and understood by anyone who learns the language. Even if you were once chased by a cow, and the word "cow" is associated in your mind with danger and violence, you can perceive, at the same time, that in the common world of the English language "cow" connotes the opposite characteristics: friendliness, placidity, and gentleness. Of course, private associations may develop into public connotations in a neighborhood, region, or nation, and at any time there will be meanings, such as poets occasionally toy with, that are on the border. But the distinction is still useful, and, indeed, you can't do without it. For when you wish to communicate with others with the help of verbal connotations, you must know which of the meanings you *think* you are communicating are only in your own mind and which are understandable to your audience.

As some of the previous examples show, the connotation of a term is most clearly brought out by comparing it with a close synonym. The terms "brother" and "male sibling" are synonyms, for example, and in many books on psychology or child development you could use them interchangeably. But in "Am I my male sibling's keeper?" there is something missing. What is missing here is the connotation of "brother," which includes a number of characteristics that are not part of the dictionary meaning of "brother," but *are* part of its full meaning in the context of Genesis. This may seem like a farfetched example, but compare some of the famous phrases in the King James version of the Bible with the translations of them in the Revised Standard version that appeared a few years ago: "affliction" (Acts 7:34) has become "ill-treatment"; "whited sepulchres" (Matthew 23:27) has become "whitewashed tombs"; and in St. Paul's phrase (1 Corinthians 13), "sounding brass" has become "a noisy gong."

To work out the connotations of a term when it is important to do so, we have to consider four things on which they depend.

First, a term acquires some of its connotations from what is generally true, or from what is generally believed to be true, about the things it comprehends. Because most cots are rather temporary resting places, "cot" can connote impermanence, though it doesn't *designate* impermanence, since a cot doesn't *have* to be temporary by definition. Because most paper is white, "paper" can connote whiteness. Because most people *think* (however unjustly) that pigs are gross, lazy, greedy, dirty, and stupid, the word "pig" connotes grossness, laziness, greediness, dirtiness, and stupidity.

Thus we discover some of the connotations of a term (not that it can have all of them in a particular context) by finding out about the things it applies to, and also by finding out what people *believe* about those things. Of course these beliefs will vary from one sector of society to another in various ways: farmers will know more about pigs than city people, and they may have different beliefs about the weather from the meteorologist's. A term can take on special connotations if it is used by people of a certain social class, financial group, political persuasion, or occupation. Not all English words are specialized in that way: practically everyone, high or low, smart or dumb, drunk or sober, uses words like "house," "chair," and "pie." But it is usually a certain sort of person who calls magazines "books"; a housewife with certain attitudes who always refers to her house as her "home"; a man of a certain vocation (or avocation) who calls a rope a "line"; a person of rather definite opinions who always expresses his displeasure with a previous administration by the phrase "pinks and minks."

Second, then, a term acquires some of its connotations from its tendency (if any) to be used by people of a certain kind. So when we care to be really thorough in grasping the subtlest connotations of a term, we want to ask what sort of person would be likely to use this term in this context, and what sort of beliefs would such a person be likely to have about the situation or object to which the term is applied. Of course, for practical purposes, we seldom have to be this meticulous. As with so many of the principles discussed in this book you can only say: it is well to know *how* to do it when you *have* to, but you don't *do* it all the time.

Third, a term acquires some of its connotations by implicit cross reference, so to speak, to other words with similar sounds. Even a combination of syllables that somebody has just made up (without yet assigning it any designation at all) can have connotations. Some of the sounds in our language that aren't words themselves turn up in several words with overlapping meanings. Take "sn" in

sneeze	snuff	snoot
snore	snoop	snooze
snort	snub	snicker
sneer	sniff	snivel
	sniffle	

—they all have something to do with noses. (Or think of words beginning with "bl" that involve a sudden, or blurred, noise.) No wonder you can make up words beginning with "sn" that will connote some connection with noses, even if they have no designation. This is of course the secret of most of Lewis Carroll's Jabberwocky words, like "slithy" and "chortle." It also helps to explain the vague but undeniable connotations of words like "Pyrex" (something to do with fire and chemistry) and "Crisco" (crispness, cleanness, efficiency).

Fourth, a term acquires some of its connotations from the contexts in which it has been used in the past. "Sepulchre" and "tomb" must have nearly the same designations. But they have different histories as English words; they have appeared in different places in the Bible, in English poetry, in essays and sermons and novels; and now their connotations are different, too. The term "bread" has appeared in many memorable contexts:

> Give us this day our daily bread . . .
> This is the bread of life . . .
> Cast your bread upon the water . . .
> Man cannot live by bread alone . . .
> A jug of wine, a loaf of bread, and thou / Beside me . . .
> I *do* like a little bit of butter to my bread! . . .

And "bread" has acquired an enormous range of potential connotation. They can't all be effective at the same time; in fact, some of the connotations of "bread" conflict. The *actual* characteristics connoted by the term in a particular context will be those that emerge from the whole context as the connotations of all the words clash, intersect, cancel out, or fuse together into a whole.

Thus each term has a range of possible connotations, but its actual connotations vary from context to context. And the range of possible connotations itself changes, of course, from time to time with the course of human history and of human knowledge. As people's beliefs about apples and ghosts change, as new stories are told, and poems are made, about them, the connotations of "apple" and "ghost" change too. You can see this clearly in the history of certain proper names. When the people who bear them have some prominent feature or some special behavior on which their fame rests, the names themselves acquire specific connotations. And if the names are often used in contexts that emphasize their connotations, the connotations become so familiar that the proper names lose their capitals and become general terms. So we get "pasteurize," "bowdlerize," "fletcherize," and "mesmerize," and "mae west" life belts. Some of these *eponyms* are given conventional definitions and hence standardized meanings, and come to *designate* fairly fixed characteristics: "boycott," "lynch," "quisling." Others seem to resist any such pinning-down, at least for a time: who can find a satisfactory conventional definition for "napoleonic" or "mccarthyism"?

Poetry is the best place to study word connotations. Indeed, what makes a poem a poem (not just verse) is in part the complexity and coherence of its connotations. But that, you might say, is an advanced course. For a general grasp of how they work, and how they can lead to confused thinking, we will do better to turn to the language of politics, and the language of advertising.

One of the important ideas in politics is that of *coming to terms with someone through willingness to modify one's original demands.* This way of putting it precisely makes it sound technical, but the basic situation it refers to can be illustrated in a thousand ways: for example, one child wants another to push him on a swing, and the other wants to be the one that gets pushed; they agree to take turns. Now, this very general idea is the common core of meaning in a whole series of familiar terms: "compromise," "mutual concessions," "mutual adjustment," "appeasement," "arbitration," "conciliation," "horse-trading," "give-and-take," "meeting each other half way." Not that all these terms have exactly the same designation, but that their designations overlap, and in some cases coincide.

Now, the kernel of these terms is a process that nearly everyone can recognize to be a part of normal democratic human and social relations. But they have nice shades of difference in meaning as regards (1) the degree to which one party gives in to another, (2) the amount of advantage gained by giving in, (3) the extent to which threats of force are hinted at, (4) the amount of reasonable discussion and deliberate thought involved in the process. Now suppose the United States Government reaches an agreement with another government after negotiations in which each side has made some concessions to the other in order to achieve a working arrangement—on fishing rights, oil, armaments, air bases, or disputed boundaries.

Several words might be used to describe this agreement, and they will all cover the essential facts. But each will also, unless the context guards against it, import a judgment about the case—that the United States gave in too far, or got too little in return, or was too spineless, or too hasty. These judgments, or some of them, may be true; the point to notice here, however, is that they are not stated explicitly so that they can be discussed on their merits; they are brought in slyly, via the connotations of the word selected, and they are easily overlooked by the unwary. Because the term "appeasement" is *roughly* apposite, its *extra* hints are accepted uncritically. Someone might call the agreement a "Munich," but that would be less subtle. Call it "appeasement" and people will half think of Munich without taking time to ask themselves exactly what are the respects in which it is, or is not, like Munich; call it "appeasement" and the damage may be done.

It is no wonder that sometimes, during a given election campaign or while a certain issue is before Congress, certain terms come to be repeated over and over by one side or another because their very useful connotations afford a chance to make all sorts of insinuations that would not survive careful scrutiny if they were baldly stated. After a time, of course, these words ("Isolationism," "New Dealism," "Fair Dealism") begin to wear thin; they are tossed about so carelessly that they no longer stand for anything very definite or identifiable. In the end they often wear out; but by that time a new set of terms has begun to take their place.

The same search for richly connotative words is carried on constantly by the advertising copywriters. Think of the names and descriptions of some of the most highly-touted products, and the key words of the most incessant commercials. What is meant by the injunction to be a "Dawn girl," to wear a "Dentosweet smile," to develop an "English complexion?" What is hinted at by saying that a cereal is "shot from guns," that a cigaret is "toasted," that a club soda has "pinpoint carbonation," or that a car has a "dynaflow" transmission or "floating power?" Without spelling things out, such words conjure up all sorts of desirable characteristics. Some words seem almost indispensable; whether you are selling pastes, lotions, oils, greases, or unguents, they must be called some kind of "cream": skin cream, hair cream, dental cream, or suntan cream.

For a more careful study of connotation, it is instructive to look among advertisements for groups of words that all have connotations of a similar sort. For example, there are the scientific-connotation terms: terms that carry with them the intimation that the product is the result of "laboratory research," is recommended or approved by doctors and druggists, is used by people "in the know," has been tested by the most delicate instruments and the tests coordinated by the most advanced statistical techniques, or contains some new, secret, complicated, marvellously effective ingredient. If you aren't a chemist, and if you haven't read impartial reports, say in *Consumer's Union*, you don't get much information (in terms of designation) when an advertisement tells you that something contains "Solium," "Solv-ex," "Duratex," "Aquasil," or "*Activated* Seismotite." Even if it gave the chemical formulas, that would mean nothing to most of us. Suppose a gasoline does contain platinum or "Petrox"; how do we know whether this is a good thing or a bad thing? Still, these terms have a strong flavor of the chemical laboratory and of industrial research, and they make a ready appeal to anyone who thinks that what is vaguely "scientific" must be good.

Now maybe that car, that hair lotion, or that whiskey actually does have not only the characteristics designated, but also the characteristics connoted, by the words used to describe it. But very often, of course, it does not. And if you were out to do a subtle and legally safe job of misrepresentation—if you wanted to promise more than you could deliver without making the promise open enough so that you could be held to it—you would pick your words largely for their connotations. It's no wonder that in some quarters the use of highly connotative words comes to be thought of as inevitably a form of lying, that people mistrust them and yearn for a plain unvarnished statement. But you don't have to be that cynical; you merely have to be a little wary. When you are asked to buy or do something on the ground that something is true, you always have a right to know what it is that is said to be true, and to know this clearly and fully you have to be aware of the connotations of the words in which it is stated.

But as a writer or speaker, also, you have to be sensitive to connotations. Otherwise you will find too late that you have said what you didn't want to say, and didn't even *know* you said. Sometimes the effect is merely goofy. A newspaper headline, for example, says

IOWA'S AUTOMOBILE
DEATH TOLL LAGGING

The subhead explains that there have been no deaths in two days, but "lagging" has the connotation of failing to reach a desired goal. The Giants can lag, but they are in there *trying*; to say the death toll is lagging is, implicitly, to say it's too bad the Iowa drivers can't kill more people than *that*.

The same insensitivity to connotations, and to fine distinctions between one term and another, may be observed in what has been called the "Elongated Yellow Fruit" school of writing. The principle of this school is to avoid using the same term twice in the same discourse, by means of Elegant Variation; the banana becomes an "elongated yellow fruit," the cow becomes a "bovine milk factory," the tennis ball a "furry sphere," the oyster a "succulent bivalve," and so on. Not that these are synonyms; they are merely alternate ways of referring to the same things. But the variation in terminology is purposeless and misleading; the only safe principle here is that if you are talking about the same thing, you do well to stick to the same word.

Of course, these examples are merely ludicrous. The same sort of mistake in misjudging the connotations of a term, when it is made in a letter, or a diplomatic message, or a contract, may be disastrous.

A CHECK-UP QUIZ. Complete the following advertisement in two different ways: first, by choosing the term in each parenthesis that gives the whole passage the greatest snob appeal (that is, the term that connotes approval by, or use by, people with pretensions to social prestige); second, by choosing the term in each parenthesis that gives the passage the most pronounced air of being scientific (that is, the term that has a scientific connotation).

Ladies! No more (1: flabby, stout, overstuffed, inflated, unhealthily fat) figures! Now (2: on the market, available, perfected, ready) at last, a revolutionary new (3: product, formula, blend, discovery) that we (4: guarantee, assure you, have established by test, claim) will (5: take off, eliminate, remove, cut down, decrease) (6: unwanted, excess, extra, bulging) flesh in a short time. No (7: dieting, starving yourself, depriving yourself of food, counting calories)! Just get (8: Reduco, Sylphine, Decrex, Lard-off)—start taking it today. Within a few days your (9: poundage, weight, effect on the scales) will begin to (10: drop, fall off, disappear, decrease to normal).

See also Exercises 25 and 26, pp. 257-58.

FURTHER READING: Edward A. Tenney and Ralph M. Wardle, *A Primer for Readers*. New York: Appleton-Century-Crofts, Inc., 1942, ch. 2. Cleanth Brooks and Robert Penn Warren, *Modern Rhetoric*. New York: Harcourt, Brace and Co., 1949, ch. 10.

§ 26. INTERPRETING A METAPHOR

If words had no connotations, we could all talk very plainly to each other, but we could not do some of the things with language that we now do. In a language especially invented for certain scientific purposes—a language like mathematics or symbolic logic—the terms have their designations fixed exactly and unambiguously, and they are not permitted to acquire connotations. Even when the physicist or sociologist uses the English language, he will, if he is skillful, select and arrange his words so that they cancel out each other's connotations and keep the sense steadily to a level of designation. Not that you must eliminate connotations to be clear; it's just easier to be clear without them. But such a language as this, though perhaps indispensable for some technical purposes, lacks some of the conveniences that we rely a good deal upon in ordinary affairs of life. One of these conveniences is *figurative language*, which would be impossible without connotations.

Rhetoricians have distinguished, and named, a large variety of figures of speech, though these have never been very systematically classified. There are, for example, similes, metaphors, analogies, parables, tropes, myths, and symbols. And besides these there are more special kinds of figure, as when we speak of a thing as a person (personification), a part as a whole (synecdoche), or one thing as another thing that is associated with it (metonymy). Such distinctions can be useful for analyzing certain kinds of discourse; a student of poetry needs to know about them. But in this book we are concerned with less specialized features of speech and writing, and it's not necessary for us to deal with them individually and in detail.

There are two things common to all figurative ways of speaking. In the first place, a figure of speech is a *condenser*: it compresses a lot of meaning into a few words. This is its economic aspect. When the poet says, "My love is like a red, red rose," he is saying that she is young, and fair, and lovely, and that her beauty, which is at its peak, will probably not last very long, but while it lasts it is wonderful, . . . and he is saying much more besides. The paraphrase of this simile differs in several ways from the simile itself; one way it differs is in being a good deal more wordy. In the second place, a figure of speech accomplishes its condensation of meaning by importing into the description a *picture* of some kind. This is not to say that the poet asks us to imagine his love as looking something like a rose (the way pansies are given human faces in a children's storybook); but in describing his love, he calls our attention to roses (roses in full bloom) and invites us, so to speak, to read off the relevant qualities of roses that are to be attributed to his love.

No doubt this sketchy account of figurative language is oversimple; the whole process is pretty complicated, and there is much about it that is not well understood. But so far as it goes, it is correct. And these two points will help us understand, as we go on, both the *usefulness* of figurative language, not only to poets but to all of us, and the *misuses* of it that can happen in the hands of a careless or unscrupulous writer.

The significant features of figurative language can be seen most clearly in metaphor, which is probably the commonest sort of figure in ordinary speech and writing. There are certain points about metaphor that we need to understand so that we can manage them well, both as readers and as writers.

The first step is to define "metaphor." Now, a metaphor can be a *statement* ("The wind is sharp") or a *phrase* ("The sharp wind of the North"). This distinction is not important here, so we shall use a single term to cover both sorts; let us call them *metaphorical attributions*. In every such attribution there is a term to which some other term is applied (the term "wind" in the examples above), and there is another term that is applied *to* it (the term "sharp"). It is convenient to have a name for the latter term; let us call it the *qualifier*. A metaphorical attribution, then, is a metaphor whether the qualifier is a noun ("He is a *wolf*"), an adjective ("a *wolfish* appetite"), or a verb ("He *wolfs* his food"). For the most part we shall discuss statements, but what is true of them can be extended to metaphorical phrases as well.

We commonly distinguish between metaphorical and *literal* attributions. The literal meaning of the word "pig" is just its designation: that is, the characteristics of being an animal, having four legs, having a snout, and so forth. If you say, "The animal in that pen is a pig," this statement *can* be literally true; an animal can have four legs. Of course, it *may* be false; but it need not be. Now, if you say, "That man over there is a pig," it is clear that this statement *cannot* be literally true. The designation of "man" includes the idea of two-leggedness; the designation of "pig" includes the idea of four-leggedness. And these are contradictory ideas. So it's impossible for a man to be *literally* a pig. If he *is* a pig, he can only be one *metaphorically*.

To say that a man is (metaphorically) a pig is, briefly, to say that he has the characteristics *connoted*, but not the characteristics designated, by the word "pig." He is *not* four-legged, snouted, tailed. He *is* greedy, gross, lazy, dirty. Or, at least, he has whichever of these characteristics the whole context admits: if you say he is an "industrious pig," that cuts out one of the connotations.

A **metaphorical statement,** then, is a statement that has two paradoxical aspects. (1) It cannot be literally true, because some of the characteristics designated by its predicate-term are inconsistent with some of the characteristics designated by its subject-term. In other words, it is self-contradictory on the level of designation. Take, for instance, the Marxist slogan: "Religion is the opiate of the masses." "Opiate" designates a narcotic chemically derived from opium; that is its literal meaning. And religion cannot be an opiate in *this* sense. (2) It is not self-contradictory (though it may be *false*) on the level of connotation. That is, the predicate-term connotes other characteristics that can be meaningfully applied to the subject-term, for example, the characteristics of inducing lassitude, unconcern, inaction, and sleep. And religion could *conceivably* have some of these characteristics, even if it doesn't. This metaphorical statement, then, *must* be literally false; whether it is metaphorically true or false depends on whether religion does have, or does not have, the characteristics connoted by "opiate of the masses."

A metaphor is a special feat of language, like juggling several plates in the air at one time. It is easy to find clear-cut examples of obviously metaphorical phrases and sentences. Some of them, indeed, have contributed much to the clarity and confusion of recent history: "Fair Deal," "bottleneck," "Communist underground," "fifth column," "book-burning," "containment," "brainwashing," "chain reaction."

But, as with all the most useful distinctions about our language, the term "metaphor" has some vagueness around its edges.

Metaphors are bounded on one side by "dead metaphors": phrases and statements that once were metaphorical but have solidified into new literal meanings. "Leg of a table," "head of a cabbage," and "eye of a needle" are no longer living metaphors. Though the word "sincere" comes from a Latin expression that meant "without wax" and referred to coins that haven't been nicked of some of their metal and the holes filled with wax, the metaphorical root of "sincere" is hidden, and you don't need to know anything about its etymology in order to understand its present designation.

Metaphors are bounded on the other side by one kind of nonsense. Take the metaphor about religion; you can imagine dropping out the word "opiate" and trying a series of other words, say, "music," "whiskey," "monkey wrench," "ash tray," "double-entry bookkeeping," or "broccoli." Some of these words will still make a metaphor: "whiskey," for example, has some connotations that could (however falsely) be attributed to religion. (Compare "Music is the brandy of the damned," in Shaw's *Man and Superman*.) Some of the others at first seem to be utterly inapplicable, but after you think about them, you can hit upon one or two connotations that could apply, and though the statement (for example, "Religion is the ash tray of the masses") may be pretty queer and strained, it might still have some slight metaphorical meaning. But "broccoli" seems to have no connotations at all that can be connected with religion. And in that case the statement, "Religion is the broccoli of the masses," is no metaphor at all; it doesn't say anything, even anything false; it is just nonsense.

Because a metaphor is an indirect way of speaking, much of its meaning is generally not on the surface, evident at a glance. It needs to be looked at with a little extra care. It may have to be *interpreted*.

To interpret a metaphorical statement is to paraphrase it in literal terms. "He is a pig" means he is lazy, gross, greedy, etc. These terms make explicit what is implicitly connoted, in this context, by "pig." But note the "etc." It might be possible to list all the characteristics connoted by "pig" in this very simple and crude metaphor: that would be a *complete interpretation* of the statement. But many metaphors are a good deal richer than this. "She was a phantom of delight": perhaps it would be impossible to list all the characteristics connoted by such a metaphor, and in such a case we have to be content with a *partial interpretation*. That is why we need the "etc."

When a metaphor appears in a poem, it is important to understand all you can of the meaning. Here the function of a partial interpretation is that, even if it only gives part, it can set you on the right path for feeling your way further into the complexities of the metaphor. The rest depends on experience, readings and rereadings of the poem. When a metaphor appears in an *argument* (and this is what we're concerned with), the situation is somewhat different. If the metaphorical statement is a conclusion, we want to know whether the reasons given are good enough to prove it; if it is a reason, we want to know how good a reason it is. But to do this, we don't need to know everything that the metaphor can mean; we only need to know what bearing it has on the point of the argument, or what bearing other statements have upon it. Thus the function of the partial interpretation is to bring out as explicitly as possible, so there can be no mistake about it, exactly what the metaphor says that is relevant. Or if it is ambiguous in some respect, we want to note that too.

The method of interpreting a metaphor is clear cut in itself, but it takes imagination to apply. Consider the sentence, "Russia has drawn an iron curtain across Europe." The first thing to do is to get the *terms* of the metaphor straight. In this sentence we have a double metaphor. In the main metaphor, Russian diplomatic behavior toward Western Europe is said to be a case of drawing a curtain, but within the metaphorical term of the main metaphor, the curtain is said to be an iron one.

The second step is to consider the range of *possible* connotations of the qualifiers, beginning with the smallest units and working out to larger contexts. You think of the characteristics of curtains (the kind you draw): their tendency to shut out air, light, and sound, to billow in a wind, to get dusty, etc. Next you think of the characteristics of iron: its hardness, brittleness, its uses for war, etc. When you try to put these two groups of connotations together, some of them (for example, dustiness) cancel out, whereas others coalesce into the idea of something that is strong, guarded, hard to penetrate, etc. When you add the connotations of "drawing a curtain" (the secrecy and suspense), you have the complicated skein of characteristics that are all wound up together in the meaning of this metaphor. The sentence says (whether truly or falsely) that Eastern and Western Europe are being prevented from communicating with one another; that this is keeping information from getting into and out of Eastern Europe; that the lack of communication is the fault of the Russians; that the boundary line is manned by armed troops, and so forth.

The full meaning of a metaphor, then, depends on (a) the possible connotations of the metaphorical qualifier, (b) the designation and connotations of the term to which it is applied, and (c) the whole context. This can be made clearer by two sorts of comparison. First, compare two different metaphorical uses of the same term:

(1) The car was *crawling* through the fog.
(2) "What should such fellows as I do *crawling* between heaven and earth?"

Crawling things can't see far ahead, and they are generally thought to be contemptible; the first of these characteristics is emphasized in 1, but not in 2; the second characteristic is emphasized in 2 but not in 1. Second, compare two different metaphors with overlapping meanings in the same context:

(3) "We are threatened by Creeping Socialism."
(4) "No, I call it Seeping Socialism."

These are both rather loose metaphors, but they have some meaning. Both say that Socialism is coming slowly; 3 says that it is being deliberately, though secretly, promoted by people who can easily be stopped once their aims are recognized; 4 says that it is taking place without anyone's really wanting it, by default, and cannot be stopped without careful examination of the economic system.

You can see why metaphor is so useful to our writing and speaking —and also why it is sometimes so dangerous. Apart from its aesthetic aspects, it is one very handy way of quickly extending our stock of words to new situations. If we can find a word that designates the particular quality, and degree, of tenseness widely felt before, or during, an important international conference, then we can use that word. But when there is no such word, we turn naturally to a comparison. Of course we can make comparisons without speaking metaphorically, or using any figure of speech: "I was as mad as you were." But a literal comparison doesn't say very much until we develop it at some length; you put more into a few words if you say, "I was as mad as a hornet." So in describing the tenseness of the international situation, we may say it was the tenseness of a ball game tied up in the ninth, or the tenseness of a man at the dentist's, or the tenseness of the beginning of the development section in the finale of Mozart's G minor symphony. These are different kinds of tenseness. We don't have any general terms for them, but we can apply them metaphorically to anything we like.

But the trouble with all metaphors is that they have a strong pull on our fancy. They tend to run away with us. Then we find that our thinking is directed, not by the force of the argument at hand, but by the interest of the image in our mind. It is this kind of *Picture Thinking* that makes political cartoons so effective and so confusing. The cartoon may say something very clearly—but it may say too little or too much. The mutual pressure of wages and prices in a time of inflation is startlingly like a revolving door with "John Q. Public" caught in it (you have no doubt seen such a cartoon)—but if you begin to think about economics solely in terms of revolving doors, soaring balloons, and seesaws, the effectiveness of your thinking is bound to be limited.

The same thing can happen when you use a metaphor. You can speak of the evidence against a defendant in court as a "chain of evidence," and this way of speaking is helpful. But you must take care that you and your reader don't get misled. A chain fails to hold if one link breaks—evidence is not like that. "Net" or "web" would be a better metaphor, but even this could be misleading; if a net is torn at one point, the quarry may slip through. A good case, in a trial, is more like a large tree upside down: even if you sawed off some branches, the rest could hold it up, though if you saw off too many, it will topple. But even this metaphor has connotations that don't apply to evidence.

This is the problem about metaphorical statements, then. Because they really are *bundles* of statements, like the one about the iron curtain, they usually are partly true and partly false. You could say, if you like, that one metaphor contains more truth than another if more of its connotations do actually apply. "Iron curtain" is a fair description, in some respects, of the line that divides Eastern from Western Europe. But when someone invented the term "bamboo curtain" to describe the Communist frontiers in the Orient, he was led astray by a very superficial parallel. "Bamboo curtain" is a ludicrously inappropriate description. It connotes something oriental, all right, but that's as far as its truth goes; it also connotes something thin, pliable, penetrable, decorative, and rather delicate.

But, after all, what matters to us at any particular time is not that one metaphorical statement contains more truth, or less falsity, than another. The important question is whether it is true in the respects in which it is relevant to the argument. A few years ago, a clergyman who was arguing that scientists, as well as clergymen, have to believe some things they can't prove, said, "The slip of faith is always showing beneath the skirt of science." This sounds rather witty until you interpret it, but then it turns out that the clergyman was not saying what he evidently wanted to say, and apparently *thought* he was saying. For his metaphor says, among other things, that scientists ought to conceal their faith.

Similarly, if someone says, "Literature is the mirror of life," and challenges us to agree or disagree, we can only refuse to do either. The question "Is literature the mirror of life?" is not a simple question, but a collection of questions, one for each of the connotations in the metaphor. Is a literary work in some way derived from the experience of its author? No doubt. Is a literary work ever a point-for-point copy of some actual occurrence? Very doubtful. Is one of the values of literature that it enables us to see and understand ourselves? Many would agree that this is so. Is the sole function of literature to imitate or mimic the external appearance of human behavior? Nobody would agree to this.

Managing metaphors is a bit like managing a nursery school. Even when things seem to be going well you have to be on the alert for signs of conflict, accidental bumps, or wandering off. In other words, all metaphors are nursery schools, including this one.

A CHECK-UP QUIZ. Here are two metaphorical descriptions of the same event. Ten statements are listed below. For each statement, say whether you think it states part of the meaning of A or of B, or of both, or of neither.

A: After persistent prodding by this Committee, the Administration has finally taken the lid off this unsavory situation in the Government Printing Office.

B: After some nudging by this Committee, the Administration has agreed to poke a flashlight into the questionable corners of the Government Printing Office.

1. There are spies and traitors in the Printing Office.

2. The Administration was at least somewhat reluctant to have the situation in the Printing Office publicly aired.

3. The Administration was at first very unwilling to have the situation in the Printing Office publicly aired.

4. The Administration is now taking an active part in the investigation.

5. It may well turn out, when the investigation is completed, that the situation is *not* very serious.

6. The Administration has tried hard to prevent the Committee from getting the facts.

7. If the situation is publicly exposed, it will be at least partly because of the work of the Committee.

8. The Administration has not been paying much attention to the possibility of wrongdoing in the Printing Office.

9. The Administration has been aware of the possibility of wrongdoing, but has ignored it.

10. The exposure of the situation in the Printing Office is likely to be something of a public scandal.

See also Exercises 27 and 28, pp. 258-60.

FURTHER READING: Hugh R. Walpole, *Semantics*. New York: W. W. Norton, Inc., 1941, ch. 7. Cleanth Brooks and Robert Penn Warren, *Modern Rhetoric*. New York: Harcourt, Brace and Co., 1949, ch. 11. Porter G. Perrin, *Writer's Guide and Index to English*. Chicago: Scott, Foresman and Co., 1942, pp. 229-241.

§ 27. EMOTIVE LANGUAGE

Poets, politicians, and proverb-makers have testified that there are many things you can do with words if you know how to use them. Even the old myths in which words magically move a mountain, open a cave, or wake an enchanted princess, might be regarded as a metaphorical way of recognizing that without language the pyramids, the Aztec temples, and the football bowls could never have been built.

One of the things you can do with words is arouse people's feelings. This can be done in two ways, and the distinction is important to keep in mind.

If you arouse someone's feelings by asserting something and getting him to *believe* it, that's one way of doing it. When you notify a mother that her child has been struck by a car and taken to the hospital, no doubt this will have a considerable effect upon her feelings. When a political candidate convinces his audience that the opposition party is secretly arranging to sell off, for a low price, public grazing lands to private cattle-raisers, no doubt they can be made to feel a strong moral indignation, and they will want to do something about it too, such as write letters or pull the second lever on the voting machine. In these cases, the feeling that is stirred up depends upon *believing* something; if the person spoken to did not believe what was said, it would leave him cold.

But you can also arouse feelings to some degree, though perhaps rather different feelings, without claiming anything to be true. You may be able to bring tears to people's eyes by telling a *story* of a small boy run over by a car, even if you make it quite clear that the story never really happened at all. And a politician might arouse a good deal of vague, but strong, indignation against his opposition merely by calling them certain names, even if he did not really convince his audience that his charges were true. Indeed, certain words by themselves are charged with emotions, and can quicken the pulse, produce a blush, or warm the heart just by being uttered.

It is this second kind of thing that we shall call the **emotive force** of a word: that is, its tendency to arouse feelings of a certain sort in those who read it or hear it uttered. "Sweetheart," "bird-brain," "Grade A," and "stinker" are examples of words with obvious emotive force, though the feelings they evoke are different in quality and intensity.

Nearly everyone is aware that words can arouse feelings; writers on language constantly remind us of this. But there is an equally impor- tant point that is hardly ever given the emphasis it deserves: that words arouse feelings very largely *through their meanings*. It is because a term calls to mind certain characteristics of things, and because these characteristics are loved, admired, or feared, that the term can stir up emotional responses in the reader or listener. Made-up combinations of syllables, like "probyllopoware," have no emotive force at all—unless the syllables give them connotations by cross reference to real words.

Now, there are a few words that may have some emotive force quite independent of any signification. There is some room for debate here. You could say that expletives like "Phooey!" "Damn!" "Hooray!" (you can supply more extreme examples yourself) don't signify any characteristics at all, that is, neither designate nor connote, but yet have emotive force. Sometimes what is meant is that they are a handy way of *relieving* feelings—a person who is sad may say, "Oh, dear!" But "Oh, dear!" doesn't make *other* people feel sad—that's quite a different matter. Even words like "darling" and "sweetie pie" have some *vague* signification. In any case, if there are words that have emotive force but no meaning at all, there aren't many, and their emotive force is pretty indefinite and pretty mild compared to that of other words. In most cases the meaning is at least part cause of the emotional response.

We can see this in the case of certain pairs of synonyms. It is easy to find two terms that are similar, or overlap, in meaning, but that have very different emotive force: "rash" and "brave," "cautious" and "cowardly," "spendthrift" and "generous," "miserly" and "thrifty." Because misers and thrifty people both save money, we are tempted to say that "miserly" and "thrifty" mean the same thing, though one has an unfriendly, the other a friendly, emotive force. But it is as clear as can be that "miserly" and "thrifty" do *not* mean the same thing; if a person is unwilling to spend money even for bare necessities, he is miserly, but *not* thrifty. The difference in emotive force is due at least in part to the difference in signification; that is why to be called "thrifty" is a compliment, "miserly" an insult.

If two terms comprehend the same things but have different emotive force, this difference may be due to a difference in what they *designate*. "The 1954 mess in Washington" and "the dispute between Senator McCarthy and the Army" both refer to the same events, but evidently they don't designate the same characteristics, and that is clearly the source of their difference in emotive force. Or, to take an example that has been bandied about considerably, "Grade A beef steak" and "first-class piece of dead steer" may have the same comprehension in that every Grade A beef steak is also a first-class piece of dead steer, and vice versa. But if you would put the former on a menu, and not the latter, surely that's because of a difference in what they designate.

If two terms have the same designation, their *connotations* may be different enough to give them a very different emotive force. Compare "bride" with "woman who has just been married"; "sister" with "female sibling"; "persistent idle talking about inconsequential matters" with "yammering." Corporations like to call stockholders

"shareholders," because of the latter's desirable connotations; opponents of the Mutual Security Administration wanted to *get away* from
the favorable connotations by renaming it the "Foreign Operations
Administration." If we feel a liking toward statesmen and a dislike
toward politicians, this is not due to a difference in *sound:* as
Webster's Dictionary points out, "politician" connotes "artifice or
intrigue," whereas "statesman" connotes "broad-minded and far-
seeing sagacity in affairs of state."

Thus it is important to distinguish the feelings caused by a word
from its meaning, including connotation. The feelings are *effects;* the
connotations are among the *causes* of the effect. Words with many
connotations are not necessarily emotive, nor are metaphors. But
perhaps the words with the most subtle and effective emotive force
are quite rich in connotations, and are therefore likely to be used
metaphorically. The main point is that the feeling is aroused, if at
all, by means of the *sense.*

Thus we shall not use the term "emotive meaning" that is so often
used in discussions of this subject. This term would be useful if
the emotive force of a word were parallel to its signification; the
emotive force is not, however, another *kind* of meaning at all. It is
convenient to speak of "emotive language," that is, a piece of discourse that contains enough words with emotive force to give the
whole passage a marked capacity to evoke feelings. The purpose of
the term "emotive language" is not to divide language into "emotive"
and "informative" as some writers have done. A discourse is informative if it tells you the truth about something you want to know about,
and an informative discourse may be highly emotive, or mildly
emotive, or not emotive at all, just as it can be in English or Danish,
and in prose or verse. Dividing discourses into emotive and informative is like dividing people into bartenders and drunkards. But we
can use a term to call attention to this *aspect* of a discourse, and to
the specific problems it raises for anyone who wants to be a clear
thinker and a critical reader.

Of course, the emotive force of a term is bound to vary from region
to region among those who speak a particular language. It depends
upon experience, upon beliefs, and upon the connotations of the
term that are brought out in certain contexts. Some words that shock
the British do not shock us, and vice versa. Terms like "white
supremacy," "civil rights," or "racial segregation" carry disapproval

in one part of the country and approval in another. When syphilis was widely believed to be caused only by immoral behavior, the term "syphilis" could not be printed in a newspaper or used in polite society, but it has now lost this connotation and also much of its emotive force.

Thus to speak cautiously of the emotive force of a term, we may have to refer to a particular social group at a particular time. And even then we are speaking rather generally, for a term with considerable emotive force can be cooled off a good deal by an appropriate context. It works this way. The emotive force of the key terms of a discourse has a good deal to do with its *tone:* that is, with the speaker's or writer's apparent attitude toward the subject he is writing about and toward his audience. We are describing the over-all tone of a poem, speech, or book, when we say, for example, that it is "contemptuous," "cheerful," "sullen," "angry," or "dispassionate." The discourse as a whole builds up a certain tone if a number of its terms have that sort of emotive import. But if the tone of a discourse is on the whole calm and temperate, an occasional term with emotive force in other contexts will have its sting drawn. A historian of the Russian Revolution can take away a good deal of the violence of "Communist" and "Bolshevik," just as a sociologist or medical writer can avert the usual effects of certain taboo words by a judicious arrangement of the context.

When you examine a discourse to discover the feeling it arouses, there are two things to note. You can describe the *quality* of the feeling, as irritation, pride, uneasiness, despair. Or you can compare the feeling with other feelings (roughly) with respect to the degree of *approval* or *disapproval* involved. "Intelligent person" is, for example, honorific; "intellectual" is disapproving, but not strongly; "egg-head" is derogatory. If we take any group of nearly synonymous terms, we can give them a kind of comparative rating on a scale ranging from those at one end that are most approving to those at the other end that are most disapproving. Near the middle we may be able to find a term that has very little emotive force either way; this is a *neutral term.*

Thus, taking a fairly neutral term, "candidate for public office," we can put it between the fairly honorific term "man willing to serve if elected" and the fairly derogatory term "office seeker." Or, we can compare "public servant" (honorific), "government official" (fairly neutral, but faintly derogatory), and "bureaucrat" (quite abusive). Sometimes there is a whole series of terms: "heavy drinker," "alcoholic," "problem drinker," "pathological drinker," "lush," "sponge," "old soak." Such comparisons can be illuminating if we know what we are doing, which is simply to make a rough estimate of the intensity of approval or disapproval these words can arouse under favorable conditions.

It is the emotive force of words that makes it worth while for people to engage in that familiar verbal activity known as *"name-calling,"* which so often passes as a substitute for argument. If there were no such thing as emotive force, we could still make unfair and untrue statements about one another. We can say, "George is very dishonest," when in fact George is only occasionally, and mildly, dishonest. From one point of view, a statement like "George is a crook" is only a little greater exaggeration. If George's morals could be discussed calmly, it would be possible to arrive at some agreement, perhaps, about the matter. The trouble with the emotive term, like "crook," is that it gets everyone excited, and instead of showing exactly how exaggerated the charge is, George or his friends are likely to shout back, "He is *not* a crook! He's as honest as the day is long!" In this way, emotive words, whether honorific or derogatory, have a way of bringing a discussion to a standstill. How often does "You're a Red!" evoke the retort, "You're a fascist!"

The temptation to name-calling comes from the assumption that we can make people like something or dislike something by giving it a name with favorable or unfavorable connotations. The Philadelphia *Evening Bulletin* once discussed a proposal to change the name of a House of Correction to "Pennypack Farms," which the residents of the Pennypack section were opposing. "Would 'Pennypack' remove the stigma from the House of Correction," asked the *Bulletin*, "or will the aroma of the House of Correction attach to Pennypack?" This is a nice question. Generally speaking, you don't change people's feelings about things by changing the names of the things—in the long run. *In the long run*, you wouldn't make dope peddlers more popular by calling them "ministers of spiritual relief," you would just give the word "minister" a new, unpleasant connotation. When the County Insane Asylum is renamed the "Hospital for Mental Illness," this generally shows that people have *already* begun to change their feelings about mental illness and the mentally ill.

In the *short* run, however, emotive words can be a very disruptive influence. Suppose someone admits that he believes certain government-owned grazing lands in the West should be leased cheaply for long terms to private cattlemen; and suppose someone else asks him, "You mean you're in favor of the grazing-lands giveaway?" He does approve the bill referred to, so he can't simply say No; on the other hand, this description of the bill in question is highly derogatory, so he can't simply say Yes. He can't really discuss the question at all in this form, for the term "giveaway" prejudices the answer beforehand. To let it be called a "giveaway" is to admit that you are against it, and he is *not* against it; the term, in fact, *begs the question* by making it unanswerable by either Yes or No. The discussion is balked until the two disputants agree on a more neutral term for what they are talking about.

Not that it is always easy to find such a neutral term. Sometimes there is no such term, and you can only invent a long circumlocution. Thus we have "firm" and "sticks by his guns" (honorific), and we have "stubborn," "obstinate," and "pigheaded" (derogatory in various degrees). In between, as a neutral term, we would have to put something like "given to continuing an action already begun, despite efforts to dissuade one from it." Like any neutral substitute, this does not have *all* the meaning of the emotive synonyms; it leaves out some of the connotations that give them their emotive force, but it also puts the sidetracked discussion back on the rails by confining it to what really is at issue and leaving out insults.

A somewhat fuller discussion will help to make this process clearer. Imagine the following dialogue:

A: "The Federal Government should increase its income by laying a tax on manufactured articles, to be collected from the manufacturers direct, and then added by them to the cost of the articles."

B: "What! You mean you're in favor of that Federal sales tax scheme?"

A: "What do you mean, Federal sales tax? As everybody knows, a sales tax is collected in the retail stores, and paid directly by the consumer, and it is an awful nuisance for everyone, and very hard on the low-income groups."

B: "So is it any different if the factory pays it to the government and adds it on the price? The consumer pays through the nose

> anyway. The only thing is, he doesn't realize it; it's just a shell-game sales tax."
>
> A: "I should prefer to describe it by the term 'Manufacturer's Excise Tax', which seems to me to describe it accurately."
>
> B: "Accurately! That's just a whitewash word for it, but it smells just as bad whatever you call it. The truth is, you're in favor of a hidden Federal sales tax."
>
> A: "Not at all. I'm in favor of a Manufacturer's Excise Tax."

This could go on for quite a while, but we may as well break it off here, for it is evident that the discussion is not getting anywhere. As long as A and B can only think of emotive terms for describing the tax they want to talk about, they cannot agree on which term to choose, for either term will seem like a victory for one side or the other. If A once calls it a "sales tax," he's lost; and B cannot accept A's term, for that makes it sound like a tax *on* the Manufacturer, which it is not. As long as they cannot agree on a term, they can't get around to the real issue, which is whether A's proposal is a good one or not. And the only way out is to find a neutral term that they can both accept, and go on from there. B could say:

> B: "Well, let's not quibble. As I understand your proposal, the tax is *collected by* the manufacturer *for* the government; we disagree about whether it is a tax *on* the manufacturer or *on* the consumer. Can't we call it a 'Factory-collectible tax,' as distinct from a 'Retail-store collectible tax'? For my point, as I say, is, first, that if the Factory-collectible tax is passed on by the manufacturer to the ultimate purchaser in the form of a higher price, then . . ."

Or A could say:

> A: "Well, perhaps 'Manufacturer's Excise Tax' *is* somewhat misleading; let's call it a 'Factory-collectible tax.' And my point is, first, that if the tax is collected in this way it is free of some of the most undesirable features of the ordinary 1 per cent or 2 per cent or 3 per cent tax collected at the retail outlet . . ."

Now they've got the discussion rolling. Of course, they may both feel as strongly about the issue as they ever did, but they can keep these feelings from getting in the way of dealing reasonably with a matter of great public importance.

One of the constant difficulties we all face, as speakers or writers, in discussing important issues, is that many of the terms that would be handiest have already taken on strong emotive force. Whether or not we want to fool others by manipulating emotive words, we don't want to fool *ourselves*. That is, we want to get at the truth when we can, and we want to know whether our reasons for believing it to be the truth are good reasons or not. And this is what makes it necessary to avoid overheated discourse.

We must learn how to handle hot words by insulating them in a calm context instead of letting them run away with us. If necessary we can warn the reader that the term is emotive and that we want to play its emotive force down if we can. But some words have become so highly charged that they are too hot to handle safely, and that's why we must cultivate a certain amount of flexibility in our vocabulary. It is dangerous to get too dependent upon, or too much attached to, certain emotive words—they are like a drug. If you find that you can't discuss American foreign policy without constantly falling back on terms like "isolationism," "appeasement," and "aggression," then your thinking is at the mercy of your language. If you find that you can't talk about the problems of internal security in a democratic nation without constantly using words like "Reds," "parlor pinks," "bleeding hearts," "soft on subversives," and other such emotive terms, you can be fairly sure that your thinking about this matter is not very effective. It is running in little polished grooves, well worn by emotions. You may enjoy your old familiar prejudices and comfortable stock responses, but that is not thinking. Nothing gets thinking more quickly off the point, or ties it up more tightly in logical knots, or stops it so dead as highly emotive language. More needs to be said about this in the following chapter. But at present the point to keep in mind is that there are remedies for these troubles. If you know how to manage the emotive force of a word by its context, and if you know how to get neutral substitutes for emotive words, you can be the boss of your language instead of being pushed around by it.

A CHECK-UP QUIZ. There are five approximate synonyms in each of the following sets. Number them 1 to 5 in order, from the most honorific to the most derogatory. If you think the emotive force of a particular word varies greatly, or is too vague to be sure about, put down a question mark.

  1. huckster, adman, advertising copywriter, public relations man, one who makes people aware of a useful product.

2. manufacturer, robber baron, commercial tycoon, leading industrialist, big businessman.

3. derogatory term, nasty crack, snarl word, term revealing a disapproving attitude, insult.

4. inflation, runaway prices, market adjusting itself upward, rise to higher prices, vigorous activity of price structure.

5. Light reading, escape literature, trash, entertaining book, hammock reading.

6. group, bloc, clique, gang, association.

7. philosophy, ideology, theory, point of view, opinion.

8. clever, cunning, smart, bright, quick-witted.

9. revelry, carousal, gay party, orgy, high old time.

10. agreement, covenant, compact, accord, deal.

See also Exercises 29, 30, 31, pp. 261-62.

FURTHER READING: Hugh R. Walpole, *Semantics*. New York: W. W. Norton, Inc., 1941, ch. 2. S. I. Hayakawa, *Language in Thought and Action*. New York: Harcourt, Brace and Co., 1949, chs. 7, 8, 11, 14, 15.

Outline-Summary of Chapter 6

The signification of a term (that is, the set of characteristics it refers to) has two parts: (1) the designation, or standard (dictionary) meaning, and (2) the connotation. A term ("star") *designates* those characteristics that an object must have in order for the term to be applied to it (largeness, gaseousness, high temperature, etc.). A term *connotes* other characteristics that most stars are believed to have, or seem to have (remoteness, stillness, long-lastingness, etc.). A term can also derive connotations (a) from notable contexts in which it has appeared ("Bright Star, would I were steadfast as thou art. . . ."), (b) from its tendency to be used by certain groups of people ("take," as a noun, is a newspaperman's word), and (c) from other words that sound like it ("Duraplex" makes an allusion to "endure," "durable," "complex," "pliable," "flexible"). These factors determine the potential connotation of a term; its actual connotation will vary a good deal from context to context.

A *metaphorical attribution*, whether a statement ("Rommel was a fox") or a phrase ("the desert fox"), contains two terms, one of which (the *qualifier*) is applied to the other (in "Rommel was a fox," the qualifier, "fox," is applied to "Rommel"). In a metaphorical statement, the qualifier (the predicate-term) has two features: (1) it designates some characteristics that are incompatible with the characteristics of the object referred to by the subject-term (as "fox" designates four-leggedness, while Rommel has only two legs); and (2) it connotes other characteristics (such as cunning, slyness, rapidity of movement, cleverness) that can be ascribed (either truly or falsely) to the object referred to by the subject-term. To interpret a metaphorical statement is to state which of the connotations of the predicate-term it applies to the subject, in a given context.

The *emotive force* of a term is its tendency to arouse emotions or feelings in those who hear or read the word. A term with positive emotive force (the phrase "an eloquent expression" tends to arouse a favorable feeling) may be approximately synonymous with (though differing in connotation, or in part of its designation, from) a term with negative emotive force (the phrase "a rhetorical flourish" tends to arouse an unfavorable feeling); in between them there may be other terms with less pronounced emotive force, that is, neutral terms (for example, "a feature of style that is unusual and particularly emotive"). The neutral term does not have exactly the same signification as its honorific or derogatory correlates because the emotive force of a term is usually dependent upon its signification. But when emotive terms get in the way of reasonable discussion by making it hard to state an issue in terms upon which all parties to the discussion can agree, it is often helpful to substitute neutral terms for the emotive ones.

Exercise 25

Select five of the following words or phrases, and in each case name five characteristics that belong to its range of connotation. Think of the characteristics of the things they name, and of literary contexts in which they have been used.

1. "shark"	6. "cash"
2. "plate"	7. "hand"
3. "card index"	8. "cloud"
4. "garbage"	9. "rock"
5. "well"	10. "sea"

Exercise 26

If A believes a certain statement and B believes that the statement **is** *false*, they may be said to be in "*disagreement* with one another." If they make their opinions known to each other, and at least one of them attempts to change the other's mind, they are having a dispute. There are many terms in English for distinguishing disputes of various sorts and degrees of intensity; the task in this exercise is to discriminate among these terms.

1. If the dispute involves some loud exchanges of words, is it (a) a controversy, (b) bickering, (c) an altercation?

2. If the dispute is carried on by letters, over a period of time, is it (a) a controversy, (b) a squabble, (c) a hassle?

3. If the dispute is carried on publicly, with great violence, is it (a) a brawl, (b) bickering, (c) an argument?

4. If the dispute is over something trivial, and the interchange of words is petulant, is it (a) a wrangle (b) bickering, (c) a rhubarb?

5. If the dispute is angry and concerns something that matters a good deal to the people involved, so that they break off relations as a result of it, is it (a) a quarrel, (b) an altercation, (c) a brawl?

6. If the dispute is carried on in a noisy, undignified, and confused manner, is it (a) an altercation, (b) a squabble, (c) a wrangle?

7. If the dispute spreads, so that it involves a number of people, who are all emotionally aroused, is it (a) a controversy, (b) a broil, (c) a squabble?

8. If the dispute is petty, and carried on in a childish way, is it (a) a controversy, (b) a broil, (c) a squabble?

9. If the dispute is noisy, does not concern anything very important, and appears faintly ridiculous to an observer, is it (a) bickering, (b) a hassle, (c) a brawl?

10. If the dispute concerns the question of whether a runner was safe at first, and involves a group of baseball players, coaches, and umpires, is it (a) a conflict of opinion, (b) a rhubarb, (c) a controversy?

Exercise 27

In each of the following pairs of statements you have either (a) two different, though overlapping, metaphors applied to the same thing, or (b) the same word applied metaphorically in two different contexts. For each pair, point out some of the differences in meaning between the two metaphors.

1. Jones was *tossed* out of his executive job.
   Jones was *eased* out of his executive job.

2. The Army has been *coddling* Communists.
   The Army has been *soft* on Communists.

3. In his attack on isolationism, Professor Berwickley is *flogging a dead horse.*
   He is *attacking a straw man.*

4. The Immigration Act has *put up a barbed wire fence* around America.
   The Immigration Act has *erected a long-needed screen* for America's open door.

5. "It hurts more *to have a belief pulled* than to have a tooth pulled, and no *intellectual novocain* is available." (Elmer Davis)
   A man's ideas are *cherished playthings*, which he parts from only with tears.

6. We asked our teachers for *bread*, they gave us stones.
   Man cannot live by *bread* alone.

7. To him, business is just a *game*.
   We don't want anyone on our sales team who isn't willing to play the *game*.

8. "Words are wise men's counters—they do but reckon by them— but they are the *money* of fools." (Hobbes)
   Words are fools' counters—but they are the *money* of wise men.

9. A house is a *machine* for living.
   A book is a *machine* to think with.

10. The earth is not a *gadget*.
    A government is a rather complicated *gadget*.

Exercise 28

For some time there was a certain amount of controversy regarding the activities of Senator Joe McCarthy, Republican, of Wisconsin—activities which he described as "exposing Communists, subversives, spies, and traitors." One fairly common attitude toward the Senator has been that it is important to expose Communists and make people aware of the Communist conspiracy, but that the Senator frequently made reckless public charges against innocent people, or people against whom he had insufficient evidence, and that he generally responded to criticism by charging or implying that the critic was sympathetic to, or unwittingly aiding, Communism. Thus many people have said, "I agree wholeheartedly with his *purpose*, but I deplore his *methods*."

This has been expressed, defended and attacked in an interesting variety of metaphors. Twelve of these are given below. Examine the connotations of each metaphor as applied to the problem of dealing with the internal Communist threat, and point out any ways in which you think each metaphor gives a misleading description of the problem. Since people disagree about the nature and extent of the problem itself, they will disagree about the correctness of any particular description. The point of this exercise is to see what each metaphor *does* connote, that is, to interpret the metaphor, at least in part.

1. "When you are out to catch rats, it doesn't make any difference what kind of cheese you use."

2. "Naturally, it hurts when the Communist boil is lanced, but that's the efficient way to clean out the infection."

3. "I say get on with chopping down the tree of International Communist Conspiracy, and let the chips fall where they may."

4. "When a bottle of ink gets overturned and the stain starts to spread, you have to start mopping it up fast unless you want things ruined. Who cares if you knock over a chair or two in your haste?"

5. "The point is to get the termites out of the house—any method that will work is certainly justified so long as it gets them out before the house falls down."

6. "We must be careful not to throw the baby of civil liberties out with the bathwater of subversion."

7. "When you keep ants out of the kitchen by throwing poison around freely, it may be eaten by the pet cat or by the baby."

8. "Anyone who can't hit the target more than once in 81 shots is a menace to innocent bystanders; when it comes to getting results, and not just making loud bangs, he is a rank amateur and should step down to make room for a professional marksman."

9. "Granted that a rotten apple will ruin the whole basket if you give it time; still, when you find that one apple is rotten, you don't jump to the conclusion that they are all bad without even looking at them."

10. "A person who goes around turning in false alarms may be making the public fire-conscious, but he isn't helping either the public *or* the fire department to deal with *real* fires."

11. "As someone has remarked, if you insist on burning down the barn to get rid of the rats, the rats usually escape—it is the horses that get killed."

12. "When I first began to fight that subversive organism known as poison ivy on the abandoned farm we moved into a few years ago, I found that it had infiltrated a beautiful stand of five-leaved woodbine twined in a groove of cedars. I poured over the whole area a thick spray of ammate. The result was an arid spot—it killed the ivy, the woodbine, the cedars, and everything living. I learned that this is not the way to fight subversion—but Senator McCarthy and his like have not learned it yet."

Exercise 29

In each of the following pairs, one is honorific, one derogatory. For each pair find a term that has a closely similar designation but is fairly neutral.

1. generous . . . a soft touch.
2. highly sensitive . . . squeamish.
3. delicate . . . sickly.
4. love . . . infatuation.
5. overhelpful . . . officious.
6. letting other nations run their own affairs without interference . . . retreating into isolationism.
7. government with foresight and preparedness . . . government aiming at a planned society.
8. bill permitting the President to appoint more capable Justices to the Supreme Court . . . court-packing bill.
9. technical adviser on improved methods of production engineering . . . efficiency expert.
10. humanitarian reformer . . . do-gooder.

Exercise 30

Rewrite the following passage, toning down its emotive force as much as possible by substituting neutral synonyms for the words with strong emotive force.

What now stares us in the face is that our Latin American policy is a complete bust; the howls from below the border put the finger on the rotten places. After being lame, halt, and blind for some time, the policy has finally fallen flat on its face.

According to official State Department mouthpieces, the purpose of this policy is to keep Latin American countries from going Communist; to keep them in our orbit. So what do we do? Instead of bolstering up their economic systems with trade and aid, we send them homilies about Democracy (homilies are not edible). When their economies are in trouble, and their governments are up against internal pressure, we shake our finger at them instead of reaching into our pants pocket. We preach prosperity, and talk up how we're going to encourage them, and then we slap import duties on the very goods they have to sell to survive. Statistics show that we are leaning more and more on Latin America for raw materials—oil, iron ore, manganese, etc.—but we shrug our shoulders at the fact that the total income of all the fast-growing population of Latin America is only one-eighth that of the United States.

It is glaringly evident that this policy of mixed kicks and kisses is a scheme hatched by the hard-money boys in the Treasury Department who are out to get the budget balanced, let the chips fall where they may. This is financial finagling while the world burns—and don't think our Latin American neighbors aren't burning. We just barely managed to pull the chestnuts out of the fire in Guatemala; now we have betrayed the solemn promises we made at the Caracas Conference, so that the American representatives who were at that conference or have dealt directly with Latin America are ashamed to show their faces down there.

Let us stop this wobbling, hot-and-cold policy that seems designed to knock itself out. Let us be neighbors to our good neighbors.

Exercise 31

The problem here is to tone up a fairly even-tempered discourse. Rewrite the following editorial, substituting strongly emotive terms wherever you can for the relatively calm adjectives and phrases.

A senate committee has been holding hearings on the latest idea of the not too clear-thinking Senator from North Dakota. This mistaken bill, which would restrict individual liberties to some extent, prohibits advertising for alcoholic beverages in newspapers, magazines, etc., that are carried across state boundaries.

As a group of well-informed witnesses have testified, this bill ought not to be passed on several counts. First, it shows excessive moral concern with matters of private conscience. Those who are working to get it passed are well aware that they cannot achieve what they most want, that is, a return of that unfortunate and unsuccessful experiment known as Prohibition (which is surely not desired by anyone except tenderminded people who are engaged in trying to improve the world), and their plan is to bring us as close to Prohibition as possible.

Second, it gives unequal treatment to an industry that disobeys no laws and is managed by respectable people. And third, it is in conflict with the Constitution, for it places a limitation on the prerogative of newspaper publishers to determine what they shall print in their advertising columns as well as their news columns. Drawn up by legislators who do not see far ahead and have a relatively low grade of intelligence, and supported by highly emotional but not rational people, this bill should be quickly put out of the way so that Congress can address itself to more pressing legislation.

7

The Uses of Suggestion

Here are two different newspapers reporting the same event. One report, under a two-column headline, begins:

> Asserting that he had complete confidence in Mr. J. J. A——,
> Chairman of the ——— Commission, the President nevertheless
> requested Mr. A——'s resignation today, pending the investiga-
> tion of charges of malfeasance in office. The President said at his
> press conference that he agreed that a Congressional inquiry was
> desirable, in view of the importance of the post.

The other report, under a four-column headline, begins:

> Accused of betraying the public trust in his important position as
> Chairman of the ——— Commission, J. J. A—— was fired by
> the President today. At his news conference, the President urged the
> desirability of a Congressional inquiry, though he expressed the
> opinion that Mr. A—— would be cleared of the charges.

Both of these reports may be true to a certain extent. They agree on some important points: that Mr. A—— has been accused, that he has been dismissed from his post, that the President said he thought Mr. A—— was innocent, and that the President said he was in favor of a Congressional inquiry. But when we look further, we see that the descriptions are by no means identical. There is a good deal of insinuation that lies beneath the surface, and it takes more careful reading to make it apparent. From the second passage you would gather that the proposal for the Congressional inquiry came from the

President; from the first passage you would gather that it came from someone else. "Fired" hints at a more abrupt and decisive sort of dismissal than "requested the resignation of." "Expressed the opinion that Mr. A——— would be cleared" makes the President sound a good deal more doubtful about Mr. A——— than does "asserting that he has complete confidence." "Malfeasance in office," in the first passage, becomes "betraying the public trust" in the second. And the very order in which the statements are arranged in the second passage makes a definite presumption of Mr. A———'s guilt; it has a disapproving air. If the first passage is fair and accurate, the second is a malicious misrepresentation; if the second passage is fair and accurate, the first "whitewashes" Mr. A———.

It doesn't take much skill or effort to understand in a rough way what these passages say. But anyone who reads the passages and thinks that they say "about the same thing" is missing exactly the differences that are crucial for making a good judgment about what actually is happening in the case of Mr. A———. If the reader is not consciously aware of the implicit assertions made by such a passage when he has to make up his mind about its truth or falsity, the passage will make up his mind for him, without his knowing it, and he will go away believing things he doesn't even know he believes, and has certainly not examined or tested.

The problem is again one of interpreting meanings. But the basic tools of interpretation have not yet all been provided; there is one further distinction that is quite indispensable in understanding what we read and in sifting what is honest in it from what is deceitful. This distinction, and some of the applications of it, we shall consider in this final chapter.

§28. STATING AND SUGGESTING

Whenever you utter a statement, that is, write it or speak it in such a way as to *assert* it, you show that you believe something. Even if you're lying when you tell a tennis dud you can't play with him because you have a dentist's appointment, still it's not a lie unless you put on a good appearance of believing what you say, namely that you *have* a dentist's appointment. But sometimes your statement can show that you not only believe what you *state*, but also something else that you are *not* stating. If you were asked to recommend a young lady of your acquaintance for a blind date, you might say, "Oh, she's at least as beautiful as she is witty." This shows, because it states, that you believe her beauty is no less great than her wittiness (if you can equate such different sorts of thing). But it also shows, without stating it, that you believe her beauty and wit are both considerable.

The sort of meaning we are speaking of here is familiar enough, but it gets elusive when you try to describe it. It seems pedantic to analyze anything so obvious, and yet its effects upon communication are not obvious at all; they are worth close attention. The distinction to be made here can be sharpened further by comparing the above example with another one. The sentence "She's no more witty than she is beautiful," is logically equivalent to the sentence, "She's at least as beautiful as she is witty." But it also asserts that she is *not* very beautiful and *not* very witty.

We shall say that these two statements are equivalent in what they *state*, but different in what they **suggest**. What is suggested by a sentence is anything that is not itself stated, but that the reader or listener can tell is probably believed by someone who writes or speaks the sentence. The speaker may not actually believe it himself, but if he (intentionally or unintentionally) uses a phrase or grammatical construction that would naturally be used by people who *do* believe it, then his words suggest that idea. When a secretary of state returned from a conference of foreign ministers at London a few years ago, he reported in a speech to the New York *Herald Tribune* Forum, "We avoided platitudes that were without relevancy." He thereby *suggested*, though no doubt unconsciously, that the foreign ministers confined themselves strictly to *relevant* platitudes.

What is suggested by a discourse is part of what it *says*, in the full sense. And evidently it may be vital to know exactly what is suggested in a particular case. Especially when a *promise* of some sort is involved. When someone says to you, "I won't go unless you go," is he suggesting that he *will* go if you *do*? In some contexts he surely is, but if you take that as a commitment without getting it put as a direct statement, you may be in for a disappointment. And this is exactly what happens sometimes in business contracts, diplomatic messages, and letters. Suggestion is an enormously valuable resource of language; it (along with connotation) makes poetry possible; it helps us to say a good deal in a few words; it gives us the chance to say things gently, or hintingly, or tentatively, or modestly that would be more blunt if explicitly stated. But it also gives us the chance to say things slyly, insinuatingly, or misleadingly as we shall see in the following section; and it gives our sentences the chance to run away with meanings we don't intend—as happened to the secretary of state and to the writer of this headline:

USES OF NATURAL GAS SEEN ANSWER
TO PROBLEM OF OVERPOPULATION

Therefore, it will be useful to consider rather carefully the various types of suggestion, the chief ways in which it works. The more familiar you are with these types, the more sensitive to suggestion you can become, and the more successful in using it, instead of letting it use you. This is what is called "reading between the lines" of a message: what is written between the lines is what is suggested but not stated.

The first type of suggestion depends merely on the fact that something is uttered. To say anything is to claim that it is *worth* saying, or that it is in some way called for under the circumstances. You don't go around telling people that you have one head—two would be news, but not one. So, if an advertisement proclaims boldly that "Piccadilly cigarettes have less nicotine than Ulsters" or "Glutz beer contains less sugar than Blitz," the suggestion is that the difference in nicotine or sugar content is big enough to call attention to—big enough, that is, to have some effect upon your health or your weight. Or, to take another example, when a certain senator says, "I want to make it very clear for the record that I don't believe Mr. So-and-so is a spy,"— well, this is a friendly remark, coming from the senator, but his *making* the remark suggests that it *needed* to be made, in short, that there had been, or is, some reason for his thinking, or other people's thinking, that Mr. So-and-so *is* a spy.

To consider this first type more broadly, you might say that every statement is the answer to some possible question, and one way of getting at what it suggests is to think of the question or questions it might be an answer to. Of course, it can be ambiguous in this way: "I'm here" can be an answer to two different questions, but the ambiguity is removed by stressing either word: "*I'm* here" answers "Who's there?"; "I'm *here*" answers "Where are you?" A sentence may contain such clues to its probable setting or circumstances, and these clues are part of its suggestion. That explains, by the way, the silliness of sentences like "It was with great difficulty that he dug the hole"; the implicit question this purports to answer is, "What did he dig the hole with?" but the natural answer would be "a shovel," not "great difficulty."

A second type of suggestion, quite similar to the first, depends on the fact that a statement may carry with it some implicit assumptions. That is, it may be the kind of statement that (usually) a person would make only if he were assuming certain other things to be true. If I say, "She is even taller than he," the understanding is that I wouldn't have used the word "even" unless I thought that *he* is pretty tall. But I haven't *stated* that he is tall. When you try on a shoe and can't get your foot into it, you could say, "The shoe is too small for the foot," or "The foot is too big for the shoe." Both are true as statements, but by suggestion they put the blame in different places. When you compare two things in this way, it makes a difference in which direction you go. To say, "The foot is too big for the shoe" is to suggest that the foot is abnormally large and something probably ought to be done about it.

A third type of suggestion depends on the fact that a statement may carry with it some implicit conclusions. When the conclusion to be deduced from a pair of premises is easy to see, it doesn't have to be spelled out; if you say, "Redheads are hot-tempered, and Clara is a redhead," the suggestion is clear. And if around midnight your host says, "I have to get up early tomorrow," you can take the hint and let him get to bed.

Rhetorical questions work in a similar way. A rhetorical question is a question that is asked in such a way (that is, in such a tone of voice or in such a context) that it suggests its own answer. "What is so rare as a day in June?" (Nothing.) "Who would believe what *he* says?" (Nobody.)

A fourth type of suggestion could also be regarded as depending upon implicit conclusions, although in this case the conclusion would be inductive. The general principle involved in this fourth type is that if two or more statements are set side by side, this juxtaposition can carry the suggestion that there must be some *connection* between the statements. In some cases it is not clear what the connection could be, so nothing specific is suggested. In other cases, we can easily see what the connection must be, if there is any, and it is this connection, then, that is suggested. "She's lovely! She's engaged! She uses _____!" The only plausible connection here is a *causal* one, and evidently that's the whole point of the advertisement, though it is not explicitly stated.

You have probably never seen this in a newspaper: "John Jones, 35, a white man, of 16 East St., was arrested on charges of assault and battery and breach of peace yesterday after a fight." But you may have seen this: "John Jones, 35, a Negro, of 16 East St., was arrested on charges of assault and battery and breach of peace yesterday after a fight." To put in the information that Jones is a Negro suggests that this fact has some significance in the context. It hints at a connection between fighting and belonging to a particular race. That kind of suggestion isn't exactly libelous—you couldn't sue the editor—but it's there. And the better newspapers no longer do this sort of thing.

There are other, more devious, ways of doing it. When Bishop Oxnam asked to appear before the House Committee on Un-American Activities to reply to a number of unverified accusations in the Committee's files which had been made public, he found that one of the techniques employed by the Committee's Chairman and Counsel went like this: "Did you ever belong to such-and-such an organization?" "No." "For the record, let me read into the record the facts about this organization. It was cited as a Communist organization by the California Committee on Un-American Activities; etc., etc." The printed transcript of this hearing shows that Bishop Oxnam asked several times why it was necessary to insert into the record the history of organizations that no one had proved his connection with. No satisfactory answer was forthcoming, but the Bishop was aware of what the record, so constructed, could suggest.

The importance of suggestion in establishing connections is also brought out by a feature of bad style that has been mentioned previously: Elegant Variation. A discourse would be very tedious if we had to spell out in so many words the exact connection between every clause and the one that precedes it. So, whenever there is no serious risk of misunderstanding, we are justified in merely suggesting the connection. But we can only do this by following generally-understood conventions. For example, if we use a pronoun in one sentence and the same pronoun in the next sentence, it is to be assumed that we are referring to the same person unless we have specifically supplied a new antecedent in between. And if we are referring twice to the same person, we refer to him by the same name unless there is some reason for changing.

Consider, then, the following passage from a standard work on the 17th century Flemish painter, Rubens:

> Rubens sought out his colleagues whenever he had the opportunity to do so. The exchange of views that took place was often as fruitful as simply copying the works. Adam Elsheimer was among the painters who were friends of Peter Paul; during the time they spent together in Rome the German taught him the art of engraving, and his artistic ideas may be recognized later in many of the Fleming's creations.

There is nothing complicated about the ideas here, but the passage is remarkably confusing. You have to stop and figure that it is Adam Elsheimer who is called "the German," for the difference in the description suggests that it is a different person or that there is some special point about his being a German—though this fact isn't relevant to the rest of the passage. It may take a little reflection to see that "Rubens" and "Peter Paul" and "the Fleming" are all the same person. It sounds as if there are at least five people involved here. And to add further confusion, the pronouns "him" and "his," separated by only five words, refer to two different people.

It won't do to reply that the author was only avoiding monotony by not using the same names more than once; we ought not to trade monotony for confusion. The right order in such a case is first to get the passage clear; if it is too monotonous (though actually it would not be very monotonous to use the name "Rubens" three times in a passage of 71 words), the reason is that there is too much repetition or unnecessary stating of what can be left to suggestion. The remedy is to rearrange the clauses so that the people don't have to be named so often. For example:

> Rubens sought out his colleagues whenever he had the opportunity. The exchange of views was often as fruitful as simply copying the works. During the time they spent together in Rome, his friend Adam Elsheimer taught him the art of engraving and influenced his artistic ideas, as can be seen in some of Rubens' later paintings.

A fifth type of suggestion depends upon grammatical constructions that show the parallelism or subordination of ideas. A good deal could be said about this matter, but a few distinctions will have to do here. Putting two ideas in a parallel way suggests that they are *comparable*.

Sometimes it claims (1) that they are relevant in the same way to the point at hand: hence the silliness of sentences like, "She drove off in a huff and her car," or "Edgar Allan Poe died in poverty, delirium, and a Baltimore hospital." But this can lead to more serious cases of confused writing. A report on public schools might say:

> We found that textbooks were generally out of date, and that in one school pupils were using a history book which had not been revised since 1908.

The grammar suggests that the two findings are on the same level, but the second finding is really an *illustration* of the first. In short, in this sentence, the suggested logical connection is at odds with the actual logical connection. A similar principle is involved in expressions like "human beings and children"; this suggests that the two classes of things are parallel, hence mutually exclusive (otherwise it would be superfluous to add "and children").

Sometimes the parallel grammar claims (2) that the two ideas or things are of equal importance. The suggestion is clear in Pope's couplet about the ladies in *The Rape of the Lock:*

> Not louder shrieks to pitying heaven are cast,
> When husbands or when lap-dogs breathe their last.

Pope knew what he was doing, but careless writers often fail to notice this sort of suggestion. Here is the way one committee listed the things it believed the public schools should teach children:

1. How to use the library.
2. How to think logically.
3. How to write a neat-looking assignment.
4. How to understand the responsibilities of democratic citizenship.
5. How to have good manners in using the telephone.
6. ... etc.

The suggestion is that they are of equal importance.

There are, of course, many ways of showing the relative importance you attach to a statement or a whole discourse. In print it is done by the size and position of type; a Broadway playbill or play advertisement, with its variety of type faces and its tacit conventions about the importance of left vs right and above vs below, can suggest very precise and subtle judgments about the roles of producer, director, author, and actors in the play. In speaking, it is done by the volume of tone, or the intensity of expression, or gestures. Something said in a loud voice is presumably believed to be urgent or especially note-worthy. But even slight hesitation (marked by a comma in the written version) can make a difference. A wife is testifying matter-of-factly in a divorce court if she reports:

My husband stayed out late with other women.

But if she says,

My husband stayed out late, with other women,

we understand that the other women were particularly objectionable.

In the sixth type of suggestion (the last we shall distinguish), there is usually a stress upon one word or another that makes the statement carry with it an implicit denial of what is left unsaid. If I say, "*Some* people are honest," you gather that I would have said "*All* people are honest" if I had believed it; so my statement suggests that some people are *not* honest. But I haven't strictly stated this. This type of suggestion can occur without particular stress: take the word "so-called." To use this word is to suggest that something is *wrongly* called. Everything is so-called, that is, called what it *is* called: cows are so-called "cows." But if I say that an Act of Congress is a "so-called liberalized immigration act," without being willing to call it that myself, I surely suggest that the term is a dubious one for it.

To give special emphasis to one word in a sentence is not only to call attention to that word, but to point out that *other* words that might have been used were not. It is a way of excluding something. Thus very different things can be suggested by the very same state-ment if different words are stressed:

We never said we would prosecute anyone who criticizes us. (But others may have said so.)

We never *said* we would prosecute anyone who criticizes us. (But we meant to.)

We never said *we* would prosecute anyone who criticizes us. (But we didn't deny that others would.)

We never said we would *prosecute* anyone who criticizes us. (But that doesn't mean we won't get back at them.)

We never said we would prosecute *anyone* who criticizes us. (But we will prosecute some of them.)

We never said we would prosecute anyone who *criticizes* us. (But we will prosecute them if they go any further.)

We never said we would prosecute anyone who criticizes *us*. (But we didn't deny we would prosecute those who criticized others.)

The possibilities here may remind you of that little interchange from *Ruddigore*, where Sir Ruthven Murgatroyd says that on Friday he disinherited his unborn son.

Ghost of Sir Roderic Murgatroyd: "But I don't think you can do that."

Sir Ruthven: "My good sir, if I can't disinherit my own unborn son, whose unborn son can I disinherit?"

Ghost: "Humph! These arguments sound very well, but I can't help thinking that, if they were reduced to syllogistic form, they wouldn't hold water."

It is not at all necessary for you to learn how to distinguish all these varieties of suggestion from one another; the point is to see that language can be suggestive in many different ways and to practice sensitivity to suggestion in any form.

Suggestion is, of course, an important element, or dimension, of literature. Poetry lives by it. It is part of what we mean by "style"; when we speak of the "style" of a writer, we include (1) his tendency to use a certain kind of *diction* (that is, words with certain connotations), and (2) his tendency to use phrases and constructions with certain kinds of suggestion. This can be worked out more fully and precisely, but we shall not stop to work it out now.

Irony is a feature of style, and it can be defined very clearly in terms of suggestion. A statement is *ironic* if what it suggests is in conflict with what it states. Because the statement is absurd, or improbable, or made in a certain tone of voice, or with certain facial expressions, it is clear that the speaker really does not believe what he is stating and does not expect anyone to think that he believes it. "But Brutus is an honorable man...." Irony includes *understatement*, where what is suggested is more than what is stated ("It's easy for *you* to forget, but I am told that some people were put to considerable inconvenience in the Nazi concentration camps"), and *overstatement*, where what is suggested is less than what is stated ("Oh, I realize that *you're* infallible; you're *always* right, of course"). In such cases, the stress on certain words, or the scornful tone, or the context show that what the speaker believes is something more or less than what he states.

Language that is rich in suggestion is highly economical, for it says a good deal briefly. But at the same time it is hard to control and likely to betray all but the most experienced writers. And in the hands of an unscrupulous writer it is especially dangerous, for it is by suggestion that he can get across implicit assertions without quite letting them out into the open where they can be inspected and criticized. But there is a way to deal with him. Generally speaking, whatever is suggested can also be stated. Throughout this section, as we have been analyzing each example of suggestion, we have made the suggestion explicit by putting it as a statement. "This student is as industrious as he is intelligent" suggests *that he is both industrious and intelligent.*

When, therefore, you catch a suggestion that is questionable, you don't have to let it pass. You can say, "You are suggesting that...." or, "If this is what is meant, then...." Consider this passage:

> No doubt our administration has made mistakes—after all, no one is perfect. Who can condemn us for being human? Look, rather, if you will be fair, at the positive side of the ledger....

The speaker *states* that his party has made mistakes; he *suggests* that the mistakes have been few. But he doesn't dwell on it; he plants the thought and deftly moves on to distract our attention to something more favorable. But we can say to ourselves, if not to him, "Hold on! You are suggesting that you have made only a few mistakes? Then what about...?" To do this is to *state* what is *suggested*, and stating it opens up to public gaze the important question, that is, the question whether it is true or false.

A CHECK-UP QUIZ. Read the following letter carefully to see what is suggested, but not stated, in it. Which of the ten clauses listed below contain ideas definitely suggested in the letter?

"Dear Mr. Stoker:

George Guff, who is a student in one of my courses, has asked me to recommend him for a summer job with your firm. I can assure you that Mr. Guff is a most remarkable lad, with, one might say, a variety of talents. As far as his classwork is concerned, he has been a leading light in the Players' Club, his fraternity, the college newspaper, the

Political Forum, and the lacrosse team. He has sometimes turned in his assignments on time, and I *believe* he will *pass* the course.

I judge that this letter is a mere formality, since Mr. Guff has assured me that he made a very favorable impression on you in the interview. I have *his* word that he is well suited to the job, and he is a student whose moral character is entirely free from any self-reproach. To turn to his more specific qualifications, I should say that his handwriting (or at least what I have seen of it) is very clear and readable, and his speech more than sufficiently fluent for most purposes.

Sincerely yours,
Aloysius Gorgon
Assoc. Prof. of English."

1. That George Guff does not care whether or not he gets the summer job.
2. That he is more interested in extracurricular activities than in his classwork.
3. That he does not usually get his assignments in on time.
4. That he does not do very much work.
5. That he does not do very accurate work.
6. That he will definitely not pass the course.
7. That he is an effective speaker.
8. That he is inclined to overrate himself.
9. That he is well suited to the job for which he has applied.
10. That he is not a very intelligent student.

See also Exercises 32 and 33, pp. 293-95.

FURTHER READING: Margaret M. Bryant and Janet R. Aiken, *Psychology of English*. New York: Columbia University Press, 1940, ch. 18.

§29. SLANTED DISCOURSE

In the strictest sense, presumably, a *lie* is a statement made by someone who knows it is not true with the intent of getting someone else to believe it. What people euphemistically call "white lies" are different. To tell a white lie is to make a statement that is true in itself but suggests something else that is false, and to make the statement with the intention of getting someone else to believe that what is suggested is true.

This may seem like too pedantic and fussy a way of defining these familiar terms, but the distinction is of considerable importance and has a wide application. Not that we need to discuss here the ethical aspects of the distinction, the question whether white lies are less wrong than black ones. The end result is much the same in both cases: someone is deliberately led to believe something that is not true. But the method, in its logical aspects, is different, and we mark this distinction in common speech by saying, sometimes, that a plain lie is "false," but a white lie is "misleading." When the tired traveller in a strange region asks the proverbially taciturn local resident, "Am I on the road to Stepney?", and the latter replies "Yup," the reply is perfectly true, of course. For after all the traveller *is* on the right road —he just happens to be going in the wrong direction.

The Federal Food, Drug, and Cosmetic Act condemns "misbranded" foods, drugs, and cosmetics, and prohibits labels that are "false *or* misleading." The label is *false* if it says "8 oz. net" when the package contains only 7 oz., or if it fails to note that the drug is poisonous or habit-forming or dangerous to take except on a doctor's prescription. It is *misleading* if the box or bottle is designed to look as if it held 8 oz. when it holds only 6 oz. (even if the label says "6 oz." way down in the corner), or if the label puts "GENTLE! MILD! SAFE!" in large letters, and "if taken in small doses" in tiny ones. There is a distinction between falsity and misleadingness, but quite a few people have been cheated or killed by each of them, and that's why the government looks with disfavor upon both.

The example of the traveller, however unlikely, illustrates very well a principle that holds for a great many white lies. It is easiest to fool people this way when you are replying to a question, or to an accusation. When you make such a reply, people expect you to *answer* the question, or the accusation, and not merely make a remark in response to it, so they tend to take your reply as if it were an answer, that is, to take it as stating what it merely suggests. The local resident did not *state* that the traveller was going away from his goal rather than toward it, but by stating that he was on the right road, and by *not* stating that the direction was wrong, he suggested that the direction was right.

This kind of lie has many uses, in the home, on the floor of Congress, and around the diplomatic conference tables. Take, for example, this bit of a Senate speech:

I welcome this opportunity to answer an unfounded charge that has been circulated about me—namely that I am opposed to the St. Lawrence seaway. Let me make it perfectly clear that for many years I have most earnestly been insisting that this country must develop and maintain the most complete and efficient transportation system possible. I will therefore support any transportation route, St. Lawrence or other, that is just to the American people and to those whose interests are most vitally concerned.

The Senator's constituents who read their copy of this speech, when he sends out copies (as he will), are likely to think he is going to vote for the St. Lawrence seaway bill when it comes up. What is *between* the lines is so obvious here, that it takes a close second look to see that nothing the Senator has actually *stated* will commit him to any vote. If he votes against the bill, he will say that it was not just to those railroads who would be threatened by the competition—and this is exactly what any other senator who votes against it can say too. No doubt the Senator was on the spot. But he's safe if he can do this good a job of answering a charge without answering it.

One kind of misleadingness, then, operates through suggestion; there is another kind that operates through connotation. Suppose you apply a particular term to someone who does have the characteristics *designated* by the term, but not the characteristics *connoted* by the term. For instance, he works hard at his studies, and you call him a "grind," though he does not in fact (as this term connotes) give up most friendly human contacts out of an abnormal desire to get high grades. The term is a libel in one respect, but not an outright lie. It is true, in so far as the designation of "grind" is concerned, but false in so far as its connotation is concerned.

It is convenient to think of all the meanings of a piece of discourse as being on three *levels*, from the most explicit to the least explicit. Take a simple sentence, like "Jones is more obese than Smith." On Level 1 this states that Jones has the characteristics *designated* by the term "obese" to a higher degree than Smith does. On Level 2 it states that Jones has the characteristics *connoted* by the term "obese" to a higher degree than Smith has. On Level 3 it suggests, without stating, that Smith also has the characteristics designated and connoted by the term "obese", at least to some degree.

Now a discourse that has these three levels of meaning can be true on Level 1, but false on Levels 2 or 3, or true on Levels 1 and 2, but false on Level 3. When a discourse is true on one level, but false on a higher level, and it carries the suggestion that because it is true on one level it must be true on the other level, we shall say that such a discourse is **slanted**. A slanted discourse purports to be a correct description of something, and it *is* correct in its most explicit and obvious respects. The incorrect parts are slipped in subtly, under cover of the correct parts; but in this form they are all the more capable of leading the reader astray.

Slanting poses one of the hardest tests of the first-rate reader. For a slanted discourse mingles truths and falsehoods in a subtle way that makes it difficult to sift out what is true from what is false. Yet this task is one that most of us are trying to do, in the best way we can, nearly every day: every newspaper, every magazine, every novel with "social significance," and every radio or television broadcast about current affairs presents us with exactly this problem. It would be convenient if truth and falsity always came in separate packages, each with its own label. In fact, however, they are mixed and jumbled, and we can't think straight until we know how to sort them out. A slanted statement is a half-truth which may be more dangerous than a plain lie until we discover which half is true and which is not.

The best way to see how slanting works is to try it ourselves. Suppose we start out with the following fact:

> Today the President signed the bill confirming the right of four Southern states to the oil known to lie underground off their shores in the Gulf of Mexico. This bill, known as the "tidelands oil bill," has been opposed by some senators who hold that the oil is Federal property.

Assume that our readers will accept this on our authority as reporters; we want them, however, to believe more than this fact. So we turn this statement into another statement that will say what this one says, but will also say some other things, and yet will pass with an uncritical reader as a substitute for this one. First we change some of the terms to other terms with closely similar designations, but different connotations:

> Today the President slapped his signature on the tidelands oil bill, which gives to four Dixie states the off-shore oil in the Mexican Gulf, despite a last ditch defense of Federal claims made by some senators.

Thus we hint (a) that the President is acting thoughtlessly, and (b) that the states don't deserve the oil because it really doesn't belong to them. Now we rearrange the sentence and add a few other remarks to take advantage of suggestion:

> Today the President made good one of the Republican campaign giveaway pledges by slapping his signature on a bill to turn over to four Southern states the off-shore oil previously reserved for the forty-eight states. The Federal Government's claims to the oil were maintained by several senators, whose defense was, however, overridden by a combination of Republicans and Southern senators.

Thus we insinuate (a) that this is probably only the first of a whole series of "giveaways," and (b) that the bill was passed by the Senate largely from selfish motives.

It may be that these hints and insinuations are provable; that's not the point. They are put in to mislead, and they *do* mislead if the reader thinks that because the discourse has some basic core of truth, the hints and insinuations are to be accepted as true too, without critical examination. Slanted discourse is designed to nudge the reader toward a point of view that is suggested, but not fully stated; it is slanted *toward* a conclusion. The conclusion is not put in so many words; it is rather taken in as what we might call the *total impression* of the discourse, which is built up by all the connotations and suggestions.

In terms of slanting we can understand the age-old device of the **Loaded Question.** This is a question you can't answer without committing yourself to something you don't believe. It is well known that in a public opinion poll, a question like "How do you feel about cooperating with the United Nations?" can be asked in a way that suggests that only a numbskull would be opposed to cooperation, or as if it were the most preposterous idea imaginable. It is also often remarked that a relatively slight difference in the wording of two questions, say,

> A. Should the United States pull out of the United Nations or should it go on trying to make the U. N. work?
> B. Should the United States withdraw from the U. N. or should it continue working to strengthen the U. N., for example, by limiting the veto power in the Security Council?

will make a considerable difference in the result of a poll—and obviously, in this case, the questions suggest very different things.

There are two particularly fine types of Loaded Question. A question of the first type offers you a choice of two answers but is rigged so that either of your answers will be slanted against you. The question, "Will organized labor eventually succeed in dominating the nation?" suggests that organized labor is *trying* to do this, and whichever way you answer the question, Yes or No, you are tacitly admitting that the suggestion is true. A question of the second type offers you a choice of two answers, one of which is false, and the other of which is slanted against you, so that again you don't know which way to answer. Suppose you are a manufacturer, and your company once unknowingly and unintentionally violated a Federal law, discovered the fact later, and made good on it. Someone asks you, "Did your company ever violate a Federal law? Answer Yes or No!" If you answer No, you will not be telling the truth; but if you answer Yes, you will not be exactly telling the truth either, for this answer will suggest (unless your questioner allows you to explain further) that you knew *at the time* that your company was violating the law. The only safe reply to questions like these is to refuse to answer until better questions are offered.

There are numerous techniques of slanting, that is, ways of coloring or doctoring facts so that they seem to prove something they don't prove, or seem to make a conclusion stronger than it really is. It would be too much trouble to try to catalogue them all, and, in any case, most of them can be understood in terms of the previous discussions of connotation and suggestion. But there are some aspects of the matter that are worth more careful notice. All the techniques, however varied (and new ones are constantly being invented), reduce to two general principles: they either involve *selection* (including or omitting certain facts) or *arrangement* (twisting the facts by combining them in certain ways).

If somebody asked you on a summer afternoon how the Giants were doing, and you said they had two runs without mentioning that the Dodgers had seven, this could hardly be called a fair, unbiased report of the game so far. Giving only the facts favorable to our conclusions, and leaving out the unfavorable ones, is one familiar way of loading the dice. Of course, we often do it without meaning to, and sometimes it seems as though the truth about a matter is so complicated that *any* summary statement is going to be misleading, no matter how we qualify it.

For example, suppose somebody brings up the question of the Tennessee Valley Authority's financial status. It is very one-sided to say, simply, that it pays no taxes as private utilities do. To be fair, we have to add that it does turn back money each year to the Federal government, in lieu of taxes ($24,676,977 in 1954; a total of $123,-170,667 in the 20 years since it was started). But *that* statement would be thought misleading in the opposite direction unless we add that Congress has had to appropriate large sums nearly every year for construction ($188,546,000 in 1954; a grand total of $1,785,214,581). But *that* might give a distorted picture unless we also noted that after all, the plants and dams belong to the Federal Government. Yes, but *that* might need to be corrected, too, by noting that the rate of return on the government's investment is low compared to taxes collected from comparable private industries. Yes, but it must be kept in mind, on the other hand, that the low rate of return is due to the lower prices of TVA power, and hence the benefits to the people who buy its power; and also it is due to the fact that TVA is not merely a power producer, but confers many other great benefits that it doesn't get paid for, such as flood control, land reclamation, navigation, parks and recreation areas. . . .

You see the problem here. With a complicated issue like this one, any summary runs the risk of misleadingness. An objective summary *can* be made, but not without considerable care, for there are so many facts that are relevant that if any one of them is missing, some distortion will occur. But, as we need to be reminded once in a while, this is exactly why we have to discuss things when we disagree, so that others will point out relevant facts that we have missed. When you read one of the periodic debates in the Congress on the TVA—such as the one in July, 1954—you can see how important it is that one man's facts are supplemented by another man's facts—and you can also see how hard it is, even with great good will and patience, for a group of people to get all of the important facts put into the record together.

The technique of omission doesn't work, of course, if it is obvious. There has to be a pretense that the speaker is impartial and is presenting both sides. The subtlest way of covering up omissions is for the speaker to present a few mildly unfavorable facts, and then pooh-

pooh them. In this way, he can attack his opponent only on the latter's weakest points, an leave the impression that he has refuted him down the line.

> Now, just as an example of the type of argument—and I am almost embarrassed to bring it up—advanced in favor of maintaining the Federal program of technical advice and assistance to farmers—and I take only one example, because I don't want to waste the afternoon on such arguments—one argument is that to abandon the program would put some bureaucrats out of work. Well, now, isn't that too bad! That sure is a powerful reason for continuing to lay out vast sums, . . . etc., etc.,

Unless you know the facts, you can't tell, of course, what's been left out of an argument. You can be on your guard, and if you find a completely one-sided argument about an issue that you know is controversial, you should suspect that there is probably *something* to be said on the other side, even if the other side is wrong. That doesn't mean you can never settle an issue—in the end, one side is right and the other wrong if there is a genuine conflict; or at least one side is more nearly right than the other, though we may not be able to tell for sure which is the right one. But if the matter is important (if it's going to affect the way you vote, or plan your family budget, or choose your profession), then you must look around for the missing facts, and see what they imply. Or you can find two newspapers or magazines that have different biases and try putting them together to make a less slanted picture.

Even if a newspaper gives you a true outline of the facts, it can twist them in important ways. In one paper we read that someone was a "cheerful, plump, and energetic speaker, addressing a somewhat passive but huge audience"; in another paper we find that he was a "cheery, pudgy, acrobatic speaker, addressing a good-sized but dead-pan audience." We read two reports of a theatre fire, and one suggests that the theatre manager is to blame, the other that the fire-inspection bureau of the city administration is to blame.

One of the most important kinds of distortion consists in playing up, or playing down, the importance of what is stated—the free-wheeling accusation of treason (large headlines on page one), artificially kept alive for several days by careful injections of "new angles" —followed by the evidence that the accusation cannot be made good (paragraph squeezed between two advertisements on page 18). The report of a State Department decision to withdraw its representative from a conference of foreign ministers may be elbowed into near-oblivion by the news of a sensational birth of Siamese twins.

To handle slanted discourse, you use the tools that have already been provided. First, get the total impression, or angle of the whole discourse. What does it add up to? What general judgment on persons or situations does it implicitly make? Second, take the discourse apart to find out exactly which terms and statements create that total impression through connotation and suggestion. What is *stated*, and what is merely insinuated by suggestion? What is *explicitly* stated, in clear literal terms, and what is merely hinted at by connotation of words? Third, compare it with other versions of the situation, and look carefully for omissions and distortions. Then you will know what it is that you are being pressed to believe. And you can begin to see whether the reasons are good enough to justify belief.

A CHECK-UP QUIZ. Read the following brief account of an incident, and then the statements about it listed below. Which statements (if any) are slanted in *favor* of the driver of the car ("Pro"), and which (if any) *against* ("Con")?

It was just after dark on a summer evening. A light, steady rain was falling. The car was going 25 miles an hour on a side street marked for a 25 mile an hour speed limit. The driver was on his way home from work, and had the car radio on. As he passed a corner at which he had the right of way, another car came out of the cross street, without pausing at a stop sign, and narrowly missed crashing into him. In the middle of the next block, a middle-aged man, who was later found to have been somewhat intoxicated, came suddenly from behind a parked car. He was also on his way home from work. Before the driver could stop, he hit the pedestrian, and knocked him down, without, however, doing any serious damage.

1. JAYWALKER STRUCK BY CAR.
2. Pushing the legal speed limit, and on a rainy night too, the driver was proceeding East . . .
3. The driver was heading home through a dark and rainy night . . .
4. The car was going 25 miles an hour.
5. The car was going 30 miles an hour.
6. The car, it is true, was going less than 50 miles an hour. . . .

7. The pedestrian lurched out without warning into the path of the on-coming car.

8. Within the space of a minute or two, the car almost had one crash-up, and then struck a homeward-bound pedestrian.

9. The car was cruising along, radio playing merrily away, though it could not have been possible for the driver to see far ahead through the rain.

10. In a strictly legal sense, it must be admitted, the driver of the car did nothing he could be held accountable for.

See also Exercises 34 and 35, pp. 296-303.

FURTHER READING: Richard D. Altick, *Preface to Critical Reading*. New York: Henry Holt and Co., revised ed., 1951, ch. 6. Elmer Davis, *But We Were Born Free*. Indianapolis and New York: The Bobbs-Merrill Co., Inc., 1954, ch. 3.

§30. THE APPEAL TO EMOTION

The terms "thinking" and "feeling" are often used in opposition to each other, as though these two processes couldn't go on in the same mind at the same time. But if human beings couldn't feel pretty strongly about something and still be able to think reasonably about it, they could never deal with a crisis. You are bound to feel stirred when your house is on fire, when you are in love, or when there is danger of war; but that doesn't imply that you are *necessarily* going to think ineffectively or act foolishly.

Nevertheless, it is true that our emotions often help to make our thinking less effective than it can be. They get in the way of clear thinking. And it has been known probably ever since language began to be spoken that if a speaker or writer is less interested in thinking clearly himself than he is in preventing *other* people from thinking clearly, he can make it very difficult to tell whether or not his arguments are good ones—or even whether or not they are arguments— by going out of his way to appeal to certain powerful emotions.

There is, of course, an unlimited variety of emotions that words can tap. Even a single name, like "fear," ranges over a class of emotions that are very different from one another: fear of fire, of poverty, of tigers, of foreigners, of mice, of death. But certain types of emotional appeal turn up very frequently, and are worth a good look.

What is to be called an "emotional appeal" is not just any discourse that affects people's feelings. There is a distinction here that is vital, but not precise. Suppose you convince someone of something that arouses his moral indignation—say, that a bill now before the House of Representatives, ending Federal trusteeship of certain Indian tribes (the Paiutes of Utah, the Shoshones of Nevada, or the Seminoles of Florida) will remove protection that they still badly need and will expose them to poverty and all sorts of exploitation. You are affecting his feelings all right, but his feelings are a result of what you have led him, let us assume on reasonable grounds, to believe. But suppose he asks for proof that the Paiutes will be worse off if the bill is passed, and you say something like, "Picture the poor ignorant Indians being swindled out of their land by unscrupulous white men." Now, picturing the poor Indian this way will very likely make him feel even more strongly indignant, and it *may* put him in a frame of mind where he will be less critical of your argument. But it *doesn't* give him any of the proof he asked for.

As this example shows, the emotional appeal depends not only on the use of words with strong connotations, but also on suggestion. For the suggestion is that the reply *is* an answer to the request. The *question* is whether the Indians *will* be swindled. The reply takes it for granted that they will, and thus begs the question, but by doing so it suggests that the answer has already been given, or is too obvious to need mentioning, and this suggestion is false. A speaker who does this deliberately is taking the same sort of risk that an army takes if it uses poison gas on a breezy day; speakers who make a habit of it generally show that they have succeeded in muddling themselves at least as well as anyone else. For our purpose it doesn't matter whether the emotional appeal is intentional; the point is to watch out for it and spot it when it comes.

1. *Appeal to pity.* "Widows and orphans whose only income depends upon dividends from stock. . . . a child torn from its mother's arms. . . . people driven from their homes by the super-highway. . . ." By presenting us with such scenes as these, which naturally make us sad, the speaker aims to make us feel unreasonable pity toward those whom his policy is supposed to help. Once he has aroused our sympathies, by whatever means, it is easier for him to make us accept what he suggests: that these people are really deserving of pity, and that his policy will actually help them. But he does not give any

reasons for these claims: he hopes that the very warmth of our feeling will make us willing to try any policy that is vaguely associated with charity, generosity, and an honest desire to help.

Thus if a housing bill is brought up before the House of Representatives with appropriate references to "homeless veterans returning from the wars," "the ill-housed," "sweeping out the slums," and so forth, this will persuade many people that it must be a good bill, sincerely drawn up. Yet it may be that in the bill itself these purposes are so hedged with restrictions that not 35,000 homes, as promised, but fewer than 10,000 will be built in the following year. The appeal to pity puts us in an awkward position by making us seem like crass monsters if we examine the provisions of the bill critically.

2. *Alarm.* "Crime waves sweeping across the nation in the wake of progressive education. . . . the man next to you on the bus may be a secret agent of the Kremlin. . . . the clergy, the teaching profession, the army, Hollywood—infiltrated with subversive elements." By calling up such specters as these, the speaker aims to put us in a state of unreasonable fearfulness. What he *suggests* is that the policy he opposes will inevitably lead to these fearful consequences, but he does not stop to *prove* that the consequences will follow. Instead, he makes us so frightened at the very thought of them that we will be scared to try any policy even remotely suggestive of the possibility of such consequences. He makes us so terrified of the danger that we run away from it blindly, even if into a worse danger; for when we are terrified it is hard for us to remember that all choices involve *some* risk, and it takes reasoning to discover which is the lesser risk.

Thus a speech along the lines, "Pickets marching up and down in front of the White House! Why, it's the next thing to open rebellion! . . ." may persuade the Senate to make it a crime to walk in front of the White House with a placard containing a protest or grievance. And the same technique is used, of course, in advertisements. Very often they don't give reasons to show that we will lose our jobs, or be left alone to sulk at beach parties, or be laughed at by our guests if we don't use hair tonic, avoid starchy foods, or increase our word power. They merely try to make us so unhappy at the very thought of these contingencies that we will do anything to avoid them, without stopping to ask for evidence that it will really help. This is using alarm as an emotional appeal instead of giving *reasons* that the consequences will actually follow and that they are undesirable.

3. *Flattery.* "It is a pleasure to speak to so discerning an audience. ... The great sovereign state of South Carolina. ... you, the citizens of the most powerful and best country in the world." By such phrases as these, ranging from the gentlest pat on the back to the wildest flag-waving, the speaker aims to make us feel pleased with ourselves, with our possessions, our achievements, or our heritage. What he *suggests* is that he admires us, and also that he is particularly smart because he recognizes our virtues, even if others don't. But he does this by catering to our stock responses, our smugness, our self-satisfaction, or our legitimate pride in our work. He doesn't give *reasons* to show that what he praises is praiseworthy, and that we deserve the fine compliments.

This is always hard to guard against, for nations as well as people. Some members of the United Nations are often critical of United States policy, and their criticisms hurt. But sometimes the criticisms are just, and sometimes the advice other nations give is good advice. But it is harder to take good advice from a sharp critic than to take bad advice from someone who tells us that we are perfectly wonderful, infinitely wise and courageous, and need pay no attention to any country whose leaders are so stupid or jealous as not to see this. Not that we have nothing to be proud of—every nation has something to be proud of, and some have more than others. The point is that when the problem is what stand to take on some vital world issue, we are only making ourselves groggy if we sing hymns of patriotic praise instead of thinking hard about the issue. One who is drugged, whether with opium or flattery, is in poor shape to get at the truth about anything.

4. *Identification with audience.* "You and I are just plain folks ... we see eye to eye. ... When I was a child on a farm like the ones you have here. ..." By such phrases as these a speaker aims to make us identify ourselves with him, to feel friendly toward him, and to trust what he says. What he *suggests* is that he has our true interests at heart; but the only evidence he gives is that he dresses like us, rolls up his sleeves, uses colloquial grammar and diction, and speaks in a hearty and confidential manner. He appears to be one of the boys, a man of the people, someone who shares, or has shared, our tasks and ambitions and hopes.

Of course, this is sometimes precisely true. If the candidate tells a group of mothers that he favors larger tax-exemptions for children, then they can see that he recognizes their interests and favors them. It is only when he tells them (if he does) that larger tax-exemptions would be undemocratic and probably fatal to the American Way of Life that he needs to make them feel that he is really one of them and working for them, and that therefore he must be right when he says it's all for their own good, even though the force of his argument escapes them.

5. *The ad hominem argument.* "My opponent wants to return the municipal garbage disposal plant to private hands. What are his underlying motives? Could it be that he and his friends are after a profitable monopoly?" Looking at the matter abstractly, it is obvious to all of us that it is one thing to talk about an issue, and it is another thing to talk about the people who are talking about the issue. Still, in the heat of a discussion, it is hard to keep personalities out. The *ad hominem* argument is not "to the thing" (*ad rem*) but "to the man" (*ad hominem*); it is a way of poisoning the well, that is, casting suspicion on the *source* of a statement in order to make us doubt the statement itself. The speaker aims to discredit the character, motives, family, college companions, pronunciation, grammar, dress, or any one of a thousand other characteristics of the person who disagrees with him—that is, to *abuse* his opponent in some way. And what he thereby *suggests* is that if something is wrong with a person, then what that person says cannot be true.

It is a form of the *ad hominem* argument when someone proposes to ban, or specially label, certain books because the authors are suspected of Communist sympathies. Even if the books are pro-Communist, it doesn't follow that they should be banned. But it is surely very much beside the point to condemn a book, no matter what it says, because of some information about the author. Obviously, the most despicable person in the world can say the sea is salt, and this will still be true. And if he says that the value of a product depends on the amount of labor that goes into it, we don't refute this statement by replying, "You're a Marxist." The question whether it is false is settled by investigating the statement, not by castigating the speaker. But that is the technique of the *ad hominem* arguer.

Of course, when a witness is giving testimony in a trial, the question at issue is, precisely, the reliability of the witness. Here it is legitimate to impeach the evidence by raising doubts about its source because the witness is asking us to believe it on his authority. But if we show that the witness is biased, or was in no position to observe what he claims to have observed, or is given to telling lies, we still have not proved that what he says is *false*—we have only proved that his *saying* it is no good reason for believing it. This is a very different thing.

6. *The argument from illegitimate authority.* "As the atomic scientists say.... as great men of the past agree.... as I was taught at my mother's knee." By such appeals to our readiness to be guided by those who really know more than we do, the speaker aims to bolster up his claims. What he *suggests* is that the authority he quotes is a legitimate one—that is, one whom we have good reason to trust in regard to the matter at hand because (a) he has access to the relevant information, (b) he is qualified by ability and training to think about it, and (c) he is fair and unbiased in his thinking. But the speaker may be hoping that we will transfer the respect or reverence we feel toward one who is an authority on one matter to other matters on which he is not an authority at all.

In this way our reasonable regard for the opinion of doctors and surgeons has made them a national symbol of authoritative guidance on a host of questions with which they are untrained, or poorly trained, to deal. The advertising pages are heavily populated with men in white brandishing stethoscopes or test tubes. They sometimes write columns on child psychology (without special training in that field), give opinions on cigarette smoking (without having done special research on it), and speak out on complex economic problems about health insurance (without studying economics).

When someone is quoted as an expert, the question is whether he knows what he is talking about. Sometimes we can't be sure. But we can always raise the question without succumbing blindly to prestige. We can see whether the speaker gives any *reasons* for supposing that the authority is genuine.

It would be a mistake to condemn, or even to mistrust, all discourse that appeals to our emotions. A statement can arouse emotions and still be true. Some facts are delightful and some are damnable. But to get at the truth about anything you have to do something more than feel strongly about it. And that is why it is necessary to recognize these emotional appeals. For if they do not paralyze clear thinking, they make it very difficult. As the immortal John J. McGraw (who was occasionally known to take offense at umpires' rulings during the thirty years he managed the Giants) once remarked, "When a man sees red, it's not likely he sees much of anything else." And the same goes for other emotions.

Generally speaking, there are two main ways in which our feelings affect our thinking, and they lead to two broad types of fallacious argument.

First, feelings can *narrow attention*. They limit what is grasped and remembered, and so they cut down the scope of what is taken into account in reasoning about a problem. This tendency is the source of the fallacy of oversimplification, which it is useful to define rather broadly. The facts relevant to a given conclusion are those facts which, if known, would be good reasons (though maybe not by themselves utterly conclusive reasons) either for or against the conclusion. When feelings are aroused in a dispute, they may lead one or both of the disputants to leave out of account some of the relevant facts; this is what we shall call **oversimplification.**

Second, feelings can *shift attention*. They get thinking off its course, lead it to slip from one point to another without noticing the slip, to lose its sense of direction. If there are two things we feel very strongly and similarly about, our sense of distinction is blurred, and we may fail to discriminate between them. This tendency is the source of the fallacy of distraction, which is the opposite of oversimplification. When feelings run high in a dispute, they may lead one or both of the disputants to bring in facts, or supposed facts, that are not relevant; this is what we shall call **distraction.**

It will be useful to consider each of these a little more fully.

A number of fallacies might be covered by the term "oversimplification"—the black-or-white fallacy and the argument from analogy, for example. No doubt we can never be certain that we have considered all the available information that bears upon a particular issue. But we can try not to overlook, or minimize the importance of, relevant information that is at hand, ready to be used. The oversimplifier, or Capsule Thinker, on the other hand, misses what others see. He has no patience with careful qualifications; when you try to set him straight, he calls it "quibbling." He thinks in terms of stereotyped formulas, and his discourse is full of catchwords and slogans, like "where there's smoke there's fire," and "America First." He puts his small stock of ideas into tidy pigeonholes, and sees every problem in terms of bold and extreme choices: Christianity *or* Communism, victory *or* defeat, militarism *or* pacificism. When the American delegates to the United Nations are engaged in delicate negotiating over a tricky question, the issue is plain to the Capsule Thinker: "Well, it all boils down to this—either they recognize the world leadership of the United States or we should pull out of the United Nations."

Any of the emotional appeals can be used for oversimplification. Consider this little dialogue:

> A: "Take the bill to let the Attorney General use evidence from wiretapping. The case for this bill can be put in a nutshell— it might help catch spies."
>
> B: "But don't you think that the possibility of misuse against innocent persons and the ethical aspects of invading people's privacy ought to be carefully considered?"
>
> A: "Look. Stick to the point. For all we know the country may be flooded with dangerous secret spies, poised over the jugular vein of the nation. What it boils down to is, do you want to catch them or not?"

This is fairly typical. There is a good deal of alarm (but no attempt to estimate reasonably the extent of the danger or the extent to which the wiretapping bill is likely to relieve it); by means of this alarm, A tries to focus attention on the aspect of the question that interests him and to prevent B from introducing other relevant points. If he succeeds in stirring up B, he may succeed in making B feel, as he does, that this complex problem can be boiled down to as simple a question as the question whether spies should be caught or not. In this way, oversimplification creates a one-track argument with a dead end.

The term "distraction" covers a number of different ways in which a dispute can be sidetracked. It includes equivocation and also some forms of slanting. Here is an example:

> A: "The United States merchant marine must be kept healthy and large, both for leadership in peace and for safety in case of war, even if it means Federal subsidies to shipbuilders."
>
> B: "I see. I suppose, by the way, that your opinion has nothing to do with the fact that you have investments in two shipping companies?"
>
> A: "So what? The question is whether it is to the good of the whole country—"
>
> B: "—And also the stockholders—?"

A: "Now listen to me. My investments have nothing to do with it. They are not very large, in fact, and I can prove that; here are the figures—"

A's original statement here is straightforward and arguable; it raises an important question. B counters with an *ad hominem* argument. A refuses at first to be drawn aside, and tries to get the discussion back on the rails. But when B needles him again, he becomes annoyed, and loosens his grip on the point. Now B, whether deliberately or not, has got A arguing a totally different question, namely how large A's investments are—which has nothing at all to do with the original point.

The Grasshopper Thinker frequently gets diverted from the issue, or diverts others. He is often hard to cope with, for he simply won't stick to the point. He will introduce a reference to a dubious authority and turn the discussion into a debate about the value of the authority, instead of the original question the authority was supposed to shed light on. Under cover of a barrage of alarm or sentimental pity, he will slide from one point to another so fast that only a skilled reasoner can keep track of his maneuvers.

Your best protection against the oversimplifier and the distractor is to take pains always to know the point at issue. And it helps you to do this if you keep on the watch in any discussion for the emotive appeals that tempt people into fallacy, and if you insist that relevant facts be considered when someone would keep them out, and that irrelevant facts be excluded when someone would bring them in.

A CHECK-UP QUIZ. Label each emotional appeal in the following passages, and say whether it is being used for oversimplification or distraction.

1. I don't profess, any more than I'm sure you do, to be one of those egghead professors who can make black into white, but the problem of euthanasia, when reduced to essentials, is just this: no human being can predict the future with certainty, and even if a person seems to be incurably ill with cancer, it is possible that the diagnosis is wrong, or a cure may be discovered, or he may miraculously recover. If we permit a doctor to put him out of his misery, and he would have recovered, it is cold-blooded legalized murder. Is that going to be written into the law? ...

2. ... The supporters of euthanasia say that all safeguards against

abuse of the law will be taken; that before anyone can be legally put to death to end his suffering, he must give his written permission to a specially-appointed board, and his illness certified by qualified physicians. But picture, if you will, the old man, one who has spent his life in hard work and who has amassed a fortune, surrounded by his bloodsucking relatives, who bribe and cajole the physician, and forge his signature, to have him put away, even though there is nothing wrong with him at all. It is impossible to design *any* law that will be protected against all abuses; that is the thing to keep in mind. . . .

3. . . . It seems to me that I detect in this scheme a secret conspiracy; one of those who have signed a petition to the state legislature is a brother of a man who was once indicted because his firm had dealings with a German cartel just before the last war. Can we trust a proposal supported by such a person?

4. . . . For I can smell the Nazi gas chambers in this scheme. Where will they go next? From legalized killing of the incurably ill, to killing the feeble-minded or crippled? To genocide? . . .

5. . . . No, my friends, whatever the decadent nations of Europe may do (already declining, as Spengler predicted), you in this land are too intelligent and vigorous to be carried away by these schemers. You can see the heart of the plan, behind all the smoke screen of pious and humanitarian words. It is, at bottom, a measure of defeatism, alien to America. It says to the person who is ill: don't try to get well; you might as well give up; have no faith in your doctor or in the scientific laboratory. That is what it means. . . .

See also Exercises 36 and 37, pp. 303-07.

FURTHER READING: L. Susan Stebbing, *Thinking to Some Purpose*. Pelican Books, chs. 3, 4, 5, 6, 8, 13. Robert H. Thouless, *Straight and Crooked Thinking*. New York: Simon and Schuster, Inc., 1932, chs. 3, 5, 6, 7, 11.

Outline Summary of Chapter 7

A declarative sentence, besides what it explicitly states (or an interrogative sentence, besides what it explicitly asks; or an imperative sentence, besides what it explicitly commands) can show that the person who utters it has certain beliefs that he does *not* explicitly state. These beliefs are said to be *suggested* by the sentence. Thus "Vote for Kelsey!" suggests that the speaker *wants* the hearer to vote for Kelsey; and "I will not *seek* the nomination" suggests that the speaker is not unwilling to accept the nomination if it is tendered to him.

When a true statement carries a false suggestion, or when a statement is true in what its words designate but false in what its words connote, the discourse in which that statement occurs is said to be *slanted*. The statement, "On gaining office, President Eisenhower unleashed the Chinese Nationalist troops on Formosa; thereupon, the Chinese Communists agreed to a Korean truce," is slanted because though it is true in what it states on the level of designation, nevertheless (a) it suggests a simple cause-effect relation between these two events which is not true, and (b) the term "unleash" connotes eagerness and readiness to attack the mainland on the part of the Nationalist troops, and it is not true that they were eager and ready to attack. In a newspaper report the truth may be slanted by omitting facts, exaggeration or playing down of the importance of facts, juxtaposing them to give a misleading suggestion, and in other ways.

When a speaker or writer attempts to arouse emotions without giving adequate reasons to show that the emotions are called for by the facts, he is making an *emotional appeal*. Among the most common emotional appeals are: (1) appeal to pity, (2) alarm, (3) flattery, (4) identification with audience, (5) *ad hominem* argument (attacking the person in order to discredit his assertions), and (6) the argument from illegitimate authority (quoting one who is an authority on one subject as an authority on another subject, where he does not qualify, because he has not the ability, training, unbiased point of view, or opportunity to learn the relevant facts).

By means of emotional appeals, a dispute between two people (a) can be made to exclude revelant facts—the fallacy of *oversimplification* ("Never mind all this talk about conserving natural resources; the question is a matter of states rights, and nothing else."); or (b) can be made to introduce irrelevant facts, or to slip away from the point—the fallacy of *distraction* ("You say that the Educational Conference Board voted that more money was needed for schools. Now, I don't say that the Board is *completely* dominated by New Deal free spenders and irresponsible idealistic bleeding hearts, but ...").

Exercise 32

State, as briefly as you can, what is suggested by each of the following remarks.

1. Oh, Johnny's not very good at *arithmetic*, I admit.

2. I'm afraid we'll have to work even harder to make up the time we have lost.

3. Work on the shoe factory is progressing as rapidly as can be expected under the supervision of Alton Prock and Sons.

4. She's a famous movie star. She is loved by millions. Her hair is radiant. She shampoos with Goldenglow.

5. If you want a treat, instead of a treatment, smoke ———'s.

6. You mustn't let anyone *catch* you cheating. That gives a *very* bad impression, and leads to trouble. Of course, it's not good to *cheat* either.

7. The program is scheduled to continue until next week.

8. Mrs. Jones's relatives visited the Joneses last Friday. Mr. Jones left on a trip Saturday morning.

9. Yes, we have three children; Cathie is older than Jeff, and David is older than Cathie.

10. "And there followed him a great company of people, and of women. . . ." (Luke 23:27)

11. The job of the public school teacher is not to teach arithmetic, but to teach *children*.

12. (A member of the House Committee on Un-American Activities, when Lucille Ball, the movie actress, told the Committee that she had once registered as a Communist voter to please her grandfather:) "The committee is departing from its usual procedure so that fact may be separated from rumor, and no damage done Miss Ball."

13. (A secretary of agriculture on farm price supports:) "The purpose of price supports should not be to stifle the farmer's initiative, but to protect him from undue disaster."

14. (The President of the United States, at the Commencement Exercises of Washington College, Chestertown, Md., June, 1954, with two senators and a representative of his own party sitting on the platform:) "I do want to tell this student body that no matter what they hear about Washington, D.C., I have two United States Senators and one Congressman here today with me to prove that we do need brains."

15. (From an article on "Putting Words in the Constitution's Mouth," inserted in the Appendix to the *Congressional Record*:) "The fathers of our country never intended any one man to have the power to fly off blind, half-cocked, and shamefully unprepared into a war, when there wasn't any immediate danger to our country, thousands of miles away, costing billions of dollars and in which thousands of our boys were shot down by bullets coming from Russia, a member of the United Nations, without first discussing the matter with Congress with a view to determining the advisability of engaging in an act of war."

Exercise 33

Compare the statements in each of the following pairs. What is the difference in what they suggest?

1. *Some* of the liberal members of the committee will be present.
   Some of the *liberal* members of the committee will be present.

2. My watch is slower than yours.
   Your watch is faster than mine.

3. He took his boots off and came in.
   He came in and took his boots off.

4. The candidate promised to keep the public debt at its present limit, and at the same time meet our increasing needs for national defense.
   The candidate promised to meet our increasing needs for national defense without increasing the public debt.

5. Don't be mean to old ladies. They are so defenceless.
   Don't be mean to old ladies. They may call the police.

6. Wife to friend: "My husband was drunk last night."
   Husband: "My wife was *sober* last night."

7. I *thought* you'd be ready.
   I thought you'd be *ready*.

8. You'll find cookies in the *cupboard*.
   You'll find *cookies* in the cupboard.

9. Poor Corveletto! He could not finish his novel. He drank too much.
   Poor Corveletto! He drank too much. He could not finish his novel.

10. A few of his old friends will be there.
    Few of his old friends will be there.

11. I'm afraid I can't do it now.
    I'm afraid I can't do it, now.

12. A man with an income of $4,500 a year has to work two hours and 35 minutes every day to pay his taxes; if he gets to work at eight, he doesn't begin earning his own living until 10:36 a.m.
    A man with an income of $4,500 a year is able to earn enough money to pay for his police and fire protection, public education, highway and slum clearance programs, public libraries, old age retirement, aid to the needy, parks, public playgrounds, recreational centers, welfare services, war veterans' pensions, the building of atomic and hydrogen bombs, Army, Navy, Air Force, and so on, by the work he does in less than a third of his working (eight-hour) day.

Exercise 34

Read these two newspaper reports and discuss the questions below.

A

AEC TO NEGOTIATE
GENERATING PLANT
TO SUPPLY TVA

Washington, June 17.—President Eisenhower has taken a substantial step toward fulfilling his pre-election pledge to check the "creeping socialism" of the Tennessee Valley Authority without preventing TVA from enlarging and improving its service to the people in the region it serves.

It was learned today that the President has instructed the Atomic Energy Commission to enter into partnership with private industry by negotiating a contract with a utility group for a $107,250,000 steam generating plant to be built at West Memphis, Ark. According to the plan, $5,000,000 of venture capital would be put up by private investors, who risk forfeiting heavy percentages of the anticipated profit if the actual cost of the plant goes above the estimated cost.

The new plant will feed 600,000 kilowatts into the TVA grid system to replace the amount furnished by TVA to the AEC atomic installations at Paducah, Ky. TVA will thus be able to fulfill the needs of atomic energy development, and at the same time satisfy the demands of its other customers, without the construction of any further government-owned power plants that would require heavy investment of Federal funds.

It was pointed out by witnesses at the hearing of the Joint Congressional Committee on Atomic Energy that TVA already purchases some of its power from private sources, as does AEC. In submitting its budget this year, the TVA monopoly again asked for heavy subsidies for expansion. This time they demanded $100,000,000 over the next three years to raise a steam generating plant at Fulton, Tenn., which is on the extreme edge of the TVA area, and 115 airline miles from the Tennessee River. As some of TVA's supporters in Congress have conceded, it has never been made clear on what authority TVA, which was originally set up for conserving the natural resources of the Tennessee River and its tributaries, has built the steam plants that now supply 70 per cent of its electric power, and has spread out its control to the Mississippi River.

The TVA request for the Fulton plant was not included in the Eisenhower appropriations bill when it was sent to Congress, and Republican Senators vigorously and successfully resisted attempts to slip it back into the bill on the floor of Congress. Instead, the Administration proposed that the AEC cut back its demands on TVA by 600,000 kilowatts and find another source of power, so that TVA would not need to build a new plant to get power. Half the power AEC uses at Paducah is now supplied by a privately-owned plant at Joppa. However, it later developed that it would be better not to encourage the building of another plant near Paducah, where power can be supplied to AEC from TVA's Shawnee plant.

Two companies in the region then offered to provide the needed power if the government would help them build a plant near West Memphis, which is only 30 miles from Fulton, and if the TVA would set up lines to carry the power to its own network. This proposal, which the President has had submitted to the AEC by Rowland R. Hughes, Director of the Bureau of the Budget, is reported to have the approval of two of the Atomic Energy Commissioners, including the chairman, Rear Admiral Lewis L. Strauss. The other three commissioners have expressed some doubt about the AEC's legal authority to negotiate such a contract, but have indicated that they are prepared to follow the direction of the President or Congress.

According to government spokesmen, the plan would further coordinate the two government agencies, and would also encourage private enterprise, for which the TVA itself was originally designed as a "yardstick." The contract contemplates only a 9 per cent return for the investors. When the annual cost to the AEC of the West Memphis proposal ($20,959,000) is compared with the present annual cost at Paducah of the same amount of power from TVA ($19,856,000) the difference of $1,103,000 is less than the Federal, State, and local taxes that would be paid out of the West Memphis total, but which TVA would not pay. An interesting feature of the proposed contract is that the taxes to be paid by the utility would be computed separately and paid directly by the Federal Government, instead of being paid in disguised form by being added to the rates.

B

DIXON-YATES CONTRACT
FOES CHARGE NINETY
MILLION DOLLAR GIFT

Washington, June 17.—Despite his campaign promises to voters in Tennessee that he would back the Tennessee Valley Authority's normal expansion to meet the needs of its present customers, President Eisenhower has taken an important first step toward putting the squeeze on TVA, which he once referred to (but not in Tennessee) as "creeping socialism." He has ordered a hitherto nonpolitical and independent agency of the government, the Atomic Energy Commission, to subsidize a private utility group to supply electric power in competition with TVA, thus making the AEC an unwilling tool of the utilities and forcing it into the new and unprecedented role of power broker—and that at an estimated cost to the Federal Government of over $90,000,000.

It was disclosed at today's hearing of the Joint Congressional Committee on Atomic Energy that the President has ordered the AEC to sign a contract with the Dixon-Yates power combine for a steam generating plant at West Memphis, Ark. The President's directive left no room for competitive bidding on the plant, and overrode three of the AEC commissioners (including the AEC's most vigorous exponent of private enterprise, Commissioner Thomas E. Murray) who expressed serious doubts about the matter, but said they would bow to the President's insistence.

According to the President's scheme, the AEC will underwrite all but $5,000,000 of the cost of the plant, which is expected to run at least to $107,250,000, and may run to much more. The estimated annual cost will be nearly $21,000,000, and, according to testimony before the Joint Congressional Committee, the AEC and the Bureau of the Budget predict that this will be at least $3,685,000 a year more than the TVA's alternate proposal, a steam generating plant at Fulton, Tenn.—in other words, a total loss to the government of over $90,000,000 in the 25 years the contract will run.

The growing demand for TVA power, at TVA's favorable rates, from private industries in its service area, as well as cities like Memphis and Nashville, and farm cooperatives, has in recent years led to the erection of steam generator plants to supplement the hydroelectric power, especially in low-water seasons. Many of these plants were built during the last war, when the Oak Ridge atomic installations were built in Tennessee partly because a plentiful supply of relatively inexpensive electric power was available there. This year TVA had proposed to build a new steam plant at Fulton, Tenn., to meet the increased need for power in that section of its grid system and to release more power to the vital atomic installations of the AEC at Paducah. TVA is now supplying 1,205,000 kilowatts to AEC from the steam plant at Shawnee, built a few years ago at AEC's request. The Eisenhower administration lopped the Fulton plant off its appropriations bill, and Democratic senators were unsuccessful in their fight to restore it on the Senate floor. So TVA was prevented from supplying the additional 600,000 kilowatts that AEC has announced it will need at Paducah.

This created a vacuum into which the businessmen of the Republican administration have now slipped the thin edge of the anti-TVA wedge—

perhaps without causing any surprise among some of the President's
heavier campaign contributors. The contract is well supplied with special
benefits for the Dixon-Yates group. It guarantees them 9 per cent interest
on the $5,000,000 they invest, but makes sure that they take no risk of
losing their investment. The AEC assures the new plant a customer for
600,000 watts for the life of the contract, and the private investors will
own the plant free and clear after the contract runs out. Another
precedent is set by the arrangement providing that the AEC will pay
outright the Federal, state, and local taxes of the proposed plant. The
deal is also unusual in that AEC will not be buying power for its own
use, but peddling private power to TVA. And the power will be expensive
for TVA because West Memphis is across the wide Mississippi River
from Fulton, Tenn., and TVA will be required by the contract to supply
transmission lines to bring the current across the river from Arkansas.

1. Describe briefly the total impression of each of these newspaper
   stories, including the general point of view toward (a) the proposed
   contract, (b) the TVA, (c) the President.
2. Find several pairs of approximately synonymous terms, one from each
   article, and explain briefly the important differences in connotation
   that contribute to the difference in total impression.
3. Find some statements that are given in A, but not in B, or in B, but
   not in A, and show how they affect what is suggested.
4. Analyze the position, or order, of statements given in both A and B,
   and point out the difference in what is suggested by the order.
5. Try to sort out the reliable from the unreliable parts of each report
   by, first, summarizing the information common to both reports as
   matter-of-factly as possible, and, second, writing a list of questions
   to which you would want to get answers before deciding which of the
   two reports, if either, is more nearly correct.

Exercise 35
MR. WELCH CROSS-EXAMINES MR. COHN

The "Army-McCarthy Hearing" that agitated the country so violently
in April, May, and June of 1954 was conducted by the Special Subcommittee on Investigations, a subcommittee of the Senate Committee
on Government Operations. It took 187 hours, spread out over 36 working days, and produced two million words, transcribed onto 7,424 typed
pages. It centered about Mr. G. David Schine, who had been a voluntary
assistant to the investigating staff of the Special Subcommittee and who
had been drafted into the Army on Nov. 3, 1953.

On March 11, 1954, the Secretary of the Army, Robert T. Stevens, publicly released a chronological report accusing the Committee Chairman (Senator Joe McCarthy), his chief counsel (Roy M. Cohn), and his staff director (Francis P. Carr), of having sought persistently, and by improper means (including threats to embarrass the Army and its Secretary by making it appear that they were ineffectual in combatting espionage), to obtain special consideration for Private Schine. Whereupon, Senator McCarthy countered by releasing a series of staff notes and memoranda accusing Secretary Stevens and his counsel, John G. Adams, of having tried to stop the Subcommittee's investigations of suspected espionage and alleged employment of Communists at the Army Signal Corps installations at Fort Monmouth, N.J.; of having used Private Schine as a "hostage" for this purpose; and of having released their "false" charges to prevent Senator McCarthy from exposing the Army's failure to deal properly with the situation at Fort Monmouth.

There were other charges and countercharges, but these were the central ones that the Special Subcommittee decided to investigate. Senator McCarthy stepped down temporarily as chairman, and Senator Mundt took his place. A special legal counsel and legal staff were procured, and the hearing was held in public, with on-the-spot broadcasts over radio and television to many parts of the country.

The rules of the hearing allowed ten-minute periods of examination or cross-examination. The following passage is a transcript of one of the exchanges between Mr. Joseph N. Welch, special counsel for the Army, and Mr. Roy Cohn. In reading these exchanges, bear in mind that Mr. Cohn and Mr. Welch were both experienced lawyers, and each was fully aware of the techniques of such a battle of wits.

One of the arguments made by the McCarthy side was that Secretary Stevens' charges could not be true, since some time after some of the threats against him had allegedly been made he was still on good terms with Private Schine. The McCarthy countercharges stated, and Mr. Cohn testified, that on Nov. 17, 1953, Secretary Stevens, on his way back to Washington from New York, had flown over to Fort Dix, where Private Schine was stationed, with a party including Senator McCarthy and Mr. Cohn; that Stevens had "wanted to go down to Fort Dix and say 'hello' to Dave Schine with us"; and that at the airfield Stevens had specifically asked to have his picture taken with Private Schine. Secretary Stevens denied that he had made this request, and said that his trip had been made solely for the convenience of Senator McCarthy and his staff. The Secretary was questioned closely about this point, and asked whether he had ever had his picture taken *alone* with Private Schine. On April 26, the McCarthy side introduced into the hearing an enlarged copy of a photograph showing Stevens and Schine alone together in front of a C-47. Then, the next morning, Mr. Welch produced a copy of a photograph showing Stevens, Schine, and a third man, Colonel Bradley. This second photograph had been taken by an Air Force photographer, who had given a copy to Schine, and from it the first one had evidently been cut down, by a member of Senator McCarthy's staff (as it turned out). On that day, April 27, Mr. Cohn was put on the stand for questioning solely concerning this picture, and Mr. Welch cross-examined him about it.

The problem here is to interpret the questions and answers and the relation between them. First, study the *Loaded Questions*: pick out the terms with misleading connotation, or with marked emotive force, and the clauses with misleading suggestion; show how the witness, if he answered them directly, would be forced to commit himself to something he did not want to say. Second, study the evasive replies: pick out the questions that are *not* loaded—questions that could be given a "yes" or "no" answer—and examine the places where the witness avoids answering these questions. In which cases do you think he is justified because an answer to the question could be quoted out of context in such a way as to oversimplify the situation the witness is describing? In which cases is the witness evasive because the question is asked in a way that makes it difficult for *him* to give the slanted answer he wants to give?

(from pages 294-296 of the printed transcript)

MR. WELCH: . . . My question now is this: You have referred to that picture as showing Mr. Secretary Stevens smiling at Dave Schine. Are you now close enough to the picture so that you would like to qualify that statement?

MR. COHN: Sir, I will accept your characterization of the picture.

MR. WELCH: It is a grim smile on Stevens' face.

MR. COHN: I accept it. If you want to call Mr. Stevens' smile a grim smile, sir, I fully accept what you say. To me it is a picture of Secretary Stevens. If it is a grim smile, so be it. It is a picture of Private Schine. They are standing next to each other. They are facing each other. Their eyes are meeting. They are looking at each other. If the smile is grim or if it isn't grim, I know not, sir.

MR. WELCH: Not too fast, Mr. Cohn; not too fast. Mr. Stevens is looking to his right, isn't he?

MR. COHN: Well, sir—

MR. WELCH: Isn't he? You can answer that one easily.

MR. COHN: Mr. Welch, do you want to imply that I am not answering it? You asked me a question, and then you say with the implication as though I can't answer it.

MR. WELCH: Well, answer it. Mr. Stevens is looking to his right, isn't he?

MR. COHN: Sir, if you will give me the chance, I will try to answer it.

MR. WELCH: By all means, sir.

MR. COHN: Thank you. The picture, to me, looks as though Mr. Stevens and Private Schine are looking at each other.

MR. WELCH: My question was a simple one. Mr. Stevens is looking to his right, is he not?

MR. COHN: Yes, I would say he probably is looking to his right, and Private Schine is standing to his right.

MR. WELCH: On Mr. Stevens' right are two figures, is that correct?

MR. COHN: Yes, that is correct. To Mr. Stevens' right there are two figures.

MR. WELCH: One is Private Schine?

MR. COHN: Yes, sir.

MR. WELCH: And further to Mr. Stevens' right is Colonel Bradley?

MR. COHN: Standing sideways.

MR. WELCH: It would take someone with clairvoyance to know to whom Secretary Stevens is looking, would it not?

MR. COHN: No, sir. I don't think so. It would take somebody with common sense who can look at a picture and see what is in it.

MR. WELCH: I think I observe on Colonel Bradley's face a faint little look of pleasure. Do you, sir?

MR. COHN: I would say I know that Colonel Bradley had a good steak dinner shortly afterward. Maybe he was anticipating it. I do know that Colonel Bradley looks to me as though he, too, is looking at Private Schine.

MR. WELCH: If Bradley is feeling good about a steak dinner, Schine must be considering a whole haunch of beef.

MR. COHN: Yes, sir, and Mr. Stevens, possibly you might be right, the grimness on his face might have come after Senator McCarthy told him that hearings showing what was going on in Communist infiltration in the Army would begin the next Tuesday.

MR. WELCH: Had Mr. Stevens actually said to you that he wanted to fly that big plane over there so he could see a private in the Army?

MR. COHN: If you would like me to relate the full circumstances—

MR. WELCH: No. Answer my question.

MR. COHN: Mr. Welch, I would be delighted to do so, sir. May I, Mr. Chairman?

MR. WELCH: Won't you try it "Yes" or "No"? Had Mr. Stevens actually said to you that he wanted to fly that big plane over there so he could see this private in the Army?

MR. COHN: That is one of the things which Mr. Stevens said on that day, yes, sir.

MR. WELCH: Did you also want to see Private Schine on that day?

MR. COHN: Oh, yes, sir.

MR. WELCH: Was it a surprise to you when he turned up and met the plane?

MR. COHN: Yes, it was a surprise.

MR. WELCH: A surprise?

MR. COHN: When he met the plane?

MR. WELCH: A surprise?

MR. COHN: I might say it was a surprise, yes, sir.

MR. WELCH: Didn't you expect to see him when you got there?

MR. COHN: I expected to see him—by the way, have we sufficiently described the smiles?

MR. WELCH: I may want it back, but not at the moment. We will drop it now.

That leads me to say this to you in line with Senator Dworshak's question: Wasn't it as early as July 15 that Dave Schine felt the hot breath of the draft board on his neck?

MR. COHN: I don't know the exact date, sir, when Dave Schine was reclassified.

Exercise 36

Read the following dialogue carefully. Find, and classify, the emotional appeals that are employed, and show briefly how each one is used either to oversimplify the discussion or to distract it from the point.

NARRATOR: Ladies and gentlemen, the question before us this evening is whether or not it should be made illegal for anyone to furnish to a newspaper, or for a newspaper to publish, anything about a criminal case except the formal charges before the case is brought to trial. Representative P, I understand that you are in favor of such a law. Would you explain your position?

REPRESENTATIVE P: My main reason is that it is the only way, so far as I can see, of getting an unbiased and unprejudiced jury. The courts take enormous pains to ensure that the testimony the jury hears is competent, relevant, and material, but even before the jury is picked, a sensational crime has been advertised to everyone. Headlines proclaim what the counsel for the defense or the district attorney's office have leaked to the press; alleged confessions are told about at length; and some of the testimony for one side or both has already been publicized in a distorted form. Before the juror hears even a word of evidence he has been influenced by a slanted account of the case.

SENATOR Q: But wouldn't such a law place a gag on the freedom of the press?

REP. P: I don't see that—it seems to me that—

SEN. Q: Wouldn't it restrict what newspapers could print, what information they could give the public about important pending trials?

REP. P: Yes, it would do that, of—

SEN. Q: That's exactly what I mean. A gag. A straightjacket. If I didn't know that a group of American lawyers, with no practical experience of newsgathering, dreamed up this idea, I would have thought it was Goebbels or Malenkov. One step further—picture the press blacked out, handcuffed, hog-tied—where is the Freedom of the Press then?

REP. P: The press would still be free in other respects; they could report the trial after it has begun, and the jury is locked up, away from newspapers and television. But—

SEN. Q: Oh, I can see it would be convenient for the lawyers, all right. Yes, indeed. You *are* a lawyer, aren't you?

REP. P: Yes. But what difference—

SEN. Q: I will leave it to the radio audience to draw their own conclusions. Only last year Columbia University celebrated its great 200th anniversary, a university which many members of our audience here in the studio are proud to call their alma mater. I honor that university. And do you recall the motto of that celebration? "Man's right to knowledge and the free use thereof." The *right* to knowledge: that is what is at issue here. It is threatened on all hands, but we must stand firm to defend it against all encroachments. Thus far you may go, but no further. That's the whole question here.

REP. P: Well, now, of course I agree there is such a right. But there is also a right to a fair trial, as the Bill of Rights guarantees it. And what we get now is often a mockery of it. It is a trial by press agents. Picture a young man railroaded to jail; an innocent bystander caught in the toils of sensational journalism. The evidence against him won't stand up in court—it is so flimsy, based on hearsay, that a good judge would not even admit it in evidence. So what happens? The police leak it to the press, and it is spread about; the jurors have all swallowed it. Even if it does not come out in court, they think he's guilty and condemn him. Not trial by court. Trial by television.

SEN. Q: Well, of course some juries are not very intelligent. You can't help that. You can't change human nature, you know. As *Life* magazine recently remarked in an editorial column, human nature does not change. You can't blame that on the newspapers—they didn't pick the jury. You lawyers did.

MODERATOR: Gentlemen, if I may interpose a question: what evidence, if any, is there that fairer trials would probably result from the law?

REP. P: Well, many lawyers who have studied the matter agree that it would have a very beneficial result. It is the law in England, and their trials are generally regarded as models of fairness.

SEN. Q: Now it's out—I knew it was coming. England! Nowadays, with our involvement in the U.N., and our great programs for giving away the wealth of America, everything that interested parties want to put over on the American people—whether Socialized Medicine or gags on the press —is defended because "They do it in England." Can't we stand on our own two feet true to our own great traditions? Why do we have to import these controversial schemes? I say, let's try it the American way.

REP. P: It might interest you to know, Senator Q, that the British have had a good many centuries of experience in these matters. They developed the common law, on which ours is based, and we can be proud to be the heirs of that great civilization.

MODERATOR: You said, Representative P, that it has worked in England?

SEN. Q: But, let me ask you this. Isn't it true that Maryland was the last state to have the British law? And that it gave it up a few years ago? And that when the Maryland Court of Appeals was petitioned by the national headquarters of the American Civil Liberties Union to abandon those unwarranted restraints on the freedom of the press, at the same time the Maryland Chapter of the American Civil Liberties Union filed a brief on the *other* side, asking that the restraints be kept? Do the lawyers agree, then?

REP. P: Does that prove that a fair trial is of no importance, just because some people don't see its importance? The point is that the right to a fair trial "by an impartial jury," as the 6th Amendment puts it, is one of the most important rights—and it comes down to this, in the end: is it more important to give people a fair trial or to let newspapers make a little more money by printing sensational crime news no matter how much harm it does?

SEN. Q: I have no quarrel with the 6th Amendment, though it's close to the 5th Amendment, and we all know how that has been made a cover for concealing guilt. But, never mind. I don't want to imply that any of those who quote the 6th Amendment have ulterior motives; or that those who are promoting this law, however much I disagree with them, are all trying to undermine the free press and get it shackled, as it is in Russia, so it cannot stand as a bulwark of our liberties. I don't wish to suggest this.

MODERATOR: Can you cite specific cases in which the publicity has interfered?

REP. P: Yes. In 1952 Denis W. Delaney, a dismissed Collector of Internal Revenue, was convicted of misconduct in office. Before his trial, a House Subcommittee held public hearings on alleged scandals in the Bureau of Internal Revenue; Boston newspapers played up the "revelations"; *Life* magazine did picture spreads entitled, "Hands in the Taxpayers' Pockets." Public opinion was inflamed against anyone even suspected of guilt, and no jury was in a mood to make nice distinctions about the evidence. In a historic decision, the U.S. Circuit Court of Appeals set aside the conviction, and granted a new trial, on the ground that conditions made a fair trial impossible.

SEN. Q: Well, I can only say that I am surprised to hear a member of the House of Representatives, over a nationwide hookup, express sympathy for an income tax collector convicted of misconduct in office. Surely it was vital to expose these matters, and the House Subcommittee rendered yeoman service. Would you gag the Committees of Congress, too, as well as the press? Publicity, my friend, publicity is in the end the great weapon against wrongdoing. You don't deny that, I hope? I'm no lawyer, and I don't pretend to understand those high-falutin legal terms, any more than, I dare say, most of those in our audience. But we know what's important. And what it comes down to is: do you want to expose corruption, or let it secretly do its dirty work? That's the whole question.

Exercise 37

The following specimen of anti-UNESCO prose was first published in the Jacksonville *Chronicle* and then reprinted in *Common Sense*, March 1, 1954. Read it through, and set down what you take to be the main point of the passage. Then pick out the statements that are asserted in support of this point. Which of these are actually reasons for the conclusions? Which of them are actually *distractions* from the issue? Which involve *oversimplification*? Analyze the types of emotional appeal employed.

UNESCO ALL BAD
by Cuthelbert Rittenhouse

UNESCO, which like all Communist, Socialist New Deal lingo, are the first letters of an abominable organization of the equally abominable United Nations.

This UNESCO floods the elementary, high schools and colleges like the dew. Everywhere you turn there is a book, pamphlet or speaker from UNESCO. One of the writers for it is Bertrand Russell. The renegade.

He deplores the teaching of history so as to "serve to keep alive a bigoted nationalism," which to him and his tribe—may they decrease—means anything which glorifies the great events and great men of any nation. All national anthems are taboo. Everything must glorify a great Socialist one world with barnyard morals. This was the Russell, remember him now, who advocated young men and women in college living sexually without benefit of clergy. He was once about to be a professor in New York University when Justice McGeehan said he was to head a chair of indecency.

The only thing is for us to get the U. N. out of the United States and get the United States out of the U. N. Everything about it is bad. It's a pest hole of evil. It's a stewing center of treason.

The UNESCO is not only going to color and distort the present and the future, but do over all the things which happened in the past. They have been granted $600,000 to do it. It is called the "History of Mankind." The men doing it are Julian Sorrell Huxley, Socialist to the core, Ralph E. Turner, leftie of Yale, A. L. Kroeber, leftie of University of California, and Bertrand Russell.

What is going to be the history of mankind when done by these men? It is the UNESCO history: it will have no appeal to bigoted nationalism. Free enterprise will be a monster. A world government, Socialist-Communist dictatorship will be the ideal. The UNESCO will place it in all the schools, unless you cut the throat of UNESCO immediately. Unless you get this thing out of the schools.

The people who founded the Republic of the United States, and guided its destiny for 150 years, just had a lot more sense than those of today. F. D. R. was a failure at law and a failure in business. He was a rich man's son. Truman was a failure in business and sold his soul to the most corrupt political machine in the U.S. He proved his loyalty to the Boss and went places by those who wished to use the government. Ike was without success, but grabbed up by Harry Hopkins and promoted over the heads of able but not toe-kissing generals.

The day of ability has died in high office.

When the Republic was virile and growing under men like Chief Justice John Marshall, not to be confused with that General George Marshall of infamous memory.

Chief Justice John Marshall said "When our people are free from poverty and want and malnutrition, it will be time enough to permanently suckle the world at the expense of the American taxpayer." In the days of these men there was no public debt. In the days of Roosevelt, Truman, and Eisenhower we have spent all the accumulations in our history.

Review

In order to get about with fair success in the world as it is today, there is one commodity that we must all have a constant supply of: that is, reliable information about what other people are doing and saying, and why. We need it the way we need food, clothes, and shelter.

Now, even if there were no artificial obstacles in the way of getting at the truths we need to know, and everyone were working with ingenuity and good will in the same direction, the problem would still be a formidable one. It can be thought of as a technological, or engineering, problem like developing necessary electric power sources, increasing the food supply, or organizing economic affairs in an efficient way. It is a problem for society as a whole, which must find some way to get hold of enormous quantities of information if it is to hold together and meet the challenge of its environment. Moreover, if the Federal Government is to remain under democratic control and work steadily for the common good, much of this information must be made available in usable form to all citizens, so that we can form intelligent opinions about government policies. No doubt there will always be disagreements about some particular facts, whether they should be made public—whether, for example, certain facts about the effects of hydrogen bomb explosions, facts which are certainly known in other countries, should be told to the people of the United States. But it is clear enough that in so far as information is withheld that would be significantly relevant to an important decision, to just that extent the public is prevented from making sure that its decision is reasonable and right.

The information that we usually have to deal with comes to us in moderately complicated discourses, of various lengths, nearly every one of which poses some problems in *linguistic interpretation* and/or *logical evaluation*. When these problems are hard enough so that either we can't solve them, or we can't be sure that we have solved them correctly, it is a help to have some general principles to guide us: standard questions to ask, methods of testing, techniques for making distinctions, and so forth. It is just such logical and linguistic machinery (so to speak) that this book has aimed to provide.

You don't need this machinery for simple discourses like billboards, parking tickets, and restaurant menus. And you don't need *most* of this machinery for those discourses we call "literature"—except when they claim to provide information on one of their levels of meaning. (Of course, the material on connotation and suggestion in the last two chapters is directly applicable to literature, and indispensable in analyzing it.) But for a wide variety of discourses on which our most far-reaching judgments and decisions must be based—radio programs, books, magazines, and reports—the machinery will serve well. It is by no means the whole of logic—not even of applied, or practical, logic. Like a home manual of medical care, it covers most of the common diseases of discourse, giving clues for diagnosis, methods of treatment, and also some suggestions about precautions against getting such infections in the first place.

In other words, you can use this machinery both as a *reader* (or listener) and as a *writer* (or speaker). But these roles require somewhat different logical strategies.

The Reader's Strategy

As a reader, you approach a discourse of the sort we are concerned with in the expectation (or at least the hope) that it will tell you something you want to know—that is, present you with some true statements. Perhaps you have a definite question, or cluster of questions, in mind; or perhaps you are merely picking up generalized information that may later answer some question that hasn't yet come up. Now, the task before you is a double one; you ask, first, what the discourse *says*, and, second, whether it is *convincing*.

In answering the first main question, you are *interpreting the discourse*. It is best to begin by getting a good grip on the over-all structure, deciding whether or not it is an argument, and, if it is an argument, what are its main points and lines of reasoning. If the discourse is elaborate, or its structure puzzling, it will usually be helpful to summarize or outline it, so that while you are examining the details closely you will not lose your general sense of the lie of the land.

Next, you should turn your attention to the details of the language. Are there words whose meaning is ambiguous in the context? Or too vague for the purpose at hand? Do any of them appear to shift their meaning in the course of the argument? Are any of the statements syntactically ambiguous? Often these questions can be answered fairly quickly, and the answer disposes of the problem of interpretation. But in some cases this line of examination reveals that there are a few key words that are behaving rather strangely and may be equivocal or ambiguous. Or that there are a few statements that may have more implicit in them than at first meets the eye. If the matter is important enough, you then examine the terms for hidden connotations, and the sentences for possible suggestion. Figures of speech may call for some analysis. Of course, in order to do this job well, you may also have to notice, and set aside, or neutralize, any strong appeals to emotion that the discourse contains. And if the argument hinges on technical terms that are defined in the discourse, you will have to look over those terms and their definitions with particular care to be sure that you are clear about them.

In answering the second main question, you are making a *logical evaluation:* that is, you are estimating the soundness of the argument. Is it a proof? Or, falling short of that, does it lend a solid weight of probability to the conclusion? Or does it fail completely to deserve even a tentative assent?

If the argument is *deductive,* the procedure is fairly standardized. To decide whether it is valid, you first decide which of the logical structures it has, and then apply the rules of validity for that structure. The question remains whether the premises are true: if they themselves are defended in the discourse, you have another argument to evaluate; if they are not defended, you must decide, on the basis of your own experience and knowledge, whether you think it safe to accept them.

If the argument is *inductive,* you must again classify it further before you can say it is convincing. If it shapes up as an argument from analogy, it is not convincing, but it may suggest a generalization for which the writer, or yourself, can supply some evidence. If the argument supports a generalization, you ask yourself whether the sample chosen as evidence is likely to be unrepresentative of the whole class. If the argument supports a hypothesis, you ask yourself whether the facts at hand can be better explained by some alternative hypothesis.

There is no ironclad guarantee that a discourse that passes all these stringent tests will never let you down, or even that it will wear like iron. It will merely be the best that is available at the time.

The Writer's Strategy

As a writer, you usually begin with a question too; perhaps a specific question that someone else has asked, or might ask, and that you think you can answer; perhaps (at first) a vague question that you cannot answer, but want to answer. If you are working out your ideas, not merely transcribing something you have already written out, it is a creative process with two main components, though they cannot be sharply separated.

There is the process of *discovery*. To reduce a complicated matter to its essentials, we might say this: There are two ways in which you might get the answer to your question (but of course you will try different answers, as you go along, and change your question too). Perhaps it can be *deduced* from what you know already; or perhaps it can be *induced* with the help of further facts that you don't yet have. If you can answer the question by a deductive argument, you have to follow the rules for that kind of argument. If your answer is a hypothesis, or a generalization, you must make sure your evidence is adequate to make the conclusion reasonable. But in the course of thinking the argument out, you will be checking and rechecking your own reasoning, going over it to see whether you made mistakes. And this is the process of *critical re-examination*.

When you write an argument, you are working out its details, and trying to make it as clear and convincing as you can. If it is complicated, it should probably be outlined before you start to write, so that the main parts are kept distinct in your mind while their mutual relations are posted. But the same problem holds for sentences and individual words. Where there is syntactical ambiguity, a change of grammar will take care of it; where the movement of your thought might be obscure even to an attentive reader, shifting paragraphs or sections about, or putting in cross references, may avert the danger.

When the framework of your thought is clear, you turn your attention to the words. The task here is to read your own words as much as possible from the outside, asking all the time whether there is anything that the reader could fail to understand, or could mis-understand: ambiguities and vagueness and misleading suggestions or connotations—and inadequate definitions or confused classifica-tions. Have you fallen into the temptation to substitute emotive language for thinking at some points? Can you work out the idea in a calmer way? These questions, of course, are not to be asked merely out of consideration for your reader: as you write, you are finding out what you really think; as you correct your writing, you are sharpening and straightening your thinking. The more clearly you say what you believe, the better you can see whether what you believe is worth believing.

Three General Exercises

Most of the passages you have worked on in the course of this book are short and limited to a few principles. They are all, of course, torn out of their living contexts of reflective reasoning or hot dispute, and that helps to make them manageable, but also somewhat artificial. To be sure you have got the feel of the logical and linguistic tools, you should try apply-ing them to your reading and conversations. But you can get some review of the principles, and see them a little more clearly in their relation to one another, by analyzing more complicated discourses such as the three General Exercises that follow.

The task, in appraising these passages, is not just one of fault-finding: there are good and bad arguments in each passage, or at least there are better and worse ones. Begin with the passage on the subject that interests you most; read it through quickly. Then ask of it the questions that have just been listed above as the strategy for critical reading. Finally, sum-marize, in your own words, your general judgment about what is con-vincing and what is unconvincing in it.

It may be helpful to refer to the list of Nineteen Fallacies, with definitions and examples, that appears after the Exercises. But don't be bound either by this list or by the suggested questions. They are here just to help you get your own critical thinking under way.

Exercise 38

Analyze the fallacies and confusions in the following passage.

WIRETAPPING

If the President set up a bootleg whiskey still in the White House, or the Senate operated an illegal gambling establishment in one of its caucus rooms, people would lift an eyebrow at such a wanton violation of the law on the part of those who are sworn to uphold it. But when the Attorney General announces that he would like Congress to let his FBI agents and Army security officers tap private telephone conversations, people clap their hands joyfully. Yet the principle is exactly analogous, for the Department of Justice is sworn to uphold the Constitution, with its guarantees of individual rights and freedoms, including freedom from arbitrary searches and seizures.

Of course, the Attorney General has a rationalization. This time the wire tapping is for cases involving "national security." A fine, vague expression. They don't ask for wire-tapping privileges for convicting income tax violators, kidnappers, or swindlers—they don't *ask*, though it's common knowledge that the FBI has actually had as many as 200 phone taps in operation on a single day in this country —not to mention the amount of other people's mail they read. No, the Attorney General only wants to be allowed to eavesdrop on telephone conversations where they suspect (they don't have to have *evidence*, just suspicions—and *they* want to be the ones to decide when to do it, with no interference from the courts)—where they suspect that somebody is spying or giving away secrets.

But any moron can see where this leads. Giving away secrets isn't much different from urging other people to give away secrets, or blackmailing them into giving away secrets, or threatening them, or kidnapping, or murder, or whatnot—in fact, where can you draw a line? If Congress gives them this, there's no reason for not letting them wiretap for any purpose whatsoever—including violations of the Mann Act. In short, there would hardly be an innocent conversation between a young man and his sweetheart that would be free from having a hired snoop breathing down their necks. And no doubt making a recording that could be played in court, after suitable editing, if necessary, to establish alienation of affection if the young man cools off.

I know that state courts have admitted wire-tap evidence for several years—though the Supreme Court has refused to allow it in Federal courts since 1938. It is argued that it is perfectly harmless. But the police of various states have for an even longer time used rubber hoses and the third degree—that doesn't prove they are justified. In fact, it is obvious that rubber hoses and wire taps tend to go together, and where you find one you will almost always find the other. We will do a poor job of defending the country against Communists if we adopt their methods—the methods of our enemies. If we use wire taps, as totalitarians do, then it follows that we are totalitarians too.

Of course, we must be "secure." That is exactly what the 4th Amendment says—"The right of the people to be *secure* in their persons, houses, papers, and effects against unreasonable searches and seizures shall not be violated." (Note that carefully: the 4th Amendment says there shall be no "searches and seizures.") They didn't have telephones in 1791, or telephone conversations would certainly have been added by the Founding Fathers—they are just as private and personal as papers; there is no relevant difference that I can see, and if anyone says that a telephone conversation is a "communication," whereas a diary that a man keeps in his desk is not, it is a sufficient reply to him to point out that when a man writes a diary to read it himself later, he is communicating with himself, and therefore his diary is a communication.

The 4th Amendment guarantees security, and thus implies that wire tapping is unconstitutional. And if the Attorney General is really interested in security, let him defend the 4th Amendment. Since the infamous Star Chamber was abolished in England in 1640 no greater threat to individual rights has reared its ugly head. The great American dream has come to this, then: a wire tap in every home. Everybody minding everybody's business. If the Attorney General has his way, we shall be but one step removed from that inhuman goldfish bowl or Benthamite Panoptikon prison of Orwell's *1984*, where Big Brother's agents watch every move in every home by continuous television viewers.

It has taken centuries to develop and establish safeguards against invasions of privacy by police when they are on the prowl for evidence. Search warrants are not issued unless there is positive evidence of wrongdoing—they are not for searching the homes of the innocent —and the citizen whose house is searched without a warrant can obtain redress through the courts, and when the police obtain a warrant they have to say what they are searching for, instead of going around ripping up the mattresses in the general hope of finding some evidence of wrongdoing. But in the Attorney General's wire-tapping plan, none of these safeguards applies; wire tapping is indiscriminate, it cannot be limited to only the guilty; wire tapping is to be done merely on suspicion; there would be no way for a person to obtain redress, since he will not know whether his lines are being tapped unless the police tell him (induction pickups tap a wire without even touching it); and if no warrant has to be obtained, there is no way of limiting wire tapping at all. The injustice of wire tapping is tacitly admitted by its very defenders, for they claim, in one breath, that most wire tapping will be limited to guilty persons, but they also admit that some wire tapping will inevitably be done against those who turn out to be innocent. But these two statements are flatly inconsistent with each other.   90

The Attorney General and his acolytes in the press say that the Federal officers are "handicapped" in their hunt for subversives if they cannot use wire tapping. I'm sure that's what the Gestapo or NKVD or any other secret police would say if you told them they shouldn't torture people and put them in concentration camps; this   95 would be a "handicap." But I argue this way: we all grant that whatever helps to expose spies is a right law; from which it follows logically that whatever is a right law will in the long run help to expose spies. Wire tapping, however, is not right, but wrong, and therefore in the long run it will not help to expose spies. The trouble   100 with "fighting fire with fire" in a case like this is that in doing so you might reduce the Bill of Rights to a heap of ashes.

The only explanation I can think of for this dangerous and ill-advised proposal is that the Attorney General is secretly aiming to destroy the independence of the legislative body. If he can tap wires   105 of Congressmen and Senators without anyone's being the wiser, he can dig up all sorts of dirt on them. And when it comes to disagreements between the Administration and the Congress, the Attorney General's office can apply a little quiet blackmail. Oh, I know this would be denied, but it fits the facts.   110

It is wrong for the State to take away a person's property without recompense, and this is what the wire tapper does. A person's conversations and words, just like his writings, are his own property, for what belongs to a person may be defined as the things he is given or that he makes by means of his own effort or by means of things that   115 already belong to him. The dilemma that confronts us is simple and clear: Either we strengthen ourselves against the enemy without by taking every precaution against spies, no matter what the cost; or we strengthen ourselves against the enemy within, by standing up for justice, liberty, and economic prosperity. If we do the former, we will   120 have wire tapping; if we do the latter, we shall preserve the heritage of our forefathers. It looks to me as if we are, foolishly and blindly enough, about to allow wire tapping; it follows logically and inevitably that we shall lose that heritage.

Exercise 39

Analyze the fallacies and confusions in the following passage.

TAX-EXEMPT FOUNDATIONS

Now that Representative B. Carroll Reece of Tennessee has concluded his little circus and sent the inmates of his Special Committee
on Tax-Exempt Foundations back to fall quarters, we can do what
neither he nor any of the other members of the Committee have
done, that is, take a cool look at their accomplishments.   5

We should first note that Rep. Reece has succeeded in his evident
intention of damning in the public eye the charitable foundations
which have been a main support of scholarly research in recent years.
Whether he will also succeed in cowing these foundations so that
they will hereafter support only biased and reactionary research   10
projects remains to be seen. Judging from their forthright response
to his sniping, they are not going to knuckle under, even to the
implied threat that their tax-exempt status will be taken away from
them by Congress unless they let Rep. Reece, rather than their
directors and advisory boards of scholars, decide *what* research and   15
whose research they will finance. As far as we can see, the investigation has served no useful purpose..

And why has it been summarily called off by its chairman? When
the investigation started (and it never has been clear why it was
necessary to go over the same ground the Cox Committee went over   20
a few years back), the Chairman announced that he would call witnesses to show various dubious things about the tax-exempt foundations—Communist infiltration and active support for "Fabian
Socialism" (the Chairman's term) in America—and then he would
give the foundations a chance to reply. Well, he's had *his* witnesses   25
parade before the Committee, and now he calls off the whole thing.
The foundations can send in letters, he says—but the public hearings
have already smeared them.

The cancellation was made necessary, says Rep. Reece in a statement he put into the *Congressional Record* Appendix the other day,   30
because "throughout the hearings, Mr. Hays" (that's the ranking
Democratic member, Rep. Wayne Hays of Illinois) "assumed an
attitude of aggressive suspicion and insulting distrust of the majority
members of the Committee and of the Committee staff," and in one
3-hour session interrupted a witness 246 times. It seems that the   35
Republicans were, however reluctantly, willing to put up with Rep.
Hays's interruptions, and his "disruptive tactics" of asking embarrass-

ing questions of the hand-picked witnesses (some of them probably
disgruntled academics whose applications for fellowships had been
turned down by the Guggenheim, or Ford, or Rockefeller founda-   40
tions)—the Republicans were willing to put up with Rep. Hays as
long as they were getting some dirt into the record, but when it came
the turn of the foundations to defend themselves, the Republicans
couldn't take it any longer. And now Rep. Reece has the nerve
to say that the foundations ought to be glad they won't be called   45
because they can't be cross-examined! How's that for poisoning the
well?

Now, what do Rep. Reece's charges amount to, and what evidence
does his committee have for them? Let us sort out the arguments
clearly and systematically.   50

First, he says that the foundations have been largely responsible
for the spread of "New Deal" social theories in the past two decades.
Why? First, because many of the so-called "New Deal" projects
(like slum clearance, Federal housing, GI Bill of Rights, public
works, etc.) were recommended in reports written by various social   55
scientists and educational groups supported by foundation grants.
Now, what kind of argument is that? Does Rep. Reece enjoy seeing
American cities riddled with slums, and poor people sick and hungry
in their broken-down cold water flats?

And second, he says, because much of the government planning   60
for "New Deal" legislation, and putting it into effect, was done by
social scientists who were connected with organizations partly supported by foundation funds. But granting that members of supported
organizations were dependent on the foundation, most of the
planners were members of organizations *not* supported by foundation   65
funds, and therefore they were quite independent of the foundations.

And, third, he says, the foundations profess to encourage social
science, but there is no such thing—so-called "social science," says
that great scholar Rep. Reece, "is little more than an elaborate argument that government can take better care of the people than the   70
people can take care of themselves." This is not only a crude fallacy
—for the government is after all only the instrument of the people
taking care of themselves—but it is also a slander and a malicious
libel. Sciences are systematic bodies of knowledge; social sciences
are systematic bodies of knowledge; evidently, therefore, social   75
sciences are sciences. If he wants to define "science" his own way, all
right; to me, any collection of tested propositions is a science.

Fourth, the Committee charges that the foundations have engaged
in "propaganda." Section 101 (6) of the Internal Revenue Code

grants tax exemption to any educational foundation "... no sub-   80
stantial part of the activities of which is carrying on propaganda, or
otherwise attempting, to influence legislation." Now, the committee's
reasoning, if you can call it that, is that foundation scholars have
made public recommendations for certain social projects, and thus
have published concrete proposals, but to publish concrete proposals   85
is to propagandize for them, and so the foundations have dissemin-
ated propaganda. The trouble with this argument is that it ignores
the main purpose of scholarship, which is simply to advance the
frontiers of knowledge.

Finally, Rep. Reece says he has proved his original suspicions of   90
the foundations. "I realized," he says, "that if my suspicions were
true, all of the enormous power and prestige of the foundations
would be pitted against the Committee." Now the foundations have
naturally protested his charges, and therefore his suspicions are true!
This is a transparent *ad hominem* argument.   95

What the Committee doesn't understand, or doesn't care about if
it does, is that it takes money to get at the truth, and it takes freedom. The Great Unknown is like a vast forest through which an
army slowly creeps. You don't know what is ahead, and you can't tell
each man exactly what to do—he has to use his own eyes and hands   100
to meet situations as they arise. Therefore the foundations must give
their funds to those scholars who have demonstrated their ability
to make discoveries—no matter who or how. Moreover, they must
keep their eyes on their own essential goal—the advancement of
learning—and refuse to be turned aside, even by an ex-National   105
Chairman of the Republican Party. Knowledge is indispensable for
our survival, for without it we cannot continue to preserve ourselves,
and if we do not preserve ourselves we are lost. Of course, we do not
mean to deny that it has been worth while to inquire into the status
of tax-exempt organizations like the foundations—we do not impugn   110
Congress's right to do so, or the motives of anyone involved. If
nothing else, Rep. Reece's Committee has helped, albeit unwittingly,
to make clearer the possible dangers to which such organizations are
subject. But surely they have passed the test well, and they deserve
a vote of confidence.   115

Exercise 40

Discuss the fallacies and confusions in the following exchange of letters to the editor.

PREVENTIVE PSYCHIATRY FOR CHILDREN

A

To the Editor:

As the father of three small children, I must admit that I actually shuddered when I read Louis B. Haberman's letter of Aug. 30 in which he advocates "preventive" psychiatric and psychological studies for children prior to and following entry into the elementary schools. He writes, among other things, that "a signed psychiatric   5
report will then be required for admission along with today's small-pox vaccination statement."

Zounds! Where are we heading, with another of these elaborate proposals which would badger even more the child just beginning school? Aren't matters complicated enough for the kids at this stage   10
of life without sanctioning another irksome adult intrusion to bedevil their young, impressionable minds? Isn't this, like too much government interference in our private affairs, an overdose of adult domination of the child's own private world?

Mr. Haberman writes of "reorienting" a 5- or 6-year-old. Reorient,   15
indeed! If we follow fantastic advice of this sort, we may yet see the day when our kids will be one glorious mass of screeching mental cases before they've even learned the ABC's in their padded class-rooms.

If some parents will allow their elementary schools to be turned   20
into mental institutions, as Mr. Haberman's kind of project might well succeed in doing, let us concurrently change the education laws so that other parents like myself can keep our kids home where they will have a better chance to grow up "normal."

Let us proceed slowly before we do further damage to our young-   25
sters, already hard pressed by the many adult-imposed restrictions of modern living. This is especially true in congested urban centers like New York City, where zealous and usually harmful overprotection of youngsters seems to be the rule.

                                                        Parent

B

To the Editor:

The letter you recently published from someone who was too em-   30
barrassed to use his real name, but signed himself "Parent," is a

perfect example of the smugness, willful ignorance, and blind resist-
ance to change that have always greeted every new and valuable
proposal for improving our human lot. It was the same with vaccination, antiseptics, and water fluoridation. In fact, the value of Mr. 35
Haberman's suggestion may be deduced from this response to it.
Pasteur, Semmelweis, Lister, and other medical pioneers and path-
breakers were greeted with scorn and ridicule and stubborn disbelief
—but they were right. At least Mr. Haberman's proposal deserves a
fair and reasonable hearing, rather than this emotional blast. 40

The logic of the proposal is clear and forceful. We require that
children be healthy and free of contagious diseases when they go to
school so that they will not infect others and thus be antisocial. Now,
psychological normality is like physical health, a kind of equilibrium
of adjustment to the environment that doctors help their patients to 45
obtain. We all agree that it is good to check up on the health of
school children. It follows that it is good to check up on their mental
normality.

What Mr. Haberman was suggesting is a kind of mental vaccination—a constant vigil against incipient psychological disorders, just 50
as we check periodically for tooth decay, eyestrain, blood count, or
vitamin deficiency. If "Parent" thinks mental health less important
than physical health, he is entitled to his own opinion. It is not mine.
I do not accept the "rule" he offers, that of overprotecting children
by keeping them in the home and under the parents' thumbs, and 55
I do not propose to follow this rule.

I can imagine that the reactionaries like "Parent"—who always
think *they* are mentally all right—will object to the idea of preventive
mental hygiene on the ground that "normal" is too vague a term, or
that after all nobody is normal and we don't want people to be too 60
normal. This is the kind of thing they say, "Parent" himself puts
quotation marks around the word, as though he doesn't think it's
clear. "Healthy" is vague too—but some people are healthier than
others, and more of it is better than less of it. The term "normal" can
easily be defined in any case: you are normal if you can get along in a 65
manner reasonably free from friction with other normal people.

Nor does the Haberman proposal turn the elementary schools into
"mental institutions." The schools in many cities already pay attention to their pupils' health—they have nurses in attendance. The
new idea would only add the function of being a part-time clinic in 70
preventive psychiatry. It only means having a qualified person around
to note incipient cases of mental illness so that something can be
done before it is too late and they either add more tragically wasted

lives to the overfilled and alarmingly increasing mental hospitals of
the nation—or else grow up to write letters to *The Times* attacking   75
psychiatry.

I believe I have more children than "Parent" has, and am therefore in a better position to judge what is best for them.

Parent of Six

C

To the Editor:

In reference to the recently published, unwarranted attack by
"Parent of Six" upon the wise letter sent in by "Parent"—an attack   80
that completely misfired—it should first, perhaps, be said that I
write as one who taught in a little country school for over forty years,
and, having seen more children than a parent can have, I believe I
know whereof I speak about children—including factors their own
parents may not be adequately aware of. I taught them their three   85
R's, with the aid of the hickory stick, and with no time or need for
modern high-falutin matters like giving them psychoanalysis every
morning. The upshot of all this babying them and catering to their
whims is to make them feel sorry for themselves and convince them
it's not their fault if they do wrong. Discipline (and this word means 90
to me simply obeying the Ten Commandments and keeping quiet)
flies out the window, and the three R's are neglected.

The result can be read in the newspapers every day. It is significant
that the frightening increase in juvenile delinquency in recent years
has paralleled exactly the spread of psychiatry and Freudianism—the   95
conclusion cannot be escaped by an intelligent person that the
former is caused by the latter. Just as nobody ever got well with
people standing around telling him how sick he is, so with those who
are always talking about mental health. When we are mentally well,
we do not talk about it; let us, therefore, stop talking about it, and 100
we shall be well enough.

"Parent of Six" utterly confuses the issue with his remarks about
mental health. Naturally, I am aware that there are many elaborate
and fancy finespun theories about the subconscious, and whatnot—
books by Freud, Jung, Karen Horner, Adler, and the rest. But how   105
many children did they teach school to? It is clear, at least to me,
that most of their writings only rationalize the immoralities and personal peculiarities and evil thoughts of their writers—which is,
incidentally, why I do not read them. It can be explained, without
all these ids, quids, superegotisms, Oedipus reflexes, inferiority com- 110
plexes, and so on, why children grow up to be criminals, murderers,
rapists, robbers, and thieves. They just are not disciplined; it is lack

of discipline that explains it. And this is perfectly evident from the way they behave.

The Haberman proposal amounts to this: the psychiatrist's couch 115 is to be substituted for the woodshed. Already we see the car replacing legs, the television set replacing homework, and phonograph records in school replacing spelling drills. Where we are headed for is not certain, but without doubt it is downward rather than upward. Let us halt the downward trend before it is too late! Let parents 120 gather together to turn the tide before the next generation becomes a race of raving maniacs.

Henrietta T. Whitrington

Nineteen Fallacies

(A check-list of common errors in reasoning analyzed in this book; with definitions and examples.)

1. AFFIRMING THE CONSEQUENT (§15). An invalid form of the conditional argument. It consists in (a) asserting a conditional statement ("If we travel faster than light, then we shall travel to the moon someday"), (b) affirming the truth of the part after the word "then" ("We shall travel to the moon someday"), and then (c) inferring the truth of the part before the word "then" ("Therefore, we shall travel faster than light").

2. ARGUMENT FROM ANALOGY (§9). An unsound type of inductive argument. It consists in (a) asserting that two things have certain characteristics in common ("A good writer's style, in its relationship to his thought, resembles in some ways the clothes a person wears, in relationship to his body: for example, the style may hide the thought or emphasize it; it makes it appear better or worse than it is"); (b) asserting that one of the two things has some further characteristic ("A suit of clothes can be separated from the body"); and then (c) arguing that that same characteristic probably is to be found in the other thing ("therefore, the style of a writer can be separated from the thought in what he writes").

3. BEGGING THE QUESTION (§16). An error in deductive reasoning. It consists in assuming as a premise (not necessarily in the same words) the very statement which you claim to prove as a conclusion of the argument ("That newspapers are reliable sources of information is conclusively proved by the facts given in the article in last Sunday's newspaper"; in this argument the reliability of the newspaper, which is supposed to be proved, has to be assumed in the proof itself).

4. BLACK-OR-WHITE FALLACY (§19). An unsound form of argument. It consists in arguing that there is no difference, or no important difference, between two things (say, between a cold war and a shooting war) because the difference is a difference of degree; no sharp line can be drawn, and hence the difference is a sum of many trivial differences (on the borderline of cold wars and shooting wars

there are situations with incidents and great tenseness that are hardly distinguishable from a small-scale shooting war; nevertheless, the difference between a cool cold war and a full-scale shooting war is considerable).

5. CROSS-RANKING (§8). A fallacy in classification. It consists in subdividing a class into subclasses and using two or more distinct bases of division at the same time (since degree of freshness, ingredients used to make them, and size are distinct bases for subdividing doughnuts, it is a mistake to classify doughnuts as consisting of (a) stale doughnuts, (b) raised doughnuts, and (c) large doughnuts).

6. DENYING THE ANTECEDENT (§15). An invalid form of the conditional argument. It consists in (a) asserting a conditional statement ("If we can travel faster than light, then we shall travel to the moon someday"), (b) denying the truth of the part before the word "then" ("We cannot travel faster than light"), and then (c) inferring the falsity of the part after the word "then" ("Therefore, we shall never travel to the moon").

7. DISTRACTION (§30). Turning the course of an argument or a dispute away from the point at issue by means of an appeal to emotion, and bringing in irrelevant statements (for example: "I know you don't like spinach, Johnny, but you must eat it anyway. What would you do if you were cast ashore on a desert island with nothing but cans of spinach to eat?").

8. EQUIVOCATION (§20). Changing the meaning of a word or statement in the course of an argument or dispute in such a way as to make a reason that is offered appear more relevant or more convincing than it actually is (for example, "It's a crime the way he treats his wife, but crimes are illegal, therefore he should be arrested," where in the first clause "crime" means anything morally reprehensible, but in the second clause it means a violation of law).

9. FALSE DISJUNCTION (§15). An invalid form of the disjunctive argument. It consists in (a) asserting a disjunctive statement ("Either he is making up the story or he really did go to the Ruanda Urundi"), (b) affirming the truth of one of the statements within the disjunction ("He did go to Ruanda Urundi"), and then (c) inferring the falsity of the other statement within the disjunction ("Therefore, he is not making up the story").

10. FORCED HYPOTHESIS (§10). An error in an inductive argument designed to establish the truth of a hypothesis. It consists in supposing that the evidence at hand is strong evidence for a particular

hypothesis when some alternate hypothesis that is also available would explain the same facts better, that is, more simply and in a more likely way (for example, suppose a man comes to the office in the morning with a scratch on his cheek; if he is also close-shaved, it is an error to jump to the hypothesis that his wife scratched him, instead of the hypothesis that he cut himself while shaving).

11. HASTY GENERALIZATION (§7). An error in an inductive argument designed to establish the truth of a generalization. It consists in supposing that a generalization is adequately established by evidence concerning a certain sample of the class generalized about, when there is available another generalization that shows the sample to be unrepresentative of the whole class (for example, suppose we notice that in a basket of strawberries, the ones on top are large; it would be an error to conclude that they are all large, since we know that the distributors often put the best ones on top).

12. INCONSISTENCY (§14). A discourse is inconsistent, or self-contradictory, if it contains two assertions that are incompatible with each other ("I say the Constitution is perfect as it is, and should never be amended; I am introducing a Constitutional amendment to that effect shortly").

13. NEGATIVE PREMISE AND AFFIRMATIVE CONCLUSION (§12). An invalid form of the syllogism ("Every voluntary action is one for which we are responsible, but no crimes of passion are really voluntary; therefore, we are responsible for crimes of passion"). It is a violation of the rule that if one of the premises of a syllogism is negative, then the conclusion must be negative.

14. OVERSIMPLIFICATION (§30). Excluding from an argument or a dispute important relevant considerations by means of an appeal to emotion, and thus making it appear that the question can be settled more easily and with less discussion than is really the case ("Let us not let these theological scholars mix up our plain common sense. The heart of the matter is this: either God *wants* evil in the world, in which case he is malevolent, or he can't *prevent* it, in which case he is weak. Stick to the issue, now; which do you accept?").

15. POST HOC, ERGO PROPTER HOC (§7). A form of hasty generalization. It consists in inferring that because one particular event followed another ("Shortly after we hired Billingsly, our business started to expand"), it must therefore be the *effect* of the other ("Therefore, Billingsly must be given credit for the expansion").

16. SLANTING (§29). A form of misrepresentation. It consists in (a) stating what is true, but in such a way as to suggest something that is not true (as "Caligula *did* misbehave himself" suggests that Caligula's misbehavior was not really seriously wrong), or (b) stating what is true as far as designation of the predicate-term is concerned, but permitting the predicate-term to connote something false (as "Caligula was a rake," where "rake" connotes a sort of cheerful and not really vicious sort of licentiousness).

17. TWO NEGATIVE PREMISES (§12). An invalid form of the syllogism ("None of Shakespeare's plays are easy to perform, and no plays that are easy to perform are good plays; therefore, all of Shakespeare's plays are good plays"). It is a violation of the rule that no conclusion can validly be drawn from two negative premises.

18. UNDISTRIBUTED MIDDLE (§12). An invalid form of the syllogism ("All Murgatroyd's friends admire him; Billingsly admires him; therefore, Billingsly is a friend of his"). It is a violation of the rule that no conclusion can be drawn from two premises unless the middle term ("People who admire Murgatroyd" in this case) is distributed at least once.

19. UNWARRANTED DISTRIBUTION (§12). An invalid form of the syllogism ("All injuries are misfortunes, but some apparent misfortunes are not injuries; therefore, some apparent misfortunes are not (real) misfortunes"). It is a violation of the rule that if either of the end-terms ("misfortunes" in this case) is distributed in the conclusion, it must also be distributed in the premise in which it occurs.

INDEX

Index

329

DAT